The **Rough Guide** to

Boston

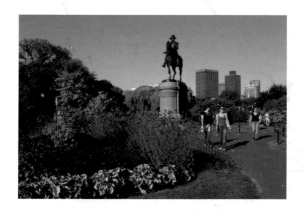

written and researched by

Sarah Hull

**ROUGH
GUIDES**

NEW YORK · LONDON · DELHI

www.roughguides.com

Contents

The sporting life color section following p.80

Yankee cooking (and drinking) color section following p.176

Color maps following p.320

◄◄ Statue of George Washington, The Public Garden ◄ Boston Harbor Hotel

Introduction to
Boston

Boston is as close to the Old World as the New World gets, an American city that proudly trades on its colonial past, having served a crucial role in the country's development from a few wayward pilgrims right through to the Revolutionary War. It occasionally takes this a bit too far – what's a faded relic anywhere else becomes a plaque-covered tourist site here – but none of it detracts from the city's overriding historic charm, nor from its present-day energy.

 The new millennium has seen a major renaissance in Boston. The completion of the seemingly never-ending Big Dig project, the Red Sox triumph in the 2004 and 2007 World Series, the Patriots' repeated Super Bowl victories and frequent openings of new restaurants, bars, clubs, and boutiques have all contributed to the feeling that Boston's future is even stronger than its past.

Despite the occasional wearisome touch, no other city in America gives a better feel for the events and persons behind the nation's birth, all played out in Boston's wealth of emblematic and evocative colonial-era sights, conveniently linked by the self-guided walking tour (one of a handful in the city) known as the Freedom Trail. As well, the city's cafés and shops, its

> No other city in America gives a better feel for the events and persons behind the nation's birth

attractive public spaces, and the diversity of its neighborhoods – student hives, ethnic enclaves, and stately districts of preserved townhouses

– are similarly alluring and go some way to answering the twin accusations of elitism and provincialism that Boston often faces.

Boston is also at the center of the American university system: more than sixty colleges call the area home, including illustrious Harvard and MIT, in the neighboring city of Cambridge, just across the Charles River. This academic connection has played a key part in the city's long left-leaning political tradition, which has spawned, most famously, the Kennedy family. Steeped in Puritan roots, local residents often display a slightly anachronistic Yankee pride, but it's one that has served to protect the city's identity. Indeed, the districts around Boston Common exude an almost small-town atmosphere, and, until the past decade or so, were relatively unmarred by chain stores and fast-food joints. Meanwhile, groups of Irish and Italian descent have carved out authentic and often equally unchanged communities in areas like the North End, Charlestown, and South Boston.

Today, Boston's relatively small size – both physically and in terms of population (eighteenth among US cities) – and its provincial feel actually serve to the city's advantage. Though it has expanded significantly through landfills and annexation since it was settled in 1630, it has never lost its core, which remains a tangle of streets over old cowpaths clustered around Boston Common (which was itself originally used as cattle pasture). Delightfully, this center can really only be explored properly on foot; for even as Boston has evolved from busy port to blighted city to the rejuvenated and prosperous place it is today, it has remained, fundamentally, a city on a human scale.

Boston nicknames, past and present

Boston has inspired many nicknames over the centuries, from the dignified to the inane. Originally called Tremontaine, after the three hills that punctuated the skyline when the Puritans arrived in the early 1600s (but which have since been razed and used for landfill), the newcomers renamed the spot Boston – itself a shortening of St Botolph – after their hometown, one hundred miles north of London. The name stuck, but other, less deferential, monikers took Boston's place. These range from the earnest ("Athens of America," after the sixty-plus universities that call the city home), to the hokey ("Beantown," reflecting its inhabitants' storied love affair with baked beans), to the overblown ("The Hub," after Oliver Wendell Holmes's famous 1857 reference to the Massachusetts State House as the "hub of the solar system").

◀ The Charles River and Boston skyline

What to see

The city's epicenter is **Boston Common**, a large public green (and the country's first public park) that orients **Downtown** and is near many of Boston's most historic sights, including the Old State House, the Old Granary Burying Ground, and the Old South Meeting House. Little, however, captures the spirit of the city better than nearby **Faneuil Hall**, the so-called "Cradle of Liberty," and the always-animated Quincy Market, adjacent to the hall. Due north, an incomparable sense of Boston's original layout can be found in the cramped, seventeenth-century **Blackstone Block**. Boston's waterfront, on the edge of Downtown, offers its fair share of diversions, mostly ideal for traveling families; the

> **Boston is the center of the American university system: more than sixty colleges call the area home**

action is centered on Long Wharf. Due east of the waterfront lies the rapidly developing **Seaport District**, home to a number of savory seafood spots as well as historic Boston icons like the larger-than-life Hood Milk Bottle (squarely in front of the Children's Museum) and the showy new Institute of Contemporary Art.

The **North End**, modern Boston's Little Italy, occupies the northeast corner of the peninsula, and was cut off from the rest of the city by the old elevated I-93 before the completion of the main section of the Big Dig in 2006. The North End is home to a few notable relics, such as **Old North Church** and the **Paul Revere House**, but is equally worth visiting for its animated streetlife, fueled, in large part, by the strong cups of espresso proffered by numerous Italian *caffès*. Just across Boston Inner Harbor from the North End lies **Charlestown**, the quiet berth of the world's oldest commissioned warship, the USS *Constitution*, as well as the site of the **Bunker Hill Monument**, an obelisk commemorating the famous battle that bolstered American morale in the fight for independence.

North of the Common, vintage gaslights and red-brick Federalist townhouses line the streets of **Beacon Hill**, the city's most exclusive residential neighborhood; it's anchored by the gold-domed **State House**, designed, as were numerous area houses, by Charles Bulfinch. Charles Street runs south from the hill and separates Boston Common from the **Public Garden**, which marks the eastern edge of **Back Bay**, a similarly well-heeled neighborhood which features opulent rowhouses alongside modern landmarks like the **John Hancock Tower**, New England's tallest skyscraper. The neighborhood also hosts some of the city's best shopping along **Newbury Street**. Additionally, the stylish enclave of the **South End**, known for its restaurants and streetlife, as well as the ornate ironwork gracing its well-maintained homes, is also worth a visit.

The Big Dig

In a city whose roads follow the logic of colonial cowpaths, the added confusion wreaked by Boston's "Big Dig" highway reconstruction project – the largest and most expensive in US history – soured the idea of driving here for more than a decade. Thankfully, that's a thing of the past, and the final phase, landscaping the space formerly occupied by the unsightly elevated Central Artery (I-93), was nearing completion at the time of writing. The Big Dig's initial budget of $2.6 billion may have more than quadrupled, but the project – as most Bostonians will tell you – was worth both the cost and the wait. Along with pumping billions of construction dollars into the city, the plan birthed new structures like the Leonard P. Zakim Bunker Hill Bridge (pictured below) and freed up 150 acres of land for park and recreational use, while supplying dirt to cap landfills where toxins once seeped into Boston Harbor. Visit Ⓦ www.bigdig.com, which has all the history, trivia, artwork, and gossip connected with the project; you can learn, among other impressive figures, that once finally finished, "more earth will [have been] moved than during the construction of the Great Pyramids."

The student domains of **Kenmore Square** and **the Fenway** are found west of Back Bay and the South End: the former is largely overrun with college kids from nearby Boston University; the latter spreads west of Massachusetts Avenue and southwest along Huntington Avenue, and is home to heavyweight local institutions like the **Museum of Fine Arts**, the **Isabella Stewart Gardner Museum**, and **Fenway Park**. Below all these neighborhoods are Boston's vast **southern districts**, home to the

The Cape and beyond

If Boston is New England's heart, then the Cape is the region's well-tanned arm. For five generations Bostonians have emerged from the city's pale winters to revel in Cape Cod's 150 miles of sugary white sand marked by lighthouses, sandy dunes, and really good ice cream. While the tone of this 63-mile peninsula varies greatly – from the old-money vibe of Chatham to the raucous good time of gay-friendly Provincetown – its beauty rarely wavers, and a piece of your own little paradise is never far. Out on the water, Martha's Vineyard and Nantucket offer enticements of their own, with gorgeous beaches complemented by breezy heaths and moorlands. The Vineyard is the more relaxed of the two islands, known for her endearing gingerbread cottages, vintage carousel (the oldest in the country), and fun mix of folks. Tiny Nantucket gets teased for her hoity-toity attitude (those pants aren't pink, they're "Nantucket reds"), but it's still a bright spot, rife with a storied whaling history and sea-salted cottages covered with roses. Wherever you go in the area, seafood is sure to be the *mot du jour*, beachcombing is a way of life, and sunny rays are the catch of the day.

▲ Cape Cod clam shack

John F. Kennedy Presidential Library and Museum and the southerly links in Frederick Law Olmsted's series of parks, known as the **Emerald Necklace**; it includes the spectacular **Arnold Arboretum** as well as **Franklin Park**, setting for the Franklin Zoo. Across the Charles River from Boston is **Cambridge**, synonymous with venerable Harvard University and tech-oriented MIT, but also boasting some of the area's best nightlife and a lively café scene, especially around Harvard Square, which spills over into neighboring **Somerville** to the north.

The waterfront's Long Wharf doubles as a jumping-off point for escaping the city altogether, on cruises to the idyllic Harbor Islands, or to happening **Provincetown**, Cape Cod's foremost destination; the rest of the Cape is also very much worth a road trip. Further afloat, sun worshippers will want to check out laidback **Martha's Vineyard** and nostalgic **Nantucket**, two islands blessed with endless beaches and fantastic seafood. Inland, nearby battle sites in **Lexington** and **Concord** make for easy day-trips, as does a jaunt up the coast to **Salem** and its witch-trials sights, or further on to seafaring towns like **Gloucester** and **Rockport**.

When to go

The city is at its most enjoyable in the **fall** (September through early November), when the weather is cooler and the long lines have somewhat abated; and in the **spring** (April through mid-May), when the magnolia trees blossom along Commonwealth Avenue and the parks spring back to life. **Summer**, meanwhile, is certainly the most popular time to visit Boston, both for the warmer weather and frequent festivals. However, July and August can be uncomfortably humid, and you'll have to contend with large student-related influxes around graduation (early June) and the beginning of school (around Labor Day, in September).

▲ Faneuil Hall

At the other end of the spectrum, Boston **winters** can be harsh affairs: they tend to run from late November through March, but, thanks to the moderating influence of the Atlantic, mild spells often break the monotony of long cold stretches, and snowfall is lighter than in the interior regions of New England. No matter when you go, though, be prepared for sudden changes in the weather in the space of a single day: a December morning snow squall could easily be followed by afternoon sunshine and temperatures in the 50s (Fahrenheit).

Boston's climate

	Jan	Feb	Mar	Apr	May	Jun	July	Aug	Sept	Oct	Nov	Dec
Average maximum temperature												
(°F)	36	39	46	56	67	77	82	80	73	62	52	42
(°C)	2.2	3.9	7.8	13.3	19.4	25	27.8	26.7	22.8	16.7	11.1	5.6
Average minimum temperature												
(°F)	22	24	31	41	50	59	65	64	57	46	38	28
(°C)	-5.6	-4.5	-0.6	5	10	15	18.3	17.8	13.9	7.8	3.3	-2.2
Average rainfall												
(in)	3.9	3.3	3.9	3.6	3.2	3.2	3.1	3.4	3.5	3.8	4.0	3.7
(mm)	99.6	83.8	97.8	91.4	82.3	81.8	77.7	85.6	88.1	96.3	101.1	94.7

things not to miss

It's not possible to see everything that Boston has to offer in one trip – and we don't suggest you try. What follows is a selective and subjective taste of the city's highlights, from impressive museums and storied ballparks to mouthwatering eateries and engaging cultural events. They're arranged in five color-coded categories to help you find the very best things to see, do, and experience. All entries have a page reference to take you straight into the text, where you can find out more.

01 Cambridge Page **132** • Funky and historic, Boston's laidback sister is known for mixing storied Ivy League culture with artful museums, cheap eats, and unique architecture like that of MIT's Stata Center.

02 **A concert at Symphony Hall** Page **194** • Home to the Boston Symphony Orchestra – going strong for more than 125 years – this gilded hall is the perfect place in which to hear classical music.

03 **Bonsais at Arnold Arboretum** Page **131** • Jamaica Plain's Arnold Arboretum boasts the largest assortment of bonsais outside Asia.

04 **Historic burying grounds** Pages **46, 48** & **136** • Holding everyone from revolutionary heroes to literary titans, Boston's colonial burying grounds are peaceful spots to contemplate their contributions.

05 **Walking the Black Heritage Trail** Page **87** • The 1.6-mile Black Heritage Trail, beginning at the striking Robert Gould Shaw Memorial, is the country's foremost site devoted to pre-Civil War African-American history.

06 A day in the Public Garden Page 93 • Take the kids down to Back Bay's idyllic Public Garden for a picnic and a ride on the Swan Boats; you might enjoy it as much as they do.

08 Shopping on Newbury Street Page 96 • Back Bay's poshest commercial stretch, with everything from colorful boutiques to hip cafés situated in elegant rowhouses.

07 Isabella Stewart Gardner Museum Page 120 • The exuberant Gardner's stunning collection is housed around a beautiful courtyard in her former mansion.

09 Trinity Church Page 98 • Step inside this 1877 Boston icon and be awed by architect H. H. Richardson's realized vision of "walking into a living painting."

10 **A game at Fenway Park** Page 111 • The country's oldest ballpark is home to the beloved Red Sox and the 37-foot-tall "Green Monster."

11 **The Omni Parker House Hotel** Page **154** • This opulent old Boston hotel – birthplace of the divine Boston cream pie – merits a look whether you stay there or not.

14

12 **The USS Constitution** Page **76** • Navy sailors give tours of "Old Ironsides," the oldest commissioned warship in the world.

13 Old North Church Page 71 •
The oldest church in Boston, this North End landmark is where the famous lanterns were hung on the night of April 18, 1775, to warn of the advancing British troops.

15 Institute of Contemporary Art Page 62 • While some exhibits may prompt the question "Is this art?" the ICA's glamorous cantilevered digs on the waterfront are not to be missed.

14 The houses of Beacon Hill Page 81 •
Be on the lookout for purple-tinted windowpanes, a former status symbol, as you stroll this elegant upper-class enclave.

16 Eating in the South End Page 174 • Boston's most gay-friendly neighborhood is also a veritable foodie paradise, with many of the city's best eats congregated here.

19 Pastries in the North End
Page **163** • Experience the vibrant cafés, bakeries, and restaurants in Boston's most authentically Italian neighborhood.

17 The Ware collection
Page **143** • The Harvard Museum of Natural History's awesome collection of glass flowers, plants, and herbs is truly one of a kind.

18 Museum of Fine Arts
Page **114** • New England's premier art space features the works of Sargent and Copley, Impressionist painters, and one of the world's best collections of art from the ancient world and Asia.

20 A visit to Provincetown
Page **259** • Though out at the tip of Cape Cod, P-town is an easy day-trip from the city, its beaches and streetlife popular with families and gay visitors alike.

Basics

Basics

Getting there

Flying is the fastest and often times the least expensive option for getting to Boston. Upon arrival, you'll be pleased to find that the Boston airport, Logan International (BOS), is conveniently situated near subways and water taxis that provide fast and efficient city access.

From **overseas, seasonal variations** in price are common, with flights at their most expensive from June to August (actually the hottest and most humid time to visit Boston). Spring and autumn are slightly less pricey, while winter (excluding the Christmas and New Year holiday period) is the cheapest time to fly.

If you're not into flying, or have already arrived from abroad somewhere in the US or Canada, **trains** can be a decent second option for getting to Boston, particularly for visitors traveling along the East Coast. **Amtrak** has a reliable high-speed service between Washington DC and Boston (which includes New York City); from elsewhere in the country, though, the approaches to Beantown are leisurely at best.

For budget travelers, the **Greyhound** and **Peter Pan bus companies** are good options, and they tend to have more flexible departure times than either train or plane. **Driving** is obviously another possibility, but if you insist on getting to Boston via car, plan on parking your vehicle once you get into the city and leaving it for the duration of your stay; you'll neither want (as Boston is a great walking city) nor need the thing again until you leave town.

On a final note, overseas visitors can buy **air**, **train**, and **bus passes** for **discounted travel** throughout the United States; these normally have to be purchased before your trip, and from within your home country. Below, all prices in this section are given in **US dollars**, unless otherwise stated.

Flights from the US and Canada

Boston's only airport, **Logan International**, is New England's busiest and has been undergoing an expansion project for the last few years: the international Terminal E opened in 2004, while Delta opened a newly refurbished Terminal A in 2005. Most service comes from **East Coast shuttles** originating at New York's La Guardia, JFK, and Newark airports (Delta Airlines; Mon–Fri every 30–60min 6am–9.30pm, Sat & Sun every 2hr 8.30am–8.30pm) and Washington DC's Dulles and Reagan National airports (US Airways; Mon–Sat every 30–60min 7.30am–9.25pm, Sun every 30–60mins 8.30am–9.25pm).

The following airlines also offer regular, **daily service** to Boston: Air Canada (from Montréal, Ottawa, Toronto, and Vancouver), American Airlines (from Chicago, Dallas, Miami, Philadelphia, and St Louis), Continental (from Houston, Chicago, Miami, Newark, and Seattle), Delta (from Atlanta, Dallas, and Tampa), JetBlue (from New York, Washington DC), United (from Chicago, Los Angeles, and San Francisco), Northwest (from Detroit, Memphis, Minneapolis, San Diego, and Vancouver), and US Airways (from Fort Lauderdale, Orlando, and Philadelphia).

Fares are lowest in the heavily trafficked Northeast corridor; a round-trip fare **from New York** can cost as little as $90–100, although $120–170 is the more usual price fare; **from Washington DC** and **Miami**, the range is usually $200–250; from **Chicago**, $260–300. The price of flights **from the West Coast** is more likely to fluctuate – round-trip fares from LA, San Francisco, or Seattle typically cost $450–550, but can go as low as $300. **From Canada**, be prepared to pay around CAN$400–500 from Toronto and Montréal, and closer to CAN$700–1000 from Vancouver.

Flights from the UK and Ireland

Five airlines make the **nonstop** seven-hour flight from **the UK and Ireland** to Boston;

most leave early to mid-afternoon and arrive in the late afternoon or evening, though the odd red-eye flight leaves the UK at 8pm and arrives later the same night in Boston. Returning to the UK and Ireland, you're looking at an early morning or early evening departure; the prevailing winds tend to make the trip back modestly shorter than the one over.

British Airways, Continental, Virgin Atlantic, and American Airlines fly from London's Heathrow Airport; travelers from elsewhere in the UK will have to connect in London. Aer Lingus and American Airlines operate nonstop services from Ireland.

As there's not a lot of price difference between the major airlines, you'll have to shop around to get the best deals. The standard option, the **Apex** ticket, is a non-refundable round-trip ticket that must be purchased 21 days in advance and requires a minimum seven-night stay, up to a maximum of one month; changing departure dates usually incurs a penalty. With or without an Apex ticket, **fares from London** hover around £200 in low season (Oct–Feb), £250 in the spring, and £300 in high season (May–Sept). All fares are subject to a £63 tax, and weekend flights incur additional surcharges. Flights **from Ireland** (Dublin, Shannon, or Cork) are somewhat cheaper, and can range from €200 in low season to €400 in high season.

Flights from Australia and New Zealand

Flights from **Australia** and **New Zealand** fly to the West Coast before continuing on to Boston, making for a pretty long trip (about fourteen hours, plus another six).

Round-trip **fares** from eastern Australian cities are usually around AUS$2000/$NZ2900 in low season (mid-Jan to Feb & Oct–Nov), while tickets from Perth and Darwin can cost up to AUS$400 more. You might do better purchasing a direct ticket to either San Francisco or LA and using an air pass to get to Boston. If you choose this route, you must buy a minimum of three flight coupons (at a cost of AUS$800 total) before leaving your home country. The best connections through the West Coast tend to be with United, Air New Zealand, and Qantas.

Trains

For those heading to Boston from within the Washington DC and New York shuttle flight radius, **train** travel is a pleasant – but not much less expensive – alternative. On the plus side, the Amtrak trains (☎1-800/USA-RAIL, ⊛www.amtrak.com) that service the Washington-to-Boston corridor are the fleet's most reliable, and usually stick to their official schedules. **Fares from New York** to Boston begin at $116 round-trip, with travel taking between four and five hours; $174 and up gets you a seat on the cushier Acela Express, which only shaves about thirty minutes off the trip time. **From Washington DC,** the regular train runs just shy of eight hours (beginning at $162 return) while the express gets you there in 6.5 hours (beginning at $274 round-trip).

Although it's possible to haul yourself long-distance **from the West Coast,** the Midwest, or the South, the trip is anything but fast – count on three days and up from California – nor is it cost-effective, at around $350 for a round-trip ticket. The same applies to visitors trying to approach Boston **from Canada** using Via Rail (☎1-888/842-7245, ⊛www.viarail.ca); you can do so only by connecting with Amtrak in Montréal, and on an indirect itinerary at best. The rail journey can take anywhere from twelve to twenty hours from Toronto and Montréal, and over three days from Vancouver. Fares start around CAN$450 return from the closer points – and at those prices, you may as well fly.

Buses

Given how expensive rail travel is in the US, getting to Boston by **bus** can be an appealing – if less comfortable – option. Boston is an especially common stop coming **from New York** or **Washington DC**; barring rush-hour traffic and highway accidents, one-way trips typically take four-and-a-half hours from New York and ten-and-a-half hours from Washington, with round-trip **fares** costing $55 and $132, respectively – though nonrefundable and seven-day advance fares from New York can drop the round-trip price as low as $30. The rates can go down even further in the summer, when the two main carriers, **Greyhound** (☎1-800/231-2222, ⊛www.greyhound.com) and **Peter Pan**

Fly less – stay longer! Travel and climate change

Climate change is a serious threat to the ecosystems that humans rely upon, and air travel is among the fastest-growing contributors to the problem. Rough Guides regard travel, overall, as a global benefit, and feel strongly that the advantages to developing economies are important, as is the opportunity of greater contact and awareness among peoples. But we all have a responsibility to limit our personal impact on global warming, and that means giving thought to how often we fly, and what we can do to redress the harm that our trips create.

Flying and climate change

Pretty much every form of motorized travel generates CO_2 – the main cause of human-induced climate change – but planes also generate climate-warming contrails and cirrus clouds and emit oxides of nitrogen, which create ozone (another greenhouse gas) at flight levels. Furthermore, flying simply allows us to travel much further than we otherwise would do. The figures are frightening: one person taking a return flight between Europe and California produces the equivalent impact of 2.5 tons of CO_2 – similar to the yearly output of the average UK car.

Fuel-cell and other less harmful types of plane may emerge eventually. But until then, there are really just two options for concerned travelers: to reduce the amount we travel by air (take fewer trips – stay for longer!), and to make the trips we do take "climate neutral" via a carbon offset scheme.

Carbon offset schemes

Offset schemes run by ⊛www.climatecare.org, ⊛www.carbonneutral.com and others allow you to make up for some or all of the greenhouse gases that you are responsible for releasing. To do this, they provide "carbon calculators" for working out the global-warming contribution of a specific flight (or even your entire existence), and then let you contribute an appropriate amount of money to fund offsetting measures. These include rainforest reforestation and initiatives to reduce future energy demand – often run in conjunction with sustainable development schemes.

Rough Guides, together with Lonely Planet and other concerned partners in the travel industry, are supporting a **carbon offset scheme** run by climatecare.org. Please take the time to view our website and see how you can help to make your trip climate neutral.

⊛www.roughguides.com/climatechange

(☎1-800/237-8747, ⊛www.peterpanbus .com) lose their best income source – college students – and tempt full-time residents with cut-rate deals. The only hitch is that these cheap tickets must be purchased in Boston; even so, you can still save by buying a one-way ticket to Boston and getting your return on arrival.

Visitors leaving **from New York City** have additional choices when it comes to bus travel with the **Chinatown** buses. Fung Wah (☎1-617/345-8000, ⊛www.fungwahbus .com) and Lucky Star (☎1-888/881-0887, ⊛www.luckystarbus.com) both leave from Canal Street in Manhattan and arrive at South Station in Boston; one-way tickets are $15 for fully air-conditioned coaches.

Coming **from Canada**, several daily buses **from Toronto** reach Boston with at least one changeover – usually in Syracuse, New York – contributing to a minimum fourteen-hour ride (CAN$186 return). Buses **from Montréal** take around twelve hours and stop in New York City first (CAN$141 round-trip). In both cases, contact Greyhound (☎1-800/661-TRIP, ⊛www.greyhound.com).

Driving

Coming into Boston by **car** used to be a nightmare, but road access has improved with the completion of the Big Dig, which has put the dreaded I-93 underground and vastly improved the flow of traffic. Despite the old flyover being

Distances and driving times to Boston

From Chicago: 982 miles
(16hr 30min)
From Miami: 1488 miles (25hr)
From Montréal: 310 miles (6hr)
From New York: 216 miles (4hr)

From San Francisco: 3100 miles
(52hr)
From Toronto: 552 miles
(9hr 30min)

torn down, construction continues on landscaping work above ground, meaning the occasional snarl-up is still possible. If driving, stay informed of road closures and re-routings by tuning in to 1030am (reports every ten minutes 5am–7pm; every half-hour 7pm–5am) and prepare for interminable jams and detours.

Two highways provide direct access to the town: **I-90** (the Massachusetts Turnpike, known locally as "The Pike" or "the Masspike"), and **I-93**, known as the Central Artery. The latter cuts north-south through the heart of Boston and provides the most majestic entrance to the city, courtesy of the newly-opened Zakim Bridge; however, don't be surprised if you get stuck in traffic for awhile here, especially if you arrive during **rush hour** (7.30-9am and 4.30-7pm). If you're coming from western Massachusetts, **I-90** is the most direct route to Boston; from points north of the city utilize I-93. Once you reach Boston, Storrow Drive is the main local drag, running alongside the Charles River and providing access to the core of the city.

Airlines, agents and operators

If you **book your tickets online**, keep in mind that you'll need to be flexible about your departure and return dates to get the best prices from these sites. Make sure you read the small print before buying, too, as it can be difficult, if not impossible, to claim refunds or change your ticket, especially on last-minute deals.

Plenty of **travel operators** offer **tours** and **camping trips** that typically feature a day or two in Boston as part of a seven-day itinerary that includes several New England destinations. Though these are considerably more expensive than a mere weekend in the city (and prices vary wildly according to what's

being offered), the Boston element of the trip makes a great backgrounder to a provincial New England vacation.

Online booking

ⓦwww.expedia.co.uk (in UK), ⓦwww.expedia.com (in US), ⓦwww.expedia.ca (in Canada)
ⓦwww.lastminute.com (in UK)
ⓦwww.opodo.co.uk (in UK)
ⓦwww.orbitz.com (in US)
ⓦwww.travelocity.co.uk (in UK), ⓦwww.travelocity.com (in US), ⓦwww.travelocity.ca (in Canada)
ⓦwww.zuji.com.au (in Australia) ⓦwww.zuji.co.nz (in New Zealand))

Airlines

Aer Lingus US and Canada ☎1-800/IRISH-AIR, UK ☎0870/876 5000, Republic of Ireland ☎0818/365 000; ⓦwww.aerlingus.com.
Air Canada US and Canada ☎1-888/247-2262, UK ☎0871/220 1111, Republic of Ireland ☎01/679 3958, Australia ☎1300/655 767, New Zealand ☎0508/747 767; ⓦwww.aircanada.com.
Air France US ☎1-800/237-2747, Canada ☎1-800-667-2747, UK ☎0870/142 4343, Australia ☎1300/390 190, SA ☎0861/340 340; ⓦwww.airfrance.com.
Air New Zealand Australia ☎13 24 76, New Zealand ☎0800/737 000; ⓦwww.airnz.co.nz.
American Airlines US ☎1-800/433-7300, UK ☎0845/7789 789, Republic of Ireland ☎01/602 0550, Australia ☎1300/650 747, New Zealand ☎0800/887 997; ⓦwww.aa.com.
ATA (American TransAir) US ☎1-800/435-9282, ⓦwww.ata.com.
British Airways US and Canada ☎1-800/AIRWAYS, UK ☎0870/850 9850, Republic of Ireland ☎1890/626 747, Australia ☎1300/767 177, New Zealand ☎09/966 9777; ⓦwww.ba.com.
Continental Airlines US and Canada ☎1-800/523-3273, UK ☎0845/607 6760, Republic of Ireland ☎1890/925 252, Australia ☎02/9244 2242, New Zealand ☎09/308 3350, International ☎1800/231 0856; ⓦwww.continental.com.

wagamama

delicious noodles ı **rice dishes** ı **fresh juices**
wine ı **sake** ı **asian beers**

wagamama faneuil hall
quincy market building
tel • 617 742 9242

wagamama harvard square
57 jfk street
tel • 617 499 0930

Cape Air US and Canada ☎1-800/352-0714 ⊛www.flycapeair.com.

Delta US and Canada ☎1-800/221-1212, UK ☎0845/600 0950, Republic of Ireland ☎1850/882 031 or 01/407 3165, Australia ☎1300/302 849, New Zealand ☎09/379 3370; ⊛www.delta.com.

Frontier Airlines US ☎1-800/432-1359 ⊛www.flyfrontier.com.

Jet Blue US ☎1-800/538-2583 ⊛www.jetblue.com.

Northwest/KLM US ☎1-800/225-2525, UK ☎0870/507 4074, Australia ☎1 300 767 310; ⊛www.nwa.com.

Qantas Airways US and Canada ☎1-800/227-4500, UK ☎0845/774 7767, Republic of Ireland ☎01/407 3278, Australia ☎13 13 13, New Zealand ☎0800/808 767 or 09/357 8900, SA ☎11/441 8550; ⊛www.qantas.com.

United Airlines US ☎1-800/UNITED-1, UK ☎0845/844 4777, Australia ☎13 17 77; ⊛www.united.com.

US Airways US and Canada ☎1-800/428-4322, UK ☎0845/600 3300, Ireland ☎1890/925 065; ⊛www.usair.com.

USA 3000 Airlines US ☎1-877/USA-3000, ⊛www.usa3000airlines.com.

Virgin Atlantic US ☎1-800/821-5438, UK ☎0870/380 2007, Australia ☎1300/727 340, SA ☎11/340 3400; ⊛www.virgin-atlantic.com.

Agents and operators

Airtech US ☎212/219-7000 ⊛www.airtech.com. Standby seat broker.

ebookers UK ☎0800/082 3000, Republic of Ireland ☎01/488 3507; ⊛www.ebookers.com. Low fares on an extensive selection of scheduled flights and package deals.

Collette Vacations US ☎1-800/340-5158 ⊛www.collettevacations.com. Boston figures in various escorted or independent tour permutations; from the seven-night "Islands of New England" option, which includes Boston, Nantucket, and Martha's Vineyard (from $1400), to the "New England Back Roads" tour, which also covers New England towns like Burlington, Vermont, and Boothbay Harbor, Maine (from $1250); prices include meals but exclude airfare/travel to Boston.

Contiki Holidays US ☎1-888/CONTIKI ⊛www.contiki.com. Trips for the 18–35-year-old crowd; the twelve-day "North by Northeast" tour (from $1615, airfare not included) takes in Boston and Cape Cod.

North South Travel UK ☎01245/608 291 ⊛www.northsouthtravel.co.uk. Friendly, competitive travel agency, offering discounted fares worldwide. Profits are used to support projects in the developing world, especially the promotion of sustainable tourism.

Now Voyager ☎1-800/255-6951 ⊛www.nowvoyager.com. San Francisco-based gay- and lesbian-friendly consolidator with Boston-based tours and packages.

Skylink US ☎1-800/247-6659 or 212/573-8980, Canada ☎1-800/759-5465; ⊛www.skylinkus.com. Consolidator with multiple offices throughout the US and Canada.

STA Travel US ☎1-800-781-4040, Canada ☎1-888-427-5639, UK ☎0870/1630 026, Australia ☎1300/733 035, New Zealand ☎0508/782 872, SA ☎0861/781 781; ⊛www.statravel.com. Worldwide specialists in independent travel; also student IDs, travel insurance, car rental, rail passes, and more. Good discounts for students and under-26s.

Trailfinders UK ☎0845/058 5858, Republic of Ireland ☎01/677 7888, Australia ☎1300/780 212; ⊛www.trailfinders.com. One of the best-informed and most efficient agents for independent travelers.

Arrival

Those traveling to Boston by airplane will arrive at the city's Logan International Airport, located on Boston's easternmost peninsula, a landfill sticking far out into Boston Harbor. From there, you can catch the subway or a water shuttle to Downtown; taking a taxi is another option. For visitors coming into Boston by bus or train, you'll arrive at South Station, near the waterfront at Summer Street and Atlantic Avenue; from there, it's just a short walk or subway ride to Downtown.

By air

Busy **Logan International** – the closest airport to a major downtown area in the US – services both domestic and international flights; it has five terminals, lettered A through E, that are connected by a series of courtesy buses. You'll find currency exchanges in terminals C and E (daily 10am–5pm), plus information booths, car rental, and ATMs in all five.

After arriving into Logan, the most convenient way downtown is by **subway**. The Airport stop is a short ride away on courtesy bus #11, which you can catch outside on the arrival level of all five terminals. From there, you can take the Blue Line to State or Government Center **T** stations in the heart of Downtown, and transfer to the Red, Orange, and Green lines to reach other points; the ride to Downtown lasts about fifteen minutes ($2).

Just as quick, but a lot more fun, is the Harbor Express **water shuttle** that whisks you across the harbor to numerous points around Boston, including Rowes or Long Wharf near the Blue Line Aquarium **T** station. Water taxis don't run in the winter, nor do they run on a set schedule; if there isn't a boat waiting in the harbor, contact them via the checkerboard call box at the Logan Dock (April–Nov Mon–Sat 7am–10pm; Sun 7am–8pm, departure times vary; $10 one-way; ☎617/422-0392; ⍟www.citywatertaxi .com). From the airport, courtesy bus #66 will take you to the pier.

By comparison, taking a **taxi** is expensive – the airport to a Downtown destination costs $20–25, plus an extra $6 or so in tolls – and can be time-consuming, given Boston's notorious traffic jams.

By bus or train

The main terminus for both **buses** and **trains** to Boston is **South Station**, in the southeast corner of Downtown at Summer Street and Atlantic Avenue. **Amtrak trains** arrive at one end, in a station with an information booth, newsstands, a food court, and several ATMs (but no currency exchange); **bus carriers** arrive at the clean and modern terminal next door, from where it's a bit of a trek to reach the subway (the Red Line), which is through the Amtrak station and down a level. Those with sizable baggage will find the walk particularly awkward, as there are no porters or handcarts. Note that despite its modernity, the bus terminal's departure and arrival screens are anything but up-to-date – confirm your gate with an agent to be sure. Trains also make a second stop at Boston's **Back Bay Station**, 145 Dartmouth St, on the **T**'s Orange Line. Lastly, Amtrak's Downeaster train – which connects Portland, Maine with Boston and points in-between – arrives at **North Station**, which is located in the West End near the TDBanknorth Garden.

By car

Driving into Boston can be stressful, and will probably put a damper on your trip if you're a first-time visitor. Boston drivers are notorious for their aggressive, impatient style of driving, and the learning curve for navigating the city by car is so steep that ability to do so has become a source of pride and cultural identity for local residents. Boston roads were built on top of colonial cowpaths (and as such are not laid out in any system per se) making them difficult to maneuver. To make matters worse, Boston signage is notoriously bad. If you are driving into Boston, just be sure to arm yourself beforehand with a good road map and a dose of patience.

Two highways provide direct access to the city, **I-90** (on which you can drive from Seattle to Boston without hitting a traffic light) and **I-93**. The latter, which cuts north-south through the heart of the city,

has been put underground by the Big Dig construction project. The completion of this ten-lane 7.5-mile tunnel has made the city less congested and vastly improved the traffic situation in Boston. A third highway, **I-95** (also known as Route-128 between Gloucester and Boston) circumnavigates the greater Boston area, affording entry points for its many suburbs (it also continues south, ending in Miami, Florida).

Getting around

Much of the pleasure of visiting Boston comes from being in a city built long before cars were invented. Walking around the narrow, winding streets can be a joy; conversely, driving around them can be a nightmare. Be particularly cautious in traffic circles known as "rotaries": when entering, always yield the right of way. If you have a car, consider parking it for the duration of your trip (see p.28) and then get around either by foot or public transit – a system of subway lines, buses, and ferries run by the Massachusetts Bay Transportation Authority (MBTA, known as the "**T**"; ☏1-800/392-6100, ⊛www.mbta.com).

The subway (T)

While not the most modern system, Boston's subway is cheap, efficient, and charmingly antiquated – its Green Line was America's first underground train, built in the late nineteenth century, and riding it today is akin to riding an underground tram.

Four **subway** lines transect Boston and continue out into some of its more proximate neighbors. Each line is color coded and passes through Downtown before continuing on to other districts. The **Red Line**, which serves Harvard, is the most frequent, inter-secting South Boston and Dorchester to the south and Cambridge to the north. The **Green Line** hits Back Bay, Kenmore Square, the Fenway, and Brookline. The **Blue Line** heads into East Boston and is most useful for its stop at Logan Airport. The less frequent **Orange Line** traverses the South End and continues down to Roxbury and Jamaica Plain.

All trains travel either **inbound** (towards the quadrant made up of State, Downtown Crossing, Park Street, and Government

Center stops) or **outbound** (away from the quadrant). If you're confused about whether you're going in or out, the train's terminus is also designated on the train itself; for instance, trains to Harvard from South Station will be on the "Inbound" platform and heading towards "Alewife."

The four lines are supplemented by a bus rapid transit (BRT) route, the **Silver Line**, which runs above ground along Washington Street from Downtown Crossing **T**. More of a fast bus than a subway, the line cuts through the heart of South End. There is also an extended, tunnelled loop connection from the South End to the airport.

Boston has recently installed a new and somewhat confusing system for subway fares. The **standard fare** to board the **T** is $2, payable by the purchase of a "CharlieTicket" (presumably named for the Kingston Trio recording of the "MTA Song," about a man named Charlie who "never returned" from his train ride due to his inability to pay an exorbitant subway exit fare), which can be purchased at any of the ATM-like machines in the stations. However, if you first pick up a free "Charlie-Card" from one of the customer services agent stations (located at most subway stops), then your fare is substantially less – beginning at $1.70 per ride. While both cards are reusable, and money can easily be added to either card at any downtown station, the difference between the two is that the CharlieCard has a credit-card thickness and thus a longer lifespan. If you're planning to use public transit a lot, your easiest and best bet is to buy a **visitor's pass** for one ($9) or seven days ($15) of unlimited subway, bus, and inter-harbor ferry use.

The biggest drawback to the **T** is the relatively limited hours of operation (Mon–Sat 5.15am–12.30am, Sun 6am–12.30am); the 12.30am closing time means you'll be stuck taking a taxi home after last-call. Free transit maps are available at most stations; there's also a subway map at the back of this book.

Buses

The MBTA manages an impressive 170 **bus** routes both in and around Boston. Though the buses run less frequently than the subway and are harder to navigate, they bear two main advantages: they're cheaper ($1.50 exact change only or with Charlie Ticket; $1.25 with CharlieCard) and they provide service to many more points. It's a service used, however, primarily by natives who've grown familiar with the byzantine system of routes. If you're transferring from the **T**, and you have a CharlieTicket, you'll have to pay the full fare, though if you have a CharlieCard you get a free bus transfer as long as you use it within two hours. Transfer-ring between buses is free, as long as you have a transfer from your original bus.

The **T**'s visitor pass includes unlimited bus access with its one or seven days package. Be sure to arm yourself with the *Official Public Transport Map*, available at most subway stations, before heading out. Most buses run from 5.30am to 1am.

Taxis

Given Boston's small scale and the efficiency (at least during the day) of its public transit, **taxis** aren't as necessary or prevalent as in cities like New York or London. If you do find yourself in need, you can generally hail one along the streets of Downtown or Back Bay, though competition gets pretty stiff after 12.30am when the subway has stopped running and bars and clubs begin to close. If desperate, go to a hotel where cabs cluster, or call the cab company directly. In Cambridge, taxis mostly congregate around Harvard Square.

Boston Cab (☎617/536-5010) and Metro Cab (☎617/782-5500) have 24-hour service and accept major credit cards. Other cab companies include Checker Taxi (☎617 /536-7000) and Town Taxi (☎617/536-5000). In Cambridge, call Yellow Cabs (☎617 /547-3000) or Ambassador Cabs (☎617/492-1100). As a general rule, the rate starts at $1.75 and goes up by 30¢ per 1/8th mile.

Ferries

Of all the MBTA transportation options, the Inner Harbor **ferry** is by far the most scenic: $1.70 gets you a ten-minute boat ride with excellent views of Downtown Boston. The boats, covered 100-seaters with exposed upper decks, navigate several waterfront routes by day, though the one most useful to visitors is that connecting Long Wharf with Charlestown (every 30min Mon–Fri 6.30am–8pm, Sat & Sun 10am–6pm).

Color scheming

Each of the **T**'s subway lines is colored after a characteristic of the area it covers. The **Red Line** evokes Harvard's crimson sports jerseys; the **Green Line** refers to the Emerald Necklace (see box, p.120); the **Blue Line** reflects its waterfront proximity; and the **Orange Line** is so named because the street under which it runs, Washington Street, used to be called Orange Street, after King William of Orange. The **Silver Line** is the only exception to the color scheme: it's colored for speed – like a silver bullet.

Another popular harbor route is the **water shuttle** between Logan Airport and Downtown's Long Wharf, a seven-minute trip that makes for a stunning arrival ($10; ☎617/422-0392, ⊕www.citywatertaxi.com); bus #66 (free) from Logan Airport will get you to the quay.

Several larger **passenger boats** cruise across the harbor and beyond to reach beach destinations such as Provincetown, at the tip of Cape Cod. Two companies make the ninety-minute trip across Massachusetts Bay. **Boston Harbor Cruises** depart from Long Wharf daily, although the hours fluctuate – check their website for the most-up-to-date times ($70 return; ☎617/227-4321, ⊕www.bostonharborcruises.com; Aquarium **T**). From the west side of the World Trade Center pier, **Bay State Cruises** leave daily late-May to early Oct departing 8am, 1pm, & 5.30pm ($69 return; ☎617/748-1428, ⊕www.baystatecruisecompany.com, World Trade Center **T**).

Commuter rail

The only time you're likely to travel by **rail** in Boston is if you're making a day trip to historical Salem, Revolutionary battle-fields in Concord, or South Shore spots like Plymouth. All have stations on the MBTA's **commuter rail** (☎617/222-3200 or 1-800/392-6100), a faster, glossier subway than the **T**, with similarly frequent service. Most lines of interest depart from **North Station T**: Salem, Gloucester, and Rockport lie on the **Rockport Line** (15min–1hr; one-way $5.25, $7.25, and $7.75 respectively), while Concord is about midway on the **Fitchburg Line** (20min; $6.25 one-way). The exception, Plymouth, is the last stop on the **Plymouth Line** that leaves from **South Station** (55min; $7.75 one-way). Tickets can be bought in advance or aboard the train itself, though doing the latter incurs a service fee of $1.50 to $2, depending on the time of day.

Driving

Thanks to the completion of the Big Dig construction project, the **driving** situation in Boston has improved greatly over the past decade. Still, should you want to pull off the road for a while, the price of parking garages is virtually a highway robbery ($25–30 per evening and more overnight). There are metered spots on main streets like Newbury, Boylston, and Charles, but the chances of finding an empty one on any given evening are slim at best.

The cheapest **parking lots** Downtown are Center Plaza Garage, at the corner of Cambridge and New Sudbury streets ($8 after 4pm Mon–Fri and all day Sat & Sun; $8/20 min. and up to $36 max on weekdays; ☎617/742-7807), and the Garage at Post Office Square, which has good weekend deals ($9 day, weekday in after 4pm and out before 8am $9), otherwise the rates are much higher ($3.50/30min up to $29 max; ☎617/423-1430). The parking limit at non-metered spots is two hours, whether posted or not. A great little parking secret can be found at the Parcel 7 garage, at 136 Blackstone St, across from Martignetti's Liquors (☎617/973-6954). The posted rates won't mention it, but if you get your ticket validated at a North End business, the rates are only $1 an hour for the first three hours; after that prices go way up. The Prudential Center (800 Boylston) has a pretty good parking deal: $10 for four hours, day-rate $20, both with a $10 purchase from the Prudential Center shops (remember to have your receipt stamped by a sales clerk; ☎617/236-3100). You can also park and ride at the safe and cheap **Alewife T** stop in Cambridge, located at the intersection of US-2 and Cambridge Park Drive; $5 a day (t1-800/392-6100).

If you must drive, bear these rules in mind: seatbelt wearing is mandatory and the ubiquitous "Permit Parking Only" signs along residential streets must be obeyed – without the requisite parking sticker, you will be ticketed $50 or towed (expect to pay well over $50 to get your car back). Should you get a ticket, you can try sweet-talking the Office of the Parking Clerk (☎617/635-4410), but it probably won't help.

As with parking, the cost of **renting a car** in Boston can add up. If you insist on getting your own wheels, the agencies we list below will happily supply them. A compact car with unlimited mileage will ring in around $50/ day ($30 plus $12 in taxes) before insurance ($20).

Car rental agencies

Alamo ☎ 1-800-522-9696, ⓦ www.alamo.com
Avis ☎ 1-800/331-1084, ⓦ www.avis.com
Budget ☎ 1-800/527-0700, ⓦ www
.budgetrentacar.com
Dollar ☎ 1-800/800-4000, ⓦ www.dollar.com
Enterprise Rent-a-Car ☎ 1-800/325-8007,
ⓦ www.enterprise.com
Hertz ☎ 1-800/654-3001, ⓦ www.hertz.com
National ☎ 1-800/227-7368, ⓦ www
.nationalcar.com
Thrifty ☎ 1-800/367-2277, ⓦ www.thrifty.com

Cycling

Cycling runs a close second to walking as the preferred mode of city transportation. It's especially popular along the riverside promenades in Cambridge, though hustling along Downtown streets is quite agreeable by bike as well. The usual precautions – wearing a helmet and carrying a whistle – are advised.

You can **rent a bike** starting at around $25/day from Community Bicycle Supply, at 496 Tremont St (☎617/542-8623, ⓦ www.communitybicycle.com; Copley **T**); Back Bay Bicycles, at 366 Commonwealth Ave (☎617/247-2336, ⓦ www.backbaybicycles.com; Hynes **T**); or Ace Wheelworks, at 145 Elm St, Somerville (☎617/776-2100; Porter Square **T**). Wheelworks and Back Bay Bicycles also do **repairs**. A copy of *Boston's Bike Map* ($5.25) is available at any decent bike store and will help you find all the trails and bike-friendly roads in the area.

 # Tours

It's hard to avoid Boston's role in Revolutionary American history – it's proclaimed by landmarks and placards virtually everywhere you go. You could very well spend your entire visit reading every last totem yourself, but a far more enjoyable way to experience the city's lore is by guided tour. Mind you, the walking and bus tours listed below aren't just limited to covering colonial-era Americana; you can also examine the architecture of Charles Bulfinch (Boston by Foot) or the city's literary legacy (Literary Trail). There are also two multi-tour passes in the city, which offer discounted packages to several attractions.

Tour companies

On the water

Boston Duck Tours ☎617/267-DUCK, ⓦ www.bostonducktours.com. Excellent tours that take to the streets and the Charles River in restored World War II amphibious landing vehicles; kids get to skipper the bus/boat in the water. Tours depart every half-hour from the Prudential Center, at 101 Huntington Ave and the Museum of Science at Science Park; reservations advised in summer. $25.

Gondola di Venezia ☎617/876-2800, ⓦ www.bostongondolas.com. Okay, so it's not Venice. But who cares when you can woo your sweetie on one of these well-loved private gondola rides? Comes complete with chocolates and a live accordion player. Per couple $100–230.

Liberty Clipper ☎617/742-0333, ⓦ www.libertyfleet.com. This 125' tall ship takes visitors on exhilarating 2hr sails leaving from Central Wharf; daily June–Sept at noon; 3pm; and 6pm; $30.

New England Aquarium Whale Watch ☎617/542-8000, ⓦ www.neaq.org Guaranteed whale sightings or you get another trip. May–June weekends only; mid-April through Oct daily at 10am, with more trips scheduled in summer; $34.

Super Duck Tours ☎1-877/34DUCKS, ⓦ www.superduckexcursions.com. There's some duck tour competition in Boston as of late. This young pipsqueak starts and ends its tour at the Charlestown Navy Yard; it, too, shows off Boston sites as well as its own amphibious prowess. Daily, 11am–4pm on the hour; $23.

Bus and trolley tours

Beantown Trolley ☎1-800/343-1328, ☎781/986 6100, ⓦ www.beantowntrolley.com. One of the oldest and most popular history tours, covering everything from waterfront wharfs to Beacon Hill Brahmins, with multiple pick-up and drop-off points around town. A 45min harbor boat tour is included. They also run tours out to Lexington/Concord, Salem, and the like. $29.

Brush Hill Grayline Tours ☎1-800/343-1328 or 781/986-6100, ⓦ www.brushhilltours.com. Day-long coach tours to surrounding towns such as Lexington, Concord, Plymouth, and Salem. Late March to Nov; $26–50.

Discover Boston Multilingual Trolley Tours ☎617/742-1440, ⓦ www.discoverbostontours .com. Tours of Boston and Cambridge in English; audio devices available with Spanish, French, German, Italian, Japanese, and Russian. Multiple pick-up and drop-off points. $28.

Liberty Ride ☎781/862-0500 ext.702, ⓦ www .libertyride.us. Run out of Lexington and Concord, this historically based trolley ride does a really good hop-on, hop-off tour covering the area's Revolutionary War and literary history; $20.

Old Town Trolley Tours ☎617/269-7010, ⓦwww.trolleytours.com. Another hop-on, hop-off trolley tour of Boston, this one on ubiquitous orange-and-green trolleys with thematic routes like Sons and Daughters of Liberty and Ghosts and Gravestones. $26.

Walking tours

Boston by Foot ☎617/367-2345, ⓦwww .bostonbyfoot.org. Well-recommended, informative 90min walking tours that focus on the architecture and history of different Boston neighborhoods such as Beacon Hill, the North End, and Victorian Back Bay. Also has "Boston by Little Feet" tours, geared toward the Freedom Trail's smaller pedestrians. $8–12.

Boston National Historical Park Visitors Center Freedom Trail Tours ☎617/242-5642, ⓦwww.nps.gov/bost/. Educational walking tours of National Landmark sites; the Black Heritage Trail tour is highly recommended. Sept–May call for hours and reservations; June–July 10am, noon, & 2pm. Free.

Hahvahd Tour ☎203/305-9735, ⓦwww .hahvahdtour.com. Fun intro to the Harvard Campus run by lively students easily spotted in their misspelled

T-shirts. Tours leave daily from outside **Harvard T**; 10.30, 11.30, 12.30, 1.30, 2.30, 3.30pm; suggested donation $10.

Literary Trail ☎617/621-4020, ⓦwww .literarytrailofgreaterboston.org. A three-hour bus tour that takes in all the local hotshots from Henry Wadsworth Longfellow to Henry David Thoreau. $25–65.

MYTOWN ☎617/536-TOWN ⓦ www.mytowninc .com. Multicultural Youth Tour of What's Now is an organization offering 90min youth-led historical walking tours of the South End; call for times. $15.

North End Market Tour ☎617/523-6032, ⓦwww.northendmarkettours.com. Award-winning walking and tasting tours of the North End's Italian salumerias, pasticcerias, and enotecas. Reserve well in advance. Wed & Sat 10am & 2pm, Fri 10am & 3pm; $48.

Photowalks ☎617/851-2273, ⓦwww .photowalks.com. Walking tours that point out the perfect places to point and shoot. Tour themes include Beacon Hill Masterpieces, Postcards of Boston, Footsteps to Freedom, and the Waterfront. Times vary. $25 each.

Bike tours

Boston Bike Tours ☎ 617/308-5902, ⓦwww .BostonBikeTours.com. Tours of Boston, Cambridge, and surrounds, departing from Boston Common. May–Oct Sat & Sun 11am; $24–30, including equipment rental and map.

Charles River Wheelmen ☎617/332-8546 or 617/325-BIKE, ⓦ www.crw.org. Organizes free weekly cycling events, ranging from delightful Wed night ice cream rides to hardcore weekend morning fitness rides.

Multi-tour passes

Boston CityPass ☎1- 888-330-500, ⓦcitypass .com. Tickets to the Museum of Science, New England Aquarium, Skywalk Observatory, Museum of Fine Arts, Harvard Museum of Natural History, and John F Kennedy Presidential Library and Museum for $39.50 – a 50 percent saving.

Go Boston Card ☎617/742-5950, ⓦwww .gobostoncard.com. Unlimited admission to fifty attractions and tours, plus discounts on shopping and dining. One day $49, two day $79, three day $92, five day $126, seven day $143. Discounted prices are available online.

The media

Despite its legacy as the birthplace of America's first newspaper (*Publick Occurences*, published in 1690), Boston hardly ranks among the country's most media-savvy cities. The better media here is intellectual rather than newsy, and you'll certainly be engaged by *The Atlantic Monthly*, one of the US's most venerable magazines, and a slew of leftist weeklies. For all that, though, Boston's real reporting strength is sports-related: a hurricane may have hit Louisiana, but if the Celtics or the Patriots played the same day, that's what will be on the front page of the city's two daily papers (and the top story on tele-vision and radio news). It makes for pretty parochial coverage but newspapers from other US cities, as well as foreign newspapers and magazines, can be bought at Out of Town News, at Harvard Square, and major bookstores like Barnes & Noble and Borders.

Newspapers and magazines

The city's oldest newspaper, *The Boston Globe* (50¢; ⓦ www.boston.com/globe) remains Boston's best general daily, with an extensive events calendar on Thursdays; its fat Sunday edition ($2) includes substantial sections on art, culture, and lifestyle. *The Boston Herald* (50¢; ⓦ www.bostonherald .com) is the *Globe*'s tabloid alternative and is best for getting your gossip and local sports coverage fix. The free and slim daily (Mon–Fri) *Metro* paper (ⓦ www.metro.lu) is available from bins outside **T** stations.

The rest of the city's print media consists primarily of listings-oriented and free weekly papers. To know what's going on, the *Boston Phoenix* (ⓦ www.bostonphoenix .com), available at sidewalk newspaper stands around town, is essential, offering extensive entertainment listings as well as good feature articles. Other freebies like *Boston's Weekly Dig* (ⓦ www.weeklydig .com), *Improper Bostonian* (ⓦ www.improper .com), the *Phoenix*'s biweekly listings magazine, *Stuff@Night*, and *The Boston Event Guide* all have good listings of new and note-worthy happenings about town (though except for the *Dig*, the features are primarily ad-driven). *Bay Windows* (ⓦ www .baywindows.com), and *In Newsweekly* (ⓦ www.innewsweekly.com) are small weeklies catering to the gay and lesbian population, are available free at most South End cafés and bars; the cover price is 50¢ otherwise. The *Cambridge TAB* has news articles and listings exclusively about local Cambridge events.

The monthly *Boston Magazine* ($5; ⓦ www .bostonmagazine.com) is a glossy lifestyle publication with good restaurant reviews and an annual "Best of Boston" round-up in August.

TV and radio

You're likely to see more **television** than you might back home just by having a drink or eating out: televisions are as common as pint glasses in Boston bars and restaurants, and they're usually airing home-team games. Most hotels have cable TV, so you'll be able to catch regular **news** on the four major networks: CBS (channel 4), ABC (channel 5), NBC (channel 7), Fox (channel 25), and CNN, as well as keep abreast of your favorite dramas and sitcoms.

The best **radio stations** are on the FM dial, including WGBH (89.7), which carries National Public Radio (NPR) shows, plus jazz, classical, and world music; WBUR (90.9), earnest, leftist talk radio; WJMN (94.5) for good hip-hop beats; WFNX (101.7) for mainstream alternative hits; and WODS (103.3), an oldies station. To get in on Boston's sports fanaticism, tune into WEEI (850AM) for day-long sports talk.

Travel essentials

Costs

Boston ranks among the top five most **expensive** cities in the US to visit. While the high cost of accommodation, food, and drink is compensated somewhat by a wealth of inexpensive (and occasionally free) activities, there's no getting around the fact that the first is going to eat up a lot of your budget. Most of your major purchases, whether hotel or car rental, will require a credit card deposit, even if you wind up paying the total in cash.

Hotels are, by far, the biggest money-grubbers: expect to fork out somewhere in the $200 range per night just for the privilege of staying in a Boston hotel. This is due somewhat to the limited accommodation the city provides, met by a fairly constant demand. The city's B&Bs cost less (around $150 a night) and often have more atmosphere than the chain hotels that make up most of Boston's market; long-term accommodation and hostels can take the price down even further.

Food costs are more reasonable – you could get by on $20 a day, if you stay in a hotel with complimentary breakfast, grab an order of scrod at Faneuil Hall for lunch, and eat only at budget restaurants for dinner. That said, scrimping on food costs when Boston has such terrific restaurants – especially seafood ones – seems almost a waste of a trip.

The best way to stretch your dollar is to book your hotel through a discount agency like Quikbook (Ⓦwww.quikbook.com) or Ⓦwww.hotels.com, and check the Greater Boston Convention and Visitor Bureau website (Ⓦwww.bostonusa.com) for deals. You'll also save on admission prices if you have a **student ID card**, including the International Student Identification Card (ISIC; Ⓦwww.isiccard.com). The ISIC is available through most student travel agencies for $22 for Americans; CAN$16 for Canadians; AUS$18 for Australians; NZ$20 for New Zealanders; and £7 for UK citizens. For the same price, an International Youth Travel Card (IYTC) is available and offers similar discounts to travelers under 26.

Otherwise, save money by traveling Oct–March, outside of peak season (although keep in mind that this is Boston's winter, so prepare for blustery days and lots of snow).

Crime and personal safety

Boston is one of the safer American cities, making solo travel, even for women, relatively worry-free. There are, as with anywhere, exceptions; at night-time especially, areas like Dorchester, Roxbury, the Fens, Downtown Crossing, and parts of the South End can feel deserted and sketchy – but you're unlikely to find yourself in many of these neighborhoods after dark, anyway. The **T** is also safe by day and, for the most part, at night; if you stick to the lines that serve the major nightlife areas (especially the Green and Red lines), you're unlikely to have any trouble.

Pickpocketing is not a huge problem, but that doesn't mean it never happens; use common sense and keep an eye on your belongings when at the ATM, on the subway, and paying up at corner stores. If you are robbed, call the police at ☎911. Note that **drugs**, including marijuana, are illegal and you will be fined and possibly sentenced to jail time if caught taking or selling them.

Electricity

As with the rest of the US, electrical outlets in Boston use 100 volts AC. Plugs are standard American two-pins.

Entry requirements

Under the **visa waiver scheme**, passport-holders from Britain, Ireland, Australia, New Zealand, and most European countries do not require visas for trips to the United States, including Hawaii, so long as they stay less than ninety days in the US, and have an

US embassies abroad
Australia 21 Moonah Place, Yarralumla, Canberra, ACT 2600 ℡02/6214 5600, ⓦusembassy-australia.state.gov
Canada 490 Sussex Drive, Ottawa, ON K1P 5T1 ℡613/238 5335, ⓦwww .usembassycanada.gov
Ireland 42 Elgin Rd, Ballsbridge, Dublin 4 ℡01/688 8777, ⓦdublin.usembassy.gov
New Zealand 29 Fitzherbert Terrace, Thorndon, Wellington ℡04/462 6000, ⓦwww .usembassy.org.nz
UK 24–31 Grosvenor Square, London, W1A 1AE ℡020/7499 9000, 24-hr visa hotline ℡09068/200 290 (60p/min), ⓦwww.usembassy.org.uk

Embassies and consulates in Boston
Australia 55 Thomson Place ℡617/261-5555
Canada 3 Copley Place, suite 500 ℡617/262-3760
Ireland 535 Boylston St ℡617/267-9330
New Zealand 57 North Main St, PO Box 1318 Concord, New Hampshire ℡603/225-8228
UK 1 Memorial Drive, Suite 1500, Cambridge ℡617/245-4500

onward or return ticket. Instead you simply fill in the visa waiver form handed out on incoming planes. Immigration control takes place at your point of arrival on US soil.

For you to be eligible for the visa waiver scheme, your passport must be **machine-readable**, with a barcode-style number. All children need to have their own individual passports. Holders of older, unreadable passports should therefore either obtain new ones or apply for visas prior to travel. For full details, visit ⓦhttp://travel.state.gov.

Canadian citizens can continue to visit the US for up to six months, as long as they present proof of citizenship (a passport or birth certificate and photo ID). Questions may be put to the US embassy at 490 Sussex Drive, Ottawa, ON, K1N 1G8 (℡613/238-5335, ⓦwww .usembassycanada.gov). If you're planning a work- or study-related visit, you will need to get a visa.

Health

Visitors from Europe, Australia, New Zealand, and Canada don't require any vaccinations to enter the US, and there aren't any out-of-the-ordinary health concerns to consider when coming to the city.

For **emergencies** or ambulances, dial ℡**911**. If you have medical or dental problems that don't require an ambulance,

most hospitals will have a walk-in **emergency room**; for the nearest hospital, check with your hotel or dial ℡**411**. Should you need to see a **doctor**, the Massa-chusetts General Physician Referral Service (Mon–Fri 8.30am–5pm; ℡617/726-5800) puts you in touch with physicians at Massachusetts General Hospital, the MGH Inter-national Patient Center (55 Fruit St; ℡617/726-2787) is geared toward helping international travellers and offers interpreting services. For immediate care, Inn-House Doctor (839 Beacon Street, Suite B, ℡617/859-1776, ⓦwww.inn-housedoctor.net) makes 24-hour house calls; rates begin at $300 and prescriptions cost more. The Fenway Community Health Center is geared particu-larly toward the gay and lesbian community but anyone can drop onto its center at 7 Haviland St (℡617/267-0900 or 1-888/242-0900, ⓦwww.fenwayhealth.org), which offers HIV testing during weekdays.

Prescriptions can be filled at the ubiqui-tous CVS **drugstore** chain. You can also pick up over-the-counter analgesics here, though international travelers should bear in mind that if you're partial to a particular brand back home, you should bring some with you – you might not find it in the US (this is especially true of codeine-based painkillers, which require a prescription in the US).

Should you be in an accident, an ambulance will take you to a **hospital** and charge you later. For walk-in emergencies, the Massachusetts General Hospital, 55 Fruit St (☎617/726-2000, ☒www.mgh .harvard.edu; Charles/MGH **T**); Beth Israel Deaconess Medical Center, 330 Brookline Ave (☎617/667-7000, ☒www.bidmc.harvard .edu; Longwood **T**); and New England Medical Center, 800 Washington St (☎617/636-5000, ☒www.nemc.org; NE Medical **T**); all have 24-hour emergency rooms. **Women travelers** with urgent needs can visit the Women's Hospital, 75 Francis St (☎617/732-5500 or 1-800/BWH-9999, ☒www.bwh.partners.org; Longwood or Brigham Circle **T**). Parents can take their kids to the Children's Hospital, 300 Longwood Ave (☎617/355-6000, ☒www .tch.harvard.edu; Longwood **T**).

Insurance

In view of the high cost of medical care in the US, all travelers visiting the US from overseas should be sure to buy some form of **travel insurance**. American and Canadian citizens should check that you're not already covered – some homeowners' or renters' policies are valid on vacation, and credit cards such as American Express often include some medical or other insurance, while most Canadians are covered for medical mishaps overseas by their provincial health plans. If you only need trip cancellation/interruption coverage (to supplement your existing plan), this is generally available at about $6 per $100.

Rough Guides has teamed up with Columbus Direct to offer you **travel insurance** that can be tailored to suit your needs. Products include a low-cost **backpacker** option for long stays; a **short break** option for city getaways; a typical **holiday package** option; and others. There are also annual **multi-trip** policies for those who travel regularly. Different sports and activities (trekking, diving, etc.) can be usually be covered if required.

For eligibility and purchasing options, see our website (☒www.roughguidesinsurance .com) . Alternatively, UK residents should call ☎0870/033 9988; Australians should call ☎1300/669 999 and New Zealanders should call ☎0800/55 9911.

All other nationalities should call ☎+44 870/890 2843.

Internet access

If you have a suitable laptop, you'll find **wireless access** is plentiful in Boston. Most hotels feature Wi-Fi hotspots, as does the public library, Faneuil Hall Marketplace, the CambridgeSide Galleria, in Cambridge, and branches of *Starbucks;* plus the city is currently undergoing an ambitious plan to have Wi-Fi citywide (check ☒boston.wifimug .org for updates).

Without a computer, the best way to check your email is to pop into a local university and use one of their free public computers. Harvard's Holyoke Center, at 1350 Massachusetts Ave in Cambridge, has a couple of stations with ten-minute access maximum. The same goes for MIT's Rogers Building, at 77 Massachusetts Ave (also in Cambridge). Boston's main public library, at 700 Boylston St, has free fifteen-minute Internet access on the ground floor of the Johnson building (as well as free Wi-Fi internet access throughout). You could also pop into one of the ubiquitous Kinko's; their Government Center location (☎617/973-9000) at 2 Center Plaza is open 24 hours from Mon–Thurs, as well as Fri 6am–10pm, Sat 8am–10pm, and Sun 8am–midnight.

Mail

Boston's **postal service** is as efficient as most US cities and has multiple outlets scattered about town. For the quickest service, use the coin-operated machines to buy books of stamps – letters and postcards within the US cost 41¢ and 24¢, respectively.

The most **central post office** downtown is at 31 Milk St in Post Office Square (Mon–Fri 7.30am–7pm; ☎617/482-1956); Cambridge's central branch is at 770 Massachusetts Ave, in Central Square (Mon–Fri 7.30am–6pm, Sat 7.30am–2pm; ☎617/876-0620). The General Post Office, 25 Dorchester Ave, behind South Station, is open 24 hours a day (☎617/654-5326). You can receive mail at the latter by having it addressed to you c/o Poste Restante, GPO, 25 Dorchester Ave, Boston MA, 02205. To collect letters, present some form of photo

ID at the window between 10am and 1pm Mon–Sat; non-acquired letters are thrown out after thirty days.

Maps

The **maps** in this book, and those given out at Boston tourism kiosks, should satisfy most of your needs; if you want something more comprehensive, best is the rip-proof, waterproof **Rough Guide Map to Boston** ($8.95), a street atlas that pinpoints recommended restaurants, bars, sights, and shops along the way. Cyclists might want to pick up *Boston's Bike Map* ($5.25), available at the Globe Corner Bookstore (28 Church St, ☎617/497-6277; Harvard **T**) and online at ⓦwww.massbike.org.

Money

Most visitors find that there's no reason to carry large amounts of cash or traveler's checks to Boston. Automatic teller machines (**ATMs**), which accept most cards issued by domestic and foreign banks, can be found almost everywhere; call your own bank if you're in any doubt.

If you do want to take **traveler's checks** – which offer the great security of knowing that lost or stolen checks will be replaced – be sure to get them issued in US dollars. Foreign currency, whether cash or travelers' checks, can be hard to exchange, so foreign travelers should change some of their money into dollars at home.

For most services, it's taken for granted that you'll be paying with a **credit card**. Hotels and car rental companies routinely require an imprint of your card whether or not you intend to use it to pay.

Banking hours typically run Mon–Fri 9am–5pm; some banks stay open later on Thursdays and Fridays, and even fewer have Saturday hours. Major banks like Sovereign and Bank of America will exchange traveler's checks and currencies at the standard exchange rate (one or two percent). Outside of banks, you're limited to exchange bureaus in Cambridge, Boston, and the airport, which set their own, often higher, commission and rates.

Opening hours and public holidays

The **opening hours** of specific attractions, monuments, memorials, stores, and offices are given in the relevant accounts throughout the guide. As a general rule, museums are open daily 10am – 5.30pm, though some have extended summer hours; a few art galleries stay open until 9pm or so one night a week. Smaller, private museums close for one day a week, usually Monday or Tuesday. Federal office buildings (some of which incorporate museums) are open Monday through Friday 9am – 5.30pm. Stores are usually open Monday through Saturday 10am – 7pm and Sunday noon–5pm; some have extended Thursday and Friday night hours. Malls tend to be open Monday through Saturday 10am – 7pm (or later) and Sunday noon – 6pm.

On the national **public holidays** listed in the box below, stores, banks, and public and federal offices are liable to be closed all day. The Museum of Fine Arts and Isabella Stewart Gardner museums, though, stay open on holiday Mondays – but no others – year round. The traditional summer tourism season, when many attractions have extended opening hours, runs from Memorial Day to Labor Day.

Boston has a huge variety of annual **festivals** and events, many of them historical

---

National public holidays

The following are public holidays on which banks, post offices, and many (although by no means all) shops and attractions will be closed:

Jan 1 **New Year's Day**	First Mon in Sept **Labor Day**
Third Mon in Jan **Martin Luther King, Jr.'s Birthday**	Second Mon in Oct **Columbus Day**
	Nov 11 **Veterans' Day**
Third Mon in Feb **Presidents' Day**	Fourth Thurs in Nov **Thanksgiving**
Last Mon in May **Memorial Day**	Dec 25 **Christmas Day**
July 4 **Independence Day**	

in scope. For a full calendar, turn to Chapter 19, "Festivals and events." It's worth noting that during all major festival periods – particularly the Head of the Charles Regatta, Easter, Memorial Day, and the Fourth of July – it can be very difficult to find accommodation in the city. Book well in advance if you plan to visit Boston at any of these times.

Phones

Boston's **area code** is ☎617; you can reach the city from elsewhere in the US or Canada by dialing ☎1-617 before the seven-digit number; from abroad, dial your country's international access code, then ☎1-617 and the seven-digit number.

Local calls cost 50¢ in coin-operated public phones; when making a local call, compose all ten digits, including the area code. Operator assistance (☎0) and directory information (☎411) are toll-free from public telephones (but not from in-room phones).

Hotels impose huge surcharges, so it's best to use a **phone card** for long-distance calls. In preference to the ones issued by the major phone companies, you'll find it simpler and cheaper to choose from the various pre-paid cards sold in almost all supermarkets and general stores.

Cell phones

If you're from overseas and want to use your **cell** phone in Boston, you'll need to check with your phone provider whether it will work

there, and what the call charges are. Unless you have a tri-band phone, it is unlikely that a cell phone bought for use outside the US will work inside the States.

Time

Boston is in the East Coast time zone, three hours ahead of West Coast America, five hours behind Britain and Ireland, fourteen to sixteen hours behind East Coast Australia (variations for Daylight Savings Time), sixteen to eighteen hours behind New Zealand (variations for Daylight Savings Time).

Tipping

Wait staff in restaurants expect tips of at least fifteen percent, in bars a little less. Hotel porters and bellhops should receive at least $2 per piece of luggage, and housekeeping staff at least $2 per night.

Tourist information

The best source of information for Boston is the Greater Boston Convention and Visitors Bureau's (GBCVB) website, ⓦwww .bostonusa.com, which maintains up-to-date information on events about town, a terrific list of special deals, and an online reservation service; agents can also make recommendations and bookings for you (call ⓦ1-888/SEE BOSTON).

The **GBCVB** produces the free *Guidebook to Boston*, a 100-page overview of restaurants, hotels, and sights, and a slimmer *Travel*

Useful telephone numbers

Area code ☎617
Directory assistance ☎411 or 1-800/555-1212 (for toll-free numbers)
Emergencies ☎911 for fire department, police, and ambulance.
Operator ☎0

International calling codes
Calling Boston from abroad international access code + 1 + 617 + seven-digit number.

To make international calls from the US, dial 011 followed by the country code (note that if you're calling Canada, you simply need to dial a 1, then the area code and number, as though you were making a domestic call):
Australia 61
Ireland 353
New Zealand 64
United Kingdom 44
For codes not listed here, dial the operator or check the front of the local White Pages.

Planner booklet; both can be mailed to you by request. For information once there, stop by the two GBCVB-run tourism centers: one is in Boston Common, west of the Park **T** stop, facing Tremont Street, and the other is in the Prudential Center, at 800 Boylston St. Both are open daily from 9am to 5pm. Across from the Old State House, at 15 State St, is a visitor center maintained by the Boston National Historical Park (daily 9am–5pm); it too has plenty of free brochures, plus a bookstore and bathrooms.

Visitors to **Cambridge** can get all the information they need from the Cambridge Office of Tourism (T1-800/862-5678, Wwww.cambridge-usa.org), which maintains a well-stocked kiosk in Harvard Square (Mon–Sat 9am–5pm).

Useful websites

Many **websites** contain travel information about Boston. What follows is a short list of both informative and irreverent sites that'll give you the low-down on what's going on around town, local trivia, neighborhood profiles, and other Boston ephemera.

Boston Globe Wwww.boston.com Perhaps the most useful Boston-related website, with extensive events listings, restaurant reviews, and (of course) local and national news.

Boston Online Wwww.boston-online.com General info on the city, including a dictionary of Bostonian English and a guide to public bathrooms.

Boston Phoenix Wwww.bostonphoenix.com Easily searched site from the city's alternative weekly, with up-to-date arts, music, and nightlife listings, restaurant reviews, and lots of cool links.

The Bostonian Society Wwww.bostonhistory.org The official historical society of the city has info on its museum (see p.50) as well as a complete transcript of the Boston Massacre trial.

Link Pink Wwww.linkpink.com Comprehensive listings of businesses, hotels, shops, and services catering for New England's gay and lesbian community.

Massachusetts Office of Travel and Tourism Wwww.massvacation.com The state-wide tourism bureau is especially useful if you're planning side trips to Cape Cod, Nantucket, or Martha's Vineyard.

Weekly Dig Wwww.weeklydig.com Website for Boston's most irreverent weekly; contains the usual reviews and events listings, less staid than other Boston publications.

Travelers with disabilities

For people with mobility impairments, getting around Boston is possible for the simple reason that the city is relatively flat and curb cuts abound. **Public transportation** can also be used: many MBTA buses and **T** stops are wheelchair-accessible; for detailed information, call T617/222-5976 or T617/222-5123, or visit Wwww.mbta.com. In addition, most major **taxi** companies have some vehicles with wheelchair lifts; Metro Cab (T617/242-8000) comes highly recommended.

Very Special Arts (T617/350-7713; Wwww.accessexpressed.net) has superior information on the accessibility of museums, sights, movie theaters, and other cultural venues in the Boston area. For everything else, contact the **Massachusetts Office on Disability**, a one-stop resource for all accessibility issues whether in Boston or further away; call T617/727-7440 or toll-free on 1-800/322-2020.

The City

The City

Downtown Boston

oston's compact **Downtown** encompasses both the colonial heart
and the contemporary core of the city. This assemblage of compressed
red-brick buildings tucked in the shadow of modern office towers may
seem less glamorous than other American big-city centers, but the
sheer concentration of historic sights here more than makes up for whatever's
lacking in flash. During the day, there's a constant buzz of commuters and
tourists, but come nightfall, the streets thin out considerably. On the upside,
many areas bordering Downtown proper remain lively come evening –
commercialized Quincy Market, which has a decent bar scene; Chinatown,
with its popular late-night restaurants; the Theater District, particularly
animated on weekends; and the waterfront, pleasantly illuminated by the lights
of harbored boats. Across the water, the Seaport District has a number of lively
dinner spots in addition to the glittery Institute for Contemporary Arts, a good
bet for evening concerts and performances.

Boston Common (a king-sized version of the tidy greenspaces at the core
of innumerable New England villages) is the starting point for the city's popular
Freedom Trail, a self-guided walking tour that connects an assortment of
historic sights by a ribbon of red brick embedded in the pavement. Abutting
the Common, several churches and old buildings are worth a peek on your way
toward **Washington Street**, where the **Old State House** and **Old South
Meeting House** provide high-water marks in pre-Revolution interest, and
over at Summer Street, **Downtown Crossing** makes for some of the best
shopping in town. Just east, the **Financial District**'s short streets still follow the
tangled patterns of colonial-village lanes, though they are now lined with all
manner of tall office buildings. A couple of blocks north stands the ever-popular
meeting place of **Faneuil Hall**.

East of Boston Common, small but energetic **Chinatown** and the nearby
Theater District are primarily of interest after dark; also in the area is the
Leather District, a chic, up-and-coming neighborhood typified by meandering
warehouse spaces. Finally, you can get the flavor of Boston Harbor, once the third
busiest in the world and enjoying a new vibrancy thanks to its reconnection to
the city with the completion of the Big Dig. Along the waterfront, scenic wharfs
jut out into Massachusetts Bay; the most bustling, **Long Wharf**, is the departure
point for **whale-watching** excursions and trips to a handful of **islands** that
make for relaxing getaways.

Though colonial Downtown boasted numerous hills, they've since been
smoothed over, and only the name of a particularly pronounced peak –
Trimountain – lives on in **Tremont Street**. **King's Chapel**, on Tremont, and
the nearby **Old State House** mark the periphery of Boston's earliest town
center, and the colonies' first church, market, newspaper, and prison were all

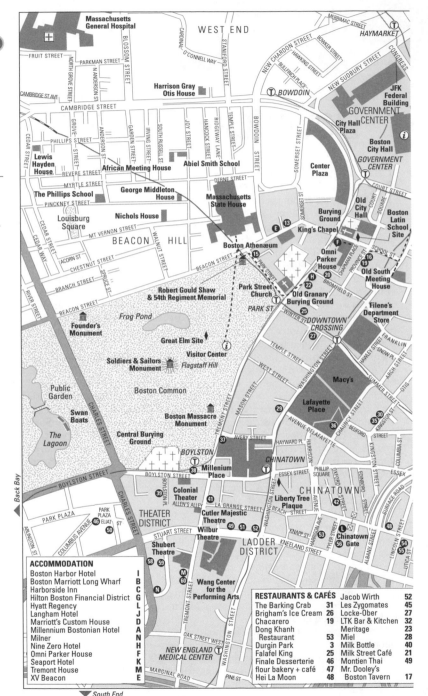

ACCOMMODATION

Boston Harbor Hotel	I
Boston Marriott Long Wharf	B
Harborside Inn	C
Hilton Boston Financial District	G
Hyatt Regency	L
Langham Hotel	J
Marriott's Custom House	D
Millennium Bostonian Hotel	A
Milner	N
Nine Zero Hotel	H
Omni Parker House	F
Seaport Hotel	K
Tremont House	M
XV Beacon	E

RESTAURANTS & CAFÉS

The Barking Crab	31	Jacob Wirth	52
Brigham's Ice Cream	26	Les Zygomates	45
Chacarero	19	Locke-Ober	27
Dong Khanh		LTK Bar & Kitchen	32
Restaurant	53	Meritage	23
Durgin Park	3	Miel	28
Falafel King	25	Milk Bottle	40
Finale Desserterie	46	Milk Street Café	21
flour bakery + café	47	Montien Thai	49
Hei La Moon	48	Mr. Dooley's	
		Boston Tavern	17

DOWNTOWN

North End
Charlestown

0   500 yds

Commercial Wharf

Harbor Islands

Holocaust Monument
Christopher Columbus Park
Long Wharf

ROSE KENNEDY GREENWAY

CROSS STREET
HANOVER ST.
NORTH ST.
FULTON STREET
COMMERCIAL STREET
ATLANTIC AVENUE
CROSS STREET
BLACKSTONE STREET
CREEK SQ ST.
UNION STREET

North Market Building

CLINTON STREET

North St.

Quincy Market

Faneuil Hall

South Market Building

AQUARIUM

CHATHAM STREET

Richards Building

Curley Memorial

Boston Massacre Site

STATE

Custom House tower

New England Aquarium

Harbor Cruises

Cunard Building

STATE STREET

India Wharf

Old State House

Fleet Bank Exchange Place

Grain and Flour Exchange Building

CENTRAL ST.

ATLANTIC AVENUE

EAST INDIA ROW

MILK STREET

CONGRESS STREET

EXCHANGE

HAWES ST.

WATER STREET

LIBERTY SQUARE

WELL STREET

BROAD STREET

CUSTOM HOUSE DISTRICT

Rowes Wharf

Post Office Square

US Post Office & Courthouse

MILK STREET

DEVONSHIRE STREET

OLIVER ST.

BATTERYMARCH STREET

WENDELL'S STREET

HIGH STREET

Post Office Square Park

FINANCIAL DISTRICT

FORT HILL SQUARE

FORT HILL

OLIVER STREET

Foster's Wharf

Verizon Building

Bank of Boston

PEARL STREET

CONGRESS STREET

GRIDLEY ST.

PURCHASE STREET

MATTHEWS ST.

FEDERAL STREET

HIGH STREET

WINTHROP SQUARE

ROSE KENNEDY GREENWAY

ATLANTIC AVENUE

PURCHASE STREET

NORTHERN AVENUE BRIDGE (PEDESTRIAN ACCESS ONLY)

EVELYN MOAKLEY BRIDGE

NORTHERN AVENUE

COURTHOUSE WAY

SEAPORT BOULEVARD

N

Federal Reserve Plaza

DEWEY SQUARE

SOUTH STATION

LEATHER DISTRICT

SUMMER STREET

South Station Transportation Center

CONGRESS STREET BRIDGE

Children's Museum

SLEEPER STREET

FARNSWORTH STREET

THOMSON PLACE

STILLINGS STREET

TUFTS ST.

EAST STREET

ATLANTIC AVENUE

DORCHESTER AVENUE

SUMMER STREET BRIDGE

Hood Milk Bottle

CONGRESS STREET

BEACH STREET

SOUTH STREET

US South Postal Annex

South Station Transportation Center

Fort Point Channel

MELCHER ST.

NECCO COURT

Red Line
Blue Line
Green Line
Orange Line
Freedom Trail

No Name Restaurant	33	Sel de la Terre	10	
No. 9 Park	15	Shabu-Zen	56	
O Ya	43	Silvertone	20	
Peach Farm	36	Sorriso Trattoria	44	
Pigalle	58	South Street Diner	61	
Pressed	18	Sultan's Kitchen	14	
Quincy Market	4	Taiwan Café	42	
Salvatore's	34	Teatro	37	
Sam La Grassa's	16	Union Oyster House	9	
Scollay Square	13	Wagamama	9	
		Walrus and Carpenter	7	

BARS & CLUBS

		The Good Life	35	The Liquor Store	39	
Beantown Pub	22	Green Dragon		Lucky's	57	
Bell in Hand Tavern	2	Tavern	2	Mr. Dooley's		
The Black Rose (Roisin Dubh)	11	Gypsy Bar	38	Boston Tavern	17	
		Houston's	12	Ned Devine's	6	
Buzz	51	Jacque's Cabaret	50	The Roxy	60	
Cheers	8	JJ Foley's	30	Umbria	24	
District	55	The Kinsale	5	Venu	59	
Felt	29	Limelight	41	Weggie's Pub	54	

43

clustered here, though much closer to the shoreline than the plaques marking their former sites. **Spring Lane**, a tiny pedestrian passage off Washington Street, recalls the springs that lured the earliest settlers over to the Shawmut Peninsula from Charlestown. The most evocative streets, however, are those whose essential characters have been less diluted over the years – **School Street**, **State Street**, and the eighteenth-century enclave known as **Blackstone Block**, near Faneuil Hall.

Boston Common and around

Boston's premier greenspace, **Boston Common**, is a fifty-acre chunk of green, neither meticulously manicured nor especially attractive, which effectively separates Downtown from its posh neighbors, Beacon Hill and Back Bay. It's the first thing you'll see emerging from the **Park Street T station**, the central transfer point of America's first subway and, unfortunately, a magnet for panhandlers.

Established in 1634 as "a trayning field" and "for the feeding of cattell," as a slate tablet opposite the station recalls, the Common is still primarily utilitarian, used by both pedestrian commuters on their way to Downtown's office towers and tourists seeking the **Boston Visitor Information Pavilion** at 147 Tremont St (Mon–Fri 8.30am–5pm, Sat & Sun 9am–5pm; ℡617/426-3115), which is the official starting point of the Freedom Trail. Along the northern side of the Common, the lovely **Beacon Street** runs from the gold-domed State House to Charles Street, opposite the Public Garden (for fuller coverage of Beacon Street, see Chapter 4).

Even before John Winthrop and his fellow Puritan colonists earmarked Boston Common for public use, it served as pasture land for the Reverend William Blackstone, Boston's first white settler. Soon after, it disintegrated into little more than a gallows for pirates, alleged witches, and various religious heretics – a commoner by the name of Rachell Whall was once hanged here for stealing a bonnet worth 75¢. Newly elected president George Washington made a much-celebrated appearance on the Common in 1789, as did his aide-de-camp, the Marquis de Lafayette, several years later. Ornate nineteenth-century iron fencing encircled the entire park until World War II, when it was taken down for use as scrap metal; it's now said to grace the bottom of Boston Harbor.

One of the few actual sights here is the **Central Burying Ground**, which has occupied the southeast corner of the Common, near the intersection of Boylston and Tremont streets, since 1754. Gilbert Stuart, best known for his portraits of George Washington – the most famous of which is replicated on the dollar bill – died penniless and was interred in Tomb 61. Among the other notables are members of the largest family to take part in the Boston Tea Party, various soldiers of the Revolutionary Army, and Redcoats killed in the Battle of Bunker Hill.

From the Burying Ground it's a short walk to **Flagstaff Hill**, the highest point on the Common, crowned with the granite-pillared Civil War **Soldiers and Sailors Monument**, which is topped by a bronze statue of Lady Liberty and encircled by four plaques displaying scenes of cap-wearing sailors and bayonet-toting infantry. A former repository of colonial gunpowder, the hill overlooks the **Frog Pond**, once home to a large number of amphibians and

▲ The Brewer Fountain in Boston Common

site of the first water pumped into the city. These days it's nothing more than a kidney-shaped pool, used for wading in summer and ice-skating in winter. From here, a path east of the pond leads to the elegant, two-tiered **Brewer Fountain**, an 1868 bronze replica of one from the Paris Exposition of 1855; the scantily clad gods and goddesses at its base are watched over by cherubs from above.

The Park Street Church

An oversized version of a typical New England village church, the **Park Street Church** (mid-June to Aug daily 8.30am–3pm, rest of year by appointment; free; ☎617/523-3383, ⓦwww.parkstreet.org; Park Street **T**) has stood at the northeast corner of Park and Tremont streets, just across from Boston Common, since 1809. Though a rather uninteresting mass of bricks and mortar, its ornate 217-foot-tall white telescoping **steeple** is undeniably impressive. To get an idea of the immensity of the building, including the spire, check out the view from tiny Hamilton Place, across Tremont. Ultimately, the structure's reputation rests not on its size but on the scope of events that took place inside: in 1819 the parish sent the country's first missionaries to Hawaii; a decade later, on July 4, 1829, William Lloyd Garrison delivered his first public address calling for the nationwide abolition of slavery (Massachusetts had already scrapped it in 1783); and on July 4, 1831, the classic patriotic song *America* ("My country 'tis of thee...") was first sung to the church rafters.

Park Street itself slopes upward along the edge of Boston Common toward the State House (see p.50). The stretch was once known as **Bulfinch Row**, for its many brick townhouses designed by the architect Charles Bulfinch (see p.85). Today only one remains, the imposing bay-windowed **Amory-Ticknor House** at no. 9, built in 1804 for George Ticknor, the first publisher of the *Atlantic Monthly*; it's now home to the first-rate restaurant *No. 9 Park* (see p.166)

The Old Granary Burying Ground

Adjacent to the Park Street Church is one of the more peaceful stops on the always-busy Freedom Trail, the **Old Granary Burying Ground** (daily 9am–5pm; free; Park Street **T**), final resting place for numerous leaders of the American Revolution. The entrance, an Egyptian Revival arch, fronts Tremont Street, and it's from the Tremont sidewalk that some of the most famous gravesites can be best appreciated. On the side closest to Park Street Church, a boulder with an attached plaque marks the tomb of revolutionary **James Otis**, known for his articulate tirades against British tyranny. A few tombs down, heading away from the church, rest the bones of **Samuel Adams**, the charismatic patriot whose sideline in beer brewing has kept him a household name. Next to his tomb is the group grave of the five people killed in the **Boston Massacre** of 1770, an event that fueled anti-Tory feeling in Boston (see p.52). From any angle you can see the stocky **obelisk** at dead center that marks the grave of Benjamin Franklin's parents.

Somewhat more secure burial vaults and table tombs – semi-submerged sarcophagi – were preferred by wealthier families. **Peter Faneuil**, who gave his money and his name to Boston's most prominent hall, is interred in one of the latter in the left rear corner of the grounds. Midway along the back path is the grave of famed messenger and silversmith **Paul Revere**. Across from Revere, in a red-toned sarcophagus, lies the infamous Salem Witch Trial Judge **Samuel Sewall**; Sewall later apologized for his "condemnation" of "innocent people." Across from the judge's grave on the Park Street Church side, a white pillar marks the resting spot of Declaration of Independence signer **John Hancock**. **Robert Treat Paine**, another signatory, lies along the eastern periphery.

The Boston Athenæum

Around the block from the Old Granary Burying Ground, the venerable **Boston Athenæum**, 101/2 Beacon St (Mon 8.30am–8pm, Tues–Fri 8.30am–5.30pm, Sat

The Freedom Trail

Boston is so permeated by history that the city often stands accused of living in its past, and tourist-friendly contrivances like the **Freedom Trail** only serve to perpetuate the notion. It originated when, like many American cities, Boston experienced an economic slump in the years after World War II as people migrated to the suburbs; in response, resident William Schofield came up with the idea of a trail highlighting historic Boston sights to lure visitors – and their money – back into town.

Delineated by a 2.5-mile-long red-brick (or paint) stripe in (or on) the sidewalk, the trail stretches from Boston Common to Charlestown, linking sixteen points "significant in their contribution to this country's struggle for freedom." It's a somewhat vague qualifier, resulting in the inclusion of several sights that have little to do with Boston's place in the American Revolution. In the relevant column, there's the Revolutionary-era **Old North Church**, whose lanterns warned of the British arrival; **Faneuil Hall**, where opposition to the Brits' proposed tea tax was voiced; the **Old South Meeting House**, wherein word came that said tax would be imposed; the **Old State House**, which served as the Boston seat of British government; and the site of the **Boston Massacre**.

Other stops on the trail, however, have nothing whatsoever to do with the struggle for Independence, like the **USS Constitution**, built fully two decades after the Declaration of Independence (but which failed, notably, to sink under British cannon fire, earning her the nickname "Old Ironsides"); the **Park Street Church**, built another fifteen years after that; and the **Old Corner Bookstore**, a publishing house for American (and some British) writers. You'll also find two instances of British dominion along the trail – the **Bunker Hill Monument**, an obelisk commemorating, ironically, a British victory, albeit in the guise of a moral one for America, and **King's Chapel**, built to serve the King's men stationed in Boston. Finally, you can check out the digs of the gilt-domed **Massachusetts State House** after visiting the gravesites of the Boston luminaries who fought for it; they lie interred in three separate **cemeteries**.

Unfortunately, some of the touches intended to accentuate the attractions' appeal move closer to tarnishing it. The people in period costume stationed outside some of the sights can't help but grate a little, and the artificially enhanced atmosphere is exaggerated by the bright red-brick trail and pseudo old signage that connects the sights. Still, the Freedom Trail remains the easiest way to orient yourself Downtown, and is especially useful if you'll only be in Boston for a short time, as it does take in many "must-see" sights. For more information and an interactive timeline of Boston's history, visit ⓦ www.thefreedomtrail.org. You can also pick up a detailed National Park Service **map** at the **Visitor Information Pavilion** (see p.44) in Boston Common, from where the trail begins, or via the affable **Boston National Park Service** visitor center at 15 State Street; a combination entrance ticket ($11) is available for three sights – the Old South Meeting House, the Old State House, and the Paul Revere House. It can be purchased from the ticket desk at any of these three attractions.

Freedom Trail sights

Boston Massacre site p.52
Bunker Hill Monument p.80
Copp's Hill Burying Ground p.72
Faneuil Hall p.55
First public school site
 (Boston Latin) p.49
King's Chapel p.48
King's Chapel Burying Ground p.48
Massachusetts State House p.84

Old Corner Bookstore p.49
Old Granary Burying Ground p.46
Old North Church p.71
Old South Meeting House p.50
Old State House p.50
The Park Street Church p.46
Paul Revere House p.68
USS Constitution p.76

9am–4pm; free; ☎617/227-0270, Ⓦwww.bostonathenaeum.org; Park Street **T**), was established in 1807, and stakes its claim as one of the oldest independent research libraries in the country. In naming their library, the Boston Brahmin founders demonstrated not only their high-minded classicism but marketing sensibility too, as the city was consequently endowed with a lofty sobriquet – the "Athens of America" – that has stuck.

Following extensive renovations in 2002 to "modernize" the edifice (a replica of the Palazzo da Porta Festa in Vicenza, Italy), only the first-floor library is open to nonmembers. It's well worth popping in, however, if only to experience its gorgeous artworks, the holdings for which were used as underpinnings for the original Museum of Fine Arts; to this day, certain works continue to travel back and forth between the two establishments. Best known are its special collections, including the original library of King's Chapel – which counts the 1666 edition of Sir Walter Raleigh's *History of the World* among its holdings – as well as books from the private library of George Washington. There is also an impressive array of paintings by the likes of John Singer Sargent and Gilbert Stuart. To get a better sense of the collection, join a docent-led art and architecture **tour** (Tues & Thurs 3pm; reservations required; free; ☎617/227-0270 ext.279, Ⓦwww .bostonathenaeum.org).

King's Chapel Burying Ground and King's Chapel

Boston's oldest cemetery, the atmospheric **King's Chapel Burying Ground**, located at the northeast corner of Beacon and Tremont streets (10am–4pm; free; Park Street **T**), often goes unnoticed by busy pedestrians. Coupled with its accompanying church, however, it's well worth a tour despite the din of nearby traffic. There are many beautifully etched gravestones here, with their winged skulls and contemplative seraphim; one of the best examples belongs to an unknown Joseph Tapping near the Tremont Street side. Among the many prominent Bostonians buried here are **John Winthrop**, the first governor of Massachusetts, and **Mary Chilton**, the first Pilgrim to set foot on Plymouth Rock; near the center of the plot is the tomb of **William Dawes**, the unsung patriot who accompanied Paul Revere on his famous "midnight ride" to Lexington. King's Chapel Burying Ground was one of the favorite Boston haunts of author **Nathaniel Hawthorne**, who visited the grave of a certain Elizabeth Pain, inspiration for the famously adulterous character Hester Prynne in his novel *The Scarlet Letter* (Hawthorne himself is buried in Concord's Sleepy Hollow Cemetery; see p.233).

King's Chapel

The most conspicuous thing about gray, foreboding **King's Chapel**, on the premises of the burying grounds, is its lack of a steeple (there were plans for one, just not enough money). But the belfry does boast the biggest bell ever cast by silversmith Paul Revere (incidentally, it's also the biggest bell in Boston), which you can't help but notice if you happen to pass by at chime time. A wooden chapel was built on this site first, amid some controversy in 1686, when King James II revoked the Massachusetts Bay Colony's charter and installed Sir Edmund Andros as governor, giving him orders to found an Anglican parish – a move that didn't sit too well with Boston's Puritan population – and resulted in the chapel being built illegally, on Puritan land. The present chapel, completed in 1754 by Peter Harrison under instructions to create a church "that would be the equal of any in England," is entered through a pillar-fronted portico added in 1789, when it became the country's first Unitarian Church.

While hardly ostentatious, the elegant Georgian interior, done up with wooden Corinthian columns and lit by chandeliers, provides a marked contrast to the minimalist adornments of Boston's other old churches. It also features America's oldest pulpit, which dates from the late 1600s, and many original pews, including a Governor's Pew along the right wall. The best time to enter the building is during one of the weekly **chamber music concerts** (Tues 12.15–12.45pm; $3 suggested donation).

The Washington Street Shopping District

To a Bostonian, Downtown proper comes in two packages: the **Washington Street Shopping District** (namely the School Street area and Downtown Crossing) and the adjacent Financial District (see p.53). The former, situated east of the King's Chapel Burying Ground, has some of the city's most historic sights – the **Old Corner Bookstore**, **Old South Meeting House**, and **Old State House** – but it tends to shut down after business hours, becoming eerily quiet at night. All can be seen in half a day, though you'll need to allow more time if shopping is on your agenda; the stretch around **Downtown Crossing** is full of stylish diversions.

Narrow and heavily trafficked today, in colonial times **Washington Street** connected the Old State House to the city gates at Boston Neck, an isthmus that joined the Shawmut Peninsula to the mainland, thus ensuring its position as the commercial nerve center of Boston. The best way to begin exploring the area is via **School Street**, anchored on its northern edge by the dignified **Omni Parker House**, the city's most venerable hotel, which has a rich history: John F. Kennedy announced his congressional candidacy here in 1946, Charles Dickens first read *A Christmas Carol* in its lobby, and Ho Chi Minh and Malcolm X both used to work here, the former in the kitchen and the latter as a busboy. If you'd like, pop in and order a slice of Boston cream pie (really a layered cake with custard filling and chocolate glaze on top): it was invented here in 1855, and the hotel reportedly still bakes 25 of them a day.

For the rest of its modest length, School Street offers up some of the best in Old Boston charm, beginning with the antique gaslights that flank the severe west wall of King's Chapel. Just beyond is a grand French Second Empire building that served as Boston City Hall from 1865 to 1969; it's near the site of the original location of the **Boston Latin School**, founded in 1635 (a mosaic embedded in the sidewalk just outside the iron gates marks the exact spot). A depiction of the school's most celebrated dropout, Benjamin Franklin, graces the courtyard (despite good marks, Franklin left school after one year because he didn't want a career in the ministry). Fellow Declaration signer John Hancock was another standout student at this, America's first public school.

The Old Corner Bookstore and around

A few doors down from the Latin School site, where School Street joins Washington, stands the gambrel-roofed, red-brick building that was once the **Old Corner Bookstore** (State Street **T**). In the nineteenth century, Boston's version of London's Fleet Street occupied the stretch of Washington from here to Old South Meeting House, with a convergence of booksellers, newspaper headquarters, and publishers; most celebrated among them was Ticknor & Fields, the hottest literary salon Boston ever had. This highly esteemed publishing house was once located in the bookstore itself and handled the likes of Emerson, Longfellow, Hawthorne, Dickens, and Thackeray. One of America's oldest literary magazines, *Atlantic Monthly*, was published upstairs here for many years; later *The Boston Globe* moved in. The building now houses a jewelry store, although a plaque outside marks its past literary glory.

At the corner of School and Washington streets is the **Irish Famine Memorial** (State Street **T**), commemorating the Irish refugees who immigrated to Boston as a result of the fungal potato crop that claimed one million lives. Its focus is an unsettling pair of statues, one depicting an Irish family holding their hands out for food, the other, a (presumably) Bostonian family that chooses to ignore them.

The Old South Meeting House

Washington Street's big architectural landmark, the **Old South Meeting House**, is one block south of the Old Corner Bookstore, at no. 310 (10am–4pm $5, kids $1; ☎617/482-6439, ⓦwww.oldsouthmeetinghouse .org; State Street **T**). The charming brick church building is recognizable by its tower, a separate but attached structure that tapers into an octagonal spire. An earlier cedarwood structure was replaced in 1729 when the size of the congregation grew, clearing the way for what is now the second-oldest church building in Boston; after Old North Church in the North End (see p.71). Its Congregationalist origins required simplicity inside and out, with no artifice to obstruct closeness to God. This also endowed Old South with a spacious-ness that made it a leading venue for anti-imperial rhetoric. The day after the Boston Massacre in 1770, outraged Bostonians assembled here to demand the removal of the troops that were ostensibly guarding the town. Five years later, patriot and doctor Joseph Warren delivered an oration to commemorate the incident; the biggest building in town was so packed that he had to crawl through the window behind the pulpit just to get inside.

More momentously, on the morning of December 16, 1773, nearly five thousand locals met here, awaiting word from Governor Thomas Hutchinson on whether he would permit the withdrawal of three ships in Boston Harbor containing sixty tons of taxed tea. When a message was received that the ships would not be removed, Samuel Adams rose and announced, "This meeting can do no more to save the country!" His simple declaration triggered the **Boston Tea Party**, perhaps the seminal event leading to the War for Independence.

Before becoming the **museum** it is today, the Meeting House served as a stable, a British riding school, and even a bar. One of the things lost in transition was the original high pulpit, which the British tore out during the Revolution and used as firewood; the ornate one currently on view is a replica from 1808. Note the exterior **clock**, installed in 1770, which you can still set your watch by. If you take the audio tour included in the admission price, you also get to hear campy re-enactments of a Puritan church service as well as the Boston Tea Party debates.

Old State House and around

That the graceful three-tiered window tower of the **Old State House** (daily 9am–5pm; $5, kids $1; ☎617/720-1713, ⓦwww.bostonhistory.org; State Street **T**), at the corner of Washington and State streets, is dwarfed by skyscrapers amplifies, rather than diminishes, its colonial-era dignity.

▲ Old State House

For years this red-brick structure, reminiscent of an old Dutch town hall, was the seat of the Massachusetts Bay Colony and consequently the center of British authority for Massachusetts and Maine; later it served as Boston's city hall. In 1880, the building was nearly demolished so that State Street traffic might flow more freely, and an unsuccessful bid was made to move it to Chicago in 1880. But while the building's predecessor met its fiery demise in 1711 (owing to a drunken woman's clumsy fire-building skills), the

Old State House has remained intact, its fate spared by the **Bostonian Society**, Boston's official historical society and founded specifically to preserve the building.

Today the site houses a small but comprehensive **museum**. An impassioned speech in the second-floor Council Chamber by **James Otis**, a Crown appointee who resigned to take up the colonial cause, sparked the quest for independence from Britain fifteen years before it was declared. Otis argued against the Writs of Assistance, which permitted the British to inspect private property at will; legend has it that on certain nights you can still hear him hurling his anti-British barbs, along with the cheers of the crowd he so energized, but museum staff has no comment. The **balcony** overlooking State Street is as famous as Otis's speech, for it was from here on July 18, 1776, that the Declaration of Independence was first read publicly in Boston – a copy having just arrived from Philadelphia. That same night the symbolic lion and unicorn figures mounted above the balcony were torn down and burned in front of the *Bunch of Grapes* tavern (see p.54); those currently on display are replicas. Just to show there were no hard feelings, Queen Elizabeth II, the first British monarch to set foot in Boston since the Revolution, made a speech from the balcony as part of the American bicentennial activities in 1976.

As for the historical society's **museum**, the permanent ground-level exhibit, "Colony to Commonwealth," has a number of well-tailored exhibits chronicling Boston's role in inciting the Revolutionary War. Displays include a bit of tea from Boston's most infamous party; the plaque of royal arms that once hung over Province House, official residence of the colonial governors; the flag that the Sons of Liberty draped from the Liberty Tree to announce their meetings; a dapper jacket belonging to John Hancock; and the most galvanizing image of the Revolutionary period, Paul Revere's propagandistic engraving of the Boston Massacre.

Adjacent to the Old State House, at 15 State Street, lies the downtown **visitor center** for the Boston National Park Service (daily 9am–5pm; free; ☎617/ 242-5642, ⓦ www.nps.gov/bost; State Street **T**), chock full of maps, facts, and particularly helpful park rangers. There are also un-crowded bathrooms.

The Boston Massacre Site

On the Devonshire Street side of the Old State House, a circle of cobble-stones embedded in a small traffic island marks the site of the **Boston Massacre** (State Street **T**), the tragic outcome of escalating tensions between Bostonians and the British Redcoats who occupied the city. Riots were an increasingly common occurrence in Boston by the time this deadly one broke out on March 5, 1770. It began when a young wigmaker's apprentice heckled an army officer over a barber's bill. The officer sought refuge in the Custom House (then opposite the Old State House), but when a throng of people gathered at the scene, the mob grew violent, hurling snowballs and rocks at arriving soldiers. When someone threw a club that knocked a Redcoat onto the ice, he rose and fired. Five Bostonians were killed in the ensuing riot – including a young black man named Crispus Attucks, considered the first casualty of the Revolution – resulting in Governor Hutchinson's order to relocate occupying troops to Castle Island in Boston Harbor. Two patriots, John Adams and Josiah Quincy, actually defended the eight soldiers in court; six were acquitted, and the two who were found guilty were branded on their thumbs.

Views of Downtown

Whether local or from out of town, people can't seem to get enough of Boston's **skyline** – its pastiche of brownstone churches and glass-paneled skyscrapers framing Massachusetts Bay ranks it among the country's finest. No wonder, then, that so many buildings have public (and often free) viewing floors. You can check out Boston from every angle by ascending the *Marriott's Custom House* (see p.57), the Prudential Tower (see p.100), on the 14th floor observation deck at 470 Atlantic Ave. (p.63), and the Bunker Hill Monument (see p.80). The best lay of the land, though, is had from the water; take a walk across the Longfellow Bridge, board the Charlestown ferry (see p.74), visit the Harbor Islands (see p.63), or take a ferry to Provincetown (see p.260) for a particularly stunning view.

Downtown Crossing

A few blocks south lies a pleasant antidote to those overwhelmed by American history. Pedestrian-friendly **Downtown Crossing**, a beloved outdoor mall area, brims with department stores and smaller shops that cater to bargain hunters of all socioeconomic stripes. Centered on the intersection of Washington and Summer streets, its nucleus is Filene's Basement, a bargain hunter's delight known for its legendary "Running of The Brides" event where frenzied brides-to-be feverishly paw their way to marked-down gowns.

The Financial District

Boston's **Financial District**, a small tract of real estate east of Washington Street and bounded by the waterfront, hardly conjures the same interest as those of New York and London, but it continues to wield influence in key fields (like mutual funds, invented here in 1925). The area is not entirely devoid of historic interest, though it's generally more manifest in plaques than actual buildings. Like most of America's business districts, it beats to an office hours–only drum, and many of its little eateries and Irish pubs are closed on weekends (some brave new restaurants have begun to make inroads, however).

The mostly immaculate streets follow the same short, winding paths as they did three hundred years ago; only now, thirty- and forty-story skyscrapers have replaced the wooden houses and churches that used to clutter the area. Still, their names are historically evocative: **High Street**, once known as Cow Lane, used to lead to the summit of the now-vanished eighty-foot-tall Fort Hill. **Arch Street** recalls the decorative arch that graced the Tontine Crescent, a block of stately townhouses designed in 1793 by Charles Bulfinch and unfortunately destroyed by the Great Fire of 1872, which began in the heart of the district. Tucked among the relatively generic skyscrapers are several well-preserved nineteenth-century mercantile masterpieces; or head down to **Franklin Street** where the curving of the street was designed by Bulfinch to reflect the turn of the Tontine Crescent.

Milk Street and Post Office Square

The most dramatic approach to the Financial District is east from Washington Street via **Milk Street**. A bust of **Benjamin Franklin** surveys the scene from a recessed Gothic niche above the doorway at no. 1; the site marks Franklin's birthplace, though the building itself only dates from 1874.

Further down Milk, the somber, 22-story **John W. McCormack Federal Courthouse** building is currently undergoing renovations, but it formally housed one of Boston's larger post offices. An earlier building on this site gave the adjacent **Post Office Square** its name; today its pretty triangular layout and cascading fountains are popular with area professionals (and area visitors, too) during the lunch hour. Though it's not officially open to the public, you might try sneaking up to the glass atrium atop the building at **One Post Office Square** for jaw-dropping views of Boston Harbor and Downtown. The city's skyline encompasses the architectural excesses of the 1980s and a few Art Deco treats, too; the best example of the former is the **First National Bank of Boston** tower at 100 Federal St, with its bulging midsection, nicknamed the "Pregnant Building."

The prime Art Deco specimen, meanwhile, is nearby at 185 Franklin St – now the **Verizon Building** – a 1947 step-top building design. If you're here during business hours, check out the fusty nook off the right-hand side of the lobby, home to a replica of the Boston attic room where Alexander Graham Bell first transmitted speech sounds over a wire in 1876; the wooden chamber is a meticulously reassembled version of the original that was installed in 1959 and, with the exception of an evocative diorama of an old Boston cityscape, it looks like nothing's been touched since. Head back to the lobby to see the impressive 360-degree mural that glorifies the exciting world of *Telephone Men and Women at Work*.

Exchange Place, at 53 State St, is a mirrored-glass tower rising from the facade of the old Boston Stock Exchange; the *Bunch of Grapes* tavern, watering hole of choice for many of Boston's Revolutionary rabble-rousers, once stood here. Behind it is tiny **Liberty Square**, once the heart of Tory Boston – the British tax office had its address here, in 1765, and was destroyed by angry colonists – and now mostly of note for its improbable bronze sculpture, called *Aspirations for Liberty*; it's an elegant depiction of rebels rising to hold a (presumably rebellious) baby in honor of the Hungarian anti-Communist uprising of 1956.

Government Center

Tremont Street's major tenant, **Government Center**, lies northwest from Exchange Place along Congress Street. Its sea of towering gray buildings on the former site of Scollay Square – once Boston's most notorious den of porn halls and tattoo parlors – is by far the least interesting section of Downtown Boston. As part of a citywide face-lift, Scollay was razed in the early 1960s, eliminating all traces of its salacious past and, along with it, most of its lively character. Indeed, the only thing that remains from the square's steamier days is the Oriental Tea Company's 227-gallon **Steaming Kettle** advertisement, which has been clouding up the sky across from the Government Center **T** stop since 1873. The area is now overlaid with concrete, thanks to an ambitious plan developed by I.M. Pei, and towered over by two monolithic edifices: **Boston City Hall**, at the east side of the plaza, and the **John F. Kennedy Federal Building**, on the north. One pretty face stands out among the concrete however, the graceful, curved nineteenth-century **Sears Crescent** building, former publishing house for the abolitionist journal "The Christian Freeman."

Unless the workings of bureaucracy get you going, Government Center is generally just a brief stopover on the walk to Faneuil Hall Marketplace.

Faneuil Hall Marketplace and around

Popular with tourists and locals alike, **Faneuil Hall Marketplace** (Faneuil rhymes with "flannel"), set on a pedestrian zone east of Government Center, is an active, bustling public gathering place that's good for a bite to eat and a bit of history (as well as free Wi-Fi Internet access). Built as a market during colonial times to house the city's growing mercantile industry, it declined during the nineteenth century and, like the area around it, was pretty much defunct until the 1960s, when it was successfully redeveloped as a restaurant and shopping mall.

Faneuil Hall

Much-hyped **Faneuil Hall** (May–Sept Mon–Sat 10am–8pm, Sun noon–6pm; Oct–April 10am–6pm, Sun noon–6pm; ☎617/523-1300, ⓦwww .faneuilhallmarketplace.com; State Street **T**) itself doesn't appear particularly majestic from the outside; it's simply a small, four-story brick building topped with a golden grasshopper weathervane – not the grandiose auditorium one might imagine would have housed the Revolutionary War meetings that earned it its "Cradle of Liberty" sobriquet.

The structure once housed an open-air market on its first floor and a space for political meetings on its second, a juxtaposition that inspired local poet Francis Hatch to pen the lines, "Here orators in ages past / Have mounted their attacks, / Undaunted by proximity / Of sausage on the racks." Faneuil Hall was where revolutionary firebrands such as Samuel Adams and James Otis whipped up popular support for independence by protesting British tax legislation. The first floor now houses a panoply of tourist **shops**; you'll also find an information desk, a post office, and a BOSTIX kiosk. The second floor is more impressive: the auditorium has been preserved to reflect modifications made by Charles Bulfinch in 1805. Its focal point is a showy – and slightly preposterous – canvas depicting an embellished version of "The Great Debate," during which Daniel Webster argued for the concept of the United States as one nation against South Carolina senator Robert Hayne. While the debate was an actual event, the painting contains a number of nineteenth-century luminaries, such as Nathaniel Hawthorne and Alexis de Toqueville, who certainly weren't in attendance – the artist simply thought this would help him sell his painting. More down-to-earth is the story of how Beantown sailors got free passage home from Britain in the War of 1812: captive Boston sailors who escaped to the American consulate were asked what flew atop Faneuil Hall as a weathervane. Those who knew it was a grasshopper were trusted as true Bostonians and given a free ride back; those who didn't were regarded with suspicion.

Dock Square, Blackstone Street, and the Holocaust Memorial

Immediately behind Faneuil Hall lies **Dock Square**, so named for its original location directly on Boston's waterfront (carvings in the pavement indicate the shoreline in 1630). The square's center is dominated by a statue of **Samuel Adams**, interesting mostly for its somewhat over-the-top caption: "A Statesman, incorruptible and fearless." A dim, narrow corridor known as Scott's Alley heads north of the market to reach Creek Square, where you enter **Blackstone Street**, the eastern edge of a tiny warren of streets bounded to the west by Union Street. Its uneven cobblestone streets and low brick buildings have remained largely untouched since the 1750s; many of them, especially those along Union Street, house restaurants and pubs (like the *Union Oyster House*, which has been serving up seafood since 1826, see p.166).

The corner of Union and North streets marks the location of the former house of **William Dawes**, one of the riders who joined Paul Revere on his midnight ride. Unlike Revere, his house has not been favorably preserved – it's now a *McDonald's* – but you can view a plaque commemorating the site. Just north on Union is the **Curley Memorial Plaza**, a small circle of benches with two statues dedicated to James Michael Curley, one of Boston's more enduring twentieth century political figures. Dubbed the "Rascal King," Curley was four times elected the mayor of Boston, and twice convicted of "official misconduct" while still in office. Just north of here lies a different sort of monument, six tall, hollow, glass pillars erected as a **memorial** to victims of the Holocaust. Built to resemble smokestacks, the columns are etched with six million numbers recalling the tattoos the Nazis gave the Jews and other victims. Steam rises from grates beneath each of the pillars to accentuate their symbolism, an effect that's particularly striking at night.

Quincy Market

The markets just behind Faneuil Hall – three parallel oblong structures and one 1970s concrete mall that house restaurants, shops, and office buildings – were built in the early eighteenth century to contain the trade that had quickly outgrown its space in the hall. The center building, known as **Quincy Market** (Mon–Sat 10am–9pm, Sun noon–6pm; ☎617/523-1300, ⓦ www.faneuilhallmarketplace.com; Government Center **T**), holds a super-extended corridor lined with stands selling a variety of take-out treats – it's the mother of mall food courts – built in 1824 under the direction of Boston's mayor at the time, Josiah Quincy. Head over to the *Walrus and the Carpenter* for a sampling of their Wellfleet Oysters; the raw bar here is an unexpected Boston best.

To either side of the market are the **North** and **South Markets**, which hold restaurants and popular chain clothing stores. The cobblestone corridors between them host a number of vendor carts offering curios and narrow specializations (one sells only purple objects, another nothing but puppets). You'll also find the usual complement of street musicians, fire-jugglers, and mimes, weather permitting. There's not much to distinguish it from any other shopping complex, though there are several good restaurants and a nice concentration of bars (including a replica of the *Cheers* set), which are scarce elsewhere in the Downtown area. Overall, sitting on a bench in the heart of it all on a summer day, eating ice cream while the mobs of locals and tourists mill about, is a quintessential, if slightly absurd, Boston experience.

The Custom House District

The not-quite-triangular wedge of Downtown between State and Broad streets and Atlantic Avenue is the unfairly overlooked, and rather loosely named, **Custom House District**, dotted with some excellent architectural draws. Chief among them is the **Custom House** itself, built in 1847 and surrounded by 32 huge Doric columns, though the thirty-story Greek Revival tower was only added in 1915. Not surprisingly, it is no longer the tallest skyscraper in New England (a status it held for forty-nine years), but it still has plenty of character and terrific views nonetheless; you can check them out from the 360-degree observation deck free of charge (or even book a room here – it now houses a *Marriott* hotel; Mon–Thurs 10am & 4pm, Fri & Sat 4pm only; ☎617/310-6300).

The **Flour and Grain Exchange Building**, a block away at 177 Milk St, is another district landmark. This fortress-like construction recalls the Romanesque-Revival style of prominent local architect H.H. Richardson. Its turreted, conical roof, encircled by a series of pointed dormers, is a bold reminder of the financial stature this district once held. **Broad Street**, which runs perpendicular to Milk Street, was built on filled-in land in 1807 and is still home to several Federal-style mercantile buildings designed by Charles Bulfinch, notably those at numbers 68–70, 72, and 102.

On **State Street**, long a focal point of Boston's maritime prosperity, get a look at the elaborate cast-iron facade of the **Richards Building** at no. 114 (a clipper ship company's office in the 1850s) and the **Cunard Building** at no. 126, its ornamental anchors recalling Boston's status as the North American terminus of the first transatlantic steamship mail service. Trading activity in the nearby harbor brought a thriving banking and insurance industry to the street in the 1850s, along with a collection of rather staid office buildings. A modern exception is the opulent **Sovereign Bank** headquarters at no. 75, a medium-sized skyscraper crowned with 3600 square feet of gold leaf and containing a six-story lobby decked out in marble, mahogany, and bronze.

The Theater and Ladder districts

Just south of Boston Common is the slightly seedy **Theater District** – the small area around the intersection of Tremont and Stuart streets. Not surprisingly, you'll have to purchase tickets in order to inspect the grand old interiors of the theaters for which it's named, but it's well worth a quick walk along Tremont Street to admire their facades. At the intersection of Washington and Avery streets you'll find the 1928 Beaux Arts **Opera House**, recently renovated after being closed for more than a decade. The **Colonial Theatre** – the oldest continuously-operating theatre in Boston – is just off **Piano Row**, a section of Boylston Street between Charles and Tremont that was the center of American piano manufacturing and music publishing in the nineteenth and early twentieth centuries. There are still a few piano shops in the area, but the hip restaurants and clubs in the immediate vicinity are of greater interest; many are tucked between Charles and Stuart streets around the mammoth **Massachusetts Transportation Building** and cater to the theater-going crowd.

Banned in Boston

Boston's Puritan founders would be horrified to find that an area called the **Theater District** exists. Their ingrained allergy to fun resulted in theatrical performances actually being outlawed in Boston until 1792, and in 1878, the Watch & Ward Society was formed to organize boycotts against indecent books and plays. Still, the shows went on, and in 1894 vaudeville was born at the lavish (now extinct) B.F. Keith Theater. Burlesque soon followed, prompting the city licensing division in 1905 to deny performances that didn't meet their neo-Puritan codes – thus the phrase "Banned in Boston." In fact, as recently as 1970, a production of *Hair* was banned for a month due to its desecration of the American flag.

Despite this censorship, Boston still managed to become the premier theater tryout town that it is today: high production costs on Broadway have dictated that hits be sifted from misses early on, and Boston has long been a cost-efficient testing ground. During the 1920s, the heyday of theater in the city, there were as many as forty playhouses in the Theater District alone. However, the rise of film meant the fall of theater, and after brief stints as movie halls, many of the grand buildings – most notably the Art Deco **Paramount**, the **Opera House** (formerly the Savoy), and the **Modern Theatre**, all on lower Washington Street – slid into disrepair and eventual abandonment. The good news is the Opera House has recently undergone a glorious renovation and reopening, and works are underway to revitalize the Modern Theatre.

South along Tremont is the beautifully ornate and restored **Cutler Majestic Theatre**. Just down the street you'll also find the porticoed **Wilbur Theatre** (see p.196), the place to go for Broadway shows; when it opened in 1914, it was the first Boston theater to have its own guest lounge, which today is used by the nightclub *Aria* (see p.196). Adjacent to the Wilbur, the old **Metropolitan Theatre**, a movie house of palatial proportions, survives as the glittering **Wang Center for the Performing Arts** (see p.196), grande dame of the theatre scene, and home to the Boston Ballet. Across the street is the darling **Shubert Theatre** (see p.196), the so-called "Little Princess of the Theater District"; its plush, 1600-seat auditor-ium is home to the Boston Lyric Opera, as well as some Broadway productions.

The tenor around Washington Street between Essex and Kneeland was relatively seedy a decade ago. Designated as an "adult entertainment zone" in the 1960s (when it replaced Scollay Square as the city's Red Light district and known, enigmatically, as "the Combat Zone," the latter-day **Ladder District** was home to a few X-rated theaters and bookshops until trendy restaurants and nightclubs designated it the new "It" spot and pushed the less reputable businesses out. PR hacks successfully renamed the area after its ladder-like layout (Tremont and Washington form the rails; Winter and Avery streets, the top and bottom rungs), but failed to alter its daylight character, which, despite the addition of a *Ritz-Carlton* at the corner of Tremont and Avery streets, remains rather desolate. At night, the place has slightly more energy, as theater-goers come here to dine, but really it's little more than an extension of Downtown Crossing's shops, home to a few nail salons and chain restaurants.

One sight of note is the plaque at the intersection of Washington and Boylston streets marking the approximation of where the **Liberty Tree** stood. This oak, planted in 1646, was a favored meeting point of the Sons of Liberty; as such, the British chopped it down in 1775. If you look up and to the right while standing at the plaque, you'll see where the oak was truly rooted – there is a bas-relief sculpture of a tree implanted in the third floor of the Registry of Motor Vehicles on Washington Street.

Chinatown and the Leather District

Boston's **Chinatown** lies wedged into just a few square blocks between the Financial and Theater districts, but it makes up in activity what it lacks in size. Just lean against a pagoda-topped payphone on the corner of **Beach** and **Tyler streets** – the neighborhood's two most dynamic thoroughfares – and watch the way life here revolves around the food trade at all hours. By day, merchants barter in Mandarin and Cantonese over the going price of produce; by night, Bostonians arrive in droves to eat in the restaurants. Walk down either street and you'll pass most of the bakeries, eateries, and indoor markets, in whose windows you'll see the usual complement of roast ducks hanging from hooks and aquariums filled with future seafood dinners. The area's at its most vibrant during various **festivals** (see Chapter 19, "Festivals and events"), none more so than **Chinese New Year** (late Jan, early Feb), when frequent parades of papier mâché dragons fill the streets and the acrid smell of firecrackers permeates the air. During the **Festival of the August Moon**, held, as you may have guessed, in August, there's a bustling street fair. Check in with the Chinese Merchants' Association for more information (☎617/350-6303; ⓦ www.chinatownmainstreet.org).

The prosperity of Boston's Chinatown has increased dramatically since the late-1990s, and consequently is expanding to the north, now bordering Downtown Crossing and even crossing over into the Leather District. Despite this growth, the heart of Chinatown contains little in the way of sights, and the atmosphere is best enjoyed by wandering around with no particular destination in mind. There are a few important landmarks, such as the impressive **Chinatown Gate**, a three-story red-and-gilt monolith guarded by four Fu dogs, located at the intersection of Hudson and Beach Streets, a gift from Taiwan in honor of Chinatown's centennial. Adjacent **Tian An Men Park** provides a place to rest, but it's poorly kept and inhabited by aggressive pigeons – although there is also a new Feng Shui-inspired park in front of the Chinatown Gate (replacing a former Central Artery off-ramp) that incorporates stones, streams, and waterfalls. Slightly west of here, at the corner of Tyler and Beach streets, is a plaque marking the site where in 1761 John Wheatley purchased eight-year old **Phillis Wheatley** to serve as his slave; twelve years later she went on to become the first published African-American woman with "Poems on Various Subjects, Religious and Moral."

The Leather District

Just east of Chinatown, the six square blocks bounded by Kneeland, Atlantic, Essex, and Lincoln streets form the **Leather District** (also known as the **Garment District**), which takes its name from the time when materials were shipped through warehouses here to keep the shoe industry – a mainstay of the New England economy – alive. Since then, the Financial District, with which it is frequently lumped, has taken over as economic hub, and the leather industry has pretty much dried up. The distinction between the Financial and Leather districts is actually quite sharp, and most evident where High Street transitions into **South Street**, the Leather District's main drag. Stout brick warehouses replace gleaming modern skyscrapers, and a melange of merchants and gallery owners take over from the suited bankers. Some of the edifices still have their leather warehouse **signs** on them; check out the Boston Hide & Leather Co at 15 East St. The nearby **South Station**, Boston's main train and bus terminus, has little to recommend it architecturally.

The waterfront

Boston's urban renewal program, sparked by the beginning of the Big Dig in the early 1990s, has resulted in a resurgence of its waterfront area. The tearing down of the John Fitzgerald Expressway, which, since the 1950s, had separated the waterfront from the rest of Downtown, has allowed the city to reconnect with the sea through a series of ambitious projects such as the expansion of the New England Aquarium and the conversion of wharf buildings into housing. You can already see the bloomy beginnings of the Rose Kennedy Greenway, a thirty-acre public park set to beautify the once car-ridden strip here between downtown Boston and the waterfront.

While the waterfront that's concentrated around **Long Wharf** is more touristy (selling T-shirts, furry lobsters, and the like), strolling the atmospheric **Harborwalk** that edges the water affords unbeatable views of Boston, and is a pleasant respite from bustling Faneuil Hall. You'll also find plenty of diversion if you've got little ones in tow at the **New England Aquarium**. Otherwise, you can do some watery exploring on a number of **boat tours**, or escape the city altogether by heading out to the **Harbor Islands**.

Long Wharf and around

Long Wharf has been the waterfront's main drag since its construction in 1710. Not surprisingly, summer is its busiest season, when the wharf is dotted with stands vending kitschy souvenirs and surprisingly good ice cream. This is also the main point of departure for Boston Harbor Cruises (☎617/227-4321, ⓦ www.bostonharborcruises.com), which runs **whale-watching** excursions, harbor cruises and ferries to Cape Cod's Provincetown (see p.259). Ferries to the Boston Harbor Islands also leave from Long Wharf; check for schedules at the Harbor Islands kiosk here or at ⓦ www.nps.gov/boha. If you're more interested in an old-school sailing experience, Boston has the recent good fortune of mooring a beautiful tall ship, *The Roseway*, at 60 Rowes Wharf. This 137-foot long national historic landmark is a former fishing yacht that functions as a non-profit school and also offers day-sails ($32, kids $25; ☎617/443-4841, ⓦ www.worldoceanschool.org; Aquarium **T**).

Situated between Long Wharf and Commercial Wharf, **Christopher Columbus Park** is a pretty green space bisected by a wisteria-laden trellis. This leisurely park also features a rose garden and kid-sized sprinkler fountain, well-loved in the summer months. In the evening, the park takes on a romantic feel, and you can walk out to the end of Long Wharf for an excellent vantage point on **Boston Harbor**, when even the freighters appear graceful against the moonlit water.

The New England Aquarium

Next door to Long Wharf is the waterfront's major draw, the **New England Aquarium** (July–Aug Mon–Thurs 9am–6pm, Fri–Sun 9am–7pm; Sept–Jun Mon–Fri 9am–5pm, Sat & Sun 9am–6pm; $19, kids $11; City Pass accepted; ☎617/973-5200, ⓦ www.neaq.org; Aquarium **T**). Especially fun for kids, the indoor aquarium has plenty of fine exhibits, such as the penguins on the bottom floor. Be sure to play with the special laser device that moves a red point of light around the bottom of their pool; the guileless waterfowl mistake the light for a fish and follow it around hopefully. In the center of the aquarium's spiral walkway is an impressive collection of marine life: a three-story, 200,000-gallon cylindrical tank packed with giant sea turtles, moray eels, sharks, stingrays,

The Harborwalk

The **Harborwalk** officially begins in Dorchester, curving eastwards into the beaches of South Boston (a whopping 47 miles in all). Obviously visitors shouldn't expect to see the whole thing, but it's quite pleasant to walk the portion that meanders through the wharves alongside the Boston waterfront. Start at Lewis Wharf, where a gravel path leads to a pretty circular garden. Continue south, passing by Christopher Columbus Park and the Aquarium. Just before the *Boston Harbor Hotel*, check out David von Schlegell's *"Untitled Landscape"* on India Wharf, two fifteen foot L-shaped bends of metal which seem to magnetically compel children (and adults, too) to run between them. Throughout, there are peaceful harbor scenes, complete with sailboats drifting on the water and scores of pulsating jellyfish below. The best scenery of the walk is contained between Lewis Wharf and 470 Atlantic Ave, former site of the Boston Tea Party and current home to a fantastic observation deck (free; daily 10am-5pm). For more information, go to the Harborwalk's extensive website at Ⓦ www.bostonharborwalk.com.

and a range of other ocean exotica that swim by in unsettling proximity. The aquarium also runs excellent **whale-watching** trips (early April–late Oct; 3–4hr, call for times and specific dates; $35, kids $29; ☎617/973-5281).

Over the last decade, a multimillion-dollar expansion program has seen the addition of a West Wing, the Aquarium Medical Center (giving visitors a look at animal care), and a showy **IMAX theater** that, at more than six stories high, has the largest screen in New England (daily 9.30am–10.30pm; $9.95, kids $7.95).

The Seaport District

The rapidly up-and-coming **Seaport District** is a spacious harborside area located across the pedestrian-only Northern Bridge, and the auto-friendly Moakley, Congress, and Summer Street bridges from Downtown. Also accessible by the Silver Line **T**, the neighborhood is full of lofty old warehouse spaces and one of the main draws is the excellent range of restaurants near **Fish Pier**, where you can also find a number of **lobster wholesalers**; if you love crustaceans, you'll avoid paying standard market price by braving the aromas at one of these seafood warehouses. The district pays equal attention to your sense of sight, too, with the affable **Children's Museum**, packed with playful and intelligent children's exhibits. But the pearl in the Seaport District's oyster is the newly-opened **Institute of Contemporary Art**, an iridescent space at the forefront of the nation's art scene, and perhaps the most important architectural design to come to Boston in nearly a century. Further in is the **Bank of America Pavilion**, a huge, half-shell amphitheater that hosts big-name musical acts in the summer.

The Children's Museum

It's hard to miss the larger-than-life 1930s-era **Hood Milk Bottle** across the Congress Street Bridge from Downtown, one of Boston's best-loved icons and a whimsical prelude to the **Children's Museum**. Doubling as a food stand, the milk bottle actually serves little dairy produce – most of its trade is in hot dogs and bagel sandwiches – though it's estimated that if the bottle was filled with milk, it would hold 58,000 gallons of the stuff.

Behind the bottle, the engaging Children's Museum, 300 Congress St (daily 10am–5pm, Fri till 9pm; $10, kids $8, Fri 5–9pm $1; ☎617/426-8855, Ⓦwww .bostonkids.org; South Station **T**), comprises four floors of educational exhibits craftily designed to trick kids into learning about a huge array of topics, from musicology to the engineering of a humongous bubble. The key here is interactivity: displays are meant to be touched rather than observed, like the three-story climbing maze in the central shaft that no one over 14 could possibly get into. Many exhibits are amusing even for adults, particularly the "Japanese House" where you can step into an authentic 100-year-old silk merchant's home, or the ball launcher on the first floor, which lets you propel a tennis ball three stories into the air. Before leaving, be sure to check out the Recycle Shop where industrial leftovers are transformed into appealing craft fodder.

The museum also hosts fun evening events, such as "Movies on the Milk Bottle," when people picnic to films projected directly onto the bottle's cream-colored exterior; check the museum's website for a full schedule of events.

ICA

Looking like a glamorous glass ice-cube perched above a chilly Boston Harbor, the **Institute of Contemporary Art**, 100 Northern Ave Tues & Wed 10am–5pm, Thurs & Fri 10am–9pm, Sat & Sun 10–5pm, closed Mon; $12, kids free, Thurs 5–9pm free; free for families the last Saturday of the month; ☎617/478-3100, Ⓦwww.icaboston.org; World Trade Center **T**), gives you a show before you've even stepped inside. Until 2006, the ICA was housed out of a nineteenth-century fire station in Back Bay; it's since moved into its new, showy digs to make room for more permanent artworks.

The ICA's permanent collection, located on the fourth floor, features late twentieth and twenty-first century artists such as photography by former Bostonian Nan Goldin, sculptural textiles by Mona Hatoum, and figures by Louise Bourgeois. Ongoing temporary exhibitions, like a melancholy collection of Philip-Lorca diCorcia photographs (best-known for his surprisingly elegant pole dancer portraits), are held in the adjacent rooms, but the best overall display is the space itself. Designed by architects Diller Scofidio + Renfro, the building features a dramatic cantilever shape that extends 80 feet into the water's edge. From the interior, this extended section functions as the "Founder's Gallery," a meditative, enclosed ledge where, if you look down from the gallery's wall of windows, you'll find yourself standing directly above a jellyfish-laden Boston Harbor.

Elsewhere, the museum houses an innovative theater space, whose glass walls alter their transparency in order to accommodate for lighting; shows here range from modern dance performances to screenings of *The Matrix*. And in summer, the gorgeous front deck plays host to live music shows and dance nights; check online for more information (Ⓦwww.icaboston.org).

Boston Tea Party Ship

For many years, in the Fort Point Channel alongside the Congress Street bridge, there was a replica of one of the three notorious ships that launched the **Boston Tea Party**. Unfortunately, the ship and its neighboring museum (☎1-800/213-2474, Ⓦwww.bostonteapartyship.com) were closed after the

The Boston Tea Party

The first major act of rebellion preceding the Revolutionary War, the **Boston Tea Party** was far greater in significance than it was in duration. On December 20, 1773, a longstanding dispute between the British government and its colonial subjects, involving a tea tax, came to a dramatic head. At nightfall, a group of five thousand waited at the Old South Meeting House to hear the governor's pronouncement regarding three ships full of tea moored in Boston Harbor. After receiving word that the governor would not remove the ships, the civil throng converged on Griffin's Wharf. Around one hundred of them, some dressed in Indian garb, boarded the brigs and threw their cargo of tea overboard. The partiers disposed of 342 chests of tea, each weighing 360 pounds – enough to make 24 million cups, and worth more than one million dollars by today's standards.

While it had the semblance of spontaneity, the event was in fact planned beforehand, and the mob was careful not to damage anything but the offending cargo. In any case, the "party" transformed protest into revolution. The ensuing British sanctions, colloquially referred to as the "Intolerable Acts," along with the colonists' continued resistance, further inflamed the tension between the Crown and its colonies, which eventually exploded at Lexington and Concord several months later.

ship was hit by lightning in August 2001; at the time of writing, the museum was several months away from reopening. Improvements will include a doubling of the museum's size and the addition of two replica ships. Spirited re-creations of the Tea Party itself will be held on occasion in the area, but don't be taken in: this is not the site of the actual event. The Tea Party actually took place on what is now dry land, near the intersection of Atlantic and Congress streets. There's a commemorative plaque at 470 Atlantic Ave, engraved with a lively, patriotic poem proclaiming "ne'er was mingled such a draught / in palace, hall, or arbor / as freeman brewed and tyrants quaffed / that night in Boston harbor." The office building at 470 Atlantic Ave also features jaw-dropping views of the city via its fourteenth-floor **observation deck**, replete with binoculars and benches – simply check in with the security guard in the lobby (free; daily 10am–5pm). There are also clean, 24hr bathrooms available here.

The Harbor Islands

Extending across Massachusetts Bay from Salem south to Portsmouth, the thirty-four islands that make up the bucolic **Harbor Islands** served as strategic defense points during the American Revolution and Civil War. It took congressional assent to turn them into a national park, in 1996, with the result that six are now easily accessible by ferry from Long Wharf (a seventh, Little Brewster Island, has a ferry that leaves from Fan Pier). Even so, they're still lightly trafficked in comparison to most Boston sights, which makes them ideal getaways from the city center, especially on a hot summer day, when their **beaches** and **hiking** trails will easily help you forget urban life altogether. Their wartime legacy has left many of the winding pathways and coastal shores dotted with intriguing fortress **ruins** and **lighthouses**, which makes for attractive scenery; the views of Boston from this distance are simply sublime as well.

Island bound

A quick fifteen-minute ride connects Long Wharf with central **George's Island** or **Spectacle Island** (May to mid-Oct daily on the hour 9am–4pm, weekends every half hour, call to confirm times; $12, kids $7; ☏617/223-8666, ⊛www.bostonislands.org; Aquarium **T**); free water taxis shuttle visitors to the other four islands from these two. Aside from George's and Spectacle, the more remote islands lack a freshwater source, so be sure to bring **bottled water**. If traveling beyond George's or Spectacle, you should also consider packing a picnic lunch (best arranged through nearby *Sel de la Terre*; see p.170), though the former two islands offer low-key **snackbars.** For a small snack, you can also go **berry-picking** on **Grape** and **Bumpkin** islands. In the interest of preserving island ecology, no bicycles or in-line skates are allowed. You can **camp** for a nominal fee on three of the islands (Lovells, Bumpkin, and Grape; May to mid-Oct; ☏1-877/422-6762); you'll need to bring your own supplies. In all cases, good walking shoes are required as most of the pathways consist of dirt roads. The Harbor Islands **information** kiosk, at the foot of Long Wharf, keeps a detailed shuttle **schedule** and stocks excellent **maps.** Visit ⊛www.bostonislands .com and ⊛www.nps.gov/boha for more information.

The Harbor Islands have seen major renovations of late, including faster ferries, artworks installed via a partnership with the ICA, and, most notably, the addition of **Spectacle Island** as an accessible spot for visitors. Spectacle has outgrown its murky past (it was formerly a horse rendering plant, then a dump for the city's trash) to become an environmentally savvy green space. In order to clean up the island, engineers cleverly solved two civic headaches at once – they disposed of the Big Dig's dirt (3.7 million cubic yards in all) and simultan-eously cleaned up the island by using the project's excavated earth to cap a landfill. The island features a small beach with lifeguard, a snack bar, a green visitor's center (complete with foul-smelling bathrooms and an intentional lack of trash cans), and pretty trails heading up its drumlins.

The most popular and best serviced of the islands is still the skipping-stone-shaped **George's Island**, a heavily used defensive outpost during the Civil War era; the remains of **Fort Warren** (April to mid-Oct daily dawn–dusk; free), a mid-nineteenth-century battle station, covers most of the island. Constructed from hand-hewn granite, and mostly used as a prison for captured Confederate soldiers, its musty barracks and extensive fortress walls are on the eerie side, while the parapets offer some stunning Downtown views. You'll get more out of a visit by taking a free Park Ranger tour, where you'll learn the legend of the Lady in Black – a prisoner's wife who was hanged while attempting to break her husband out of jail. Outside the fort, there are shady picnic benches and cobble beaches to explore. The island also hosts performances, be it jazz, children's theater, or a vintage baseball game; check the Harbor Islands website for scheduling (free; ⊛www.bostonislands.com).

If you're interested in seeing one of the remaining Harbor Islands, it's best to make a full day of it, as island hopping on the shuttle service is a little irregular. The densely wooded and sand-duned **Lovells** is a good bet, as it's home to vibrant tidepools and sand dunes near the remains of Fort Standish – an early-twentieth-century military base. The largest of all, the 134-acre **Peddocks**, is laced with hiking trails connecting the remains of Fort Andrews, a harbor defense used from 1904 to 1945, with a freshwater pond and wildlife sanctuary. Romantic **Bumpkin** was once the site of a children's hospital whose ruins, along with the casements of an old stone farmhouse, lie along raspberry bush-fringed pathways. More berries grow on **Grape**, an ideal bird-watching spot.

The most intriguing of the islands is the one furthest at sea – **Little Brewster Island**. Home to the 1783 Boston Light, it's both the oldest light station in the country and the only one that still has a Coast Guard-staffed keeper on site. Excellent tours to Little Brewster are run daily from Fan Pier by the National Park Service, where after meeting the keeper you get to traverse the lighthouse's 76 steps and two ladders in order to glimpse the seaworthy views from the top (3hrs, plan to bring a boxed lunch; $28, kids $17; ☎617/223-8666, ⓦwww .bostonislands.com; South Station **T**).

2

The North End

The **North End** is a small yet densely populated neighborhood whose narrow streets are chock-a-block with Italian bakeries and restaurants, along with some of Boston's most storied sights. While the aboveground highway that once separated the North End from downtown has been removed, the area still has a bit of a detached quality even though it's easily accessed from the Haymarket **T** station, or from the Harborwalk via the waterfront.

Once here, you can cover must-see sights like the **Paul Revere House**, **Old North Church**, and **Copp's Hill Burying Ground**, and still be sure to experience the vibrant cafés, bakeries, restaurants, and food shops in this, Boston's most authentically **Italian** neighborhood. This Italian flavor is particularly pronounced during the eight annual summer **festas** (see Chapter 19, "Festivals and events"), during which members of private charity clubs march figurines of their patron saints (usually the same as those of their home towns in Italy) through the streets. The processions, complete with marching bands, stop every few feet to let people pin dollar bills to streamers attached to the effigies.

In addition to the Italian cultural scene, the North End has more recently become known for its chic clothing boutiques and shops. If shopping is your thing, be sure to check out a number of hip stores interspersed along Hanover and Salem streets.

Some history

In colonial times, the North End was actually a peninsula. Because it was separated from Boston by a tidal creek, a series of short bridges was built to the main part of town. This physical separation bred antagonism, culminating every November 5 in **Pope's Day**, when North Enders and Bostonians on the "other side" paraded effigies of the Pope through their neighborhoods to a standoff on Boston Common, where the competing groups attempted to capture each other's pontiff. If the North Enders won, they would burn their rival's effigy atop Copp's Hill.

Spiritually, the community was dominated by **Increase Mather**, who ministered at the Old North Congregational Church and whose 1689 *Memorable Providences, Relating to Witchcraft and Possessions* probably fuelled the hysteria that led to the Salem Witch Trials (see p.235). But the North End was also the residence of choice for the wealthy merchant class; Massachusetts Bay Colony governors Hutchinson and Phips owned spacious homes here. Following the Revolutionary War, however, many British loyalists fled to Nova Scotia, and, as the North End declined, it became a magnet for free blacks known as the **New Guinea Community**, as well as immigrant groups.

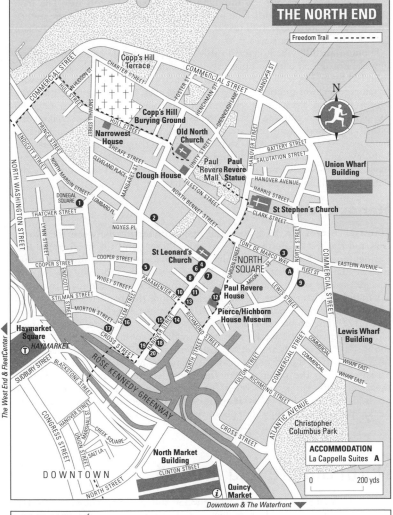

THE NORTH END

Freedom Trail --------

N

Copp's Hill Terrace

CHARTER STREET

COMMERCIAL STREET

HANOVER ST

COMMERCIAL STREET

FOSTER ST

HENCHMAN ST

GREENOUGH LANE

HANOVER STREET

BATTERY STREET

SALUTATION STREET

Union Wharf Building

HULL STREET

HUDSON ST

Copp's Hill Burying Ground

PRINCE STREET

ENDICOTT STREET

HULL STREET

SNOWHILL STREET

Narrowest House

SHEAFE STREET

Old North Church

UNITY ST

Paul Revere Mall

Paul Revere Statue

HANOVER AVENUE

NORTH WASHINGTON STREET

CLEVELAND PLACE

NORTH MARGIN STREET

MARGARET ST

Clough House

Harris STREET

St Stephen's Church

CLARK STREET

THATCHER STREET

LOMBARD PL

DONEGAL SQUARE ❶

TILESTON STREET

NORTH BENNET STREET

LYNN STREET

NOYES PL

❷

TONY DE MARCO WAY

GARDEN STREET

❸

NORTH STREET

COMMERCIAL STREET

COOPER STREET

St Leonard's Church

NORTH SQUARE

FLEET ST

Ⓐ

EASTERN AVENUE

COOPER STREET

ENDICOTT STREET

WIGET STREET

❺

❹

❻

❽ ❼

MOON

LEWIS STREET

❾

STILMAN STREET

PARMENTER STREET

SALEM STREET

❿ ❶❶

Paul Revere House

Pierce/Hichborn House Museum

MORTON STREET

❶❸

❶❷

Lewis Wharf Building

Haymarket Square

HANOVER STREET

❶❻

RICHMOND STREET

COMMERCIAL

WHARF EAST

Ⓣ HAYMARKET

CROSS STREET

❶❺ ❶❹

❶❼

NORTH STREET

COMMERCIAL

WHARF EAST

SUDBURY STREET

BLACKSTONE STREET

ROSE KENNEDY GREENWAY

❶❾ ❶❽

❷⓿

HANOVER STREET

RICHMOND STREET

FULTON STREET

ATLANTIC AVENUE

CONGRESS STREET

HANOVER STREET

MARSHALL STREET

CREEK SQUARE

SALT LA

UNION STREET

CROSS STREET

Christopher Columbus Park

DOWNTOWN

North Market Building

CLINTON STREET

NORTH STREET

ACCOMMODATION
La Cappella Suites **A**

0   200 yds

ⓘ Quincy Market

Downtown & The Waterfront ▼

The West End & FleetCenter ◄

RESTAURANTS & CAFÉS								
Bacco	5	Carmen	12	Lulu's Bake Shoppe	20	Monica's Trattoria	2
Bricco	15	The Daily Catch	7	Mare	13	Neptune Oyster	16
Caffe dello Sport	4	Galleria Umberto	11	Maria's Pastry	17	Pizzeria Regina	1
Caffe Paradiso	18	Gelateria	10	Mike's Pastry	6	Prezza	3
Caffe Vittoria	8	Hot Tomatoes	9	Modern Pastry	14	Taranta	19

The **Irish** were the first immigrants to flock to the area, putting down roots from 1840 onwards (John F. Fitzgerald, JFK's grandfather and mayor of Boston, was born on Ferry Street in 1863, and the late president's mother, Rose, on nearby Garden Court in 1890). With the onset of the potato famine in 1845, the trickle became a flood – in 1847 alone, some 13,000 new arrivals settled here. Employment opportunities for the Irish were limited, however: "No Irish Need Apply" signs were common, and a decade after their arrival the community began to disperse throughout the Greater Boston area. The Irish were succeeded in the North End by Eastern European Jews, who were in turn edged out by **southern Italians** in the early twentieth century. The Italians have, for the most part, stayed put.

Though **landfill**, which began in the 1820s, temporarily ended the district's physical isolation, it became a place apart once more when the elevated I-93 (or John Fitzgerald Expressway) tore through the city in 1954. But Boston's massive urban regeneration through the Big Dig means that, as with the waterfront, the North End has again been rejoined with the city, and what was once an unsightly highway is now a pleasant greenway. Yuppies have been overtaking the North End's waterfront and are also making inroads into the rehabilitated tenements. Though you can still see laundry dangling from upper-story windows and grandmothers chattering in Italian, younger generations aren't staying in the North End, and it's feared that it won't be long see before the neighborhood loses its distinctively Italian character.

Hanover Street

Hanover Street has long been the main connection between the North End and the rest of Boston, and it is along here – and the small streets like Parmenter and Richmond (actually a continuation of each other on either side of Hanover) – that many of the area's *trattorias* and cafés are located. It's also where you'll find a distinctly European flavor: although there are a handful of chain stores in the neighborhood, the majority of businesses remain refreshingly independent, such as bustling *Mike's Pastry*, at no. 300 (see p.171). The quieter side of the neighborhood reasserts itself on the short blocks north of the Paul Revere Mall (really a cobblestoned park), where though the restaurants are still filled up with diners, the roads are peacefully uncrowded. If in the area on a Friday or Saturday afternoon, follow Hanover Street south to the other side of the Rose Kennedy Greenway (where it meets up with Blackstone Street) to witness one of Boston's best-known open-air markets, known as **Haymarket**. Here, energetic produce sellers heckle patrons, and happy shoppers haggle right back.

North Square and around

The little triangular wedge of cobblestones and gaslights known as **North Square**, one block east of Hanover between Prince and Richmond streets, is one of the most historic and attractive pockets of Boston. Here the eateries recede in deference to the **Paul Revere House**, the oldest residential address in the city, at 19 North Square (mid-April to Oct daily 9.30am–5.15pm, Nov to mid-April Tues–Sun 9.30-4.15pm; $3; ☎617/523-2338, ⓦ www.paulreverehouse.org). A North Ender for most of his life, Revere lived here from 1770 to 1800 (except for much of 1775, when he hid out from the British in Watertown), and during these thirty years he sired a brood of sixteen. Before being restored to its seventeenth-century appearance in 1908, the small Tudor-style, post-and-beam structure, which dates from about 1680, had served in turn as a grocery store, tenement, and cigar factory. It stands on what once was the site of the considerably grander home of Puritan heavyweight Increase Mather (father of Cotton), which burned down in the Great Fire of 1676.

Paul Revere

It wasn't until decades after his death that **Paul Revere** achieved fame for his nighttime journey to Lexington to warn John Hancock and Sam Adams of the impending British march inland to seize colonial munitions. When he did, it was thanks to a fanciful 1861 poem by Henry Wadsworth Longfellow called *Paul Revere's Ride*. Its opening line, "Listen, my children, and you shall hear / Of the midnight ride of Paul Revere," is perhaps as familiar to New England schoolchildren as the Pledge of Allegiance, but during his lifetime, this jack-of-all-trades was principally known for his abilities as a **silversmith** (with a side business in false teeth) and a **propagandist** for the patriot cause – not so much as a legendary messenger.

Revere's original engraving of the Boston Massacre, on display in the Old State House (see p.50), did much to turn public opinion against the Tories, and he even went so far as to stage an exhibition of more patriotic prints at his North End home on the first anniversary of the incident. He also rode on horseback to carry news of the Boston Tea Party to New York and Philadelphia – only hours after participating in the event. After the Revolution, Revere engraved the Massachusetts currency, though a more profitable venture was his bell-and-cannon foundry in Canton, located just south of Boston. He died in 1818 at the age of 83, and rests among his Revolutionary peers in the Old Granary Burying Ground (see p.46).

The building is more impressive for its longevity than its appearance, but the third-story overhang and leaded windows do provide quite a contrast to the red-brick buildings around it. Examples of Revere's self-made silverware upstairs merit a look, as does a small but evocative exhibit about the mythologizing of Revere's famed horseback ride to warn patriots that the Regulars were coming.

The Pierce/Hichborn House and North Street

A small courtyard, the focus of which is a glass-encased 900-pound bell cast by Revere, separates the Paul Revere House from the **Pierce/Hichborn House** (tours by appointment only; $3; ☎617/523-2338). A simple Georgian-style residence – and the oldest brick house in Boston – it was built in 1710 by glazier Moses Pierce, and later owned by Paul Revere's shipbuilding cousin, Nathaniel Hichborn, who was considerably wealthier than his more famous relative. The house holds some noteworthy architectural details, including its original staircase as well as two painted fireplaces dating to the early 1700s. Also worth noting are **Baker's Alley**, which runs between the Pierce/Hichborn House and the *Limoncello* restaurant, and **Quincy Court** across the street – both prime examples of how narrow the surrounding streets would have been in colonial times.

South from North Square, Garden Court Street (on which the Revere House and the Pierce/Hichborn House are located) runs into **North Street**, which was somewhat of a red-light district in the early nineteenth century, but today is merely a pretty residential side street. Its one distinguishing feature, the **oldest sign** in Boston, is affixed to the third floor of a building at the corner of Richmond Street – the initials "SW" and "TW" refer to Susanna Wadsworth and Timothy Wadsworth, owners of the *Red Lion Inn* that stood here in 1694.

St Stephen's Church and Paul Revere Mall

Further north, at Hanover's intersection with Clark Street, sits the striking, three-story, recessed-brick arch entrance to **St Stephen's Church**. The church was built on this site in 1714 and replaced by a Charles Bulfinch design in 1804. A fire ravaged the building in 1929, but in 1964 it was restored according to Bulfinch's plan; its interior is a great example of the architect's austere Federal style. A more recent claim to fame is that the funeral ceremony for JFK's mother, Rose Kennedy, was held in the understated apse, in 1995 (her baptism also took place here, 104 years prior).

▲ Paul Revere Mall

Originally called New North Church, St Stephen's received its present-day name in 1862, in order to keep up with the increasingly Catholic population of the North End. Though it seems firmly planted today, the whole building was actually moved back sixteen feet when Hanover Street was widened in 1870.

Just across Hanover, the famous bronze **statue** of Paul Revere astride his borrowed horse marks the edge of the **Paul Revere Mall**, a tree-lined, cobble-stoned park also known as the Prado. This relaxed open space was carved out of a chunk of apartment blocks in 1933 and runs back to tiny **Unity Street** – home of the small 1712 red-brick **Clough House**, at no. 21; a private residence built by the mason who helped lay the brick of nearby Old North Church.

Continue north on Hanover for a look at local landmark "All Saint's Way," a miniature devotional alleyway squeezed in between nos. 4 and 6 Battery St. Folksy and sweet, it's decked out with images of saints and watched over by peaceful cherubim.

Old North Church

Few places in Boston have as emblematic a quality as the simple yet noble **Old North Church** at 93 Salem St (daily June–Oct 9am–6pm, Nov–May 9am–5pm; free; ☎617/523-6676; ⓦ www.oldnorth.com), rising unobstructed above the uniform blocks of the surrounding red-brick apartments. Built in 1723, and inspired by St Andrew's-by-the-Wardrobe in Blackfriars, London, it's the oldest church building in Boston, easily recognized by its gleaming 191-foot **steeple**. The weathervane perched on top is the colonial original, though the steeple itself is a replica – hurricanes toppled both its first, in 1804, and its replacement, in 1954.

It was a pair of lanterns that secured the structure's place in history, though. The church sexton, Robert Newman, is said to have hung both of them inside ("One if by land, two if by 'sea'") on the night of April 18, 1775, to signal the movement of British forces from Boston Common. The signal was intended for colonial militia in Charlestown, just in case Paul Revere was unsuccessful in his crossing of the Charles River. Revere had already learned of the impending British advance and was riding to Lexington by the time the lanterns were in place – he simply needed Newman's help to alert Charlestown in case his mission was thwarted. As it turned out, both Revere and fellow rider William Dawes were detained by British patrols; Dr. Samuel Prescott, the evening's third rider (and the one least known to history), is the only one who made it all the way to Concord.

The **interior** of the church is spotlessly white and well lit, thanks to the Palladian windows behind the pulpit. Other details include twelve bricks, set into the vestibule wall, from a prison cell in Boston, England, where an early group of Pilgrims were incarcerated, and the four seventeenth-century cherubim near the organ that were looted from a French vessel. You can also check your watch by the **clock** at the rear; made in 1726, it's the oldest one still ticking in an American public building. Have a wander, too, among the high box pews: no. 62 belonged to General Thomas Gage, commander-in-chief of the British army in North America, while descendants of Paul Revere still lay claim to no. 54. Beneath your feet, the timber on which the pews rest is supported by 37 basement-level brick crypts; one of the 1100 bodies encased therein is that of John Pitcairn, the British major killed in the Battle of Bunker Hill. His remains were tagged for Westminster Abbey, but they never made it home to England. The eight bells inside the belfry – open to the public during summer-only **tours** ($8 adults, $5 kids) – were the first cast for the British Empire in North America and have since tolled the death of every US president.

Some of Old North's greatest charms are actually outside the church itself, notably the diminutive **Washington Memorial Garden**, the brick walls of which are bedecked with commemorative plaques honoring past church members, and the inviting **Eighteenth-Century Garden**, its terraces packed with lilies and roses, as well as some curious umbrella-shaped flowers known, appropriately, as archangels.

Salem and Prince streets

While Old North Church is certainly **Salem Street's** star attraction, the lower blocks to the south between Prince and Cross streets make up the North End's most colorful thoroughfare. The actual street – whose name is possibly a bastardization of "Shalom Street," as it was known to the earlier Eastern European Jewish settlers – is so narrow that the red-brick buildings seem to lean into one another, and light traffic makes it a common practice to walk right down the middle of the road. Traveling south, an agreeable onslaught of Italian grocers, aromatic *pasticcerias*, and cafés begins rather abruptly at Salem's intersection with Prince Street, starting with *Bova's Bakery* at no. 134 (see p.207). The Neapolitan bustle ends at Cross Street; if you continue on, you'll pass the Rose Kennedy Greenway and then on to the Fanueil Hall Marketplace and Government Center in Downtown.

Bustling **Prince Street**, a narrow road cutting through the heart of the North End on an east–west axis, is also lined with *salumerias* and restaurants, but tends to be more social – locals typically while away the day along the pavement here on folding chairs brought from home. At the corner of Hanover Street and parallel to Prince Street, **St Leonard's Church**, 14 N Bennet St, was the first Italian-Catholic church in New England when it was founded in 1873. The ornate interior is a marked contrast to Boston's stark Protestant churches, while the so-called "Peace Garden" in front, with its prosaic plantings and tacky statuary, is, in a sense, vintage North End.

Copp's Hill Burying Ground and Copp's Hill Terrace

Up Hull Street from Old North Church, **Copp's Hill Burying Ground** (daily dawn–dusk) displays eerily tilting slate tombstones, stunning harbor views, and the graves of some significant sons of the North End. The first burial here, on the highest ground in the North End, took place in 1659. Among the ten thousand interred are nearly a thousand men from the "New Guinea Community," a colonial enclave of free blacks at the foot of the hill. One such notable was Prince Hall, who founded the first Black Masons lodge and played an important role in the 1783 act that abolished slavery in Massachusetts. The most famous gravesite here is that of the **Mather family**, just inside the wrought-iron gates on the northern Charter Street side. Increase Mather and his son Cotton – the latter a Salem Witch Trial witness for the prosecution – were big players in Boston's early days of Puritan theocracy, a fact not at all reflected in the rather diminutive, if appropriately plain, brick vault tomb. As for other noteworthy graves, **Robert Newman**, who hung Paul Revere's lanterns in Old North Church, is buried near the western rim of the plot, as is **Edmund Hartt**, the builder of the famous ship the USS *Constitution* ("Old Ironsides"; see p.76).

You'll notice, too, that many gravestones have significant chunks missing – a consequence of British soldiers using them for target practice during the 1775 Siege of Boston. The grave of one Captain Daniel Malcolm, toward the left end of the third row of gravestones, bears particularly strong evidence of this: three musketball marks scar his epitaph, which hails him as a "true son of liberty" and an "enemy of oppression." The burying ground suffered further damages in the mid-nineteenth century when its gravestones were used as hearthstones for baking, making it a real possibility that you would find the imprint of an epitaph on the bottom of your loaf of bread. As you exit the burying ground, keep an eye out for the **narrowest house** in Boston, a private residence merely ten feet in width; it's located at 44 Hull St.

The granite **Copp's Hill Terrace**, a plateau separated from the burial ground on the northern side by Charter Street, was the place from which British cannon bombarded Charlestown during the Battle of Bunker Hill. On a sweltering day in 1919, a 2.3-million-gallon steel storage tank of molasses – used in the production of alcoholic beverages – exploded nearby, creating a syrupy tidal wave thirty feet high that engulfed entire buildings and drowned 21 people along with a score of horses. Old North Enders – the kind you'll see playing bocce in the little park at the bottom of the terrace – claim you can still catch a whiff of the stuff on an exceptionally hot day.

3

Charlestown

Across Boston Harbor from the North End (see Chapter 2), upscale, historic Charlestown stands quite isolated from the city, despite its annexation more than a century ago. The Big Dig has dramatically reshaped its landscape for the better, and the new Leonard P. Zakim Bridge, with its towering, obelisk-style suspension poles, pays architectural homage to the local Bunker Hill Monument.

There are two main ways to get to **Charlestown**: one is to take the **T** to North Station and walk over the Charlestown Bridge – which affords great views of both Boston Harbor and the Zakim Bridge. The other is to take the short $1.70 ferry trip from the waterfront's Long Wharf, which deposits you on the eastern outskirts of the Charlestown Navy Yard, where the area's big draw, the **USS Constitution**, is berthed.

Just a few minutes' walk northwest from the Navy Yard, Charlestown's center, **City Square**, is the point from which most notable streets in the area radiate out. Directly north is the neighborhood's other major sight, the **Bunker Hill Monument**, the northern terminus of the Freedom Trail, which runs across the Charlestown Bridge from the North End. Otherwise, the rest of the district is simply a pretty, tree-lined neighborhood, although it gets a bit dodgier on its outskirts. This shouldn't cause much worry, as if you stick to the USS *Constitution* and the monument, you needn't spend more than a morning in Charlestown, although the area's romantic environs and posh restaurants, such as *Olives* or the hookah-savvy *Tangierino* (see Chapter 11, "Eating"), may tempt visitors back for the evening.

Some history

The earliest **Puritan settlers** had high hopes for developing Charlestown when they arrived in 1629, but an unsuitable water supply pushed them over to the Shawmut Peninsula, which they promptly renamed Boston. Charlestown grew slowly after that, and had to be completely rebuilt after the British burned it down in 1775; almost as many houses were lost in that blaze as had been torched in the entire Revolutionary War.

The mid-1800s witnessed the arrival of the so-called "lace-curtain Irish" (those who were somewhat better off than their East Boston brethren), and the district remains an **Irish** one at heart. The long-time locals, known as "townies," have acquired a reputation for being standoffish, due to such episodes as their resistance to school desegregation in the 1970s. The neighborhood was once a haven for criminals, too: if a bank was robbed in Boston, the story goes, police would simply wait on the Charlestown Bridge for their quarry to come home. Today, though, the criminal element has all but disappeared from the area, since urban professionals took over many of the Federal- and Colonial-style

CHARLESTOWN

ACCOMMODATION
Bed and Breakfast Afloat — B
Constitution Inn YMCA — A
Residence Inn Boston Harbor — C

RESTAURANTS & CAFÉS
Figs — 5
Olives — 6
Sorelle Bakery & Café — 4
Tangierino — 3
Warren Tavern — 2

BARS & CLUBS
Tavern on the Water — 1

Pier 9
Pier 8
Pier 7
Pier 6
Pier 5
Pier 4
Pier 3
Pier 2
Pier 1

Foundary
Charlestown New Yard
Shipyard Park
Ropewalk Building

MBTA ferry to Long Wharf, Downtown

USS Constitution Museum
USS Constitution (Old Ironsides)
USS Cassin Young
Boston National Historical Park
Bunker Hill Pavilion

Breed's Hill
Bunker Hill Monument
Monument Square

33 Cordis Street
Larkin House
John Harvard Mall
City Square

Warren Tavern
Charlestown Public Library
Charlestown Five Cents Savings Bank Building

Phipps Street Burying Ground
Bunker Hill Community College

500 yds
0

N

North End
West End & Downtown

Freedom Trail

93

COMMUNITY COLLEGE

Street names:
3RD AVENUE
2ND AVENUE
4TH AVENUE
TOBIN BRIDGE
CHELSEA STREET
DECATUR STREET
MEDFORD STREET
OXFORD STREET
5TH STREET
8TH STREET
1ST AVENUE
2ND AVENUE
BUNKER HILL ST
VINE STREET
HAYES SQUARE
WAY
TUFTS STREET
WALFORD WAY
TREMONT STREET
PROSPECT ST
MT VERNON STREET
CHESTNUT STREET
MONUMENT SQUARE
LEXINGTON ST
LEXINGTON AVE
MONUMENT STREET
O'REILLY WAY
BUNKER HILL ST
CONCORD ST
JEFFERSON AVE
TRENTON STREET
CEDAR STREET
CROSS STREET
ELM STREET
GREEN STREET
BARTLETT STREET
HIGH STREET
WOOD ST
SCHOOL STREET
PEARL STREET
SALEM STREET
SULLIVAN STREET
HIGH STREET
LAWRENCE ST
SCHOOL STREET
WEST SCHOOL STREET
DUNSTABLE STREET
AUSTIN STREET
RUTHERFORD AVENUE
NEW RUTHERFORD AVENUE
WASHINGTON STREET
UNION STREET
DEVEN'S STREET
PRESCOTT ST
HARVARD STREET
MAIN STREET
WARREN STREET
SOLEY STREET
WINTHROP SQUARE
ADAMS STREET
COMMON STREET
PARK STREET
ROSE KENNEDY GREENWAY
CHELSEA STREET
2ND AVENUE
CONSTITUTION ROAD
MONUMENT AVENUE
CORDIS STREET

townhouses south of the Bunker Hill Monument. The resulting mood in Charlestown is one of amiable if quiet affluence, especially along the southern blocks of Main Street, where the better restaurants are found.

③ The Charlestown Navy Yard and the USS Constitution Museum

Opened in 1800, the sprawling **Charlestown Navy Yard** was one of the first and busiest US naval shipyards – riveting together an astounding 46 destroyer escorts in 1943 alone – though it owes most of its present-day liveliness to its grandest tenant, the frigate USS *Constitution* at Constitution Wharf. Today, the ship is well cared for by the Navy and the Boston National Historical Park, an umbrella association that preserves nationally significant Boston sights.

It's a good idea to visit the **USS Constitution Museum** (April to late Oct Tues–Sun 10am–5.50pm, Nov–March Thurs–Sun 10am–3.50pm; free; ⊤617/426-1812, Ⓦwww.ussconstitutionmuseum.org), located in a substantial granite structure a short walk from the *Constitution* and across from Pier 1, before you board the ship itself. Its excellent exhibits help contextualize the vessel and her unparalleled role in American maritime history. The history of the ship is covered downstairs, including the story of how, in the 1920s, US schoolchildren contributed $154,000 in pennies toward its preservation; you can also glimpse the ship's original logbooks and examine the drafting tools used by the *Constitution's* designer. Upstairs is perhaps more fun, with hands-on exhibits putting you in the role of a sailor: determine whether your comrades have scurvy or gout, attempt to balance yourself on a shifting footrope, and ponder whether you would be willing to eat a biscuit "as hard as a brick."

The USS Constitution ("Old Ironsides")

As tall as a twenty-story building and three hundred feet long from bowsprit to back end, the **USS Constitution** (daily 10am–4pm; free; ⊤617/242-5671; Ⓦwww.ussconstitution.navy.mil) is impressive from any angle. Launched in 1797 to safeguard American merchant vessels from Barbary pirates and, later on, the French and British navies, she earned her nickname during the War of 1812; cannonballs fired from the British HMS *Guerrière* bounced off the hull (the "iron" sides were actually hewn from live oak, a particularly sturdy wood from the south-eastern US), leading to the first and most dramatic American naval conquest of that war. The *Constitution* went on to win 33 battles – never losing one – before she was retired from active service in the 1830s; stints as flagship with Mediterranean and African squadrons were followed by use as a training ship until her full naval commission was returned in 1940, making her the oldest commissioned warship afloat in the world. When, in 1997, the *Constitution* went on her first unassisted voyage in 116 years, news coverage was international in scale, a measure of the worldwide respect for the symbolic flagship of the US Navy.

Though authentic enough in appearance, the *Constitution* has certainly taken its hits (roughly ninety percent of the ship has been reconstructed). Even after extensive renovations, though, Old Ironsides is still too frail to support sails for extended periods of time, and the only regular trips she makes are annual Fourth of July turnarounds in Boston Harbor. There's often a line to visit the ship, especially in the summer, and access has been further slowed by increased security checks, but it's nonetheless worth the wait to get a close-up view of the elaborate rigging that can support some three dozen sails totaling almost an acre in area.

After ambling about the main deck, you can scuttle down nearly vertical stairways to the lower deck, where there's an impressive array of cannons, many of them christened with fun fighting names like Raging Eagle or Jumping Billy. Most of the ship's 54 cannon are actually replicas – when Old Ironsides ceased to be a fighting vessel, its munitions were removed for use in battle-worthy ships – but two functional models face downtown from the bow of the main deck. They still get a daily workout, too, shooting off explosive powder to mark mast-raising and -lowering (dawn and dusk, respectively); were they to fire the 24-pound balls for which they were originally outfitted, they'd topple the Customs House tower across the bay in downtown Boston.

The rest of the Navy Yard

Berthed in between Old Ironsides and the museum is the hulking gray mass of the World War II destroyer **USS** *Cassin Young* (same hours as the *Constitution*; free; ☎617/242-5601). While several similar destroyers were made in Charlestown, the *Cassin Young* was built in San Pedro, California, and served primarily in the Atlantic and Mediterranean before eventually being transferred to the National Park Service for use as a museum ship in 1978. There's not too much to see here, though, aside from the expansive main deck's depth chargers and tiny infirmary. The cramped chambers below – the Captain's rooms and the ship's barber shop, among them – are mostly of interest to World War II buffs, who can inspect them by taking a 45-minute guided **tour** (11am, 2pm, 3pm; must be over 4ft tall, arrive ten minutes early to secure a ticket; free).

At the northern perimeter of the Navy Yard is the **Ropewalk Building**. Between 1830 and 1970 "ropewalkers" made every single strand of rope used by the US Navy in this narrow, quarter-mile-long granite building, the only one of its kind still standing in the country; unfortunately it's not open to the public. At the opposite end of the Yard, near the point where you access the Charlestown Bridge, the **Bunker Hill Pavilion,** run by the Boston National Park Service, offers helpful information and screens a rather dated, twenty-minute program entitled *The Whites of Their Eyes* (daily 9.30am–4.30pm; $4; ☎617/241-7575), which attempts to recreate the Battle of Bunker Hill via blinking lights and voiceovers.

City Square and around

Charlestown's center is a few minutes' walk northwest of the Navy Yard. At the end of a scenic, harborfront walk is **City Square** – a park space that doubles as a traffic circle. The square is anchored at its northern tip by *Olives*, one of Boston's most popular restaurants, and the 1913 yellow-brick three-story Charlestown Municipal Building on its east side.

Harvard Street, which runs off the square's northwest side, was posthumously named for John Harvard, the young Charlestown-based minister whose library and funds launched the country's first university, in Cambridge. The street curves through the small **Town Hill** district, site of the neighborhood's first settled community. Here you'll also find John Harvard Mall and Harvard Square (not to be confused with the celebrated one in Cambridge), both lined with well-preserved homes.

Main, Devens, and Cordis streets

Main Street extends north from the square; at no. 55 you'll find the wooden 1795 house of **Deacon John Larkin**, who lent Paul Revere his horse for his famous ride to Lexington, and he never got it back. You can't go inside, so press on to the quaint **Warren Tavern**, at no. 105, a small three-story wooden structure. Both Larkin's house and the Warren Tavern were built soon after the British burned Charlestown in the Battle of Bunker Hill. The tavern, named for doctor Joseph Warren, personal physician to the Adams family (as in President John Adams) before he was killed in the Battle of Bunker Hill, still functions as a popular watering hole today (see Chapter 12, "Drinking").

West of the tavern, the monumental 1876 **Charlestown Five Cents Savings Bank Building**, at 1 Thompson Square, boasts a steep mansard roof, Victorian Gothic ornamentation, and a 1000lb clock; the modest external vault belonging to its original tenants still protrudes from the eastern wall. A good ten minutes' walk further west takes you to the **Phipps Street Burying Ground**, dating from 1630, which has an unusual layout allegedly corresponding to that of Charlestown itself, and quirky gravestones like that of Prince Bradstreet, memorialized as "an honest man of color." While many Revolutionary soldiers are buried here, it lacks the historical resonance of some other burying grounds along the Freedom Trail.

Retrace your steps to the Warren Tavern and head down crooked **Devens Street** to the south (called Crooked Lane in 1640) and **Cordis Street** to the north, which are packed with historic, private houses, many of which are lovely to look at, though they don't offer anything in the way of tours. Of these, the

The Battle of Bunker Hill

The Revolutionary War was at its bloodiest on the hot June day in 1775 when British and colonial forces clashed in Charlestown. In the wake of the battles at Lexington and Concord two months before, the British had assumed full control of Boston, while the patriots had the upper hand in the surrounding countryside. The British, under the command of generals Thomas Gage, William Howe, and "Gentleman Johnny" Burgoyne, intended to sweep the area clean of "rebellious rascals." Colonials intercepted the plans and moved to fortify **Bunker Hill**, the dominant hill in Charlestown. However, when Colonel William Prescott arrived on the scene, he chose to occupy **Breed's Hill** instead, either due to a mix-up – the two hills were often confused on colonial-era maps – or tactical foresight, based on the proximity of Breed's Hill to the harbor. Whatever the motivation, more than a thousand citizen-soldiers arrived during the night of June 16, 1775, and fortified the hill with a 160-foot-long earthen redoubt by morning.

Spotting the Yankee fort, the Redcoats, each carrying 125 pounds of food and supplies on their backs, rowed across the harbor to take the rebel-held town. On the patriots' side, Colonel Prescott had issued the celebrated order that his troops not fire "'til you see the whites of their eyes," such was their limited store of gunpowder. When the enemy's approach was deemed near enough, the patriots opened fire; though vastly outnumbered, they successfully repelled two full-fledged assaults, the even rows of under-prepared and overburdened redcoats making easy targets. Some British units lost more than ninety percent of their men, and the few officers that survived had to push their troops forward with their swords to make them fight on. By the third British assault, the Redcoats had shed their gear, reinforcements had arrived, and the colonial's supply of gunpowder was dwindling – as were their chances of clinching victory. The rebels continued to fight with stones and musket butts; meanwhile, British cannon fire from Copp's Hill in the North End was turning Charlestown into an inferno. Despite their eventual loss, the patriots were invigorated by their strong showing, and the British, who had lost nearly half of their men in the battle, became convinced that victory over the determined rebels would only be possible with a much larger army.

▲ Bunker Hill Monument

worn Revival mansion at 33 Cordis St is the most striking, with its white Ionic columns standing tall amidst its quaint New England neighbors.

Monument Avenue and Winthrop Square

North from Main Street toward the Bunker Hill Monument, the red-brick townhouses along **Monument Avenue** are some of Boston's most exclusive residences. Though no house really stands out, strolling past the medley of

Federal and Revival structures en route to the Bunker Hill monument makes for scenic meandering. Nearby along Winthrop Street, **Winthrop Square** is Charlestown's unofficial common; the prim rowhouses overlooking it from another upscale enclave. Appropriately enough, considering its proximity to Bunker Hill, the common started out as a military training field; a series of bronze tablets at its northeastern edge list the men killed just up the slope in the Battle of Bunker Hill.

The Bunker Hill Monument

Commemorating the Battle of Bunker Hill is the **Bunker Hill Monument** (daily 9am–4.30pm; free; ☎617/242-5641), a gray, dagger-like obelisk that's visible from just about anywhere in Charlestown, thanks to a position atop a butte confusingly known as Breed's Hill (see box, p.78). It was here that the New England militia positioned themselves on the night of June 16, 1775, to wage what was ultimately a losing battle – despite its recasting by US historians as a great moral victory in the fight for independence. The obelisk is notable for being both the country's first monument funded entirely by public donations, and the first to popularize the dagger-like style epitomized by the Washington Monument in DC. The tower is centrally positioned in **Monument Square** and fronted by a strident, sword-bearing statue of Colonel William Prescott, who commanded the colonial troops; a lodge at its base houses dioramas of the battle, while inside, 294 steps ascend to the top of the 221-foot granite shaft. Hardy climbers will be rewarded with sweeping views of Boston, the Harbor, surrounding towns, and, to the northwest, the stone spire of the **St Francis de Sales Church**, which stands atop the real Bunker Hill.

The sporting life

Boston is undeniably a sports town. Ever since the Boston Red Stockings scored their first run in 1871, the city's devotion to baseball has raged to a nearly religious fervor. And while baseball fever is Boston's best-known sports affliction, there's no shortage of Patriots football, Bruins ice hockey, or Celtics basketball fans. College sports, too, have an almost maniacal following, particularly with the Harvard–Yale football rivalry and the Boston Beanpot, a well-loved February ice hockey tournament for local colleges. If spectator sports aren't your thing, Boston also has a seventeen-mile bike path, outdoor skating ponds in winter, and a mind-boggling number of picnic-worthy public parks.

Title town

You'd be hard-pressed to find a city as fanatical about its sports as Boston. As a result tickets for some of the more popular teams can be difficult, if not impossible, to find at a reasonable price. Love for the Red Sox has only intensified in recent years with World Series wins in 2004 and 2007. Tickets for the regular season (which starts in April) sell out fast, but it's possible to score pricey resale tickets. And though they play in a stadium a long drive away, seeing a New England Patriots game live is a rare treat for non season ticket holders. Their Super Bowl victories in 2002, 2004, and 2005 have gone a long way to making locals forget that the Celtics haven't won a NBA championship since 1986, and the Bruins haven't brought home the Stanley Cup since 1972.

All is not lost for crowd seekers, however. If a big game is on, the whole city comes to attention, and it's easy to join in on the fun; even upscale restaurants often have a television or two on so their patrons can catch the game.

▲ Paul Pierce of the Boston Celtics

Fenway Park

No team in professional baseball has as distinct a **home-field advantage** as the Boston Red Sox. The oldest Major League ballpark in the country (it dates to 1912), **Fenway Park** is rife with old-school charms like a manually-operated scoreboard, it's own trademarked color ("Fens Green"), and a whimsically angled playing field known for its crazy caroms. All this is in addition to the legendary 37ft high **Green Monster** wall in left field, originally built because homeruns were breaking the windows of the adjacent Lansdowne Street businesses.

To get in on the action, your best bet is to head toward the neighborhood where the game is playing – Kenmore Square for Red Sox revelry, and the West End for Celtics and Bruins events. Be sure to hit your chosen bar early so you can nab a good seat, then order a local brew and get ready for a wild night spent with an animated crowd.

The race is on

Not all of Boston's biggest sporting events require a ticket. Indeed, two of the city's largest and most loved annual events cost nothing to attend. The iconic **Head of the Charles Regatta** is the world's largest two-day rowing race, taking place every October and attracting more than 7500 athletes from around the world – not to mention the 300,000 picnicking spectators who angle for views of it from both the Boston and Cambridge sides of the Charles River. Another international attraction, the endearing **Boston Marathon**, is the oldest marathon in the world (dating back to 1897) and lures some 20,000 runners to town every April. The 26.2-mile course curves through the suburbs – lined by legions of cheering residents – before culminating on Boylston Street just before The Old South Church. While the events themselves are a sight to be seen, best is the local camaraderie that urges the competitors on from start to finish.

Park it

Perhaps it's because Boston winters are so arduous, but when warm weather hits the town is positively abuzz with people strolling, biking, sailing, and rowing. When you're ready to take a breather, you'll find that the city's greenspaces are as much fun for lounging as they are for exercising – see our list below for some of the area's most affable picnic spots.

Arnold Arboretum p.131
Over 260 beautiful acres of rolling lawns, flowering trees, and a particularly striking bonsai collection; there's also a number of pretty bike paths.

Boston Public Garden p.93
This flower-filled oasis functions as the lungs of the city; the breezy lagoon at its center is home to Boston's beloved Swan Boats.

Charles River Esplanade p.88
In summer, the affable Boston Pops play free concerts here at the Hatch Memorial Shell; the rest of the year sees biking, strolling, and rollerblading by the river.

Christopher Columbus Park p.60
This North End beauty is loved by locals at lunchtime thanks to its wisteria-laden trellis and superb waterfront views.

Post Office Park p.54
Smaller than a postage stamp, the benches at this flowery financial district hotspot are frequented by businessmen on their lunch break.

◀ The Public Garden

Beacon Hill and the West End

No visit to Boston would be complete without an afternoon spent strolling around delightful **Beacon Hill**, a dignified stack of red-brick rising over the north side of Boston Common. This is the Boston of wealth and privilege, one-time home to numerous historical and literary figures – including John Hancock, John Quincy Adams, Louisa May Alcott, Oliver Wendell Holmes, and Nathaniel Hawthorne – and still the address of choice for the city's elite. And, looking around, it's not hard to fathom why. The narrow, hilly byways are lit with **gaslamps** that burn 24/7 (historically it was cheaper to leave them on than to snuff them out and relight them on a daily basis) and lined with quaint, nineteenth-century **townhouses**, all part of an enforced preservation that prohibits modern buildings, architectural innovations, or anything else from disturbing the carefully cultivated atmosphere of urban gentility. (Even *Starbucks* has been forced to adopt the neighborhood's distinctive signage.)

It was not always this way. In colonial times, Beacon Hill was the most prominent of three peaks, known as the Trimountain, which formed Boston's geological backbone. The sunny south slope was developed into prime real estate and quickly settled by the city's political and economic powers, while the north slope was traditionally closer in spirit to the **West End**, a tumbledown port district populated by free blacks and immigrants; indeed, the north slope was home to so much salacious activity, that outraged Brahmins – Beacon Hill's moneyed elite – termed it "Mount Whoredom."

By the end of the twentieth century, this social divide was largely eradicated and clever real estate agents and developers have been quick to bracket the West End with Beacon Hill. Condominiums have recently been built on Bowdoin Street – one of the arteries joining the two neighborhoods – and businesses up to ten blocks from the Hill itself have taken on a "Beacon Hill" prefix as part of their names. The result is that Beacon Hill has lost a bit of its exclusionary feel (though members of polite society still refer to the south slope as "the good side"). Both sides, in fact, have much to offer: on the south slope, there's the grandiose **Massachusetts State House**, residences of past and present luminaries, and attractive boulevards like **Charles Street** and **Beacon Street** (the former is Beacon Hill's main thoroughfare, and full of boutiques, antique shops, and cafés; the latter is snugly crowded with prim townhouses). The north slope is home to the first-rate **Black Heritage Trail** (see box, p.87) – a walking tour that explores the history of Boston's nineteenth-century

African-American community – and takes in the superb **African Meeting House**, the stellar **Robert Gould Shaw/54th Regiment Memorial**, and a warren of alleyways used by fleeing slaves to escape arrest.

Beacon Street

Running along the south slope of Beacon Hill above Boston Common, **Beacon Street** was described as Boston's "sunny street for the sifted few" by Oliver Wendell Holmes in the late-nineteenth century. This lofty character remains today: a row of stately brick townhouses, fronted by ornate iron grillwork, presides regally over the area. The ground level of one of these homes holds what might be the most famous address on the block, **Cheers** (see p.183) home of the *Bull & Finch* pub. This ultra-touristy bar, whose setting inspired the hit TV series, unabashedly trades on the association and has added a gift store at street level.

Continuing along, look for **purple panes** in some of the townhouses' windows, especially at nos. 63 and 64; the story behind this odd coloring evinces the street's long association with Boston wealth and privilege. When panes were installed in some of the first Beacon Street mansions, they turned purple upon exposure to the sun, due to an excess of manganese in the glass. At first an irritating accident, they were eventually regarded as the definitive Beacon Hill status symbol due to their prevalence in the windows of Boston's most prestigious homes; some residents have gone so far as to shade their windows purple in imitation.

Prescott House, the Founder's Monument, and Somerset Club

While it lacks the purple-tinted panes, the elegant bowfronted 1808 **Prescott House**, at no. 55 (May–Oct Wed, Thurs, & Sat noon–4pm, tours every 30min; $5; ⓣ617/742-3190, ⓦwww.nscda.org/ma; Park St **T**) is still worthy of a visit. Designed by Asher Benjamin, one of Charles Bulfinch's most prolific understudies, its most distinguished inhabitant was Spanish historian William Hickling Prescott, whose family occupied its five floors from 1845 to 1859. Hung above the pastiche of Federalist and Victorian furniture inside is a photograph of two crossed swords that once belonged to Colonel William Prescott and British Captain John Linzee – the historian and his wife's respective grandfathers. The men fought against each other at Bunker Hill, and the sight of their munitions here inspired William Thackeray, a frequent houseguest, to write his novel, *The Virginians*.

Across the street, the **Founder's Monument** commemorates Boston's first European settler, William Blackstone, a Cambridge-educated loner who moved from England with his entire library to a piece of wilderness he acquired for next to nothing from the Shawmut Indians – the site of present-day Boston. A stone bas-relief depicts the apocryphal moment in 1629 when Blackstone sold most of his acreage to a group of Puritans from Charlestown (and marks the year, 1630, when Boston was founded).

Back on the north side of Beacon Street, and a few steps past Spruce Court, is the last of a trio of **Charles Bulfinch houses** (see box, p.85) commissioned by lawyer and future Boston mayor Harrison Gray Otis over a ten-year period; the four-story Neoclassical house has been home to the American Meteorological Society since 1958. Just east of here, it's hard to miss the twin-swelled granite building at nos. 42–43, built for Colonel David Sears's family by

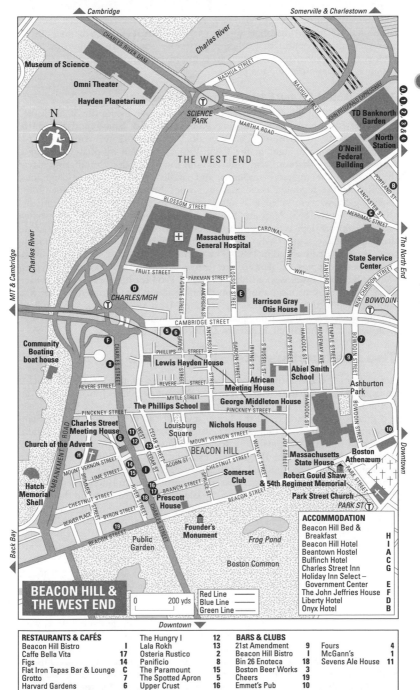

▲ Cambridge   Somerville & Charlestown ▲

Charles River

Charles River Dam

CHARLES RIVER DAM

Museum of Science

NASHUA STREET

Omni Theater

Hayden Planetarium

NASHUA STREET

JOHN FITZGERALD EXPRESSWAY

Ⓐ ① ② ③ & ④

N

SCIENCE
PARK

Ⓣ

MARTHA ROAD

**TD Banknorth
Garden**

**North
Station**

Ⓑ

PORTLAND ST

THE WEST END

**O'Neill
Federal
Building**

LANCASTER ST

Ⓒ

MERRIMAC STREET

The North End ►

BLOSSOM STREET

CARDINAL

O'CONNELL

WAY

STANIFORD STREET

**State Service
Center**

NEW CHARDON STREET

⬥ MIT & Cambridge

Charles River

+ **Massachusetts
General Hospital**

FRUIT STREET

PARKMAN STREET

BLOSSOM STREET

BOWDOIN

Ⓔ

N ANDERSON STREET

N GROVE STREET

**Harrison Gray
Otis House**

Ⓣ

Ⓓ

CHARLES/MGH

Ⓣ

CAMBRIDGE STREET

ANDERSON STREET

GARDEN STREET

IRVING ST

S RUSSELL ST

JOY STREET

HANCOCK ST

RIDGEWAY AVE

TEMPLE STREET

BOWDOIN STREET

Ⓕ

⑤ ⑥

GROVE STREET

PHILLIPS STREET

Ⓖ

**Community
Boating
boat house**

REVERE STREET

Ⓖ

Lewis Hayden House

REVERE STREET

**African
Meeting
House**

**Abiel Smith
School**

⑦

⑨

Ⓗ

MYTLE STREET

George Middleton House

**Ashburton
Park**

The Phillips School

PINCKNEY STREET

PINCKNEY STREET

HANCOCK ST

BOWDOIN STREET

Downtown ►

**Charles Street
Meeting House**

Ⓖ ⑪ ⑫

**Louisburg
Square**

Nichols House

⑩

Church of the Advent

Ⓗ

⑬

CEDAR ST

MOUNT VERNON STREET

WALNUT STREET

JOY STREET

**Massachusetts
State House**

PARK STREET

**Boston
Athenæum**

EMBANKMENT ROAD

MOUNT VERNON STREET

⑭

WEST CEDAR ST

ACORN ST

BEACON HILL

CHARLES STREET

BRIMMER STREET

LIME STREET

⑮

Ⓘ

CHESTNUT STREET

**Somerset
Club**

**Robert Gould Shaw
& 54th Regiment Memorial**

🏛

**Hatch
Memorial
Shell**

CHESTNUT STREET

⑯ ⑰

BRANCH STREET

RIVER STREET

SPRUCE ST

BEACON STREET

Park Street Church

✝

⑱ **Prescott
House**

PARK ST Ⓣ

BEAVER PLACE

BYRON STREET

CHARLES STREET

BEACON STREET

⬥ Back Bay

⑲

**Public
Garden**

🏛 **Founder's
Monument**

Frog Pond

Boston Common

**BEACON HILL &
THE WEST END**

0   200 yds

Red Line ——
Blue Line ——
Green Line ——

Downtown ▼

Alexander Parris of Quincy Market fame (see p.56). Its stern Greek Revival facade has welcomed members of the exclusive **Somerset Club** since 1872, an organization so elitist that when a fire broke out in the kitchen in 1945, firemen who arrived were ordered to come in via the cumbersome servants' entrance, a heavy iron-studded portal.

Robert Gould Shaw/54th Regiment Memorial

Further up Beacon Street, on the edge of the Common facing the State House, is the majestic monument honoring **Robert Gould Shaw** and the **54th Massachusetts Regiment**. The memorial commemorates America's first all-black company to fight in the Civil War, a group led by Shaw, scion of a moneyed Boston Brahmin clan. Isolated from the rest of the Union army, given the worst of the military's resources, and saddled with menial or dangerous assignments, the regiment performed its service bravely; most of its members, including Shaw, were killed in a failed attempt to take Fort Wagner from the Confederates in 1863. Augustus Saint-Gaudens' outstanding 1897 high-relief bronze sculpture depicts the regiment's farewell march down Beacon Street, with the names of the soldiers who died in action listed on its reverse side (though these were belatedly added in 1982). The wistful angel that presides over the men carries both poppies and laurels, the former a symbol of death, the latter of victory. Robert Lowell won a Pulitzer Prize in 1964 for his poem, *For the Union Dead*, which took its inspiration from the monument; the regiment's story was also depicted in the 1989 film *Glory*, starring Matthew Broderick as Shaw. The monument serves as the starting point of the excellent National Park Ranger-led walking tour of the **Black Heritage Trail** (see box, p.87).

The Massachusetts State House

Across from the memorial rises the large gilt dome of the Charles Bulfinch-designed **Massachusetts State House** (Mon–Fri 10am–4pm, last tour at 3.30pm; free; ☎617/727-3676; ⓦwww.sec.state.ma.us; Park Street **T**), the scale and grandeur of which recall the heady spirit of the then newly independent America in which it was built. Of the current structure, only the central section was part of Bulfinch's original 1795 design; the huge wings jutting out toward the street on either side and the section extending up Bowdoin Street behind the State House were all added much later. An all-star team of Revolution-era luminaries contributed to the original construction: built on land purchased from John Hancock's estate, its cornerstone was laid by Samuel Adams, and the copper for its dome was rolled in Paul Revere's foundry in 1802 (though it was covered over with 23-karat gold leaf in the 1870s). Its front lawn is dotted with statuary honoring favorite sons such as Henry Cabot Lodge and JFK; to the right of the State House is a statue of Civil War General Joseph Hooker, best-known for his frequent procurement of "hookers" for his troops. There is also a statue of Mary Dyer, who became a symbol for religious freedom when she was put to death in 1660 for adhering to her Quaker faith. The statue overlooks a spot on Boston Common where her gallows may have stood.

Once inside the labyrinthine interior, make your way up a flight to the second floor, where 40-minute tours start from **Doric Hall** – though you'd do as well to grab a free map and show yourself around. The best section is the sober and impressive **Memorial Hall**, a circular room surrounded by tall columns of Siena marble, displaying transparencies of the original flags carried by Massachusetts soldiers into battle and lit by a vaulted stained-glass window bearing the state seal. On the third floor, a carved wooden fish known as the **Sacred Cod** hangs

The architecture of Charles Bulfinch

America's foremost architect of the late-eighteenth and early nineteenth centuries, **Charles Bulfinch** (1763–1844) developed a distinctive style somewhere between Federal and Classical that remains Boston's most recognizable architectural motif. Mixing Neoclassical training with New England practicality, Bulfinch built residences characterized by their rectilinear brick structure and pillared porticoes; examples remain throughout Beacon Hill, most notably at **87 Mount Vernon St** and **45 Beacon St**. While most of his work was residential, Bulfinch, in fact, made his name with the design of various government buildings, such as the 1805 renovation of **Faneuil Hall** and, more significantly, the **Massachusetts State House**, whose dome influenced the design of state capitols nationwide.

Bulfinch's talents also extended to urban planning. He designed the layout of Boston's **South End**, as well as the now demolished **Tontine Crescent**, a half-ellipse crescent planned around a small park that won Bulfinch praise but ruined him financially; what vestiges remain are found around the Financial District's **Franklin** and **Arch streets**. Bulfinch was also adept at designing massive greystone mercantile warehouses in both Victorian and Federal styles as well as churches – the North End owes **St Stephen's** to Bulfinch. Furthermore, his wide-ranging skill caught the attention of President James Monroe, who in 1818 commissioned Bulfinch to serve as the architect of Washington DC's **US Capitol**.

above the public gallery in the House of Representatives. The politicos take this symbol of maritime prosperity so seriously that when Harvard pranksters stole it in the 1930s, the House didn't reconvene until it was recovered.

Behind the State House, on Bowdoin Street, lies pleasant, grassy **Ashburton Park**, centered on a pillar that is a replica of a 1789 Bulfinch work. The column indicates the hill's original summit, which was sixty feet higher and topped by a 65-foot post with the makeshift warning light – constructed from an iron pot filled with combustibles – that gave Beacon Hill its name.

Louisburg Square and around

If you head north on Joy Street and take a left onto Mount Vernon Street, you will come across **Louisburg Square** (which will have a silent "s" or not, depending on whom you ask) regally poised between Mount Vernon and Pinkney. The gilded geographic heart of Beacon Hill, it's central lawn, surrounded by wrought-iron fencing and flanked by statues of Columbus and Aristides the Just, is owned by local residents, making it the city's only private square. On either side of this oblong green space are rows of stately brick townhouses, though the square's distinction is due less to its architectural character than to its long history of illustrious residents and the sense of elite civic parochialism that has made this Boston's most coveted address. Among those to call the area home were novelist Louisa May Alcott and members of the Vanderbilt family; it's currently home to former presidential candidate Senator John Kerry, and his wife, ketchup heiress Teresa Heinz.

A jaunt down Mount Vernon Street brings you past some of Beacon Hill's most beautiful buildings. The **Nichols House** (May–Oct Tues–Sat noon–4pm; Nov–April Thurs–Sat noon–4pm, tours start 15min past the hour; $7; ℗617/227-6993, ⓦwww.nicholshousemuseum.org; Park Street **T**), at no.55, is yet another Bulfinch design, and the only Beacon Hill residence open year-round to the public. The building was most recently the home of landscape designer and pacifist Rose Standish Nichols, the favorite niece of sculptor

Augustus Saint-Gaudens (the man behind the **54th Regiment Memorial** on Beacon Street see p.84). Miss Rose, as she is known to posterity, lived in the house until her death in the early 1960s – though the faint odor of roses lingering in the air here today is supposed to imply that she may still be haunting the hallways. The detailed thirty-minute tours are best for those with an abiding interest in antique furnishings and decorations (there are some striking Asian tapestries, Federal-period furniture, and an original self-portrait by John Singleton Copley), though the home does lend some perspective on the interior life of leisure led by Beacon Hill's moneyed elite.

Acorn and Chestnut streets

A block south of Mount Vernon Street (and squeezed in between Willow and W. Cedar streets) narrow **Acorn Street** still has its original early nineteenth-century cobblestones. Barely wide enough for a car to pass through, it was originally built as a minor byway to be lined with servants' residences. Locals have always clung to it as the epitome of Beacon Hill quaint; in the 1960s, residents permitted the city to tear up the street to install sewer pipes only after exacting the promise that every cobblestone would be replaced in its original location. One block further south, **Chestnut Street** features some of the most intricate facades in Boston, notably Bulfinch's **Swan Houses**, at nos. 13, 15, and 17, with their recessed arches, Doric columns and delicate touches like wrought-iron lace balconies.

Pinckney Street

North of Louisburg Square runs **Pinckney Street**, once the sharp division between the opulent south and ramshackle north sections of Beacon Hill – original developers planned it as such, arranging their stables and estates so that only the back entrances fringed the street. In the 1920s, resident Robert Lowell expressed shock at the proximity of his home at 91 Revere St to these shadier environs, claiming that while he lived only fifty yards from Louisburg Square, he

▲ Acorn Street in Beacon Hill

In 1783, Massachusetts became the first state to declare slavery illegal, partly in recognition of black participation in the Revolutionary War. Not long after, a large community of free blacks and escaped slaves swiftly sprang up in the North End and Beacon Hill. The neighborhoods' proximity to the shipyards was convenient to the men, while the nearby upper-class houses meant domestic work for the women. Very few blacks live in either place nowadays, but the **Black Heritage Trail** traces Beacon Hill's key role in local and national black history and is the most important historical site in America devoted to pre-Civil War African-American history and culture.

The 1.6-mile loop takes in fourteen historical sights, which are detailed in a useful **guide** available at the **Museum of African American History** (as well as the information centers in Boston Common and State Street; see p.44 and 52). The best way to experience the trail is by taking a National Park Service **walking tour** (Mon–Sat 10am, noon, & 2pm; call to reserve; free; ☎617/742-5415, Ⓦwww.afroammuseum .org; Park St **T**).

Starting from the **Robert Gould Shaw Memorial** (see p.84), the tour passes the **George Middleton House** and the **Phillips School**, which in 1855 became Boston's first racially-integrated school. Near the end of the walk, you'll find the **Lewis and Harriet Hayden House** at 66 Phillips St, whose owner, a former escaped slave himself, regularly opened his door to fugitive slaves as part of the Underground Railroad (and slept with a rifle in his arms in case anyone tried to interfere with his guests), and **Smith Court**, home to the **African Meeting House** and **Abiel Smith School** at the end of **Holmes Alley**, a common escape route used by runaway slaves.

was nevertheless "perched on the outer rim of the hub of decency." The distinction is no longer so sharp, and now Pinckney is yet another picturesque Beacon Hill street, all the more worth a stroll thanks to its location at the crest of the hill; on a clear day, its intersection with Anderson Street affords partial views of the West End and across the Charles River to Cambridge – not the clearest vista, but good for getting the lay of the land.

Two historically important if aesthetically modest sights on the Black Heritage Trail can also be found on Pinckney: the 1797 clapboard **George Middleton House**, Beacon Hill's first African-American-built private dwelling, is at nos. 5-7, while the red-brick **Phillips School**, one of the first integrated schools in Boston, is at the street's intersection with Anderson.

The African Meeting House and around

Continue north on sloping Joy Street from Pinkney and you will intersect with tiny **Smith Court**, once the center of Boston's substantial pre-Civil War black community, and now home to a few crucial stops on Boston's **Black Heritage Trail**.

The **African Meeting House**, at no. 8 (Mon–Sat 10am–4pm; donations welcomed; Ⓦwww.afroammuseum.org; Park Street **T**) is the oldest black church structure in the country, and in its heyday served as the spiritual and political center for Boston's black community. It is also the birthplace of abolitionism: in 1832, William Lloyd Garrison founded The New England Anti-Slavery Society here, the first group of its kind to call for the immediate abolition of slavery; in 1860 Frederick Douglass gave an anti-slavery speech here after being run out of Tremont Temple. The place is currently being remodeled to look as it did in 1854, with plans to be finished in 2009.

At the end of Smith Court, walk along part of the old Underground Railroad used to protect escaped slaves, who once ducked into the doors along narrow **Holmes Alley** that were left open by sympathizers to the abolitionist cause. The **Abiel Smith School**, at 46 Joy St (same hours as above), built in 1834, was the first public building in the country established for the purpose of educating black children. Today, along with the African Meeting House, it comes under the aegis of the **Museum of African American History** and rotates a number of well-tailored exhibits centered on abolitionism and African-American history.

Charles Street

Located west of Joy Street, Charles Street is the commercial center of Beacon Hill, lined with scores of restaurants, antiques shops, and hip boutiques. The Federal-style **Charles Street Meeting House**, with its set-back, cupolaed roof, stands on the corner of Mount Vernon and Charles Street. Although it has since been repurposed as an office space and sidewalk café, the Meeting House was a hotbed of political activity in the nineteenth century. Just off Charles Street, where Mount Vernon intersects with Brimmer Street, you'll find the vine-covered **Church of the Advent**; with its pointed arches and starkly contrasting stone and red-brick facade, it's a striking example of High Victorian Gothic. If you poke your head in during one of their frequent weekly masses, you can check out the decadent gold altar and detailed grillwork along the apse.

The Esplanade

Spanning nine miles along the Charles River, the **Esplanade** is another of Boston's well-manicured public spaces, complete with requisite playgrounds, landscaped hills, lakes, and bridges. The nicest stretch runs alongside Beacon Hill and continues into Back Bay, providing a unique, scenic way to appreciate the Hill from a distance, as well as being a leading hotspot for the city's young and attractive. On summer days the Esplanade is swarming with well-toned joggers and rollerbladers, many of them seemingly on the prowl for a partner. Just below the Longfellow Bridge (which connects to Cambridge, across the river; see Chapter 9) is the Community Boating Boathouse, the point of departure for sailing, kayaking, and windsurfing outings on the Charles (April–Oct Mon–Fri 1pm–sunset, Sat & Sun 9am–sunset; two-day visitor's sailing pass $100 and must be able to prove sailing abilities; ☎617/523-1038, ⓦwww.community-boating.org).

The white half-dome rising from the riverbank along the Esplanade is the **Hatch Shell** (☎617/227-0627, ⓦwww.hatchshell.com; Charles **T**), a public performance space best known for its Fourth of July celebration (see p.225), which features a free concert by the Boston Pops, a pared-down, snappy version of the Boston Symphony Orchestra. Free movies and jazz concerts occur almost nightly in summer; check their website for a schedule of events.

The West End

North of Cambridge Street, the tidy rows of townhouses are replaced by a more urban spread of office buildings and old brick structures, signaling the start of the **West End**. Boston's main port of entry for immigrants in post-Colonial times, this area was populated by a broad mix of ethnic groups as well as transient sailors who brought a rough-and-tumble sex-and-tattoo industry with them. Unfortunately, the West End was razed during 1960s urban renewal, which did much to efface the district's once-lively character.

A vestige of the old West End remains in the small tangle of byways (currently being reinvigorated as the "Bulfinch Triangle") – namely Friend, Portland, and Canal streets – behind the high-rise buildings of Massachusetts General Hospital. Here urban warehouses are interspersed with numerous Irish bars that swell to a fever pitch after Celtics basketball and Bruin hockey games at the nearby **TDBanknorth Garden**, the slick, corporate-named arena on top of North Station at 150 Causeway St (℗617/624-1000; ⓦwww .tdbanknorthgarden.com). Within the arena is the affable **Sports Museum** (Mon–Sun 11am–5pm; admission on the hour at 11pm, 12pm, 1pm, 2pm with last tour at 3pm; hours fluctuate according to events – call to confirm; $6; ℗617/624-1234; ⓦwww.sportsmuseum.org; North Station T). Visitors can glimpse Bostonian sports classics like statues of Celtic Larry Bird and Bruin Bobby Orr, as well as the American League Championship banner from when the Red Sox finally beat the hated New York Yankees in 2004. There are also old school uniforms and equipment, like a prim woman's basketball uniform from the 1890s, but best of all is the hockey penalty box from the old Boston Garden, which visitors are invited to climb into.

The Harrison Gray Otis House

Back along Cambridge Street at no. 141, the brick **Harrison Gray Otis House** (Wed–Sun 11am–4.30pm, tours every half hour; $8; ℗617/227-3956, ⓦwww.historicnewengland.org; Charles T), originally built for the wealthy Otis family in 1796 by Bulfinch, sits incongruously among modern stores and office buildings (another of the family's three houses can be seen on Beacon Street; see p.82). In the 1830s, this building served as a medical facility offering "Champoo Baths" (a sort of old-fashioned aromatherapy treatment) before its later transformation into a boarding house. In 1925, the structure was literally rolled back from the present-day median strip in order to make way for the street. Its first two floors have been painstakingly restored – from the bright wallpaper right down to the silverware sets – in the often loud hues of the Federal style. Tours offer a glimpse into the lifestyle of Boston's elite following the American Revolution.

The Museum of Science

Situated on the Charles River Bridge, at the northernmost part of the Esplanade, Boston's stellar **Museum of Science** (July to early Sept daily 9am–7pm, Fri till 9pm, Sept–June daily 9am–5pm, Fri till 9pm; $17, kids $14; CityPass accepted; ℗617/723-2500, ⓦwww.mos.org; Science Park T) consists of several floors of well-loved interactive exhibits illustrating basic principles of natural and physical science. There's enough here to entertain kids for most of a day, though that doesn't make it off-limits to fun-loving adults, too.

The best exhibit is the **Theater of Electricity** in the Blue Wing, a darkened room full of optical illusions and glowing displays on the presence of electricity in everyday life; the world's largest Van de Graaff generator utilizes 2.5 million volts of electricity and gives daily electricity shows in which simulated lightning bolts flash and crackle. More cerebral is Mathematica, in which randomly dropped balls fall neatly into a bell curve to demonstrate the notion of prob-ability, and Virtual FishTank, an underwater exhibit that encourages visitors to create and care for their own virtual sea-life. Be sure to check out the Big Dig exhibit on the lower level, where videos and interactive displays provide an engaging chronicle of Boston's Sisyphean attempt to put the unsightly elevated I-93 underground.

The museum also houses a five-story **IMAX theater** and the **Charles Hayden Planetarium** (schedule varies; $9, kids $7; ⓣ617/723-2500, ⓦwww .mos.org); along with its standard starry productions, the latter also features a number of semi-rocking laser shows, including the infamous "Laser Floyd: Dark Side of the Moon." The **3-D theater** ($4 in addition to museum admission; ⓣ617/723-2500, ⓦwww.mos.org) is a welcome new addition, screening larger-than-life movies on planets, stars, and bugs; best is the chance to wear those retro-cool 3-D glasses.

5

Back Bay

Meticulously planned **Back Bay** is Boston at its most cosmopolitan. The neighborhood's elegant, angular, tree-lined streets form a pedestrian-friendly area that looks much as it did in the nineteenth century, right down to the original gaslights and brick sidewalks. A youthful population helps offset stodginess and keeps the district, which begins at the **Public Garden**, buzzing with chic eateries, trendy shops, and an aura of breezy affluence. Besides the café culture, its other main draw is a trove of exquisite Gilded Age rowhouses; walking around, it seems as if there's no end to the fanciful bay windows and ornamental turrets. With a few exceptions, the brownstones get fancier the farther from the garden you go (the order in which they were built), a result of architectural one-upmanship.

Running parallel to the Charles River in neat rows, Back Bay's east–west thoroughfares – **Beacon**, **Marlborough**, **Newbury**, and **Boylston streets**, with **Commonwealth Avenue** in between – are transsected by eight shorter streets. These latter roads have been so fastidiously laid out that not only are their names in alphabetical order, but trisyllables are deliberately intercut by disyllables: Arlington, Berkeley, Clarendon, Dartmouth, Exeter, Fairfield, Gloucester, and Hereford (though Gloucester, purists protest, only looks trisyllabic) – until Massachusetts Avenue breaks the pattern at the western border of the neighborhood. The grandest rowhouses are to be found on Beacon Street and Commonwealth Avenue, while Marlborough is perhaps more atmospheric. Boylston and Newbury are the main commercial drags and a shopping excursion on the latter is a must-do Boston experience. In the midst of it all is a small greenspace, **Copley Square**, surrounded by the area's main sights: **Trinity Church**, the imposing **Boston Central Library,** and the city's skyline-defining **John Hancock Tower**.

Some history

The fashioning of Back Bay (as was its neighbor, the South End; see Chapter 6) occurred in response to a shortage of living space in Boston. An increasingly cramped Beacon Hill prompted developers to revisit a failed dam project on the Charles River that had made a swamp of much of the area. With visionary architect and urban planner **Arthur Gilman** at the helm of a huge landfill job, the sludge began to be reclaimed in 1857.

Taking his cue from Georges Eugène Haussmann's new wide boulevards in Paris, Gilman decided on an orderly street pattern extending east to west from the Public Garden, which itself had been sculpted from swampland only two decades before. By 1890, the once-cramped peninsula of old Boston could claim 450 new acres, on which stood a range of churches, townhouses, and schools.

BACK BAY

Downtown

Beacon Hill

Cambridge

Kenmore Square

The South End

RESTAURANTS & CAFÉS

Aujourd'hui	H
Café Jaffa	5
Croma	7
Emack & Bolio's	10
Grill 23 & Bar	29
India Samraat	1
JP Licks	11
Kashmir	6
L'Aroma Café	8
Legal Seafoods	25, K & Q
The Other Side Cosmic Café	3
Parish Café & Bar	20
Skipjacks's	24
Sonsie	4
Sorellina	26
Stephanie's on Newbury	13
Summer Shack	27
Tapeo	12
Tealuxe	14
Trident Booksellers & Café	9

BARS & CLUBS

Bristol Lounge	H
Bukowski Tavern	22
Cactus Club	17
Dillons	16
Excelsior	21
Flash's	28
Kings Bowling	23
Match	2
Oak Bar	J
The Rattlesnake Bar & Grill	19
Saint	15
Top of the Hub	25
Whiskey Park	K
Whiskey's	18

ACCOMMODATION

463 Beacon Street Guest House	J
Back Bay Hilton	I
Boston Park Plaza Hotel & Towers	K
Charlesmark Hotel	P
The College Club	G
The Colonnade	Q
Copley House	E
Copley Inn	O
Copley Square Hotel	D
Eliot	M
Fairmont Copley Plaza	A
Four Seasons	H
Hotel 140	N
Jurys Boston Hotel	P
Marriott at Copley Place	R
The Lenox	T
Newbury Guest House	S
Sheraton Boston Hotel	L
Taj Boston	C
Westin	

Green Line
Orange Line

Charles Street

Public Garden

Ducklings Statue

Ether Memorial

George Washington Statue

Swan Boats

Storrow Lagoon

Arlington Street

Boylston Street

Gibson House Museum

First Lutheran Church

Emmanuel Church of Boston

Baylies Mansion

Arlington ST Church

Church of the Covenant

First and Second Church in Boston

New England Mutual Life building

Trinity Church

John Hancock Tower

First Baptist Church

Copley Square

Boston Public Library

New Old South Church

Newbury Street Mural

Ames-Webster Mansion

Oliver Ames Mansion

Burrage Mansion

Newbury St Shops

Stable

Prudential Center

Hynes Convention Center

Christian Science Mother Church

Christian Science Center

Reflecting Pool

Mapparium

Berklee College of Music

Copley Place

Tent City

BAY VILLAGE

BACK BAY

Beacon Street
Marlborough Street
Commonwealth Avenue
Newbury Street
Boylston Street
Hereford Street
Gloucester Street
Fairfield Street
Exeter Street
Dartmouth Street
Clarendon Street
Berkeley Street
Arlington Street
Chestnut Street
Beacon Street
Byron St
Beaver Place
Chestnut Street
Branch St
Charles Street
Swan St
Brimmer Street

Massachusetts Avenue
Massachusetts Turnpike
Haviland Street
Edgerly Road
Westland Avenue
Norway St
St Cecilia St
Belvidere Street
St Germain Street
Clearway Street
Dalton Street
Scotia St
Huntington Avenue
Ring Road
West Newton St
Follen St
Garrison St
West Canton St
Belvoke St
Yarmouth Street
Cumberland St
Columbus Avenue
Chandler Street
Lawrence Street
Providence Street
Stuart Street
St James Avenue
Park Plaza
Columbus Avenue

HYNES/ICA
COPLEY
PRUDENTIAL

N

0   200 yds
0   200 m

Not surprisingly, Back Bay quickly became one of the city's most sought-after addresses, although its popularity subsided somewhat during the Great Depression, when single families were unable to afford such opulence. During this period, developers converted many of the spaces into apartments, often gutting the interiors in the process; other properties were purchased by colleges and universities.

Due largely to landmark preservation laws, the exteriors of most buildings remain unaltered, and many retain their old wood ornamentation and Victorian embellishments. All in all, the neighborhood's authentic charm, as well as the pervasive grace of the bowfronts and wrought-iron terraces, proffers an air of well-heeled serenity that makes Back Bay perfect for boutique browsing, afternoon strolling, and frothy cappuccino runs.

The Public Garden

The value of property in Boston increases the closer its proximity to Back Bay's lovingly maintained **Public Garden**, a 24-acre park founded in 1837 and earmarked for public use since 1859. Of the garden's 125 types of trees – many identified by little brass placards – most impressive are the weeping willows that ring the picturesque man-made lagoon. Here you can take a fifteen-minute ride in one of six **Swan Boats** (April to late June daily 10am–4pm; late-June to early Sept daily 10am–5pm; early to mid-Sept Mon–Fri noon–4pm, Sat & Sun 10am–4pm; $2.75; ☏617/522-1966; ⓦwww.swanboats.com), which trace gracious figure-eights in the oversized puddle. The elegant, pedal-powered conveyances, inspired by a scene in Wagner's opera *Lohengrin*, have been around since 1877, long enough to become a Boston institution. The boats carry up to twenty passengers at a time, and in the height of summer there is often a line to hop on board; instead of waiting, you can get just as good a view of the park from the tiny suspension bridge that spans the lagoon.

The park has another fowl-related draw: a cluster of popular bronze bird sculptures collectively called **Mrs Mallard and Her Eight Ducklings**. The sculptures were installed in 1987 to commemorate Robert McClosky's 1941 *Make Way for Ducklings*, a children's tale set in the park (it's unlikely you'll ever pass the sculptures without seeing someone "riding" one of the ducks). Of the many other statues and monuments throughout the park, the oldest and oddest is the thirty-foot-tall **Good Samaritan** monument along the Arlington Street side; the granite and red-marble column is a tribute to, of all things, the anesthetic qualities of ether. Controversy as to which of two Boston men invented the wonder drug led Oliver Wendell Holmes to dub it the "Either Monument." Finally, a dignified equestrian statue of **George Washington**, installed in 1869 and the first of the general astride a horse, watches over the garden's Commonwealth Avenue entrance.

Beacon Street

As a continuation of Beacon Hill's stately main thoroughfare, **Beacon Street** was long the province of blueblood Bostonians. Despite being so close to the Charles River, however, its buildings turn their back to it, principally because in the nineteenth century the river was a stinking mess. One such building, the Italian Renaissance townhouse at no. 137, holds the remarkable **Gibson House Museum** (Wed–Sun 1–3pm, tours hourly, ring bell on hour for entry; $7; ☏617/267-6338, ⓦwww.thegibsonhouse.org; Arlington **T**), which preserves the home built for Catherine Hammond Gibson in 1860, twenty years after the

▲ Gibson House Museum

death of her well-to-do husband. In the ornate interior, there's a curious host of Victoriana, including a still-functioning dumbwaiter, antique clocks, and writing paraphernalia (one of the Gibsons was a noted travel writer), and gilt-framed photos of Catherine's relatives. Notable among the various chinoiserie is the stunning gold-embossed "Japanese Leather" wallpaper that covers a good portion of the abode, and a sequined pink velvet cat house or, if you prefer the Gibsons' term, "pet pagoda."

Things get less interesting at the far end of Beacon Street (furthest from the Public Garden); the one structure of note is the turreted **Charlesgate Building** at no. 535, a former hotel that's been nicknamed "The Witch's Castle," for obvious reasons, by the Boston University students who now call it home.

Marlborough Street

Sandwiched between Beacon Street and Commonwealth Avenue, quiet **Marlborough Street** is one of the most prized residential locales in Boston – with its brick sidewalks and vintage gaslights – after Beacon Hill's Louisburg Square and the first few blocks of Commonwealth Avenue. Even though the townhouses here tend to be smaller than elsewhere in Back Bay, they display a surprising range of styles when it comes to ornamentation, especially along the blocks between Clarendon and Fairfield streets.

Back at the crossroad with Berkeley Street, no. 66 is one of Boston's more bizarre buildings: a Gothic-Modern hybrid that houses the **First and Second Church in Boston** (opening times vary, ☎617/267-6730, ⊛www.fscboston .org). As its name suggests, the church represents the First and Second churches in Boston, which have been amalgamated since 1870. The First Church's covenant was signed on July 30, 1630 by prominent members of the Massachusetts Bay Colony, and the Second Church was founded in the North End in 1649. A fire in 1968 destroyed much of the original church, designed by renowned Boston architects William Ware and Henry Van Brunt. The present edifice – added to the old facade in 1972 – is the work of Paul Rudolph; the two very different styles clash in an eye-jarring way.

Commonwealth Avenue

The Public Garden leads into the tree-lined parkway of **Commonwealth Avenue**, modeled after the grand boulevards of Paris and Back Bay's showcase street. The 100-foot-wide leafy median at its center forms the first link in Frederick Law Olmsted's so-called **Emerald Necklace**, which begins at Boston Common and extends all the way to the Arnold Arboretum in Jamaica Plain. The snazzy *Taj Boston* hotel on Arlington Street forms a fittingly upscale backdrop to the promenade, itself peppered with several elegantly placed **statues**; one particularly interesting trio, that of **Abigail Adams, Lucy Stone, and Phyllis Wheatley** is located between Fairfield and Gloucester streets; there is also a curious statue of **William Lloyd Garrison** seated over a book between Dartmouth and Exeter streets. "Comm Ave," as locals irreverently call it, is at its prettiest in early May, when the magnolia and dogwood trees are in full bloom, showering the brownstone steps with their fragrant pink buds.

One set of these steps – the first as you walk along the avenue – belongs to the **Gamble Mansion**, at no. 5, which has housed the Boston Center for Adult Education since 1941. Feel free to slip inside for a look at the opulent Louis XV ballroom built expressly for Baylies's daughter's coming-out (in the old-fashioned sense) party. You'll have to be content to see the Queen Anne-style **Ames-Webster Mansion**, a few blocks down at 306 Dartmouth St, from the outside. Built in 1872 for railroad tycoon, Massachusetts's governor, and US congressman Frederick Ames, it features a two-story conservatory, central tower, and imposing chimney. Farther down Comm Ave is the **Burrage Mansion**, at no. 314, a fanciful synthesis of a Vanderbilt-style mansion and the French château of *Chenonceaux*. The exterior of this 1899 urban palace is a riot of gargoyles and carved cherubim; inside it's less riotous – it serves as a retirement home. Further on, the Beaux Arts chateau at no. 355 is the **Oliver Ames Mansion** (no relation to the railroad tycoon), topped by multiple chimneys and dormer windows; its interior now comprises offices and, as such, is not open to the public.

The First Baptist Church of Boston

Rising above the avenue at no. 110 is the landmark belfry of the **First Baptist Church of Boston** (Mon–Fri 11am–3pm; ☎617/267-3148; ⓦwww.firstbaptistchurchofboston.org), designed by architect H.H.Richardson in 1872 for a Unitarian congregation, though at bill-paying time only a Baptist group was able to pony up the necessary funds. The puddingstone exterior is topped off by a 176-foot **bell tower**, which is covered by four gorgeous friezes by Frédéric-Auguste Bartholdi of Statue of Liberty fame; a product of his friendship with Richardson that developed at the École des Beaux Arts in Paris. More interesting than what the tableaux depict (baptism, communion, marriage, and death) are some of the illustrious stone-etched visages, particularly those of Emerson, Longfellow, Hawthorne, and Lincoln. Trumpeting angels protrude from each corner, inspiring its inglorious nickname, "Church of the Holy Bean Blowers."

Richardson's lofty plans for the interior never materialized, again for lack of money, but its high ceiling, exposed timbers, and Norman-style rose windows are still worth a peek if you happen by when someone's in the church office.

Newbury and Boylston streets

Take a walk down **Newbury Street** and it's hard to imagine this was once considered one of Back Bay's least fashionable addresses. Thought of as a poor relation to nearby Commonwealth Avenue, Newbury was almost exclusively residential when the earliest buildings were constructed in 1857, and its first retail shop didn't open until 1905. Today the street comprises eight atmospheric blocks of Victorian-era brownstones housing more than three hundred boutiques, art galleries, and restaurants, plus chain stores like the Gap and NikeTown. Despite the occasional nod to pretentiousness in some of its swankier spaces, it remains an atmospheric and surprisingly inviting place to wander around. And not all is shopping: Newbury and neighboring **Boylston** are home to most of the old schools and churches built in the Back Bay area.

The Emmanuel Church of Boston and Church of the Covenant

On the first block of Newbury Street, sandwiched between fancy hair salons and upscale retail stores, is the **Emmanuel Church of Boston**, an unassuming rural Gothic Revival building. Of greater interest is the full-blown Gothic Revival **Church of the Covenant**, further down the street on the same side. Most passersby are too intent on window shopping to notice the soaring steeple, so look up before checking out the interior, famous – like its neighbor, the Arlington Street Church – for its Tiffany stained-glass windows, some of which are thirty feet high. The **Gallery NAGA** (Newbury Associated Guild of Artists), in the chapel (Tues–Sat 10am–5.30pm; ☎617/267-9060, ⓦwww .gallerynaga.com), is one of Boston's biggest contemporary art spaces, and stages new exhibits of works by artists from Boston and New England; it's also a nice setting for chamber music performances – the Boston Pro Arte Chamber Orchestra was founded here.

The rest of Newbury Street

Designed as an architect's house, the medieval flight-of-fancy at **109 Newbury St** is more arresting for its two fortress-like brownstone turrets than the Cole Haan footwear inside. A block down and across the street, **271 Dartmouth**, houses a *Papa Razzi* restaurant, but again the burnt sienna-colored building with mock battlements hunkered over it steals the show: originally the *Hotel Victoria* in 1886, it looks like a combination Venetian-Moorish castle.

Newbury gets progressively funkier west of Exeter Street, with alternative record stores and an excellent used bookstore catering to a more low-key, student-centered crowd. On the final block, between Hereford Street and Massachusetts Avenue, a span of nineteenth-century **stables** has been converted to commercial space; check out the cavernous Patagonia clothing shop at no. 346 for the best example.

Arlington Street Church and the New England Financial building

Right on the corner of Boylston and Arlington streets is Back Bay's first building, the squat **Arlington Street Church** (Mon–Fri 10am–5pm, Sun 10am–3pm ☏617/536-7050, ⓦwww.ascboston.org), a minor Italianesque masterpiece designed in 1859 by Arthur Gilman, chief planner of Back Bay; its host of Tiffany stained glass windows (believed to be the largest assemblage of Tiffany windows unified under one church) were added from 1898 to 1933. A history of progressive rhetoric has also earned it some note: abolitionist minister William Ellery Channing intoned against slavery here just a year before the Civil War erupted, and the church was a favored venue of peace activists during the Vietnam War; nowadays there's an active gay congregation. A block down is the prison-like **New England Financial building**, now bearing the corporate moniker "The Newbry"; it's worth nipping inside for a look at the **murals**, which depict such historic regional events as John Winthrop sailing from Old to New England aboard the *Arbella*, Paul Revere sounding his famous alarm, and the Declaration of Independence being read in Boston for the first time, from the balcony of the Old State House.

The New Old South Church

On the corner of Boylston and Dartmouth streets stands one of Boston's most attractive buildings, the **New Old South Church** (Mon–Fri 9am–5pm; ☏617/536-1970, ⓦwww.oldsouth.org). There's actually some logic to the name: the congregation in residence at Downtown's Old South Meeting House outgrew it and decamped here in 1875. The names of former Old South members reads like a who's who of Boston historical figures: Benjamin Franklin, Phyllis Whealey, Samuel Adams, and even Mother Goose all congregated here. You need not be a student of architecture to be won over by the Italian Gothic design, most pronounced in the ornate, 220-foot bell tower, its copper-roof lantern, replete with metallic gargoyles in the shape of dragons. The dramatic zebra-striped archways on the Dartmouth Street side are, unfortunately, partially obscured by the entrance to the Copley **T** station. The church isn't just to be admired from the outside, either: its interior is an alluring assemblage of dark woods set against a rose-colored backdrop, coupled with fifteenth-century, English-style stained-glass windows. Old South is locally known as the "Church of the Finish Line" due to its cheer-worthy location just beyond Boston Marathon's official finish line.

Copley Square and around

Bounded by Boylston, Clarendon, Dartmouth, and St James streets, **Copley Square** is the busy center of Back Bay. Various design schemes have come and gone since the square was first filled in the 1870s; the present one is a remnant from 1984, a square, grassy expanse anchored by a fountain on the Boylston Street side. In the summer, children and locals cool their feet in the fountain, whose twin obelisks mimic the Bunker Hill monument and Zakim Bridge. Close by, kid-sized bronze statues of the tortoise and the hare honor Boston Marathon runners, a 26-mile Boston tradition held every April. A **farmers' market** materializes opposite the *Fairmont Copley Plaza Hotel* on Tuesday and Friday mornings from May through October.

Trinity Church

The star of the square is **Trinity Church**, 206 Clarendon St (daily 9am–5pm; $5; includes guided tour, call for times; ☎617/536-0944 Ⓦ www.trinitychurchboston .org; Copley **T**), whose original interior design concept was to create the experience of "walking into a living painting." The result is H.H. Richardson's 1877 Romanesque masterpiece, a breathtaking display of polychromatic eye candy fashioned by legendary stained glass artist John La Farge. The majestic central tower reaches an eye-opening ten stories, and is situated between sweeping arches and a glamorous golden chancel. While it's all quite lovely, Trinity's finest feature is La Farge's aquamarine *Christ in Majesty* triptych, a bold, multi-dimensional stained-glass window. Aim to make your visit when the sun is setting and the stained glass is at its most brilliant, or during one of the **free organ recitals** (Fridays at 12.15pm).

The Central Library

A decidedly secular building anchors the end of Copley Square opposite Trinity Church, in the form of the **Boston Public Library** (Mon–Thurs 9am–9pm, Fri–Sat 9am–5pm; ☎617/536-5400, Ⓦ www.bpl.org; Copley **T**). It's the largest public research library in New England and the first one in America to permit the borrowing of books. McKim, Mead & White, the leading architectural firm of its day, built the Italian Renaissance Revival structure in 1852. The Copley Square facade, with its sloping red tile roof, green copper cresting, and huge arched windows, is quite magnificent, while the visibility of the entrance is heightened by the presence of the spiky yet sinuous lanterns overhanging it. The massive inner bronze doors were designed by Daniel Chester French (sculptor of the Lincoln Memorial in Washington DC); inside, a musketeer-like statue of Sir Henry Vane stands guard. This early governor of the Massachusetts Bay Colony believed, or so the inscription relates, that "God, law and parliament" were superior to the king, which apparently didn't do much for his case in 1662, when his freethinking head got the chop.

Beyond the marble grand staircase and signature lions and underneath the coffered ceilings are a series of **murals**, most impressive of which is a diaphanous depiction of the nine Muses. Just to the right is the **Abbey Room**, named for Edwin Abbey's murals depicting the Holy Grail legend, and where Bostonians once took delivery of their books. Most of these were kept in the imposing **Bates Reading Room**, which, with its 218-foot-long sweep, 50-foot-high barrel-vaulted ceiling, dark oak paneling, and incomparable calm, hasn't changed much since its debut more than a century ago. The library's most remarkable feature is tucked away on the top floor, however, where the darkly lit **Sargent Hall** is covered with more than fifteen astonishing murals painted by John Singer Sargent between 1890 and 1916. Entitled the *Triumph of Religion*, the works are a mastery of detail incorporating appliquéd metal, paper, and jewels – most striking in the north end's stunning twin *Pagan Gods* ceiling vaults – and plaster relief, evident in Moses' twin tablets which project from the east wall. First-time visitors should pick up a floor plan and explanatory pamphlet at the top of the stairs to guide you through the works; they're quite overwhelming without. Afterwards, you can take a breather in the library's open-air central **courtyard**, modeled after that of the Palazzo della Chancelleria in Rome and centered on a statue of a smiling, naked woman holding a baby in one hand and a bunch of grapes in the other.

The John Hancock Tower

At 62 stories, the **John Hancock Tower**, at 200 Clarendon St, is Boston's signature skyscraper – first loathed, now loved, and taking on startlingly different appearances depending on your vantage point. In Back Bay, the characteristically angular edifice is often barely noticeable, due to deft under-statement and wafer-thin design in deference to adjacent Trinity Church and the old brownstones nearby. This modern subtlety in the face of historic landmarks is a signature quality of architect I.M. Pei (of the Louvre Pyramid and Bank of China, Hong Kong fame). From Beacon Hill, the tower appears broad-shouldered and stocky; from the South End, taller than it actually is; from across the Charles River, like a crisp metallic wafer. One of the best views is from the **Harvard Bridge**, which connects the western edge of Back Bay and Massachusetts Avenue with MIT in Cambridge; from there, you'll be able to see clouds reflected in the tower's lofty, fully mirrored coat. With such a seamless facade, you'd never guess that soon after its 1976 construction, dozens of windowpanes popped out, showering Copley Square with glass, due to a design flaw that prompted the replacement of over 10,000 panes.

Today, most of the building is given over to offices, and its sixtieth-floor **observatory**, which afforded some of the most stunning views around, is permanently closed due to security concerns arising after the events of September 11, 2001. (You'll have to head instead to the Prudential Skywalk for deluxe Boston vistas; see p.100.) Next door is the old Hancock Tower, which cuts a distinguished profile in the skyline with its truncated step-top pyramid roof. It's locally famous for the neon weather beacon on top, which can be decoded with the help of the jingle, "Solid blue, clear view; flashing blue, clouds are due; solid red, rain ahead; flashing red, snow instead" (except in summer when red signifies the cancellation of a Red Sox game). In October of 2004, the beacon flashed blue and red together for the first time to commemorate the Red Sox World Series win: "flashing blue and red, the Curse is dead!"

Copley Place

On the corner of Huntington Avenue and Dartmouth Street, **Copley Place** (☎617/369-5000, ⓦwww.simon.com) isn't a spot to venture into without a credit card. Not only is this mall home to the *Westin* and *Boston Marriott* hotels (see Chapter 10, "Accommodation"), but it also contains numerous high-end stores. The 9.5-acre site is slightly garish – all indoor waterfalls and potted trees – but its two floors are packed with sleek shops like Jimmy Choo and Barneys New York. The mall is linked to the more low-key shops at the Prudential Tower via a series of enclosed skywalks.

The Prudential Tower

Not even the darkest winter night can cloak the ugliness of the **Prudential Tower** ("The Pru"), at 800 Boylston St, just west of Copley Square. The 52-story gray intruder to the Back Bay skyline is one of the more unfortunate by-products of the urban renewal craze that gripped Boston and most other American cities in the 1960s.

Apart from being one of the starting points for a number of Boston tours (see p.29), its chief selling point is its fiftieth-floor **Skywalk** (daily 10am–10pm; $11; ℡617/859-0648, Ⓦ www.prudentialcenter.com; Copley **T**), offering the only 360-degree aerial view of Boston. On a clear day you can make out Cape Cod across the waters of Massachusetts Bay and New Hampshire to the north. If you're hungry (or just thirsty) you can avoid the admission charge by ascending two more floors to the *Top of the Hub* restaurant (see p.185); your bill may well equal the money you just saved, but during most daytime hours it's fairly relaxed, and you can linger over coffee or a drink. Well below, the first-floor **Shops at Prudential Center** is a lively shopping mall, adjoining the hulking mass of the **Hynes Convention Center**.

The Christian Science buildings

People gazing down at Boston from the top of the Prudential Tower are often surprised to see a 224-foot-tall Renaissance Revival basilica vying for attention amidst the urban outcroppings lapping at its base. The rather artificial-looking structure is the central feature of the world headquarters of the **First Church of Christ, Scientist**, 175 Huntington Ave (Mon–Sat 10am–4pm; free; ℡617/450-2000, Ⓦ www.tfccs.com; Symphony **T**), which was founded by Mary Baker Eddy in 1879. With seating for 3000 (and an enormous pipe organ), it dwarfs the earlier, prettier Romanesque **Christian Science Mother Church** just behind it, built in 1894 and decked out with spectacular opalescent stained-glass windows. There may be no better place in Boston to contemplate the excesses of religion than around the center's 670-foot-long, red-granite-trimmed

▲ Christian Science buildings

reflecting pool, which, through some high-tech miracle, manages to cool water for the complex's air-conditioning system.

The highlights of a visit here, though, are on the ground floor of the **Mary Baker Eddy Library**, in the Christian Science Publishing Library at 200 Massachusetts Ave (Tues–Sun 10am–4pm; $5; ☎1-888/222-3711, ⓦwww .marybakereddylibrary.org; Symphony **T**). The library's original Art Deco lobby has been transformed into the grandly named Hall of Ideas, home to a wild glass and bronze fountain that appears to cascade with words rather than water; the sayings – a diverse collection of inspiring tidbits – are projected from the ceiling for an effect that verges on holographic. Tucked behind the Hall of Ideas is the equally marvelous **Mapparium**, a curious stained-glass globe whose thirty-foot diameter can be crossed on a glass bridge. The technicolor hues of the six hundred-plus glass panels, illuminated from behind, reveal the geopolitical reality of the world in 1935, when the globe was constructed, as evidenced by country names such as Siam, Baluchistan, and Transjordan. Intended to symbolize the worldwide reach of journalism, the Mapparium has a more immediate payoff: thanks to the spherical glass surface, which absorbs no sound, you can whisper, "What's Tanganyika called today?" at one end of the bridge and someone on the opposite end will hear it clear as a bell – and perhaps proffer the answer (Tanzania).

Bay Village

Back near the Public Garden, one of the oldest sections of Boston, **Bay Village**, bounded by Arlington, Church, Fayette, and Stuart streets, functions as a small atmospheric satellite of Back Bay. This warren of gaslights and tiny brick houses has managed to escape the trolley tours that can make other parts of the city feel like a theme park; of course, that's in part because there's not all that much to see. The area is, however, popular with Boston's gay population, who colonized it well over a decade ago, before nearby South End came into favor.

The neighborhood's overall resemblance to Beacon Hill is no accident; many of the artisans who pieced that district together built their own, smaller houses here throughout the 1820s and 1830s. A few decades later, water displaced from the filling in of Back Bay threatened to turn the area back into a swamp, but Yankee practicality resulted in the lifting of hundreds of houses and shops onto wooden pilings fully eighteen feet above the water level. Backyards were raised only twelve feet, and when the water receded many building owners designed **sunken gardens**. One of the most unusual remnants from the nineteenth century is the **fortress** at the intersection of Arlington and Stuart streets at Columbus Avenue. Complete with drawbridge and fake moat, it was built as an armory for the First Corps of Cadets (a private military organization); today it houses Boston's branch of the upscale New York steakhouse *Smith & Wollensky*.

The obvious streets to explore are **Piedmont**, **Winchester**, and **Church**, which radiate out from the *Boston Park Plaza Hotel* anchoring the neighborhood. Footsteps beyond, lightly trafficked **Melrose and Fayette streets** are also worth inspection: it's here you'll find the neighborhood's last remaining sunken gardens – tiny, and often gated, private lawns lying just below street level. Bay Village's proximity to the theater district made it a prime location for **speakeasies** in the 1920s, not to mention a natural spot for actors and impresarios to take up residence; indeed the building at **48–50 Melrose Street** originally housed a movie studio. Around the corner is the site of the Coconut Grove Fire of 1942, in which 490 people perished in a nightclub because the exit doors were locked. There are few other actual sights, although you could stop by the delightful *Rachel's Kitchen* (12 Church St; ☎617/423-3447; see p.175) for an iced cappuccino.

The South End

Over the last decade, **the South End**, which extends below Back Bay from Huntington Avenue to where I-93 emerges above ground, has gone from being a predominantly residential neighborhood to one of Boston's most happening areas. Quaint and trendy in equal measure, the rise to prominence of a number of hip restaurants, art galleries, and theaters, coupled with a vibrant multicultural population has made it *the* place to live in the city.

The neighborhood's heart is bounded by Tremont Street, Dartmouth Street, and Columbus Avenue. This posh enclave boasts a spectacular concentration of Victorian architecture, unmatched anywhere in the US. In fact, the sheer number of such houses earned the South End a **National Landmark District** designation in 1983, making the 500-acre area the largest historical neighborhood of its kind in the country. In addition to its architecture, the South End is also known for its well-preserved ironwork – a French botanical motif known as Rinceau adorns many of the houses' stairways and windows (see box, p.107). Unsurprisingly, details like these made the area quite popular with upwardly mobile Bostonians (among them a strong gay and lesbian contingent), who moved in and gentrified the neighborhood in the mid-1990s. The upshot has been some of the most happening streetlife in town, while the South End has become the breeding ground for chefs looking to push the boundaries of haute cuisine. The activity is most visible on **Tremont Street** and on pockets of **Washington Street**, a few blocks below the Back Bay **T**, the neighborhood's only subway stop.

A couple of yet to be gentrified areas do exist, namely in a small quadrant below Tremont Street, which is home to most of Boston's Puerto Rican community, and a patch along Dartmouth Street near Copley Place, where the low-income housing co-op of **Tent City** presides. As well, surrounding areas such as Roxbury are a little rough around the edges. Along the outer reaches of the neighborhood, appropriate caution should be taken, especially at night.

Some history

Like Back Bay, the South End was originally a marshland that now sits on landfill. Though the mud-to-mansion process kicked off in 1834 – predating Back Bay by more than twenty years – the neighborhood really took shape between 1850 and 1875, when it was laid out according to plans designed by **Charles Bulfinch** some fifty years earlier; its similarity to Beacon Hill, completed just two years prior to development here, is striking, though the South End "look" is more homogeneous and streamlined, dominated by red-brick bowfront townhouses that are modestly taller than their Beacon Hill predecessors. As for greenspace, quaint slivers like Union Park Square were created to attract wealthy buyers who had progressively been moving to the

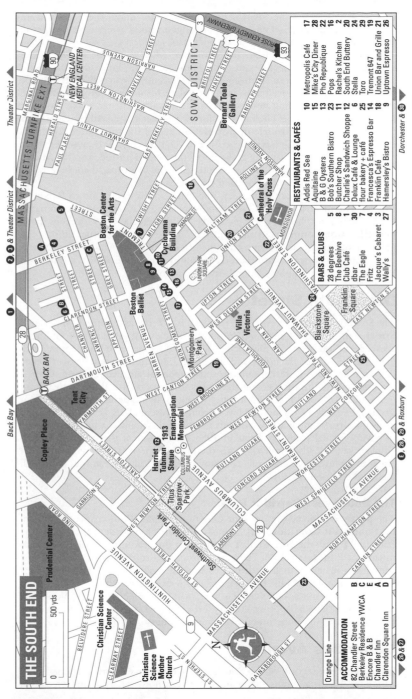

THE SOUTH END

0	500 yds

Orange Line ───

Boston countryside; the marketing campaign to draw them southward included, among other schemes, naming neighborhood arteries like Appleton and Chandler streets after well-to-do merchant families.

This initial success began to flag, however, when many of these families experienced financial decline after the **Panic of 1873**. Following the Panic, what nouveau riche were left headed for the recently created Back Bay, while waves of immigrants moved in to take their place, turning numerous South End townhouses into boarding homes, or razing them altogether to make room for low-income living space. The lure of affordable housing attracted large numbers of the city's **African-American population**, too, at the turn of the twentieth century, who left expensive Beacon Hill digs to install themselves here; consequently, Sammy Davis Jr grew up in the neighborhood, and Dr Martin Luther King Jr and his wife, Coretta Scott King, rented an apartment here while the future civil rights leader attended Boston University.

In the 1970s, as African-American populations were migrating to Roxbury, **Puerto Rican and Dominican** populations began moving in and initiated local community housing projects like Villa Victoria. Two decades later, **gentrification** commenced in earnest, leading to, among other things, the opening of several art galleries in the streets south of Washington Street, a geographical concentration latterly going by the name of SoWa (South of Washington), recalling Manhattan's trendy SoHo.

Dartmouth Street

The South End's main access point, the Back Bay **T**, opens up onto **Dartmouth Street**, which becomes increasingly upscale the closer it gets to Tremont Street, a few blocks southeast. To the north is Copley Place (see p.99), a shopping mall that's on the cusp of Back Bay and the South End. Immediately below Copley Place, at no. 130, is Dartmouth's most important occupant, **Tent City** – a mixed-income housing co-op that owes its name to the 1968 sit-in protest (tents included) staged on the formerly vacant lot by residents concerned about the neighborhood's dwindling low-income housing. This activism thwarted plans for a parking garage to be built here, and the result is a terrific example of environmental planning. Built in 1988, the section of the co-op closest to Copley Place blends seamlessly with the mall's modern facade, while the part closer to Columbus Avenue incorporates a series of Victorian houses for which the neighborhood is known.

The Southwest Corridor Park

The pocket of land separating Tent City from Copley Place marks the start of the **Southwest Corridor Park**, a grassy 4.7-mile promenade that connects the Back Bay **T** with the Forest Hill **T** station near the beautiful Arnold Arboretum in Jamaica Plain (see p.131). The park runs parallel to the Orange MBTA line and was designed with low shrubs to increase visibility and give an "open" feeling. Around Forest Hill, the park includes recreational facilities such as tennis and basketball courts, but here it serves mainly as the start of a biking and walking path. Part of another creative urban project, the park expertly covers the tracks of a long-gone nineteenth-century railroad corridor.

Columbus Avenue

In the northern section of the South End, **Columbus Avenue** is lined with handsome Victorian houses; the main interest, however, is a tiny wedge of parkland known, obviously enough, as **Columbus Square**. The square, more or less the outer boundary of the triangle, contains two bronze relief sculptures, commemorating Boston's role as part of the Underground Railroad. The nine-foot-tall **Harriet Tubman "Step on Board" Memorial**, by Boston sculptor Fern Cunningham, depicts the strident abolitionist leading several weary slaves to safety, while the nearby 1913 **Emancipation Memorial** is a more harrowing portrait of the slaves' plight: the foursome here are achingly thin and barely clothed. More African-American history is found behind the park, along Warren Avenue; the Gothic red-brick **Concord Baptist Church**, at no. 190, welcomed Martin Luther King Jr as a guest minister during his Boston University days.

Appleton and Chandler streets

Cobblestoned **Appleton Street** and quiet **Chandler Street**, which jut off to the northeast from Dartmouth, are some of the most sought-after South End addresses. The appeal is obvious: the tree-lined streets are graced with refurbished flat- and bowfronted rowhouses that would easily be at home in London's Mayfair. In addition, unlike many of their neighbors, the houses here have an extra (fourth) story, and are capped off by mansard roofs. Keep an eye out for the Frisbee-sized bronze discs embedded in the sidewalk in front of the houses, too – they're remnants of coal-heating days, when the stuff was delivered through the portals and straight into the basement. The best way to see the houses in this area is to take the South End Historical Society's annual October **house tour** (price varies; ☏617/536-4445, ⊛ www.southendhistoricalsociety .org), in which residents open their doors to the public.

Clarendon and Tremont streets

South End's architecture is more working-class along **Clarendon Street**, one block northeast of Dartmouth Street. There's little to see here until you reach Warren Street, anchored by a 1991 arch-windowed red-brick building used as a practice space by the renowned **Boston Ballet** (call ☏617/695-6950 to schedule a studio tour). The building gets some of its architectural inspiration from the substantial red-brick **Second Baptist Church** across the way, with its late-1860 Gothic facade. It no longer serves as a church, however, since the interior was razed by fire and its surviving walls were incorporated into a condominium in 1991.

The heart of the South End is at the intersection of Clarendon and **Tremont** streets, where an upmarket pseudo-square is flanked by some of the trendiest restaurants in Boston; the acclaimed *Hamersley's Bistro* (see p.175), at 553 Tremont St, holds fort at the square's southern corner. The only real sight is smack in the middle: the domed **Cyclorama Building**, built in 1884 to house an enormous, 360-degree painting of the Battle of Gettysburg (since moved to Gettysburg itself). It was later used as a carousel space, a boxing ring, and even the site of the Boston Floral Exchange in 1923; the repurposing continued until 1972, when its current tenants, the **Boston Center for the Arts** (☏617/426-7700, ⊛ www.bcaonline.com), moved in providing a home for more than a dozen low-budget theater troupes (see Chapter 14, "Performing arts and film"). Under the aegis of BCA, the celebrated **Stanford Calderwood Pavilion** (☏617/266-0800, ⊛ www.huntingtontheatre.org) is home to two brand-new theater spaces – the first new theaters to be built in Boston in over seventy-five years. The two vary widely in their design: the Wimberly is a luxurious proscenium theater favored for contemporary productions, while the Roberts Studio employs a black-box, flexible stage set-up and is generally used for smaller productions.

The rest of Tremont Street carries on the high-end restaurant theme set by *Hamersley's*, especially at luxurious eateries like *Aquitaine* and *B & G Oysters* (see Chapter 11, "Eating"). Worth a quick peek en route to gastronomic heaven is the old **St Cloud Hotel**, at 567 Tremont St, a French Second Empire building dating from 1872 that still boasts a facade of white marble and green bay windows; most of the building now houses private apartments.

Union Park Square

Charming **Union Park Square**, east of Tremont along Union Park Street, is a tiny decorative park which, in typical English fashion, you can walk around but not through – an elegant wrought-iron fence encircles it to make sure you keep off the grass. The oval-shaped park is framed by about twenty refined brownstone rowhouses, representing a pastiche of styles from Italianate to Greek Revival, all of them with bigger windows and more elaborate cornice-work than houses on surrounding streets. Of these, the residence at **4 Union Park St** is worth a nod for its particularly pretty ironworks.

Just past the square along Union Park Street is the whitewashed **St John the Baptist Church** (open for Sunday mass only); a pretty blue-hued Nativity mosaic on its facade adds the only splash of color. Edward Everett Hale, author of *The Man without a Country*, a short story about a self-exiled man sentenced to a lifetime alone at sea (made into a film in 1973), was minister here from 1856–1909; a statue of him can be seen in the Public Garden (see p.93).

Washington Street and around

The South End's other major artery (along with Tremont), **Washington Street**, intersects with Union Park Street and extends southwest to Roxbury. Though intended to resemble a French grand boulevard, the only real similarity is its

▲ Union Park Square

Know your irons

As you walk around the South End, you'll notice a slew of brownstones adorned with curlicued **cast iron** on everything from stairway railings and flower boxes to windowsills and balconies. A distinctive South End feature, the fancy ironwork was, like the area's street-naming convention, intended as a perk to attract upwardly mobile residents back from the suburbs. The arboreal-themed lacing is known as the **Rinceau style** (from the French, and meaning "small branch"), and the neighborhood boasts around seven variations on the serpentine scroll, ranging from a simple run of acanthus leaves to elaborate arabesques sprouting off from a central rosette. Some of the best can be seen on **West Canton Street** (a few blocks southwest along Tremont Street), where a series of sandstone stairways are trimmed with a wavy version inset with garden roses. Don't let their intricacy fool you, though – by the mid-1850s, technological innovations meant that scrolls such as these were about as easy to stamp out as notebook paper.

width; the street itself is worn and devoid of the bustle of Tremont Street. What activity exists tends to focus on its major tenant, the 1875 **Cathedral of the Holy Cross**, at no. 1400, which in 2002 unfortunately found itself at the center of the Catholic priest sex abuse scandal. Distinguished by uneven and truncated twin towers – intended as steeples until the parish ran out of money – the vast neo-Gothic interior seats two thousand and boasts some fine stained-glass work, including a multicolored rose window depicting the Bible's King David.

The only other sight nearby is a few blocks southwest, at the corner of West Brookline Street, where the charmless **Blackstone Square**, named for Boston's original settler William Blackstone, occupies a city block. Like much in the neighborhood, it, too, is laid out in English fashion, with diagonal spokes leading to a central fountain. This public space, with equally ramshackle **Franklin Square** across the street, was once the official entry-point to Boston, but nowadays is rather seedy, and really not worth your time, unless you're popping by for a meal at chic *Stella* (see p.175).

Villa Victoria and around

North from Blackstone and Franklin squares, a rather bland bronze **plaque** at the corner of Washington and West Dedham streets commemorates the 65th infantry of World War II, a largely Puerto Rican regiment, and along with two large metal "V"s, serves as an unofficial marker of the community's southern frontier.

The real heart of the enclave, though, is two blocks up West Dedham at **Villa Victoria**, a housing project serving 3000 members of the community. This place, like Tent City, was also the result of late-1960s public activism. And though the buildings suffer from 1970s architectural aesthetics, their purple brick hues and setting around a central square, **Plaza Betances**, suggest a Hispanic influence that sets them apart from the rest of the South End's Victor-iana. The main draw here is in the square itself, where the **Ramón Betances Mural** occupies wall space measuring a whopping 45 feet long by 14 feet high. Created in 1977 by 300 local teenagers, the brightly colored mosaic has less to do with its namesake (a leader in Puerto Rico's fight for independence from Spain) than with simple hope and optimism, as demonstrated by the cheerful faces and flowers that surround a massive sun; a Spanish inscription asserts "let us know how to fight for our honor and our liberty." Meticulously executed and yet unexpected, it may be Boston's best piece of public art.

Harrison and Thayer streets

Around the intersection of **Harrison** and **Thayer** streets, near the eastern edge of the South End, a handful of **art galleries** have showrooms in cavernous loft spaces. Wandering around the self-styled **SoWa** district could easily distract you for an hour or so. Certainly, the **Bernard Toale Gallery**, at 450 Harrison St (Tues–Sat 10.30am–5.30pm, ☎617/482-2477, ⓦwww.bernardtoalegallery.com), is worth a peek; when its namesake and owner, one of Boston's foremost art connoisseurs, moved here from his tony Newbury Street digs in 1998, he effectively sanctified the area as the new arts hotspot. Two other happening art spaces, the artist-owned **Bromfield Art Gallery** (Wed–Sat noon–5pm, ☎617/451-3605, ⓦwww .bromfieldartgallery.com) and the **Kingston Gallery** (Tues-Sat noon–5pm, ☎617/423-4133, ⓦwww.kingstongallery.com), are situated in the same enclave. A sort of gallery in its own right, **Bobby From Boston,** filled with a beautifully executed collection of vintage wares, also holds court in this lot (see p.206 for a full review). The best time to visit is on **First Fridays** (first Friday of month 5–9pm, ☎617/482-2477, ⓦwww.sowaartistsguild.com), when the galleries ply visitors with wine and spaces are abuzz with artists and fans. For a more complete list of galleries, see Chapter 16, "Shopping."

On Sundays from May to October, the **South End Open Market Gallery** (10am–5pm, ☎617/481-2257, ⓦwww.southendopenmarket.com), is held just south of here at 540 Harrison Ave. Fronted by a gorgeous old warehouse building, it's run Portobello Market-style, with artists and local food purveyors selling the likes of vintage clothes, hand-sewn crafts, potted herbs, and sweet jars of honey from underneath bright white tents.

Kenmore Square, the Fenway, and west

A t the western edge of Back Bay (see Chapter 5), the decorous brownstones and smart shops fade into the more casual **Kenmore Square** and **Fenway** districts. While both areas are somewhat removed from the historical-sights-of-Boston circuit, they're good fun nonetheless, exuding a youthful vibe and, perhaps surprisingly, some of the city's more notable cultural landmarks. The Fenway spreads out beneath Kenmore Square like an elongated kite, taking in a disparate array of sights ranging from **Fenway Park**, where the Red Sox play ball, to some of Boston's finest high-culture institutions, like **Symphony Hall**, the **Museum of Fine Arts**, and the **Isabella Stewart Gardner Museum**. Further west, and more residential, are the communities of **Allston-Brighton** and **Brookline**; the former is home to a young, hip crowd of students, thanks to its proximity to Boston University, the latter boasts the birthplace of JFK. While visitors won't find much here in the way of sights, both have a number of good eating establishments, and Allston-Brighton (or A-B, as it's known locally) has a good bar scene by night.

Kenmore Square and around

Kenmore Square, at the junction of Commonwealth Avenue and Beacon Street, is the unofficial playground for the students of Boston University, as most of its buildings can be found here. Back Bay's Commonwealth Avenue leads right into this lively stretch of youth-oriented bars, record stores, and casual restaurants catering to the late-night cravings of local students; as such, the square is considerably more alive when school is in session. Many of the buildings on its north side have been snapped up by BU, such as the bustling six-story Barnes & Noble bookstore at 660 Beacon St, on top of which is perched the monumental **Citgo Sign**, Kenmore's most noticeable landmark. This 60-square-foot neon advertisement, a pulsing red-orange triangle that is the oil company's logo, has been a popular symbol of Boston since it was placed here in 1965.

Southwest along Brookline Avenue from the square, you can cross over the Massachusetts Turnpike (via a bridge) to the block-long **Lansdowne Street**, on the northeast side of Fenway Park, a popular stretch of show-your-ID bars and

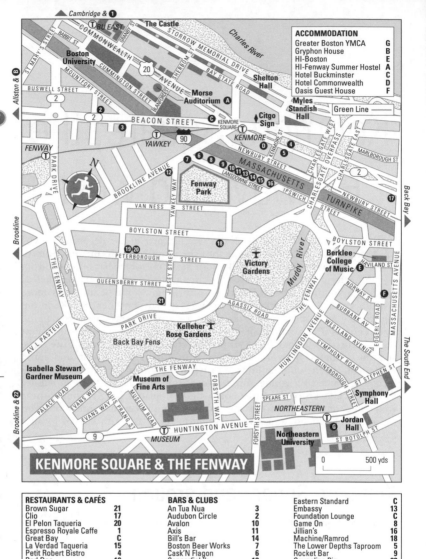

ACCOMMODATION

Greater Boston YMCA	G
Gryphon House	B
HI-Boston	E
HI-Fenway Summer Hostel	A
Hotel Buckminster	C
Hotel Commonwealth	D
Oasis Guest House	F

Green Line ━━━

KENMORE SQUARE & THE FENWAY

0   500 yds

RESTAURANTS & CAFÉS		BARS & CLUBS			
Brown Sugar	21	An Tua Nua	3	Eastern Standard	C
Clio	17	Audubon Circle	2	Embassy	13
El Pelon Taqueria	20	Avalon	10	Foundation Lounge	C
Espresso Royale Caffe	1	Axis	11	Game On	8
Great Bay	C	Bill's Bar	14	Jillian's	16
La Verdad Taqueria	15	Boston Beer Works	7	Machine/Ramrod	18
Petit Robert Bistro	4	Cask'N Flagon	6	The Lower Depths Taproom	5
Rod Dee	19	Copperfield's	12	Rocket Bar	9
				Squealing Pig	22

nightclubs (see Chapter 13, "Nightlife"). There's little point in coming here during daylight hours, though, as most of the action takes place once the sun goes down.

Boston University

One of the country's largest private schools, **Boston University** has its main campus alongside the Charles River on the narrow stretch of land between Commonwealth Avenue and Storrow Drive, extending down Comm Ave all the way to the Brighton and Brookline borders. Though it boasts a few Nobel Prize winners among its faculty, such as Derek Walcott and Elie Wiesel, the school is more interesting for its creative reuse of old buildings, such as the dormitory **Myles Standish Hall**, at 610 Beacon St, a scaled-down version of New York's Flatiron Building that once was a hotel where notables like Babe Ruth camped out. One of its rooms also served as the fictional trysting place of Willy Loman in Arthur Miller's *Death of a Salesman*. Behind the building on Bay State Road, many of the turn-of-the-century brownstones serve as BU graduate institutes and smaller residence buildings, such as **Shelton Hall**, another hostelry-turned-dorm where playwright Eugene O'Neill made his long day's journey into night in 1953. Bay State Road ends at **The Castle**, an ivy-covered Tudor mansion now used for university functions, and housing a BU-only pub. Just beyond is one of BU's few green spaces, the **Warren Alpert Mall**, and its so-called "BU Beach," a sliver of lawn that's been purposefully upswept at the edge to shield busy Storrow Drive from view.

Back on Commonwealth Avenue, the domed **Morse Auditorium**, formerly a synagogue, is currently a performance space for BU events. One long block down is the closest thing the BU campus has to a center, **Marsh Plaza**, with its Gothic Revival chapel and memorial to Martin Luther King Jr, one of the university's more celebrated alumni.

Fenway Park

Baseball is treated with reverence in Boston, with the **Red Sox** being virtually every Bostonian's – if not every New Englander's – favorite team. It's appropriate then that baseball is played here in what is arguably the country's most storied stadium, the unique **Fenway Park**, whose giant 37-foot-tall leftfield wall, known as the **Green Monster**, is an enduring symbol of the quirks of early ballparks. Only Chicago's Wrigley Field, and to a lesser extent Yankee Stadium in New York City, can compete with Fenway for overall tradition and atmosphere. Fenway was constructed in 1912 in a tiny, asymmetrical wedge just off Brookline Avenue, resulting in its famously awkward dimensions, which also include an abnormally short rightfield line (302 feet) and a fence that doesn't at all approximate the smooth arc of most outfields. That the leftfield wall was built so high makes up for some of the short distances in the park and also gives Red Sox leftfielders a distinct advantage over their counterparts – it takes a good deal of playing time before one gets accustomed to the crazy caroms a ball hit off the wall might take.

In the past, it was rumored that the Red Sox were planning to move from Fenway, one of the few ballparks from its era that has not been replaced by a more commercially conscious park. Indeed, it's the oldest Major League ballpark still in use. Nearly universal nostalgia along with pressure from preservation-minded fans, however, has made such a move highly improbable. Instead, updates like building seats atop the Green Monster in 2003 have been implemented by renowned architect Janet Marie Smith. To sit in one of these seats yourself, you can take an hour-long **tour of the park** (daily year-round 9am–4pm or up to three and a half hours before a game; $12; ☏1/877-RED-SOXX, ⊛www.redsox.com; Kenmore or Fenway **T**), the highlight of which is

The Curse: Reversed!

With the Boston Red Sox having won baseball's coveted World Series in both 2004 and 2007, the curse that once hung over the team is quickly becoming distant memory. In 1903, the **Boston Pilgrims** (as they were then called) became the first team to represent the American League in baseball's World Series, upsetting the heavily favored Pittsburgh Pirates to claim the championship; their continued financial success allowed them to build a new stadium, **Fenway Park**, in 1912. During their first year there, Boston won the Series again, and repeated the feat in 1915, 1916, and 1918, led in the latter years by a young pitcher named **George Herman "Babe" Ruth.** Along with strikeouts, Ruth also demonstrated an eye-opening penchant for hitting home runs.

The team was poised to become a dynasty when its owner, **Harry Frazee,** began a fire sale of the team to finance a Broadway play that was to star his ingénue girlfriend. Most of the players went for bargain prices, including Ruth, who was sold to rival **New York Yankees.** While the Yankees went on to become the most successful franchise in professional sports history, and Frazee's play, *No, No, Nanette* garnered warm reviews, his baseball team floundered.

After Ruth's departure, the Red Sox embarked upon a long period in the wilderness, with 86 demoralizing years at bat without a World Series win. Over the years, this drought began to be blamed on the **"Curse of the Bambino"** (aka Babe Ruth), punishment meted out by the baseball gods for selling off one of the game's greatest players. Before finally breaking the curse in 2004, the Sox had come maddeningly close to the title many times – most notably in **1986**, when they were one strike away from clinching the Series before a ground ball rolled through the legs of first baseman **Bill Buckner**. More recently, with the Sox leading game seven of the **2003 American League Championship Series**, poor pitching from Martinez allowed the Yankees – of course – to tie the game in the eighth inning, before **Aaron Boone**, in the 11th inning, hit a home run to culminate another season of Red Sox heartbreak.

The Sox reached the ALCS again in 2004, and this time, when their opponent would be either the Minnesota Twins or the New York Yankees, the *Boston Globe* taunted the team's archrivals with the front-page splash of "Go Yankees. We want to kick your butt on the way to the World Series." The Yankees obliged, setting up one of the most extraordinary chain of events in Major League Baseball history.

Before the ALCS game one at Yankee Stadium, the Sox's new star pitcher, **Curt Schilling**, said: "I'm not sure of any scenario more enjoyable than making 55,000 people from New York shut up." Unbeknownst to the fans, Schilling was injured and pitched like a drain, and the Sox fell behind three games to none, following a humiliating 19-8 loss at Fenway. But a surprising Boston win carved in the bottom of the ninth in game four galvanized the team, and they went on to defeat the Yankees 4-3 – the only time a major league baseball team has reversed a 3-0 score in postseason history. By the time the Sox came up against the Cardinals in the **World Series**, they were a juggernaut: In a **four-game sweep**, the Red Sox ended the 86-year-old curse, which Sox owner John Henry called "the biggest thing since the Revolutionary War." In 2007, the Red Sox began a new tradition of World Series sweeps, beating the Colorado Rockies in four straight games to win their **second championship** in four years.

To read more about the Curse of the Bambino, pick up local sportswriter Dan Shaughnessy's book of the same name (see Contexts, p.300).

getting up close with the Green Monster, as well as hearing stories about Red Sox greats like Ted Williams, Carl Yastrzemski, and Babe Ruth, before he became a Yankee. More so than touring the park, seeing a game is a must for any baseball fan, and a reasonable draw for anyone remotely curious. The season runs from April to October, and tickets can be quite affordable, though you'll have to book well in advance: since winning the 2004 World Series, Red Sox hysteria has surpassed even its own mind-boggling standards for fan devotion. Check out Chapter 17, "Sports and outdoor activities," for more details on tickets and the team.

The Back Bay Fens

The Fenway's defining element is the snakelike **Back Bay Fens** (daily 7.30am–dusk; Ⓦwww.emeraldnecklace.org/fenway.htm), which occupies land due east of the stadium, starting where the prim Commonwealth Avenue greenway leaves off. This segment of Frederick Law Olmsted's **Emerald Necklace** was fashioned from marsh and mud in 1879, a fact reflected by frequent vistas of swaying reeds and the name of the waterway that still runs through the park space today – the **Muddy River** – a narrow channel crossed in its northernmost part by an H.H. Richardson-designed medievalesque puddingstone bridge. In the northern portion of the park, local residents maintain small garden plots in the wonderfully jumbled **Victory Garden**, the oldest community garden in the US. Nearby, below Agassiz Road, the more formally laid out **Kelleher Rose Garden** boasts colorful hybrid species bearing exotic names like Marmalade Skies, Glowing Peace, and Climbing White Iceberg. The area also makes an agreeable backdrop for some of Boston's smaller colleges, such as Simmons and Emmanuel, as well as the Harvard Medical School. Though pretty, the Fens has become a bit unkempt over the years and as such gets a bit dodgy at night – it's best to head onwards before it gets dark.

The Berklee College of Music and Symphony Hall

The renowned **Berklee College of Music** makes its home east of the Fens near Back Bay, its campus buildings concentrated mostly on the busy stretch of Massachusetts Avenue south of Boylston Street, an area with several appropriately budget-friendly eateries. In addition to coordinating the BeanTown Jazz Festival every September, there's nearly always something musical on in the Berklee environs – check Ⓦwww.berklee.edu/events for a list of current (and often very inexpensive) performances. Looming a few short blocks south, **Symphony Hall**, home to the **Boston Symphony Orchestra** (see p.194), anchors the corner of Massachusetts and Huntington avenues. The inside of the 1900 McKim, Mead and White design, modeled after the no longer extant Gewandhaus in Leipzig, Germany, resembles an oversized cube, apparently just the right shape to lend it its perfect acoustics. **Jordan Hall**, venue for the **New England Conservatory of Music**'s chamber music concerts (see p.194), is a few blocks down on Huntington, at nos. 290–294. The modern campus of **Northeastern University** spreads out on both sides of the avenue about a half-mile further south, though it lacks the collegiate atmosphere of Boston's better-known universities.

The Museum of Fine Arts

Rather inconveniently located in south Fenway – but well worth the trip – the **Museum of Fine Arts**, at 465 Huntington Ave (Mon & Tues, Sat & Sun 10am–4.45pm, Wed–Fri 10am–9.45pm, Thurs & Fri West Wing and selected galleries only after 5pm; $17, by contribution Wed after 4pm; CityPass accepted; ☎617/267-9300, ⓦwww.mfa.org; Museum **T**), is New England's premier art space. Founded in 1870, the MFA boasts one of the most distinctive art collections in the country, while it continues to be a privately supported and administered institution. In 1909, the museum was moved from its original location in Copley Square to its permanent, Neoclassical home on Huntington Avenue.

Most recently, the sprawling three-floor granite complex has proven too small for its **extensive collection**, despite measuring almost 550,000 square feet, and is in the throes of a remedial expansion period – the ninth such enlargement since the museum's opening. At the time of writing, there was only room for ten percent of the museum's collection to be on view at any given point. One projected goal is the improvement of museum "wayfinding" – navigating the labyrinthine corridors and galleries is a bewildering experience, even with the museum map in hand – but a better layout to come means more inconvenience in the interim, with gallery closures and relocations scheduled well into 2009. Consequently, if you're looking for a particular piece, be sure to ask where it is; well-informed staffers maintain ground-floor **booths** near the Huntington Avenue and West Wing entrances and float around the galleries as well.

Trying to see all of the massive collection in one day is a daunting prospect at best; conveniently, the **entrance fee** entitles you to visit the museum twice in a ten-day period provided you keep the original ticket. Perhaps the easiest way

▲ Museum of Fine Arts

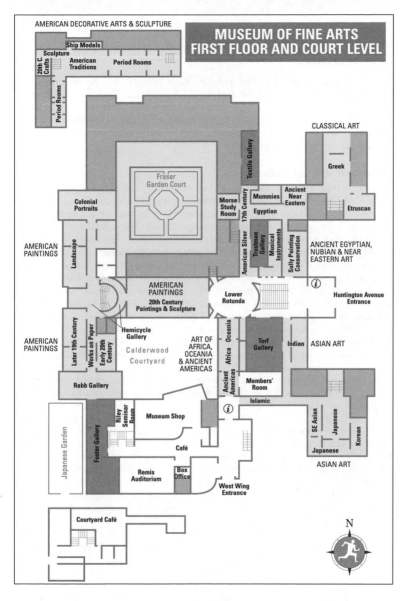

AMERICAN DECORATIVE ARTS & SCULPTURE

**MUSEUM OF FINE ARTS
FIRST FLOOR AND COURT LEVEL**

Ship Models

Sculpture

20th C. Crafts

American Traditions

Period Rooms

Period Rooms

CLASSICAL ART

Greek

Textile Gallery

Fraser Garden Court

Colonial Portraits

Morse Study Room

Mummies

Ancient Near Eastern

17th Century

Egyptian

Etruscan

American Silver

Trustman Gallery

Musical Instruments

Sully Painting Conservation

ANCIENT EGYPTIAN, NUBIAN & NEAR EASTERN ART

AMERICAN PAINTINGS

Landscape

AMERICAN PAINTINGS

20th Century Paintings & Sculpture

Lower Rotunda

Huntington Avenue Entrance

AMERICAN PAINTINGS

Later 19th Century

Works on Paper

Early 20th Century

Hemicycle Gallery

Calderwood Courtyard

ART OF AFRICA, OCEANIA & ANCIENT AMERICAS

Oceania

Africa

Torf Gallery

Indian

ASIAN ART

Rabb Gallery

Ancient Americas

Members' Room

Islamic

Riley Seminar Room

Museum Shop

SE Asian

Japanese

Korean

Japanese Garden

Foster Gallery

Café

Japanese

ASIAN ART

Remis Auditorium

Box Office

West Wing Entrance

Courtyard Café

N

to stay focused is by concentrating on one particular main building: the **West Wing** holds the marvelously dense American painting collection, substantial Impressionist art, and blockbuster **special exhibits**, while the adjoining **Huntington Building** contains one of the best collections of arts of the ancient world and Asia. The two buildings are joined by interconnecting galleries, which culminate in the Huntington Avenue-side **rotunda**, the second floor of which is a must-see for the outstanding John Singer Sargent **murals** decorating its walls and ceilings. Completing the current layout are several smaller wings with an emphasis on decorative arts.

West Wing

The modern, graystone, I.M. Pei-designed **West Wing** lacks a bit of personality, but it draws the bigger crowds of the two MFA buildings thanks to its important collection of American paintings, Impressionist works, and stellar temporary exhibits. The first takes up most of the ground floor starting chronologically, but annoyingly, layout-wise, near the rear, in the Colonial Portraits gallery; the latter two are housed on the second floor.

American art collections

The **American** gallery features important paintings from the two major figures of the Colonial period – **John Singleton Copley** and **Gilbert Stuart**. Copley, one of Boston's favorite sons and after whom Copley Square is named, is best represented by portraits of revolutionary figures like Paul Revere, John Hancock, and Sam Adams. His other works include likenesses of Boston notables such as Nicholas Boylston, the Boston merchant after whom the town's prominent street is named, and Massachusetts Solicitor General Samuel Quincy. One of Copley's most celebrated works, the gruesome narrative *Watson and the Shark*, is also on display here (though it's a full-scale replica made by the artist of the original, which is on permanent display at the National Gallery of Art in Washington DC). The dramatically vivid piece was an immediate success when first exhibited at London's Royal Academy in 1778 and is notable for two reasons: no other American artist had yet attempted "reportage-style" painting, and this was Copley's first work to not include a person of note (though Brook Watson did survive his encounter with the shark and go on to become Lord Mayor of London). Gilbert Stuart is represented by the nationalistic *Washington at Dorchester Heights*, which is displayed along with his portrait of the first US president that graces the one-dollar bill.

The works lining the long hallway that leads back to the front entrance are of lesser interest than what's in the adjoining rooms, such as the Romantic naturalist **landscapes** from the first half of the nineteenth century. **Albert Bierstadt**'s quietly majestic *Lake Tahoe, California,* a particular standout, mingles with Neoclassical representations of sea battles, such as **Thomas Birch**'s jubilant *The Constitution and the Guerrière*, which depicts the engagement from whence the USS *Constitution*'s nickname, "Old Ironsides," originates.

Standout pieces from the latter half of the nineteenth century include **James Abbott McNeill Whistler**'s moody *Nocturne in Blue and Silver: the Lagoon* and several works from the Boston School, notably **Childe Hassam**'s evocative *Boston Common at Twilight* and several works by **John Singer Sargent**. Sargent's work, on display here with that of other American Impressionists, is from early in his career, before he decided that murals, and not portraiture, were the way forward (see Shapiro Rotunda, p.119). Included in the collection is the touching *Mrs Fiske Warren and Her Daughter*, with the Boston socialite pictured in Fenway Court (now the Isabella Stewart Gardner Museum); and the simple *Nude Study of Thomas E McKeller*, a Boston hotel bellman and Sargent's favorite model. Also on display are various studies for Sargent's Boston Public Library murals, such as *Frieze of the Prophets*.

The era's highlights, a trio of haunting seascapes painted by **Winslow Homer** shortly before his death in 1910, hang in the first-floor rotunda. Early twentieth-century American work is displayed in the last room on the left, where **Edward Hopper**'s dour *Drugstore* hangs beside his uncharacteristically upbeat *Room in Brooklyn*. Provided renovations are completed upon your visit, other standout works from twentieth century American artists to search out include iconic pieces by **Jackson Pollock** and **Georgia O'Keefe**.

European art collections

The stairs leading from within the American galleries to the second-floor **European** galleries put you smack in the middle of the collection. Like the first floor, it actually begins chronologically to the far right, in a room showcasing Dutch paintings from the Northern Renaissance, including two outstanding **Rembrandt** works, which emphasize his mastery of light and shadow, *Artist in his Studio* and *Old Man in Prayer*. A gruesome work by **David Teniers the Younger**, *Butcher's Shop*, hangs nearby. Several rooms of grandiose Rococo and Romantic work from the eighteenth and early nineteenth centuries lead off to the right of the central hallway; most interesting are **Pannini**'s self-referential *Picture Gallery with Views of Modern Rome*, Jean-Baptiste Greuze's erotic *Young Woman in White Hat* (note the scandalous, unveiled breast), **Tiepolo**'s complex allegory *Time Unveiling Truth*, and **Turner**'s renowned fire and brimstone *Slave Ship*. The rooms across the hall contain a good survey of European modern art, among them **Henri Matisse**'s striking *Carmelina*, and **Ernst Ludwig Kirchner's** colorful *Reclining Nude*.

The culmination of the wing is the late-nineteenth-century collection, which begins with works by early Impressionists: **Degas**'s *Edmond and Thérèse Morbilli* exhibits the stark use of color and interest in common subjects that went on to influence other French artists. The subsequent Impressionist room contains **Monet**'s heavily abstracted *Grainstack (Snow Effect)* and *Rouen Cathedral (Morning Effect)*, though his tongue-in-cheek *La Japonaise*, a riff on Parisian fashion trends, steals the show. Degas figures prominently here again with his agitated *Pagans and Degas' Father* and a bronze cast of the celebrated *Little Fourteen-Year-Old Dancer*, as does **Renoir**, whose radiant *Dance at Bougival* looks onto *Psyche*, a delicate Rodin marble. The room's highlight, however, is its selection of Post-Impressionist art, best of which is **Van Gogh**'s richly hued *Lullaby: Madame Augustine Roulin Rocking a Cradle (La Berceuse)*, and **Gauguin**'s sumptuous display of existential angst *Where Do We Come From? What Are We? Where Are We Going?*.

The Koch Gallery

Halfway back along the main corridor, the **Koch Gallery**, which connects the West Wing with the second floor of the Huntington Building's rotunda, ranks among the MFA's more spectacular showings. Designed to resemble a European palace hallway, its wood-inlaid ceilings cap walls hung two-high with dozens of portraits and landscapes of varying sizes. The southern wall finds largely **religious** pieces, three of which belong to **El Greco**, whose sparse *Fray Hortensio Felix Paravicino* contrasts sharply with **Francesco del Cairo**'s *Herodias with the Head of St John the Baptist*, a macabre depiction that'll have you thinking twice about tongue-piercing.

The opposite wall showcases predominantly **portraits** and **landscapes**, most emblematic of which is **Velazquez**'s austere *Philip IV, King of Spain*, dating from the artist's time as court painter. Another standout is **Poussin**'s harmonious *Mars and Venus*, which provides an uplifting counterpoint to the nearby **Rubens** piece *Head of Cyrus Brought to Queen Tomyris*, an epic story of retribution in

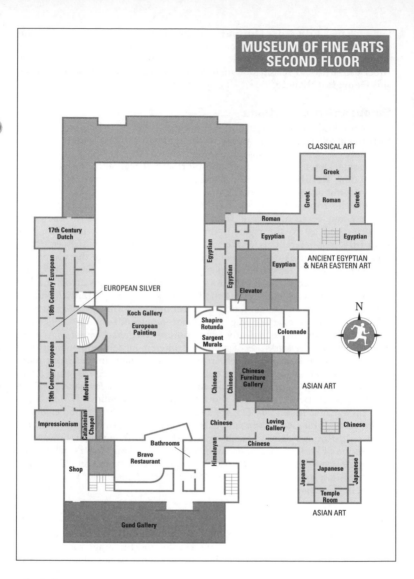

MUSEUM OF FINE ARTS
SECOND FLOOR

CLASSICAL ART

Greek

Greek Roman Greek

Roman

Egyptian Egyptian Egyptian

Egyptian

17th Century
Dutch

Egyptian

18th Century European

ANCIENT EGYPTIAN
& NEAR EASTERN ART

EUROPEAN SILVER

Egyptian

Elevator

Koch Gallery

European
Painting

Shapiro
Rotunda

Sargent
Murals

Colonnade

N

19th Century European

Medieval

Chinese

Chinese

Chinese
Furniture
Gallery

ASIAN ART

Impressionism

Catalonian
Chapel

Chinese

Loving
Gallery

Chinese

Bathrooms

Himalayan

Chinese

Bravo
Restaurant

Japanese

Japanese

Japanese

Shop

Temple
Room

Gund Gallery

ASIAN ART

which the artist's sons served as models for the Queen's pages. The doors at the far end put you in the upper Rotunda, under John Singer Sargent's superb murals (see opposite).

Huntington Avenue Building

Connected to the West Wing by both the Lane and Koch galleries, the 500-foot granite-faced **Huntington Avenue Building** was the first MFA structure to open on this site in 1909. It's a bit gloomier than the West Wing addition, due to a lack of natural light, but here you'll find the museum's impressive – and often overwhelming – collection of **ancient world** and **Asian** arts.

Ancient world and Musical Instruments galleries

A series of MFA-sponsored digs at Giza have made its **Egyptian collection** not only the standout of the museum's **ancient world** holdings, but also one of the finest and most extensive of its kind in the world. Eight galleries over two floors feature some 40,000 objects, including sculpture, pottery, and sarcophagi ranging from prehistoric times to the Roman period. Best among the first-floor findings is the small gallery on **Egyptian Funerary Arts**, with gorgeous blue canopic jars, pristine shrouds, and mummies – including one for a baby crocodile that likely served as a well-to-do family's pet. The **Classical** section is also worth a glance mostly for its numerous Grecian urns, a fine Cycladic *Female Figure*, and several Etruscan sarcophagi with elaborately wrought narrative bas-reliefs.

Just inside the museum's Huntington Street entrance, the **Nubian collection's** exhibit space is (rather anachronistically) currently being used toward the restoration of *Passage of the Delaware*, Thomas Sully's elegant, massive depiction of George Washington crossing the Delaware River on December 25, 1776. The painting is getting a facelift before serving as centerpiece for the new American wing; in the meantime, patrons can peek into the glass-enclosed space and watch the artful surgery at work. Across the hall, it's worth popping into the **Musical Instruments** gallery, even if just to glimpse item #12 – one of the world's first saxophones, made by Adolphe Sax himself.

The Shapiro Rotunda

Between the second-floor Egyptian and Asian galleries is the outstanding **Shapiro Rotunda**, its dome and en-suite colonnade inset with twenty **murals** and fourteen **bas reliefs** by John Singer Sargent, who undertook the commission following his Boston Public Library work (see p.98). Operating under the belief that mural painting – not portraiture – was the key to "artistic immortality," this installation certainly guaranteed the artist a lasting place in the MFA and some controversy to boot: when the ten-year project was completed shortly before Sargent's death in 1925, his Classical theme was falling out of vogue and his efforts were considered the "frivolous works of a failing master." Today, after a 1999 refurbishment that revitalized the works – much of which depict debates between Classical and Roman Art using figures from Greek mythology – it's clear that what many had described as a confused set of subjects (art, theater, philosophy, mythology, and architecture) is actually a brilliant representation of the museum's collections, portrayed through a visual feast of fluid lines and color schemes.

Asian galleries

South of the rotunda, the **Asian galleries** – though they're among the best of their kind in the world – don't get nearly the attention they deserve, in all likelihood due to their awkward layout and hard-to-find galleries. A few are well worth ferreting out, none more so than the magnificent recreation of Japan's oldest surviving **Buddhist temple**, complete with gray stone floors, tapered wooden columns, and coffered ceiling. Seven Buddhas dating to the ninth century recline inside the darkened temple; two of them represent the Buddha of Infinite Illumination. The antechambers contain a marvelous array of Japanese scrolls and screens, including ornamental munitions – such as

Frederick Law Olmsted and the Emerald Necklace

The string of urban parks that stretches through Boston's southern districts, known as the **Emerald Necklace**, grew out of a project conceived in the 1870s, when landscape architect **Frederick Law Olmsted** was commissioned to create for Boston a series of urban parks, as he had done in New York and Chicago. A Romantic naturalist in the tradition of Rousseau and Wordsworth, Olmsted conceived of nature as a way to escape the ills wrought by society, and considered his parks a means for city-dwellers to escape the clamor of their everyday life. He converted much of Boston's remaining open space, which was often disease-ridden marshland, into a sequence of meticulously manicured outdoor spaces beginning with the **Back Bay Fens**, including the **Riverway** along the Boston–Brookline border, and proceeding through **Jamaica Pond** and the **Arnold Arboretum** to Roxbury's **Franklin Park**. While Olmsted's original skein of parks was limited to these, further development linked the Fens, via the Commonwealth Avenue greenway, to the Public Garden and Boston Common, all of which now function as part of the Necklace. By 2009, when the landscaping of the Big Dig is complete, a thirty-acre park will be added to the Necklace around Quincy Market in Downtown. Pretty as it is, the Necklace's sense of pristine natural wonder has slipped in the century since its creation – the more southerly links in the chain, starting with the Fens, have grown shaggy and are unsafe at night.

The **Boston Park Rangers** organize free walking tours (daily 9am–5pm; ☎617/635-7383, ⓦ www.cityofboston.gov/parks/ParkRangers) that cover each of the Necklace's segments, and Olmsted fans won't want to miss the **Frederick Law Olmsted National Historic Site** at 99 Warren St (see p.123).

Samurai swords – that date back to the thirteenth century. The woodblock print cityscapes of Ando Hiroshige, with their sharply delineated chromatic schemes, influenced Van Gogh, Gauguin, and Whistler. Changes in twentieth-century Japanese culture are depicted through wonderful displays of Meisen kimonos, the advent of which heralded the first time the lower classes were allowed to wear silk.

The **Chinese** section is equally superb, with scrolls decorated with spare naturalist abstractions as well as finely detailed graphic narratives, and several life-size statues; that of *Guanyin, Bodhisattva of Compassion* is one of the best-preserved pieces from the twelfth-century Jin Dynasty. Don't leave before checking out the remarkable **Chinese Furniture Gallery**, a dull name for what is in fact a life-size staging of an upper-class Chinese house. Arranged beneath its pagoda-style roof are ornate examples of sixteenth- and seventeenth-century Chinese furniture, such as handsomely carved teak day beds, lacquered tables inlaid with birds and flowers, and household items like the strategy game Wiegi, in which the goal is to surround other players' pieces.

The Isabella Stewart Gardner Museum

Less broad in its collection, but more distinctive and idiosyncratic than the MFA, is the neighboring **Isabella Stewart Gardner Museum**, 280 The Fenway (Tues–Sun 11am–4.45pm; $12, $2 off with an MFA admission receipt (within two days), free admission for those named "Isabella"; Citypass accepted; ☎617/566-1401, ⓦ www.gardnermuseum.org; Museum **T**). Eccentric Boston socialite Gardner (1840–1924) collected and arranged more than 2500 objects in the four-story Fenway Court building she designed herself – right down to the marbleized paint technique she demonstrated to her workers atop a ladder – making this the country's only major museum that is entirely the creation of a single individual. The fine-art collection, including works by Titian, Rembrandt, and Whistler, alongside a hodgepodge of furniture, textiles and objects from around the globe, is presented without much attention to period or style; Gardner's goal was to foster the love of art rather than its study, and she wanted the setting of her pieces to "fire the imagination." Your imagination does get quite a workout: there's art everywhere you look, with most of the objects unlabeled, placed in corners or above doorways, for an effect that is occasionally chaotic, but always striking. Gardner's will stipulated that every piece in the galleries stay put, or else the entire kit and kaboodle was to be shipped to Paris for auction and the proceeds given to Harvard.

The key to getting the most out of a visit is to engage as Ms Gardner wished, speculating on why an artwork is placed where it is, and looking for relationships with surrounding objects. If possible, aim to join the hour-long Friday **tours** (free; 2.30pm), but get there early as only twenty people are allowed at a time, and places are allocated on a first-come-first-served basis. Alternatively, the **gift shop** sells a worthwhile **guide** ($5) detailing the location and ownership history of every piece on display, while self-guided audio tour equipment can be rented for $4.

The first floor

The Gardner is best known for its spectacular central **courtyard** styled after a fifteenth-century Venetian palace; the second-century Roman mosaic of Medusa at its center is fittingly surrounded by stone-faced statuary and fountains, and brightened up, year round, by flowering plants and trees. However, the museum's greatest success is the **Spanish Cloister** flanking the courtyard, a long, narrow corridor just through the main entrance that perfectly frames **John Singer Sargent**'s ecstatic representation of flamenco dance, *El Jaleo* (meaning "The Ruckus"), and also contains fine seventeenth-century Mexican tiles, as well as Roman statuary and sarcophagi. A door nearby leads discreetly to the **Monks Garden**, a Mediterranean outdoor space bursting with palms and bougainvillaea.

The first floor's remaining side-rooms hold Gardner's small collection of European modern art: **Degas**'s tiny and austere portrait of a Parisian actress

Heist at the Gardner

In one of the most famous unsolved **art thefts** of all time, the Isabella Stewart Gardner Museum was robbed on March 18, 1990. At around 1.30am, as the city's St Patrick's Day celebrations were coming to a close, two men dressed as police officers knocked on the side door of the museum and were allowed to enter by security guards. Within minutes, the guards were overpowered and the men pillaged some $300–500 million worth of art, including three Rembrandts and a Manet. The empty frames are still on display, an homage to the works and a placeholder for their return. Despite the lure of a $5 million reward and numerous leads that have implicated everyone from the IRA to the Mafia to a notorious art thief, the paintings have yet to be recovered. Adding insult to injury, if the thieves were captured today they possibly wouldn't face prosecution, owing to the Massachusetts statute of limitations on robberies.

called *Madame Gaujelin* and **Matisse**'s sunstreaked *The Terrace, St Tropez*, are in the **Yellow Room**, while **Manet**'s stern portrait of his mother, *Madame Auguste Manet*, is in the appropriately dim **Blue Room**. The floor's final room, the **Macknight**, was Gardner's writing room when she was in residence and frequently doubled as Sargent's guestroom; atop one of the bookshelves is a poignant late-life portrait of his hostess, *Mrs Gardner in White*, which reveals the closeness of their friendship.

The second floor

Up one level, a first-rate display of **seventeenth-century Northern European** works was diminished by a 1990 **art heist** in which three Rembrandts and a Vermeer were among thirteen artworks stolen (see box, p.121). You can spot the missing works by their empty frames. Even with these glaring absences the second-floor **Dutch Room** retains **Rembrandt**'s early *Self-Portrait* across from **Rubens**'s heavily ornamented *Thomas Howard, Earl of Arundel*.

Next door, the magnificent **Tapestry Room** is hung with rich mid-sixteenth-century Brussels tapestries, including the *Abraham Series*, illustrating the life of the prominent Bible figure; it's a sumptuous backdrop for the weekend chamber orchestra concerts held here from September to May (☎617/566-1401). The **Short Gallery** extending north from the Tapestry Room is devoted primarily to **etchings**, many of which hang on hinged wooden panels; one bears a sign noting the theft of four Degas works from its spot – his chalk *Racehorse* remains at the bottom of the rear panel. Rounding out the floor, the colorful **Raphael Room** finds its namesake's officious *Portrait of Tommaso Inghirami*, the Vatican's rotund chief librarian, above his early *Lamentation over the Death of Christ*, which sits, unassumingly, on the desk below. The nearby walls find a couple of works by **Botticelli** as well, most notably his highly stylized *Tragedy of Lucretia*.

The third floor

Gardner had an affinity for **altars**, and her collection contains several, cobbled together from various religious artifacts. A dramatic concentration of these surrounds the third-floor stairwell and includes a medieval stone carving of the beheading of John the Baptist, a particularly agonized twelfth-century wood carving of *Christ from a Deposition Group* from Spain, and **Giovanni Minelli**'s maudlin painting, *Entombment of Christ*. Perhaps the most notable sacred art on display is in the **chapel**, also on the third floor, which incorporates sixteenth-century Italian choir stalls and stained glass from Milan and Soissons cathedrals, as well as assorted religious figurines, candlesticks, and crucifixes, all surrounding **Paul-César Helleu**'s moody representation of the *Interior of the Abbey Church of Saint-Denis*.

Between the stairwell and the chapel is the **Gothic Room**, a somberly decorated chamber whose chief attraction is **John Singer Sargent**'s controversial life-size *Portrait of Isabella Gardner* that prompted the public to rename her "Saint Isabella," thanks to the halo effect of the background. The portrait was considered so "provocative" by Gardner's husband that he asked that it not be displayed until after her death (when it did indeed cause a stir). Completing the third floor, the **Titian** and **Veronese rooms** comprise a strong showing of Italian Renaissance and Baroque work, including Titian's famous *Europa* (which was voted Boston's most important work of art by other museum directors in 2002) and **Crivelli**'s Mannerist *St George and the Dragon*. Also in the **Veronese Room** are four minute **Whistler**s, including *Little Note in Yellow and Gold*, yet another portrait of the museum's doyenne, albeit a softer and more feminine version.

Allston-Brighton and Brookline

There's little doing west of the Fenway – just a few largely residential areas, accessible on the Green Line, that seem more or less extensions of Boston and Cambridge. In fact, **Allston–Brighton**, a triangular community that spreads south from the Charles River down to Beacon Street, was originally conceived as a Cambridge adjunct. Nowadays, it's a funkier community than its neighbor across the river, with laid-back restaurants, a plethora of Jewish delis and bakeries (hit up *Kupel's*, at 421 Harvard St, for exceptional bagels), innovative shops, and hipster bars crammed into a couple of blocks along Harvard Street. It doesn't really rank as a destination in its own right, however.

Much of the activity in the affluent town of **Brookline** is focused around bustling **Coolidge Corner**, at Beacon and Harvard streets. Of note in these parts is the **Coolidge Corner Theater**, at 290 Harvard St, a refurbished arthouse cinema sustained by the many students living in the area. The main draw, though, is the nearby **John F. Kennedy National Historic Site**, at 83 Beals St (mid-May to late-Oct Wed–Sun 10am–4.30pm, closed winter; $3; ℡617/566-7937, ⓦwww.nps.gov/jofi), which preserves the outwardly unremarkable home where JFK was born on May 29, 1917. Inside, a narrated voiceover by the late-president's mother, Rose, adds some spice to the roped-off rooms; another option is the park ranger tours that are given every half an hour. To get to the heart of Brookline, take the Green Line's C branch to Coolidge Corner or D branch to Brookline Village.

It's a bit of a hike to the last of Brookline's attractions; along the suburb's southern fringe is the **Frederick Law Olmsted National Historic Site**, at 99 Warren St (Fri–Sun 10am–4.30pm; free; ℡617/566-1689 ⓦwww.nps.gov/frla). Known as Fairsted, this expansive house doubled as Olmsted's family home and office. Almost one million landscape schemes are archived here, ranging from his work on Yosemite Valley to New York's Central Park, and while the surrounding grounds are (unsurprisingly) quite idyllic, the park site is closed for renovations until 2010.

8

The southern districts

The parts of Boston most visitors see – Downtown, Beacon Hill, Back Bay, and the North End – only comprise a small portion of the city. To the south of the city center lies a vast spread of residential neighborhoods known collectively as the **southern districts**, including largely Irish **South Boston**, historical **Dorchester** and **Roxbury**, and pleasant, trendy **Jamaica Plain**. Though they do offer a more complete picture of urban life, these areas are unlikely to divert your interest for long (or at all), especially if you're short on time. Nevertheless, JFK-junkies will be rewarded by Dorchester's worthwhile **John F. Kennedy Library and Museum**, and no one should miss Jamaica Plain's superb **Arnold Arboretum**, with its world-renowned array of bonsai trees; the two combine to make a terrific half-day outing, and are easily accessible by the **T**.

Once rural areas dotted with the swank summer homes of Boston's elite, in the late-nineteenth century the southern districts became populated by middle- and working-class families pushed from increasingly crowded Downtown. Three-story rowhouses soon replaced mansions, and the moniker **"streetcar suburbs"** – after the trolley that debuted in 1899 and connected these once remote areas with Downtown – was coined as a catchall for the newly redefined neighborhoods. Following World War II, each was hit to varying degrees by economic decline, and the middle class moved farther afield. Today, the districts retain a vibrant immigrant, blue-collar, young family and student population – all seeking the lower rents and less-harried vibe that accompanies life lived just outside a major city.

South Boston

Across Fort Point Channel from Downtown and east into Boston Harbor lies **South Boston**, affectionately referred to as "Southie" by its large Irish-American population. Originally a peninsula separated from Boston proper by waterways, it was connected to the city by bridge in 1805, and throughout the nineteenth century it grew in size, augmented by landfills, and in population, thanks to a steady influx of immigrants. South Boston remained solidly blue-collar and Irish until just after World War II, when it was particularly hard hit by recession, and its makeup began to change. Despite some economic revival – especially in the shipbuilding industry – and some gentrification over the last decade, the area is still tainted by the reputation of being Boston's hotbed of racial tension, owing to friction between its old timers and the

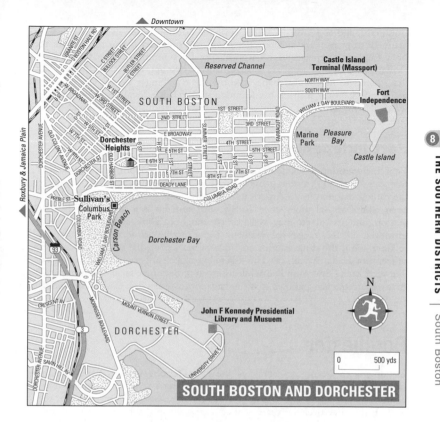

SOUTH BOSTON AND DORCHESTER

newer communities of African–Americans, Hispanics, and gays. Indeed, during the 2004 Democratic Convention, held in Boston, an attempt to promote the city's outlying neighborhoods was almost scuppered when New York Democrats expressed concern about their welcoming party being held in Southie. New York State Democratic Committee Chairman Herman "Denny" Farrell Jr went so far as to say: "For those of us who were on the frontlines of that struggle [for civil rights], the prospect of celebrating in a neighborhood that so fiercely opposed integration is very troubling." Fortunately, however, the residents of Southie put on a great party, and Farrell Jr apologised for "putting his foot in his mouth."

The area's Celtic heritage is quite evident on the main commercial boulevard, **Broadway**, where seemingly every laundry, convenience store, and even Chinese restaurant has a sign plastered with shamrocks. You'll also find an unsurprising profusion of Irish bars along West Broadway that make up in enthusiasm for the mother country what they lack in authenticity.

Castle Island

South Boston narrows to an end in Boston Harbor on a 22-acre strip of land called **Castle Island**. The island was once only connected to the mainland via a causeway bridge, but landfill projects in the nineteenth century fashioned it into a peninsula. Castle Island lies just off the terminus of William J. Day

Boulevard, and is a favorite leisure spot for Southie residents and, in fact, for many Bostonians. Park and beaches cover the spit, and if you can handle the New England temperatures, it's a good spot for swimming. Here, the views of Downtown and the harbor are spectacular, and best appreciated via the walkway that, thanks to its circular shape, is known as the "Sugar Bowl." Closer to the mainland, *Sullivan's*, a snack bar founded in 1951, is a local institution. Here a seasonal army of young employees serves tasty portions of seafood and grilled fare, while the $1.45 hot dogs are said to be the best in New England.

Fort Independence

Fort Independence (guided tours Sat & Sun noon–3.30pm; free; Broadway **T**, then bus #9 or #11), a stout granite edifice just north of Castle Island, was one of the earliest redoubts in the Americas, originally established in 1634, though it has been rebuilt several times since. Today, what remains is a skeleton of its 1801 version, and its granite-gray walls aren't much to look at from the outside. However, the free ranger-led weekend tours provide some decent history and folklore about the dank interior corridors. One legend has it that friends of an officer shot dead in a duel sealed his killer alive in a chamber in the fort's dungeons. Ten years later, Edgar Allan Poe, while assigned to duty here as an officer in the US Army, heard the tale and used it as the basis for his story, *The Cask of Amontillado*.

Dorchester

Occupying the southeast corner of the city, **Dorchester** lies beneath South Boston, below Columbia Road. North Dorchester was from its earliest days a center of trade and is still a largely industrial area. South Dorchester has seen more turbulence over the years – once a coveted spot for upper-class country homes, it followed the streetcar suburb pattern of the southern districts and remained relatively affluent until after World War II, when the middle class left; property values soon plummeted, and crime and unemployment rose. Things are brighter today, with both parts of Dorchester now home to a broad ethnic mix, notably Irish, Haitians, Vietnamese, Caribbeans, and African-Americans, as well as a yuppyish blend. Save for the **John F. Kennedy Presidential Library and Museum** (JFK's mother lived in Dorchester as a girl), as well as some hip restaurants and shops along "Dot" (Dorchester) Ave, there's not too much here in the way of sights.

John F. Kennedy Presidential Library and Museum

The **John F. Kennedy Presidential Library and Museum**, at Columbia Point (daily 9am–5pm; $10, CityPass accepted; ☎1-866/JFK-1960, ⓦwww .jfklibrary.org; JFK/UMass **T**; free shuttle every twenty minutes, free parking), stands out for providing a fascinating glimpse into the culture of a recent, storied, era, while being spectacularly situated in a stunning, glass-fronted, curvilinear I.M. Pei-designed building – allegedly the architect's favorite commission – offering panoramic views over Boston Harbor.

    The museum opens with a well-done eighteen-minute **film** covering Kennedy's political career up until the 1960 Democratic National Convention, and is narrated with soundbites from Kennedy himself. On leaving the auditor-ium and entering the exhibition space, other displays cover the presidential campaign of 1960 and the highlights of the brief Kennedy administration against a backdrop of stylized recreations of his campaign headquarters, the CBS studio that hosted the first televised presidential debate between him and Richard Nixon, and the main White House corridor. The campaign exhibits are most interesting for their television and radio ads, which illustrate the squeaky-clean self-image America possessed at that time. The section covering the Kennedy administration is more serious, animated by a 22-minute film on the Cuban Missile Crisis that evokes the tension of the event, while possibly exaggerating Kennedy's heroics. Most sobering is the darkened hallway towards the end where a televised announcement of the president's assassination plays in a continuous loop. Lighter fare is on display in the **Jackie Kennedy exhibits**, which trace her evolution from young debutante to First Lady-cum-popular icon; items on display include her outfits, her camera, and her baby brush.

The final section of the museum is perhaps the best: a 115-foot-high glass **atrium** overlooking the harbor, where a majestic American flag presides over modestly presented excerpts from Kennedy's *Profiles on Courage* – affecting enough to move even the most jaded JFK critic. The research **library**, open to any member of the public with advance notice of specific archival requests, holds JFK's papers (some 8.4 million pages in all) from his curtailed term in the Oval Office. The archives is also the repository for Ernest Hemingway's original manuscripts; Kennedy helped Hemingway's wife get the papers out of Cuba following her husband's 1961 suicide (call ☎1-866/JFK-1960 for an appointment to see them).

Dorchester Heights Monument

At the convergence of South Boston and Dorchester rises the incline of **Dorchester Heights** (Broadway **T** to bus #11 to G St stop), a neighborhood of three-story rowhouses whose northernmost point, Thomas Park, is crowned by a 70ft tall square marble Georgian revival **tower** commemorating George Washington's bloodless purge of the Brits from Boston. After the Continental Army had held the British under siege here for just over a year, Washington wanted to put an end to the whole thing. On March 4, 1776, the general amassed all the artillery around and placed it on the towering peak of Dorchester Heights, so the tired redcoats could get a good look at the patriots' firepower. Intimidated, they swiftly left Boston – for good.

Thomas Park, generally empty and pristinely kept, still commands the same sweeping views of Boston and its southern communities that it did during the Revolutionary War. The best vista is from the top of the monument itself, though it's only open by appointment (free; ☎617/242-5642). Next to the park is South Boston High School, the location of nationally televised racial turmoil during desegregation busing in the 1970s.

Roxbury

Vibrant **Roxbury**, historically an African-American neighborhood, occupies much of south central Boston below the South End, between Dorchester and Jamaica Plain. This formerly pastoral region was one of the city's most coveted addresses in the seventeenth and eighteenth centuries, when wealthy families built sumptuous country homes here. Around the 1950s, the area hit hard times, and the urban blight has left its scars, although ongoing attempts to restore some of the impressive, if neglected, properties in the area have been slowly successful, drawing in former South Enders who've been pushed out by that neighborhood's skyrocketing real estate prices. For exploring by day, the area holds some historical interest around **Dudley Square**, where a couple of African-American institutions have been preserved, but the main attraction here, especially if you have children in tow, is the **Franklin Park Zoo**, located in yet another of Frederick Law Olmsted's greenspaces. To learn more about Roxbury's history, or to hop on a tour of its best sights, check in with "Discover Roxbury" (☏617/427-1006, ⓦ www.discoverroxbury.org), run by a group of well-informed Roxbury residents, whose tours take in the Dillaway Thomas House as well the home of Ella Collins Little, where a young Malcolm X spent a number of formative years.

Dudley Square and around

Roxbury's commercial center is **Dudley Square** – the intersection of Dudley and Warren streets – which is little more than the usual mix of restaurants and shops. If you're in the area, check out the **Dillaway Thomas House**, at 183 Roxbury St between Dudley Square and the Roxbury Crossing **T** stop (Wed–Fri 10am–4pm, weekends by appointment; donations welcome), a structure built in 1750 as a parsonage and subsequently used as the main headquarters for Brigadier General Thomas and the continental army in the Revolutionary War. Its first floor is remarkably well-preserved, featuring many details of its original construction, such as exposed beams; the best part, though, may be the serene apple orchard surrounding it, enhanced by incredible city views. Across the street is John Eliot Square, from where William Dawes began his ride to Lexington on April 18, 1775, to warn of the British arrival by "sea."

Further south, the **Museum of the National Center for Afro-American Artists**, at 300 Walnut Ave (Tues–Sun 1–5pm; $4; ☏617/442-8614, ⓦ www .ncaaa.org), housed in a Victorian Gothic "Oak Bend" mansion, has a decent collection of African-American visual art from throughout the twentieth century, highlighted by some richly textured linocuts by Elizabeth Hatlett.

Franklin Park and the zoo

The southernmost link in the Emerald Necklace (see box, p.120), **Franklin Park** was one of Olmsted's proudest accomplishments when it was completed, owing to the sheer size of the place, and its scale is indeed astounding: 527 acres of greenspace, with countless trails for hikers, bikers, and walkers leading through the hills and thickly forested areas. That's about it, though, as much of the park has unfortunately become overgrown from years of half-hearted upkeep. It's quite easy to get lost among all the greenery and forget that you're still in the city, though this is perhaps not such a hot idea – the park borders some of Boston's more dangerous areas, and the place can feel quite threatening, especially at night.

The **Franklin Park Zoo**, on the far eastern edge of Franklin Park (April–Sept Mon–Fri 10am–5pm, Sat & Sun 10am–6pm, Oct–March daily 10am–4pm; $11, kids $6; ☏617/541-LION, ⓦ www.zoonewengland.com; Forest Hills **T**) is much like any other zoo, and is really only essential if you're traveling with kids, who'll definitely get a kick out of the Serengeti Crossing, where they'll interact with zebras, ostriches, and ibex along four-acres of rolling, wooded hills. Adults may enjoy the array of exotic fauna, much of which is contained in the African Tropical Forest, an impressively recreated savannah that's the largest indoor zoo design in North America, housing gorillas, warthogs, and pygmy hippos. More fun is had at Bird's World, a charming relic from the days of Edwardian zoo design: a huge, ornate wrought-iron cage you can walk through while birds fly overhead.

Jamaica Plain

Diminutive **Jamaica Plain** – "JP" in local parlance – is one of Boston's more successfully integrated neighborhoods, with a good mix of students, immigrants, and working-class families crowded into its relatively cheap apartments. Located between Roxbury and the section of the Emerald Necklace known as the Muddy River Improvement, the area's activity centers on, appropriately,

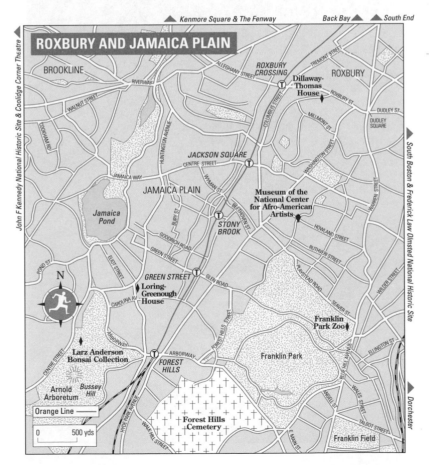

ROXBURY AND JAMAICA PLAIN

Kenmore Square & The Fenway   Back Bay   South End

John F Kennedy National Historic Site & Coolidge Corner Theatre

South Boston & Frederick Law Olmsted National Historic Site

Dorchester

Centre Street, which holds some inventive, and remarkably inexpensive, cafés and restaurants (see chapter 11, "Eating"). While you might call in at the historic estate just off the street or indulge at one of those eating establishments, the more likely bet is to head straight for the neighborhood's star attraction, the **Arnold Arboretum**, on its southwestern edge.

Loring-Greenough House

At Centre Street's foot stands the fusty **Loring-Greenough House**, 12 South St (Sat 10am–noon, Sun noon–2pm; $3 donation requested; ☎617/524-3158, Ⓦ www.lghouse.org; Forest Hills **T** or Green Street **T** to bus #39), built in 1760

▲ Arnold Arboretum

for Loyalist Commodore Joshua Loring and confiscated by colonial troops in 1775 for use as a Revolutionary War hospital. Restored to private use in 1780, the mid-Georgian mansion house was occupied by lawyer David Stoddard Greenough's family until 1926, when it was designated a historic site. The house's significance – as the last of JP's country estates from that period – does more for it than its refurbished chambers, whose highlights are unrelated exhibits of jeweled handbags and ornate calling-card cases collected by the women of the Tuesday Club, the organization that manages the house.

Arnold Arboretum

The 265-acre Harvard University-run **Arnold Arboretum**, 125 Arborway (daily dawn to dusk; donations welcome; ☎617/524-1718, ⓦwww.arboretum .harvard.edu; Forest Hills **T**), is the most spectacular link in the Emerald Necklace and the southern districts' only real must-see sight. Its collection of over 14,000 flowering trees, vines, and shrubs has benefited from more than 100 years of both careful grooming and ample funding, and is now one of the finest in North America. The plants are arranged along a series of paths populated by runners and dog-walkers as well as serious botanists, though it certainly doesn't require any expert knowledge to enjoy the grounds.

The array of Asian species – considered one of the largest and most diverse outside Asia – is highlighted by the **Larz Anderson Bonsai Collection**, brilliantly concentrated along the Chinese Path walkway at the center of the park. The arboretum also has more than 700 trees that are over 100 years old; eighteen of them (including an 1881 silver maple that, at over 120ft, is the tallest tree here) have been chosen as part of a self-guided Centenarian tour (the trees and plants are labeled with a gold tag, and you can pick up helpful guide maps from the visitor's center).

Although the staff does an impressive job of keeping the grounds looking fabulous year-round, it's best to visit in spring, when crab-apples, lilacs, and magnolias complement the greenery with dazzling chromatic schemes. "Lilac Sunday," the third Sunday in May, celebrates the arboretum at its most vibrant (and busiest), when its collection of **lilacs**, the second largest in the US, is in full bloom. **Fall** is also a good time to visit, when the arboretum becomes a glorious mass of blazing oranges, reds, and browns.

One of the best ways to appreciate the scope of the place is to make your way to the top of 198-foot **Bussey Hill** in the arboretum's center, where you can overlook the grounds in their impressive entirety and, on a clear day, catch a great view of Downtown Boston as well.

Cambridge

Just across the Charles River from Boston, **Cambridge** is altogether more unbuttoned and laid-back than its big city counterpart, and populated by a younger, more bohemian type of resident. Highlighted by two of the most illustrious institutions of higher learning in the country, its denizens, including clean-cut college students, disaffected punks, starched business people, and street artists performing magic tricks, manage to support a buzzing streetlife and café culture that can either be seen as a refreshing change from provincial Boston or just a continuation of it.

A walk down Cambridge's colonial-era brick sidewalks and narrow, crooked roads takes you past plaques and monuments honoring literati and revolutionaries who lived and worked in the area – some hailing from as early as the seventeenth century. Nevertheless, Cambridge manages – perhaps even better than Boston itself – an exhilarating mix of colonial past and urban present; the extensive range of residents and activities, and the sheer energy that pervades its classrooms and coffeehouses, are all enough to make it an essential stopover on your trip.

Cambridge resembles a bow tie, with Harvard Square forming the knot. On its southern border is the sinuous Charles River, with Boston on the opposite bank, while the concave northern side is shared with the large, mostly residential town of **Somerville**, popular with locals for its restaurant and café scene centering on the alternative vibe of **Davis Square**. Cambridge proper, meanwhile, is loosely organized around a series of squares – actually confluences of streets that are the focus of each area's commercial activity. By far the most important of these is **Harvard Square**, which radiates out from the **T** stop along Massachusetts Avenue, JFK Street, and Brattle Street. Roughly coterminous with Harvard Square is **Harvard University**; together, these two areas make up the cultural and academic heart of Cambridge. This is where people converge to check out the famous Ivy League institution, historical monuments, a lively coffeehouse-and-bookstore scene, and a disgruntled counterculture. Its total area – only a single square mile – is small in comparison with the entirety of Cambridge, but the density of attractions here make it one part of town not to be missed.

Old Cambridge, the clean, impeccably kept colonial heart of the city, is easily accessible from Harvard Square; sights here include impressive mansions – most notably the **Longfellow House** – and peaceful **Mount Auburn Cemetery**. East from here, on the other side of the university, **Central** and **Inman squares** represent the core of **Central Cambridge**, and are of primary interest for their atmospheric bar scene. As with Central Cambridge, **East Cambridge** grew up around industry rather than academia, but its proximity to Downtown Boston has led to increasing real estate prices and an "upscaling" of residents; there's not too much to see here, as this area is known mainly for its shopping mall – the CambridgeSide Galleria. East Cambridge draws most of its modern-day interest from the **Massachusetts Institute of Technology**, one of the world's premier science and research institutions. Home to some innovative – if at times peculiar – architecture and an excellent museum, MIT spreads out below **Kendall Square**, which itself is home to a cluster of stalwart high-tech companies. Finally, above Harvard, **Northwest Cambridge** is an ill-defined corner of the city, a catchall term for some of the places not identified with its more happening districts – and as such is easily overlooked. Despite some good shopping and decent restaurants, especially along **Huron Avenue** and around **Porter Square**, the area is more of interest to residents than to travelers.

Some history

Cambridge began inauspiciously in 1630, when a group of English immigrants from Charlestown founded **New Towne** village on the narrow, swampy banks of the Charles River. These Puritans hoped New Towne would become an ideal religious community; to that end, they founded a college in 1636 for the purpose of training clergy. Two years later, the college took its name in honor of a local minister, **John Harvard**, who bequeathed his library and half his estate to the nascent institution. New Towne was eventually renamed **Cambridge** after the English university where many of its founders were educated, and became one of the largest publishing centers in the New World after the importation of the printing press in the seventeenth century. Its university and printing industry established Cambridge as an important center of intellectual activity and political thought, and during the late eighteenth century its population became sharply divided between the many artisan and farmer sympathizers of the revolution and the moneyed Tory minority; when fighting began, the Tories were driven from their mansions on modern-day Brattle Street (then called "Tory Row"), their place taken by Cambridge intelligentsia and prominent Revolutionaries.

In 1846, the Massachusetts Legislature granted a city charter linking Old Cambridge (the Harvard Square area) and industrial East Cambridge as a single municipality. Initially, there was friction between these two very different neighborhoods; in 1855, citizens from each area unsuccessfully petitioned for them to be granted separate civic status. Though relations improved, the distinctive characters remain. The late nineteenth and early twentieth centuries brought substantial growth to the town. A large, mainly Irish immigrant population was drawn to opportunity in the industrial and commercial sectors of East Cambridge, while academics increasingly sought out Harvard, whose reputation continued to swell, and the **Massachusetts Institute of Technology**, which moved here from Boston in 1916. The fact that nearly half of its 90,000-plus residents are university affiliates ensures that it will remain one of America's most opinionated cities.

Harvard Square and around

The Harvard **T** station marks Cambridge's center, opening up onto **Harvard Square** and the square's main tenant, Out of Town News, where an

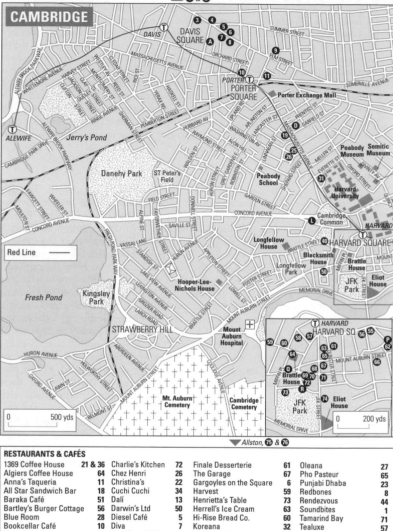

CAMBRIDGE

Red Line ——

Allston, **75** & **76** ▼

RESTAURANTS & CAFÉS

1369 Coffee House	21 & 36	Charlie's Kitchen	72	Finale Desserterie	61	Oleana	27
Algiers Coffee House	64	Chez Henri	26	The Garage	67	Pho Pasteur	65
Anna's Taqueria	11	Christina's	22	Gargoyles on the Square	6	Punjabi Dhaba	23
All Star Sandwich Bar	18	Cuchi Cuchi	34	Harvest	59	Redbones	8
Baraka Café	51	Dalí	13	Henrietta's Table	50	Rendezvous	44
Bartley's Burger Cottage	56	Darwin's Ltd	50	Herrell's Ice Cream	63	Soundbites	1
Blue Room	28	Diesel Café	5	Hi-Rise Bread Co.	60	Tamarind Bay	71
Bookcellar Café	10	Diva	7	Koreana	32	Tealuxe	57
Boca Grande	19	East Coast Grill	16	LA Burdick Chocolates	40	Toscanini's	56
Café Pamplona	62	Emma's Pizza	30	Midwest Grill	12	True Grounds	2
Central Kitchen	39	EVOO	15	Olé Mexican Grill	14	Upstairs on the Square	70

enthusiastic youth brigade (led by Harvard's "Unofficial Tours" guides) rallies visitors in the shadow of the Harvard Yard buildings. A small **tourism kiosk** run by the Cambridge Tourism Office (daily 9am–5pm; ☏617/441-2884 or 1-800/862-5678, Ⓦwww.cambridge-usa.com) faces the station exit, but more of the action is in the adjacent sunken area known as **The Pit**, a triage center for fashion victims of alternative culture – teens can spend entire days sitting here admiring each other's green hair and body

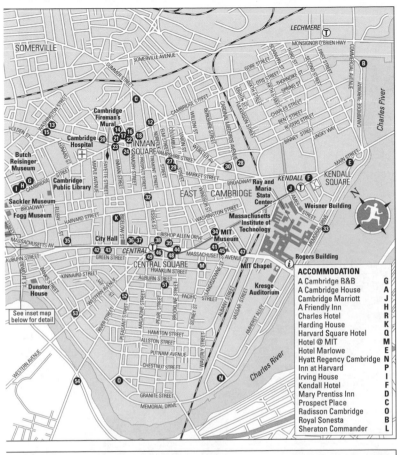

LECHMERE

ACCOMMODATION

A Cambridge B&B	G
A Cambridge House	A
Cambridge Marriott	J
A Friendly Inn	H
Charles Hotel	R
Harding House	K
Harvard Square Hotel	Q
Hotel @ MIT	M
Hotel Marlowe	E
Hyatt Regency Cambridge	N
Inn at Harvard	P
Irving House	I
Kendall Hotel	F
Mary Prentiss Inn	D
Prospect Place	C
Radisson Cambridge	O
Royal Sonesta	B
Sheraton Commander	L

BARS & CLUBS

Abbey Lounge		20	The Field		38	Miracle of	
B-Side Lounge		29	Grafton Street		55	Science	
Bukowski's			Great Scott		75	Model Café	
Tavern		17	Green Street		49	Muddy Charles	
Burren		4	Grendel's Den		68	Noir	
Cantab Lounge		37	Johnny D's		3	Paradise Café	
Cellar		35	Lizard Lounge		31	People's Republic	
Club Passim		58	The Middle East		48	Phoenix Landing	
Daedalus		66	Middlesex			Plough & Stars	
Enormous Room		39	Lounge		45	Regattabar	

Rialto	73
River Gods	52
Ryles	24
Scullers	54
Shay's Pub and	
Wine Bar	74
Temple Bar	25
Thirsty Scholar Pub	9
T.T. the Bear's Place	48
Western Front	53

piercings. This is also the beginning of the **street music scene**, where folk diva Tracy Chapman (a graduate of Tufts University, in nearby Somerville) and country maven Bonnie Raitt (a Radcliffe alumna) both got their starts. The square reaches its most frenetic state on Friday and Saturday nights and Sunday afternoons, when all the elements converge – crowds mill about while magicians, acrobats, and bands perform on every corner.

▲ The Pit, Harvard Square

The Old Burying Ground

Facing Harvard Square to the north along Massachusetts Avenue is one of Cambridge's first cemeteries, the **Old Burying Ground**, whose style and grounds have scarcely changed since the seventeenth century. You're supposed to apply to the sexton of nearby **Christ Church** for entry, but if the gate at the path beside the simple, graywashed, eighteenth-century church is open (as it frequently is), you can enter so long as you're respectful of the grounds.

The epitaphs have an archaic ring to them ("Here lyes..."), and the stone grave markers are adorned in a style blending Puritan austerity and medieval superstition: inscriptions praise the simple piety of the staunchly Christian deceased, but are surrounded by death's-heads carved to ward off evil spirits. Its most famous occupants include several of Harvard's first presidents as well as two black veterans of the Revolutionary War, Cato Stedman and Neptune Frost. Be sure to check out the **milestone** marker (at the northeast corner, where Garden Street meets Massachusetts Avenue) found just inside the gate, whose 250-year-old inscription is still readily visible. Originally set to mark the then-daunting distance of eight miles to Boston. the letters A.I. identify the stone's maker. Abraham Ireland.

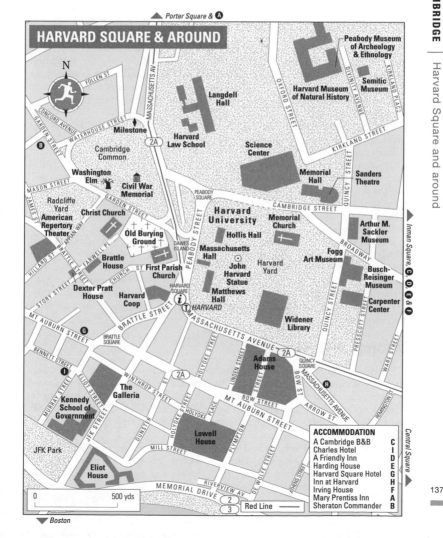

Dawes Island

A triangular traffic island squeezed into the intersection of Massachusetts Avenue, Garden Street, and Peabody Street, **Dawes Island** is anything but bucolic – the wedge of concrete serves as a bus stop. The island is named after the patriot who rode to alert residents that the British were marching to Lexington and Concord on April 19, 1775 – the *other* patriot, that is, William Dawes (see p.48). While Longfellow opted to commemorate Paul Revere's midnight ride instead, Cantabrigians must have appreciated poor Dawes's contribution just as much. In reality, there was also a third rider, Dr Samuel Prescott, who's generally credited as the only one to complete the ride. Bronze hoof marks in the sidewalk mark the event, and several placards provide information on the history of the Harvard Square/Old Cambridge area.

Cambridge Common and Radcliffe Yard

A trapezoidal patch of green between Massachusetts Avenue, Garden Street, and Waterhouse Street, **Cambridge Common** has been a site for recreation and community events since the area's earliest settlers used it as a cow pasture. Visitors flock here for its historical interest, but locals congregate for Frisbee and sunbathing – although after dusk it can be an altogether lonelier, and somewhat dodgier, place.

Early Harvard commencements took place here, as did public debates and training exercises for the local militia. You can retrace a portion of the old **Charlestown–Watertown path**, along which the British Redcoats beat a sheepish retreat to Watertown during the Revolutionary War, and which still transects the park from east to west. A broad range of **statuary** dots the southeast corner of the park, and you can't miss the towering monument to Lincoln and the Civil War dead, which all but overshadows the tableau of two emaciated figures nearby, wrought as an unsettling memorial to the Irish Potato Famine.

Just across Garden Street from Cambridge Common is a less crowded park, **Radcliffe Yard**, originally the center of Radcliffe College, established in 1878 to give women access to (then exclusively male) Harvard; the two colleges merged in the 1970s. The yard itself is a picturesque, impeccably preserved quadrangle; enclosed by brick buildings upheld by Ionic columns, it's dotted with statues and pathways, making it a great place for a summer picnic or stroll.

Along JFK Street

The stretch of **JFK Street** below Harvard Square holds more of the city's many public spaces, including **Winthrop Square**, site of the original New Towne marketplace and since converted into a tiny, well-shaded park, presided over by restaurants and shops and strewn about with benches. Cross the park and walk down Winthrop Street to the right to get a sense of the sloping topography and narrow street design of early Cambridge.

John F. Kennedy Park, located where JFK Street meets Memorial Drive, was only finished in the late 1980s. Though certainly not the first pious shrine to Boston's favorite modern son, this one is cleaner and more spacious than most other parks in the area. The unusual **memorial** to Kennedy in its center is worth a look; a low, pink-granite pyramid inscribed with Kennedy platitudes, covered constantly but imperceptibly by a thin film of flowing water.

Harvard Yard and the university

The transition from Harvard Square to **Harvard Yard** – the proper center of the university – is dramatic: in a matter of only several feet, the buzz of car traffic and urban life gives way to grassy lawns and towering oaks, pervaded by an aura of Ivy League academia. The atmosphere is more mythological than real, however, as the Yard's narrow, haphazard footpaths are constantly plied by preoccupied students and camera-clicking tour groups, who can make the place feel more like an amusement park than a staid university campus. You can join the hullabaloo by taking a free one-hour student-guided walking tour from the Harvard Events & Information Center in the **Holyoke Center**, 1350 Massachusetts Ave (June–Aug Mon–Sat 10am, 11.15am, 2pm, & 3.15pm; Sept–May Mon–Fri 10am & 2pm, Sat 2pm; no tours during breaks in the academic calendar; ☎617/495-1573, ⓦwww.hno .harvard.edu/guide/to_do/index.html), where you can also pick up maps and brochures detailing everything Harvard-related. You could also hop on one of the less reverential "Unofficial Tours" (daily 10.30am, 11.30am, 12.30, 1.30pm, 2.30pm, 3.30pm; free, tips appreciated; ☎203/305-9735, ⓦwww .hahvahdtour.com), departing from the Cambridge information kiosk, just outside the Harvard **T** station; tour guides are easily spotted by their crimson "Hahvahd" t-shirts.

The Old Yard

The most common entrance to Harvard Yard is the one directly across from Harvard Square proper, which leads by **Massachusetts Hall** (holding the office of the university president) to the **Old Yard**, a large, rectangular area dating from 1636, when it was created as a grazing field for university livestock. In front of stark, symmetrical, marble-hued **University Hall** is the yard's trademark icon, the **John Harvard statue**, around which chipper student guides inform

The Washington Elm

Perhaps the prettiest feature on Cambridge Common is the revered **Washington Elm**, under which it's claimed George Washington took command of the Continental Army. The tree is at the southern side of the park, almost facing the intersection of Garden Street and Appian Way, and is predictably accompanied by a wealth of commemorative objects: three cannons captured from the British when they evacuated Boston, an engraving of Washington standing in the shade of the elm, and monuments to two Polish army captains hired to lead revolutionary forces. What the memorials don't tell you is that the city of Cambridge cut down the original Washington Elm in 1946 when it began to obstruct traffic; it stood at the intersection of Mason and Garden streets. The present tree is actually the offspring of that tree, raised from one of its branches. To further confuse the issue, the Daughters of the American Revolution erected a monument commemorating the southeast corner of the park as the spot where Washington did his historic thing. And recently, American historians have adduced evidence strongly suggesting that Washington never commissioned the troops on the common at all, but rather in Wadsworth House at Harvard Yard.

For another memorial to the tree, check out the Washington Elm marker embedded in the intersection of Mason and Garden streets. What looks like an ordinary manhole actually bears the inscription "Here Stood the Washington Elm" – just be careful not to get honked at (or injured) by oncoming traffic.

tour groups of the oft-told "three lies" (it misdates the college's founding; erroneously identifies John Harvard as the college's founder; and isn't really a likeness of John Harvard at all). While it's a popular spot for visitors to take pictures, male students at the college covet the statue as a site of public urination; it's a badge of honor around here, and as a result there are surveillance cameras trained on the statue.

Along the northwest border of the yard, stout **Hollis Hall** is the dormitory where Henry David Thoreau lived as an undergraduate. The architectural contrast between modest Hollis, which dates from 1762, and its grandiose southern neighbor, **Matthews Hall**, built around a hundred years later, reflects Harvard's transition from a quiet training ground for ministers to a wealthy, cosmopolitan university. The **indentations** in Hollis's front steps also hold some historical interest: students used to warm their rooms by heating cannonballs, and when it came time to leave their quarters for the summer, they would dispose of them by dropping them from their windows rather than having to carry them down the stairs. Harvard's first chapel, the charming 1744 **Holden Chapel** to the rear, is also worth a quick peek for its attractive Georgian architecture and provincial blue-and-white pediment.

The New Yard

To the east of the Old Yard lie the grander buildings of the Tercentenary Theatre, colloquially known as the **New Yard**, where a vast set of steps leads up to the enormous pillars of **Widener Library**. Named after Harvard grad and *Titanic* victim Harry Elkins Widener, whose mother paid for the project, it's the center of the largest private library collection in the US, boasting a first folio of Shakespeare and a Gutenberg Bible among its holdings (you'll need Harvard student ID to see them). At the opposite side of the New Yard is **Memorial Church** (℡617/495-5508, ⓦwww.memorialchurch.harvard .edu), whose narrow, white spire strikes a balancing note to the heavy pillared front of Widener; its 172-foot-high steeple, topped by a medieval pennant-shaped **weathervane**, is a classic postcard image of Harvard Yard. Inside the church, the nave bears the names of alumni who've died at war; the organ at the rear is a much fancier affair, adorned with gilded carvings of starfish, kelp, cod, and crab.

The Science Center and Law School

The immense structure facing the New Yard is Harvard's **Science Center**. The big lecture halls on the first floor are home to some of Harvard's most popular classes; one celebrity professor who taught here was the late evolutionary biologist Stephen Jay Gould. A popular myth has it that the center was designed to look like a camera, since one of its main benefactors was Polaroid magnate Edwin Land, but any likeness is purely accidental.

Up Massachusetts Avenue, on the east side of Cambridge Common, lies the main quad of the famed **Harvard Law School**, founded in 1817. The campus focuses on the stern gray pillars of **Langdell Hall**, an imposing edifice on its western border, whose entrance bears the inscription "*Non sub homine, sed sub deo et lege*" ("Not under man, but under God and law"). Inside is the renovated **Harvard Law Library**, where you can practically smell the stress in the air.

Memorial Hall and the Carpenter Center

The rest of the campus lies east of the Science Center, starting with the pointed arches and flying buttresses of **Memorial Hall**, built to commemorate the Harvard students who died during the Civil War. While it resembles a church, right down to its central vaulted **narthex**, which is bathed in filtered sunlight through Tiffany and La Farge stained-glass windows, the space actually serves as **Sanders Theater**, undoubtedly Harvard's most impressive public lecture space.

The conspicuously modern **Carpenter Center** is hard to miss as you continue past Memorial Hall and look down Quincy Street: the slate-gray granite slab stands out amidst Harvard's ever-present brick motif. Completed in 1963 as a center for the study of visual art at Harvard, the Carpenter Center is the only building in America designed by modernist French architect Le Corbusier (known for Zurich's Centre Le Corbusier and avant-garde furniture design), and its jarring difference from its surroundings has drawn a great deal of criticism from staunch Harvard traditionalists. Still, it's a striking and reasonably functional space; be sure to traverse its trademark feature, a **walkway** that leads through the middle of the building, meant to reflect the path worn by students on the lot on which the center was constructed. The modest **Sert Gallery**, on the third floor (Mon–Sat 10am–5pm, Sun 1–5pm; free; no phone, Ⓦwww.artmuseums.harvard.edu/sert), puts on rotating contemporary art exhibits culled from Harvard's collections, while the lower floors of the building frequently display student art exhibits. Also downstairs is the **Harvard Film Archive** (Ⓣ617/495-4700, Ⓦhttp://hcl.harvard.edu/hfa), which screens old-school, foreign, and contemporary classics such as *Whatever Happened to Baby Jane* or *La Femme Infidèle* – check their website for scheduling, or pick up a calendar from inside the building.

Harvard University art museums

Harvard's three art museums – the **Fogg Art**, the **Busch–Reisinger**, and the **Sackler** (Mon–Sat 10am–5pm, Sun 1–5pm; $9; free Sat 10am–noon and daily after 4.30pm; Ⓣ617/495-9400, Ⓦwww.artmuseums.harvard.edu) – have benefited from years of scholarly attention and donors' financial generosity. Largely under-appreciated and under-attended by most visitors – not to mention the students themselves – the collections are easily some of the finest in New England; certainly the Fogg has the most important collection of Picassos around.

The Fogg Art Museum

Housed on two floors surrounding a lovely mock sixteenth-century Italian Renaissance courtyard, the **Fogg Art Museum**, 32 Quincy St, showcases the highlights of Harvard's substantial collection of Western art. Much of the first floor is devoted to **medieval** and **Renaissance** material, mainly religious art with the usual complement of suffering Christs, mostly housed in the far room to the right, below a marvelous *circa* 1540 oak ceiling carved with scrolls and arabesques. This part of the collection is best for a series of capitals salvaged from the French cathedral of Moutiers-Saint-Jean, which combine a Romanesque predilection for classical design with medieval didactic narrative. Additional first-floor chambers are devoted to **portraiture** of the seventeenth and eighteenth centuries, featuring five Rubens, an artwork from the school of Rembrandt, and three Poussins, among them the startling *Hannibal Crossing the Alps*, which depicts the great Carthaginian instructing his troops from atop a massive tusked elephant. There is also an atmospheric exhibit devoted to the clay sculptures, or "sketches," of Gian Lorenzo Bernini (1598–1680), precursors for final pieces that would later be cast in marble or bronze and harbored around Rome's Saint Peter's Basilica. Blissfully filled with delicate, ecstatic angels, the space documents Bernini's task of "making manifest the intangible realms of saints and angels" by modeling them "in the humblest of materials."

The second floor houses rotating exhibits, as well as smaller rooms displaying the museum's well-chosen **Impressionist, Post–Impressionist,** and **Modernist** works. There's an especially strong showing from the late-nineteenth-century French contingent of Dégas, Monet, Manet, Pissarro, and Cézanne. You'll also see Picasso's *Mother and Child,* famously exemplary of his blue period, a sickly *Self-Portrait, dedicated to Paul Gauguin* by Van Gogh, and Toulouse-Lautrec's queasy *The Hangover (Suzanne Valadon).* But it's the focus on American counterparts to European late-nineteenth- and early-twentieth-century artists that truly distinguishes the collection, from the fine range of John Singer Sargent portraits, his solitary *The Breakfast Table* among them, to an ethereal Whistler *Nocturne* in blue and silver tints. Modernism is represented by, among others, Jackson Pollock's narrow beige and black *No. 2,* and Ellsworth Kelly's cheerful *City Island,* a jovial yellow flower sunburst. Fine examples of lesser-known nineteenth-century sensualist works are also displayed throughout the museum; look for Rodin's downright sexy *Iris, Messenger of the Gods* statue, and Gustave Moreau's highly eroticized *Apparition.*

The Busch-Reisinger Museum

Secreted away at the rear of the Fogg's second floor is the entrance to Werner Otto Hall, home of the rich collection of the **Busch–Reisinger Museum**. Despite its small size, it's one of the finest collections of German Expressionists and Bauhaus works in the world. Its six rooms contain *fin de siècle* art, including Klimt's *Pear Tree,* a dappled meditation on the natural environment, and several Bauhaus standouts like Feininger's angular *Bird Cloud* and Moholy-Nagy's *Light-Space Modulator* – a quirky sculpture-machine set in motion for ten-minutes just once a week (Wed 1.45pm) due to its fragility. The gallery is strongest in Expressionist portraiture, notably, Kirchner's sardonic *Self-Portrait with a Cat* and Beckmann's garish *The Actors,* a narcissistic triptych that features a self-portrait as its centrepiece.

The Arthur M. Sackler Museum

Right out of the Fogg and dead ahead, is the five-floor Arthur M. Sackler Building, 485 Broadway, the first, second and fourth floors of which make up the **Sackler Museum**, dedicated to the art of **classical**, **Asian,** and **Islamic** cultures. The museum's holdings have far outgrown its available space, which is why the first floor is devoted to rotating exhibits based on permanent collection holdings. Islamic and Asian art are featured on the second floor and show illustrations from Muslim texts, Chinese landscapes from the past several centuries, and an outstanding collection of Indian watercolors called "Pavilions of Love," which depict a number of heartfelt rendezvous held amidst gloriously gilded pavilions. The fourth floor is best known for its excellent array of sensuous **Buddhist sculptures** from ancient China, India, and Southeast Asia; one of them is housed in an ornate gilt and bronze portable shrine and, like a set of gilded, spiritual action figures, comes equipped with two removable bodhisattvas. You'll also see a number of gorgeous bronze ritual bells, dating from 5–3rd BC and decked out with elaborate inlay work that has aged to a lovely turquoise patina.

Harvard Museum of Natural History and Peabody Museum of Archeology and Ethnology

North of the Sackler, Divinity Avenue holds the beloved **Harvard Museum of Natural History** (☎617/495-3045; Ⓦwww.hmnh.harvard.edu), as well as a separate entity, the **Peabody Museum of Archeology and Ethnology** (☎617/496-1027; Ⓦwww.peabody.harvard.edu), linked to the HMNH via a walkway. Entry to both is via a common ticket (daily 9am–5pm; $9, free to Massachusetts' residents Sun 9am–noon year round and Wed 3–5pm Sept–May). Favored by youngsters, but also a worthy visit for adults, the museums are the public front for Harvard University's natural history institutions, and as such feature comprehensive collections of North American and Mayan archaeology, interactive exhibits related to meteorites, gemstones, and climate change, and lots of funhouse-sized dinosaur skeletons and bones.

The Peabody Museum of Archeology and Ethnology

Although considered a separate body, the **Peabody Museum of Archeology and Ethnology**, 11 Divinity Ave, displays materials culled from the university's anthropological and archeological expeditions. The strength of the museum lies in its collection of pieces from **Mesoamerica**, ranging from digs in the pueblos of southwestern United States to artifacts from Incan civilizations. Best are the enormous, carved Copan stelæ on which practical information such as birth, death, and bloodletting are all recorded in ancient Mayan. The ground-floor centers on the indigenous cultures of North America, including the only surviving Native American artifacts collected by Lewis and Clark, as well as colorful kachina dolls crafted by Arizona Hopi for their children, and stupendous examples of Northwest Coast ceremonial masks with pronounced bird beaks.

Harvard Museum of Natural History

A second-floor passageway connects the Peabody with the **Harvard Museum of Natural History**, at 24 Oxford St. Start at "Minerals, Gems, and Meteorites," a visual feast of sparkly rocks and gemstones, with a stunning 1600-pound amethyst-encrusted cavity serving as its centerpiece. Reputed to be one of the world's finest mineral collections, most of the gems are truly gorgeous, and even if you don't know anything about geology, there's plenty of eye candy to keep you occupied. While here, seek out the small display devoted to **meteorites**, where you can glimpse rocks that not only survived their fall from outer space, but also have been in existence for 4.5 billion years.

The adjacent gallery houses the museum's *pièce de resistance,* the stunning **Ware Collection of Glass Models of Plants.** This project, the work of a father-and-son team from Dresden, Germany, began in 1887 to serve as a teaching collection and terminated almost fifty years later in 1936, leaving the museum with an absolutely unique and visually awesome collection of flower models constructed to the last detail, entirely from glass; it's really not to be missed. Down the hall, the **zoological galleries** are home to some gloriously huge dinosaur fossils, including a 42-foot-long prehistoric marine reptile, the *Kronosaurus*, the teeth of which (as the museum proudly proclaims) "are the size of bananas." Around the corner is the *Glyptodont*, which looks like an inflated armadillo.

The Harvard Semitic Museum

Catecorner to the Peabody Museum entrance is the **Harvard Semitic Museum**, 6 Divinity Ave (Mon–Fri 10am–4pm, Sun 1–4pm; free; ☎617/495-4631, ⓦwww.fas.harvard.edu/~semitic), which lacks the magnetism of its neighbors but holds some Near Eastern archeological artifacts that are worth a look. Pieces range from Egyptian tombs to Babylonian cuneiform, and include a particularly appealing collection of tiny stone-cut votive figurines from ancient Cyprus. There is also a set of Egyptian amulet and funerary figurines, which were buried with the dead along with a magical charm so that they could later reawaken and "perform the agricultural labor that was required in the afterlife."

Harvard houses

Harvard's fancy upperclassmen residences, most of which are nested in the area east of JFK Street and south of Massachusetts Avenue, are a visible – and sometimes ostentatious – reminder of the university's legacy. Nearest the Yard, at 46 Plympton St, **Adams House** has the most rebellious history of the lot, having been used as a revolutionary prison for General "Gentleman Johnny" Burgoyne, and later serving as a speakeasy during Prohibition. Just south of Adams juts the graceful, blue-topped bell tower of **Lowell House**, at 2 Holyoke Place, which boasts one of Harvard's most beautiful courtyards, surrounded by a compound of sober brick dormitories and fastidiously manicured grounds. Further southwest, along the banks of the Charles, rises the purple spire of **Eliot House**, at 101 Dunster St, formerly a blueblood bastion of social privilege that can count David Rockefeller and Leonard Bernstein as former residents. To the east, at 945 Memorial Drive, lies **Dunster House**, whose red Georgian tower top is a favorite subject of Cambridge's tourist brochures; it was modeled after Christ Church College's Big Tom in Oxford. Alongside Adams, Dunster was historically considered a center for radical culture: while the other residences were often praised for their building of a "house spirit," Dunster had no rules or regulations, but rather a reputation for "extreme informality."

Old Cambridge: Upper Brattle Street

After the outbreak of the American Revolution, Cambridge's patriot dissidents ran the Tories out of town, leaving their sumptuous houses to be used as barracks for the Continental Army. What was then called Tory Row is modern-day **Brattle Street**, the main drag of the **Old Cambridge** district. Extending west from Eliot Street and Harvard Square, Brattle runs through a tree-lined neighborhood of expansive, impeccably kept lawns foregrounding stately mansions, many of which have been labeled with blue oval plaques commemorating their former owners.

The Brattle House and Farwell Place

The first of several noteworthy residences along Brattle Street, the **Brattle House**, at no. 42, doesn't reflect the unabashedly extravagant lifestyle of its former resident, the Revolutionary War commander General William Brattle. Dwarfed as it is by surrounding shops and restaurants, it currently houses the Cambridge Center for Adult Education; they don't mind if you pop in for a look.

Down the street and to the right, tiny **Farwell Place** features several modest Federal-style houses dating to the early nineteenth century and is the best (and only remaining) example of the square's residential character before it became a teeming center of activity. The restored house at no. 17 is one of the best examples of the genre; it now houses Christ Church's thrift shop (Tues, Wed, Thurs, Sat 10am–4pm; ☎617/492-3335).

The Dexter Pratt House

A marker on the corner of Brattle and Story streets commemorates the site of a tree that once stood near the **Dexter Pratt House**, at 56 Brattle St. The house is the former home of a village blacksmith celebrated by Longfellow in a popular poem that began, "Under a spreading chestnut tree / The village smithy stands, / The smith a mighty man is he, / With large and sinewy hands; / And the muscles of his brawny arms / Are strong as iron bands." In 1876, the chestnut was cut down, despite Longfellow's vigorous opposition, because it was spreading into the path of passing traffic. The city of Cambridge fashioned a chair out of the felled tree and presented it as a birthday present to Longfellow, who then composed a mawkish poem about the whole affair ("From My Easy Chair"), and all was forgiven. These days the Federal-style building is home to the *Hi-Rise Bread Company* (see p.178), a good stop for tasty sandwiches and granola. Beyond the house, at the intersection of **Mason** and **Brattle streets**, a neighborhood of elite mansions signals the edge of Old Cambridge proper.

Longfellow National Historic Site

One worthy sight on Brattle Street is the recently renovated **Longfellow National Historic Site**, 105 Brattle St (April–Oct Wed–Sun 10am–4.30pm, tours hourly 10.30–11.30am & 1–4pm; $3; ☎617/876-4491, ⓦwww.nps .gov/long; Harvard **T**). Erected for Royalist John Vassal in 1759, who promptly vacated it on the eve of the Revolutionary War, and used by George Washington as headquarters during the Siege of Boston, it later became home to poet Henry Wadsworth Longfellow, who moved in as a boarder in 1837. When he married the wealthy Fanny Appleton, her father purchased the house for them as a wedding gift in 1843, and Longfellow lived here until his death in 1882.

Preserved to recall the styles of the era, the result is a solid example of Brattle Street opulence during the nineteenth century. The halls and walls are festooned with Longfellow's furniture and art collection, including portraits of fellow writers like Ralph Waldo Emerson and Nathaniel Hawthorne. Most surprising is the wealth of nineteenth-century pieces from the Far East amassed by Longfellow's renegade son, Charlie, on his world travels; four of his Japanese screens are included, the best of which, a two-panel example depicting geishas in spring and winter costumes, is in an upstairs bedroom. His other son, Ernie, stayed at home to make a name for himself as a landscape and portrait painter; a number of his works adorn the walls of the house. Just outside, a lovely garden space features labyrinthine shrubs, snapdragons, and roses all laid out with historical accuracy from plans dating to 1904.

The Hooper-Lee-Nichols House

The second Brattle Street mansion open to the public is the bluewashed **Hooper-Lee-Nichols House** at no. 159 (Tues & Thurs 2–4pm, tours every hour; $5; ☎617/547-4252, ⓦwww.cambridgehistory.org), half a mile west of the Longfellow House. While a bit out-of-the-way, the house – one of the area's oldest residences – does give an intimate sense of colonial Cambridge life. It's particularly unusual for its various architectural incarnations: it began as a stout, post-medieval farmhouse and underwent several renovations until it became the Georgian mansion it is today. Rooms have been predictably restored with period writing tables, canopy beds, and rag dolls, but knowledgeable tour guides spice things up a bit, opening secret panels to reveal centuries-old wallpaper and original foundations.

The Mount Auburn Cemetery

Past the Hooper-Lee-Nichols House, at the intersection of Brattle and Mount Auburn streets, is the **Mount Auburn Cemetery** (ⓦwww.mountauburn .org), made to pay tribute to "the great and good." When founded in 1831, it was America's first landscaped cemetery; today its 170 acres of grounds are more like a beautifully kept municipal park than a necropolis – Isamu Noguchi called it "the best little sculpture garden in the world." The best way to get a sense of the cemetery's scope is to ascend the **tower** that lies smack in its center atop a grassy bluff; from the top you can see not only the entire grounds but all of Downtown Boston and its environs. Of course, like most cemeteries in the Boston area, Mount Auburn also has its share of deceased luminaries, most notably the painter Winslow Homer and art patron Isabella Stewart Gardner; ask the folks in the main office for a map of famous graves if you're interested.

Central Square

A mile east of Brattle Street, **Central Square**, bordered by Massachusetts Avenue, Prospect Street, and Western Avenue, is roughly in the geographical center of Cambridge, and is the city's civic center as well. The square is an interesting mix of cultural and industrial Cambridge – a working-class area that's steadily being gentrified, with an ethnically diverse population and little of the hype that surrounds other parts of town. There's nothing much to see, but this is a good place to shop and eat, and home to some of the best **nightlife** in Cambridge. Indeed, you'll find substantially more activity here after dark, especially along Massachusetts Avenue, as denizens flock to hear live music.

The Gothic quarters of **City Hall**, 795 Massachusetts Ave (Mon–Fri 8.30am–5pm), house Cambridge's municipal bureaucracy and act as an occasional venue for town meetings or public events, and the imposing marble **Clifton Merriman Building** across the street, 770 Massachusetts Ave, houses a post office (Mon–Fri 7.30am–6.45pm, Sat 7.30am–2pm; ☎617/575-8700, ⓦwww.usps.com), but little else stands out here.

Inman and Kendall Squares

Overshadowed by Cambridge's busier districts, **Inman Square** marks a hip stretch directly north of Central Square that's centered on the confluence of Cambridge, Beacon, and Prospect streets. There's not much of note here, either – just a pleasant, mostly residential neighborhood where much of Cambridge's working-class, Portuguese-speaking population resides alongside students and hipster types. What does make Inman worth a visit, though, is its café culture and broad range of excellent restaurants, where you can enjoy some of the town's finest food without breaking the bank. Look out for *Punjabi Dhaba*, arguably the best Indian spot in town (see p.179). While in the area, check out the **Cambridge Firemen's Mural**, on the front of the Inman Square Firehouse at 1384 Cambridge St. This piece of public art was painted by a young local artist named Ellary Eddy in 1976 and depicts then-members of Engine No. 5; it also includes images of Benjamin Franklin, who founded the country's first volunteer fire department, and George Washington, who stayed in Cambridge during the Siege of Boston.

Adjacent to the Massachusetts Institute of Technology, **Kendall Square** grew from the ashes of the post-industrial desolation of East Cambridge in the 1960s and 1970s to become a glittering testament to the economic revival that sparked Massachusetts in the 1980s. By day, Kendall bustles with tech students and programmers lunching in low-key eateries; at night, the business crowd goes home and the place becomes largely deserted. The exception to this is the Kendall Square Cinema (see p.197), which draws large crowds to see some of the best arthouse and second-run movies in the area.

The Massachusetts Institute of Technology

Eastern Cambridge is mostly taken over by the **Massachusetts Institute of Technology** (**MIT**), which covers more than 150 acres alongside the Charles River, and provides an intellectual counterweight to the otherwise working-class character of the area. Originally established in Back Bay in 1861, MIT moved to this more auspicious campus across the river in 1916 and has since risen to international prominence as a major center for theoretical and practical research in the sciences. Both NASA and the Department of Defense pour funds into MIT in exchange for research and development assistance from the university's best minds.

The campus buildings and geography reflect the quirky, nerdy character of the institute, emphasizing function and peppering it with a peculiar notion of form. Everything is obsessively numbered and coded: you can, for example, go to 1-290 (the Pierce Laboratory) for a lecture in 1.050 (Engineering Mechanics 1), which gets you closer to a minor in Course 1 (Civil and Environmental Engineering).

The Rogers Building

Behind the massive pillars that guard the entrance of MIT's main building, the **Pierce Laboratory**, at 77 Massachusetts Ave, you'll find a labyrinth of corridors – known to Techies as the **Infinite Corridor** – through which students can traverse the entire east campus without ever going outside. Just inside Pierce's entrance you'll find the **MIT Information Center** (Mon–Fri 9am–5pm, campus tours at 10.45am & 2.45pm), while atop the nearby McLaurin Building is MIT's best-known architectural icon, a massive gilt hemisphere called the **Great Dome**.

The Ray and Maria Stata Center

Despite looking like a set of egg timers designed by Salvador Dalí, the **Ray and Maria Stata Center**, which houses the Computer, Information, and Intelligence Sciences departments, is the $200 million work of renowned

▲ The Ray and Maria Stata Center at MIT

architect Frank Gehry and was partly funded by Bill Gates of Microsoft. Opened in May 2004, self-guided tours of the public spaces on the first and third floors are possible Mon–Fri 9am–5pm. There are several entrances to the building, all of which lead to Student Street, bizarrely located *in* the building. An information desk is conspicuous by its location under a huge question mark hanging from the ceiling.

The Kresge Auditorium and MIT Chapel

MIT has drawn the attention of some of the major architects of the twentieth century, who have used the university's progressiveness as a testing ground for some of their more experimental works. Two of these are located in the courtyard across Massachusetts Avenue from the Rogers Building. The **Kresge Auditorium**, designed by Finnish architect Eero Saarinen, resembles a large tent, though its real claim to fame is that it puzzlingly rests on three, rather than four, corners; the architect allegedly designed it over breakfast by cutting into his grapefruit. In the same courtyard is the red-brick **MIT Chapel**, also the work of Saarinen, and shaped like a stocky cylinder with an abstract sculpture crafted from paper-thin metals serving as a rather unconventional spire; inside, a delicate metal screen scatters light patterns across the floor.

A couple of blocks back toward Kendall Square, the I.M. Pei-designed **Weisner Building** hosts the **List Visual Art Center** (Tues–Thurs, Sat & Sun noon–6pm; free), which displays contemporary artworks that utilize a wide range of media.

The MIT Museum

Of perhaps greater interest than the Art Center is the **MIT Museum**, near Central Square at 265 Massachusetts Ave (daily 10am–5pm; $7.50; ☎617/253-4444, ⓦweb.mit.edu/museum). The museum has a number of standout permanent displays, including "Holography: the Light Fantastic," a collection of seriously cool eye-trickery, as well as "Robots and Beyond," where those of the humanoid persuasion can interact with robotic displays such as *Kismet*, a "sociable robot" who utilizes an eye-opening range of emotional expression and physical gestures.

Northwest Cambridge and Somerville

Off any university-oriented or colonial heritage sightseeing circuit, **Northwest Cambridge** has more residential charms on offer. The area's financial center, **Porter Square**, is a mile north of Harvard Square along Massachusetts Avenue. The walk from Harvard will take you past some of Cambridge's most chic lounges and boutiques, while Porter Square itself is hard to miss – look for the 46-foot red kinetic sculpture *Gift of the Wind*, by Susumu Shingu; it's right outside the subway stop.

Davis Square

Beyond Porter Square, **Somerville**'s ongoing "discovery" by young residents is reflected in the area's central plaza, **Davis Square**, a former working-class stronghold, and now the beating heart of Northwest Cambridge. You're unlikely to make it this far out, however, unless you're angling to jump on the scenic **Minuteman Bike Trail**, which begins nearby, at the Alewife **T** stop, and continues through Arlington and Lexington to Bedford (☎617/542-BIKE, Ⓦwww.massbike.org), or heading to a performance at the stellar Somerville Theatre (55 Davis Square; ☎617/625-5700, Ⓦwww.somervilletheatreonline .com), which screens first and second-run films in a former 1914 vaudeville house. Still, if you've got the time to spare, the square itself is a fun place to kick around for an afternoon, and is easily accessible from the Davis Square **T** stop on the Red Line. Homey coffee shops, restaurants, and bookstores face the square's central plaza, which, on weekends, is typically occupied by folksy musicians and street performers.

Listings

Listings

Accommodation

D espite the opening of some new hotels and B&Bs over the last few years, Boston has a surprisingly limited range of reasonably priced **accommodation**. Though there are still bargains to be found, prices at many formerly moderate hotels have inched into the expense-account range: you're looking at spending upwards of $200 just to stay the night during **high season** – which, while not unanimously agreed upon, is often late summer and early fall.

Your best bet to save money is to make your booking Online: most hotels offer discounted rates on their websites, as do discount **booking agencies** like Orbitz (ⓦ www.orbitz.com) or Expedia (ⓦ www.expedia.com). If calling a hotel direct, be sure to inquire about special packages when reserving a room. Additional discounts of around ten percent can often be had with an AAA membership. Your other option, if you don't mind braving the sharp East Coast winter, is to come in the **off-season**, usually November through April, when many hotels not only have more vacancies but also offer weekend package discounts. At any other time of year, be sure to make reservations well in advance. September (start of the school year) and May through June (gradu-ation) are particularly busy months, due to the large student population here. October, when leaf-peeping season starts, is also expensive.

In response to the hotel crunch, some visitors turn to less-expensive **bed and breakfasts**, many of which are tucked into renovated brownstones in Back Bay and the South End; other good B&B choices can be found outside the city center, in Brookline and Cambridge. Short-term **furnished apartments**, spread throughout the city, are another option, though most have two-week minimums. There are also a handful of decent **hostels** if you're looking for truly budget accommodation.

Throughout this chapter we give a price for hotels, B&Bs, and hostels. It reflects the lowest listed price for a standard double room for most of the year – depending on availability and season, you may end up paying twice as much, or you might pay half the listed price by snagging a great deal online.

Finally, all accommodations are **keyed** to the relevant **chapter maps** in the "Guide" portion of this book.

Hotels

Boston and Cambridge combined have an underwhelming fifty or so **hotels** between them, a shortage that helps to explain their exorbitant prices.

Hotels in Boston range from the usual assortment of chains to some excellent independently run hotels, the highest concentration of which – including some of the best – are in **Back Bay**. Not surprisingly, most of the business hotels are located in or around the **Financial District**.

Modestly cheaper rates can be found at **Cambridge**'s hotels, though rates at these, too, go sky-high around college commencement and during the fall. A handful of gay-friendly hotels and B&Bs, mostly in the **South End**, are listed in the "Gay Boston" chapter on p.199.

Downtown

Hilton Boston Financial District 89 Broad St ☎617/556-0006, ⊛www.hilton.com; **Downtown Crossing T**. Housed within a luxuriously renovated 1928 skyscraper, this *Hilton* splurges with high ceilings, large rooms, and Art Deco details. There's also an attractive reading room and Wi-Fi throughout. $270.

Hyatt Regency 1 Avenue de Lafayette ☎617/912-1234, ⊛www.hyatt.com; **Downtown Crossing T**. The *Hyatt* is just one of the reasons for Downtown Crossing's regeneration over the past years. The plush hotel is beautifully furnished with antiques, and there's a fantastic array of services. Wi-Fi access available. $350.

Langham Hotel 250 Franklin St ☎617/451-1900, ⊛www.langhamhotels.com; **State T**. This stern granite building in the heart of the Financial District is the former Federal Reserve Bank of Boston and was, until 2004, the home of Boston's *Le Meridien*. The hotel's spacious rooms are decorated in a contemporary French style, and each one features, cable TV, Internet access, and Italian marble bathrooms. $245.

Marriott's Custom House 3 McKinley Sq ☎617/310-6300 or 1-888/236-2427, ⊛www.marriott.com; **Aquarium T**. All the rooms at this Downtown landmark-turned-hotel are high-end, one-bedroom suites with spectacular Boston Harbor and city views; there's also a great gym on the top floor. $330.

Millennium Bostonian Hotel Faneuil Hall Marketplace ☎617/523-3600 or 1-866/866-8086, ⊛www.millenniumhotels.com; **State T**. Right in the heart of Downtown, the *Millennium Bostonian* has splendid quarters, some with fireplaces and – unusual for Boston – balconies. The rooms and lobby are festooned with portraits of famous colonial-era figures; common areas have Wi-Fi access. $350.

Milner 78 Charles St South ☎617/426-6220 or 1-877/MILNERS, ⊛www.milner-hotels.com; **Boylston T**. An uninspiring but affordable

hotel, the *Milner* is convenient to the Theater District, Bay Village, and the Public Garden. All room rates include a continental breakfast, served in a European-style nook in the lobby. $160.

Nine Zero Hotel 90 Tremont St ☎617/772-5800 or 1-800/434-7347, ⊛www.ninezerohotel.com; **Park St T**. Executive-class boutique hotel with 190 polished quarters equipped with Wi-Fi, CD players, plush linens, and a complimentary morning paper. $260.

Omni Parker House 60 School St ☎617/227-8600 or 1-800/843-6664, ⊛www.omniparkerhouse .com; **Park T**. Though the present building only dates from 1927, the *Omni Parker House* is the oldest continuously operating hotel in the US. The lobby, decorated in dark oak with carved gilt moldings, recalls the splendor of the original nineteenth-century building. The rooms, which have free Internet access, are a bit small, however. $390.

Tremont House 275 Tremont St ☎617/426-1400, ⊛www.marriott.com; **NE Medical Center T**. The opulent lobby of this *Marriott*-managed 1925 hotel, the former national headquarters of the Elks Lodge, somewhat compensates for its rather small rooms; and if you want to be in the thick of the Theater District you can't do better. $370.

XV Beacon 15 Beacon St ☎617/670-1500 or 1-877/XVBEACON, ⊛www.xvbeacon.com; **Park St T**. Ultra-decadent boutique hotel across from the Boston Athenaeum, with 61 spectacular rooms equipped with marble bathrooms, Kiehl toiletries, CD player, beautiful upholstery, and working gas fireplaces; some rooms even have four-poster beds. All rates include access to your own chauffeured Mercedes for the length of your stay. $575.

Waterfront and Seaport District

Boston Harbor Hotel 70 Rowes Wharf ☎617/439-7000 or 1-800/752-7077, ⊛www .bhh.com; **Aquarium T**. Opulent accommodation in an atmosphere of studied corporate elegance. There's a health club, pool,

▲ Boston Harbor Hotel

gracious concierge staff, and rooms with harbor and city views; the former are substantially pricier. $450.

Boston Marriott Long Wharf 296 State St ☎617/227-0800 or 1-888/236-2427, ⓦwww .marriott.com; Aquarium **T**. All the rooms here boast harbor views, but the stunning vaulted lobby is what really makes this *Marriott* stand out. The rooms themselves are standard business-class affairs, with the expected Internet access, in-room movies, and generic furnishings. $350.

🏃 **Harborside Inn** 185 State St ☎617/723-7500, ⓦwww.harborsideinnboston.com; State **T**. This small hotel is housed in a renovated 1890s mercantile warehouse across from Quincy Market. The (relatively) reasonably priced rooms – with exposed brick, hardwood floors, and cherry furniture – are a welcome surprise for this part of town. $175.

Seaport Hotel 1 Seaport Lane ☎617/385-4000, ⓦwww.seaportboston.com; South Station **T**. A luxurious Boston newbie out on the waterfront, this hotel offers access to the Institute of Contemporary Art and convention center, as well as business travel standards like cozy linens and Internet access. $380.

Charlestown

Constitution Inn YMCA 150 Second Ave ☎617/241-8400 or 1-800/495-9622, ⓦwww .constitutioninn.com; North Station **T**. Despite its billing as a YMCA, this inn, which is easily connected to Downtown by ferry, has 150 private rooms equipped with cable TV, a/c, and private baths; there's also an on-site weight room, sauna, and pool. Though predominantly servicing military personnel, civilians are more than welcome, though they pay significantly more. $150.

Residence Inn Boston Harbor 34 n – 44 Charles River Ave ☎617/242-9000, ⓦwww.marriott .com; Community College **T**. The Marriott's *Residence Inn* is an all-suiter close to some of the main sights along the Freedom Trail. The amazing views of Boston's skyline over the river more than make up for the slightly sterile atmosphere. Wi-Fi available. $300.

Beacon Hill and the West End

🏃 **Beacon Hill Hotel** 25 Charles St ☎617/723-7575 or 1-888/959-BHHB, ⓦwww.beaconhillhotel.com; Charles **T**. A luxurious boutique hotel occupying two mid-1800s brownstones. Its thirteen sleek chambers are decked out with flat-screen televisions and balconies. Internet access is available in all rooms. $265.

🏃 **Bulfinch Hotel** 107 Merrimac St ☎617/624-0202, ⓦwww.bulfinchhotel .com; North Station **T**. A beautiful and fresh addition to the West End, this sleek newbie housed in a vintage triangular – or flatiron-shaped – building has pretty wool-toned rooms brightened with contemporary paintings, Internet access, and an exercise room; the *Bulfinch* also hosts the fabulous *Flat Iron Tapas Bar & Lounge* (see p.172). $180.

Holiday Inn Select – Government Center 5 Blossom St ☎617/742-7630 or 1-800/HOLIDAY, ⓦwww.holidayinn.com; Bowdoin **T**. Somewhat misleadingly named – it's located in the West End and more convenient to Beacon Hill than Government Center – this Holiday Inn-standard property has all the modern accoutrements, including a weight room and pool. $250.

🏃 **The John Jeffries House** 14 David G Mugar Way ☎617/367-1866, ⓦwww .johnjeffrieshouse.com; Charles **T**. A little gem with some of the best prices in town and clean and tasteful rooms to match. A midscale hotel at the foot of Beacon Hill, it features a cozy lounge and rooms done up in Victorian style, with cable TV, Wi-Fi, and a/c; single-occupancy studios include kitchenettes. Singles from $95.

Liberty Hotel 25 Charles St ☎617/224-4000, ⓦwww.libertyhotel.com; Charles **T**. A welcome if expensive newcomer to Boston's accommodation scene, the *Liberty Hotel* has taken over the labyrinthine digs of an 1851 prison in Beacon Hill and fashioned it with lush details and modern accoutrements such as same-day laundry service, a fitness and business center, and overnight shoeshines. $375.

Onyx Hotel 155 Portland St ☎617/557-0005, ⓦwww.onyxhotel.com; North Station **T**. The stark, glass-paneled front of this small luxury hotel belies an opulent interior. The *Ruby Room* bar is great for a nightcap, but beware the hotel's "Britney Spears" room – designed by the singer's mom, it looks as you would have expected the singer's childhood room to look – complete with pink bible and fairy statuettes. $360.

Back Bay

Back Bay Hilton 40 Dalton St ☎617/236-1100 or 1-800/874-0663, ⓦwww.hilton.com; Hynes **T**. Though this chain hotel is fairly charmless, it does have good weekend packages, a fitness room and pool, as well as a guaranteed good American-style breakfast at the hotel's informal restaurant, *Boodle's*. It's actually a bit away from Back Bay, closer to the bohemian area of the Berklee College of Music than the shops of Newbury Street – a plus in some folks' eyes. $300.

Boston Park Plaza Hotel & Towers 64 Arlington St ☎617/426-2000 or 1-800/225-2008, ⓦwww .bostonparkplaza.com; Arlington **T**. This hotel's old-school elegance and hospitality – plus its central location – make it stand out; the high-ceilinged rooms, complete with Internet access, are comfortable, too. The *Park Plaza* is known for its spacious digs; it was dubbed a "city within a city" when it first opened in 1927 and now houses a beauty salon, airline offices, and three restaurants. $250.

🏃 **Charlesmark Hotel** 655 Boylston St ☎617/247-1212, ⓦwww.thecharlesmark .com; Copley **T**. A great little European-style hotel boasting some of the best prices around. The 33 cozy, smallish rooms feature beechwood furnishings and modern accoutrements, such as Wi-Fi and CD/DVD players, plus there are speakers in your bathroom so you can sing as you shower. $145.

The College Club 44 Commonwealth Ave ☎617/536-9510, ⓦwww.thecollegeclubofboston .com; Arlington **T**. The College Club was founded in 1890 by 19 women wanting to create a space of "sociability and companionship" for college-educated women. Now the oldest woman's club in the country, the *Club* is home to eleven well-priced guestrooms (available to both male and female visitors), many with shared baths, all

decked out with antique furnishings. The smart location by the Public Garden and Newbury Street goes a long way. In summer, single rooms with shared baths start at $105; doubles with private baths $180.

The Colonnade 120 Huntington Ave ☎617/424-7000 or 1-800/962-3030, ⓦwww.colonnadehotel .com; Prudential **T**. With its beige poured-concrete shell, the *Colonnade* looks weirdly like a parking garage. Still, there are spacious rooms (if at a price) and, in summer, a rooftop pool – the only one in Boston. Its currently undergoing an $18 million renovation, aimed for completion in 2008. $350.

Copley Square Hotel 47 Huntington Ave ☎617/536-9000 or 1-800/225-7062, ⓦwww .copleysquarehotel.com; Copley **T**. Situated on the eastern fringe of Copley Square, this family-run, low-key hotel is popular with a predominantly European crowd. The rooms won't win any style awards, given their dowdy linens, but they're spacious enough and equipped with modem hook-ups, cable TV, and coffeemakers. $180.

Eliot 370 Commonwealth Ave ☎617/267-1607 or 1-800/442-5468, ⓦwww.eliothotel.com; Hynes **T**. West Back Bay's answer to the *Ritz-Carlton*, this plush, nine-floor suite hotel has sizable rooms with kitchenettes, luxurious Italian marble baths, huge beds with Egyptian cotton sheets, and Wi-Fi access. $250.

Fairmont Copley Plaza 138 St James Ave ☎617/267-5300 or 1-800/795-3906, ⓦwww .fairmont.com; Copley **T**. Built in 1912, the *Fairmont* has long boasted Boston's most elegant lobby, with its glittering chandeliers, mirrored walls, and *trompe l'oeil* sky. Most rooms are decorated in a French Neoclassical style and have Internet access (Wi-Fi is available in the lounge). Even if you don't stay here, be sure to have a martini in the fabulous *Oak Bar* (see p.184), with its high-coffered ceilings and mahogany chairs. $450.

Four Seasons 200 Boylston St ☎617/338-4400 or 1-800/332-3442, ⓦwww.fourseasons.com; Arlington **T**. The tops in city accommodation, with 288 large rooms. The penthouse-level health spa has an indoor pool that seems to float over the Public Garden, and the superlative *Aujourd'hui* restaurant (see p.173) is housed here, too. $450.

Hotel 140 140 Clarendon St ☎617/585-5600, ⓦwww.hotel140.com; Back Bay **T**. Completely renovated in 2005, this 54-room boutique hotel offers accommodations that range from budget to "superior," as well as some twin bed options – a welcome respite from many Back Bay prices. $170.

Jurys Boston Hotel 350 Stuart St ☎617/226-7200, ⊛www.jurysdoyle.com; Copley Square **T**. Set in a 1920s building that used to be Boston Police headquarters, the 220 smallish rooms in this lavishly furnished hotel have huge beds, marble bathrooms, multi-head showers, and heated towel racks. The function rooms are named after the celebrated Irish writers Shaw, Yeats, Beckett, Joyce, and Wilde; displays in the lobby show old police memorabilia. $425.

The Lenox 710 Boylston St ☎617/536-5300 or 1-800/225-7676, ⊛www.lenoxhotel.com; Copley **T**. Billed as Boston's version of the New York's *Waldorf-Astoria* when its doors first opened in 1900, the *Lenox* – after a recent renovation – is still one of the most upscale hotels in the city, with 212 rooms featuring high ceilings, walk-in closets, and, in some, working fireplaces. $310.

Marriott at Copley Place Copley Place ☎617/236-5800 or 1-800/228-9290; ⊛www.marriott.com; Copley **T**. There's not a whole lot of character here but it's modern, clean, and well-located, with an indoor pool. Ask about lower weekend rates that include full breakfast. $350.

Sheraton Boston Hotel 39 Dalton St ☎617/236-2000 or 1-800/325-3535; ⊛www.starwoodhotels.com; Hynes **T**. After a major renovation, the Sheraton is looking less like a chain and more like a Back Bay boutique. Featuring sleigh beds with pillow-top mattresses and an expanded in-room work area, the *Sheraton* mostly plays host to convention-goers – the Hynes Convention Center and Prudential Center are both connected to the hotel. $330.

🏃 **Taj Boston** 15 Arlington St ☎617/536-5700, ⊛www.tajhotels.com; Arlington **T**. Replacing (albeit lovingly) Boston's historic Ritz-Carlton, *Taj Boston* is the ultimate in luxurious, old-school Boston accommodation, with wood-burning fireplace suites, gilded antique furniture, and a not-to-be-beat location across from the Public Garden. $345.

Westin Copley Place ☎617/262-9600 or 1-800/228-3000, ⊛www.westin.com; Copley **T**. Rooms are modern and spacious at this well-located hotel. Always hopping with convention-goers (it's connected to the convention center), the *Westin* offers a fitness center with pool and "unwinding

activities" from 5–7pm, such as making your own chocolate-dipped strawberries. Be sure to request a room facing the Charles River. $310.

Kenmore Square and the Fenway

Hotel Buckminster 645 Beacon St ☎617/236-7050 or 1-800/727-2825, ⊛www.bostonhotelbuckminster.com; Kenmore **T**. Though renovated not so long ago, the 1905 *Buckminster*, with its antique furnishings, retains the feel of an old Boston hotel. Its Kenmore Square location also puts it within easy walking distance of Fenway Park and Boston University. Good rates, too. $170.

Gryphon House 9 Bay State Rd ☎617/375-9003 or 1-877/375-9003, ⊛www.innboston.com; Kenmore **T**. This hotel-cum-B&B around the corner from Fenway has eight wonderfully appointed suites equipped with working gas fireplaces, cable TV, CD player, connection, continental breakfast, and free parking (a big plus in Boston). You won't want to leave your room. $150.

🏃 **Hotel Commonwealth** 500 Commonwealth Ave ☎617/933-5000, ⊛www.hotelcommonwealth.com; Kenmore **T**. Old-world charm mixed with modern decor makes this a welcome addition to Boston's luxury hotel scene, with nice touches like choice linens and L'Occitaine products, as well as the Eastern Standard (see pp.176 & 185) and the fabulous Foundation Lounge (see p.185). $400.

The South End

Chandler Inn 26 Chandler St ☎617/482-3450 or 1-800/842-3450, ⊛www.chandlerinn.com; Back Bay **T**. Comfortable, 55-room, European-style hotel above the popular *Fritz* bar (see p.200, "Gay Boston"); perks like satellite TV, in-room wireless Internet, and continental breakfast are included in the rates. $175.

Cambridge

Cambridge Marriott 2 Cambridge Center ☎617/494-6600 or 1-800/228-9290, ⊛www.marriott.com; Kendall **T**. Stately, well-appointed rooms with a minimum of pretension. Many have views of the river, while the rest look out onto industrial Kendall Square. Some weekend packages include a sumptuous brunch. $210.

Charles Hotel 1 Bennett St ☎617/864-1200 or 1-800/882-1818, ⓦwww.charleshotel.com; Harvard **T**. Clean, bright rooms, some overlooking the Charles, that come with an array of amenities: cable TV, Shaker furniture, and access to the adjacent WellBridge Health Spa. There's also an excellent jazz club, *Regattabar*, iconic restaurant, *Henrietta's Table*, and a sultry bar, *Noir*, on the premises – see p.178 and p.187 for reviews. $200.

Harvard Square Hotel 110 Mt Auburn St ☎617/864-5200 or 1-800/222-8733, ⓦwww.harvardsquarehotel.com; Harvard **T**. The rooms here are are pretty standard – clean, plain, and on the small side – although there is Wi-Fi in all the rooms, and the Harvard Square location is just right. $200.

Hotel Marlowe 25 Edwin H Land Blvd ☎1-800/825-7140, ⓦwww.hotelmarlowe.com; Kendall Square **T**. The funky décor at this hotel is cozy and plush, with faux-leopard print rugs and bright, boutiquey designs in the rooms. Pet friendly (they'll even order a birthday cake for your pup), and there is Internet access available. $250.

Hotel @ MIT 20 Sidney St ☎617/577-0200 or 1-800/524-2538, ⓦwww.hotelatmit.com; Kendall Square **T**. Contemporary hotel anchoring an office tower near MIT, with a lobby festooned with AI robots created by the university's tech-savvy students. The modern rooms have nice touches like louvered window shades and muted color schemes, and come with Internet access, both wired and Wi-Fi. $190.

Hyatt Regency Cambridge 575 Memorial Drive ☎617/492-1234 or 1-800/233-1234, ⓦwww.cambridge.hyatt.com; Kendall **T**. This brick ziggurat-like monolith, with luxurious rooms, pool, health club, and a patio with a gazebo, has a picturesque location on the Charles, but it's a hike from Cambridge's major points of interest. $275.

Inn at Harvard 1201 Massachusetts Ave ☎617/491-2222 or 1-800/222-8733, ⓦwww.theinnatharvard.com; Harvard **T**. Harvard University owns this red-brick, European-influenced hotel, set directly on its campus. Its four-story atrium was inspired by a Venetian piazza, and its rooms, while small, have huge writing desks and look out onto Harvard Square. A wide range of rates, from $125 to $475.

Kendall Hotel 350 Main St ☎617/577-1300, ⓦwww.kendallhotel.com; Kendall Square **T**. This hotel near MIT occupies a former 1894 fire station. Its 65 quaint rooms are country-chic with quilts and reproduction antiques; modern ameneties include Internet access and gym access. $250.

Radisson Cambridge 777 Memorial Drive ☎617/492-7777 or 1-800/333-3333, ⓦwww.radisson.com; Central or Harvard **T**. The business-class rooms at this chain hotel, located between Harvard and MIT, are nothing extraordinary, but many come with terrific views of the Charles and Back Bay; also, there's an indoor pool and gym. Wi-Fi access available. $180.

Royal Sonesta Cambridge Parkway ☎617/491-3600 or 1-800/SONESTA; ⓦwww.sonesta.com; Kendall Square **T**. Luxury quarters with good views of the Boston skyline. The fancy rooms have big, sparkling bathrooms, and the hotel's public spaces are festooned with striking (and some strikingly bad) art. $275.

Sheraton Commander 16 Garden St ☎617/547-4800 or 1-800/535-5007, ⓦwww.sheraton.com/commander; Harvard **T**. The hotel's name refers to George Washington, who, legend has it, took command of the Continental Army on nearby Cambridge Common. Rooms are luxurious and with charming frills such as terrycloth robes, nightlights, and even an umbrella service (should you have forgotten to pack yours). $245.

Bed and breakfasts

The **bed and breakfast** industry in Boston is thriving, for the most part because it is so difficult to find a hotel room here for under $200 a night – and some B&Bs offer just that, at least in the off-season. On the other hand, many B&Bs cash in on the popularity of their old-world charm, meaning their prices may hover near those of the swankier hotels. One plus is that breakfast is typically included with the price of your stay; while this can vary greatly (from self-serve milk and cereal to fresh omelettes with home-made scones), it's still a thrifty perk.

Some of the best B&Bs are outside the city, in either **Cambridge** or **Brookline**, though there are nice in-town options as well. You can make reservations directly with the places we've listed; there are also numerous B&B **agencies** that can do the booking for you and find you a room in an unlisted house (see box below).

Charlestown

Bed & Breakfast Afloat 28 Constitution Rd ☎617/241-9640, ⊛www.bedandbreakfastafloat .com; Community College **T**. Guests at this unusual B&B get to hole up on their own personal houseboat, sailboat, or yacht, right in Boston Harbor; the fancier vessels come with DVD players and deck-top hot tubs. All come with continental breakfast and access to the marina pool. From $135 to $375.

Beacon Hill

Beacon Hill Bed & Breakfast 27 Brimmer St ☎617/523-7376, ⊛www.lanierbb.com/inns /bb1384.html; Charles **T**. Only two spacious rooms with fireplaces are available in this well-situated 1869 brick townhouse. There are sumptuous full breakfasts; two-night minimum stay, three on holiday weekends. $200.
Charles Street Inn 94 Charles St ☎617/314-8900, ⊛www.charlesstreetinn.com; Charles **T**. An intimate nine-room inn with lavish rooms styled after the (presumed) tastes of various Boston luminaries; the Isabella Stewart Gardner room features a Rococo chandelier, while Oliver Wendell Holmes's chamber boasts a king-sized sleigh bed. All rooms come with working fireplaces –

it's one of Boston's best romantic getaways. $300.

Back Bay

463 Beacon Street Guest House 463 Beacon St ☎617/536-1302, ⊛www.463beacon.com; Hynes **T**. The good-sized rooms in this renovated brownstone, in the heart of Back Bay, are available by the night, week, and month, and come equipped with kitchen-ettes, cable TV, and various hotel amenities (though no maid service); some have a/c, hardwood floors, and ornamental fireplaces. Ask for the top-floor room. $80.
Copley House 239 W Newton St ☎617/236-8300 or 1-800/331-1318, ⊛www.copleyhouse .com; Prudential **T**. Furnished studios and one-bedroom apartments on an attractive edge of Back Bay, across from the Copley Plaza shopping center; rented by the week or month. $80.
Copley Inn 19 Garrison St ☎617/236-0300 or 1-800/232-0306, ⊛www.copleyinn.com; Prudential **T**. Comfortable rooms with full kitchens, friendly staff, and a great location make this an ideal place to stay in Back Bay. If you stay six days, the seventh night is free. $105.
Newbury Guest House 261 Newbury St ☎617/437-7666, ⊛www.newburyguesthouse

B&Bs and short-term rental agencies

Bed & Breakfast Agency of Boston 47 Commercial Wharf, Boston, MA 02110 ☎617/720-3540 or 1-800/248-9262, UK ☎0800/895 128, ⊛www.boston-bnbagency. com. Can book you a room in a brownstone, a waterfront loft, or even aboard a yacht.
Bed & Breakfast Associates Bay Colony Ltd PO Box 57166 Babson Park Branch, Boston, MA 02157 ☎781/647-4949 or 1-888/486-6018, ⊛www.bnbboston.com. Features some real finds in Back Bay, the South End, and Cambridge. Friendly and helpful staff.
Bed & Breakfast Reservations ☎617/964-1606 or 1-800/832-2632, ⊛www .bbreserve.com. Lists B&Bs in Greater Boston, North Shore, and Cape Cod.
Boston Reservations/Boston Bed & Breakfast, Inc ☎617/332-4199, ⊛www .bostonreservations.com. Competitive rates at B&Bs as well as at leading hotels. Reservation packs include maps and directions from Logan airport and to local sights. Will also book rooms in many other cities worldwide.
Greater Boston Hospitality ☎617/393-1548, ⊛www.bostonbedandbreakfast.com. Rentals in homes, inns, and condominiums. Good for booking out-of-town accommodation.

.com; **Copley T.** Big Victorian brownstone that still fills up whenever there's a big convention in town, so be sure to call ahead. The 32 rooms range from cramped chambers with overstuffed chairs to spacious bay-windowed quarters with hardwood floors and sleighbeds. Continental breakfast included, and all rooms have wireless Internet access. $150.

The North End

La Cappella Suites 290 North St ☎617/523-9020, ⓦwww.lacappellasuites.com; **Haymarket T.** Accommodation has opened up in the North End with this lovely new arrival – three cozy, modern rooms, two with private balconies, and all with Wi-Fi and a public seating area. Be prepared for a five floor walk-up. $130.

The South End

82 Chandler Street 82 Chandler St ☎617/482-0408 or 1-888/482-0408, ⓦwww.82chandler.com; **Back Bay T.** Basic rooms with minimal service in a restored, 1863 brownstone that sits on one of the most up-and-coming streets in the South End. Breakfast is served on the sunny top floor – where you'll also find the best room in the house, with a working fireplace and great views. Wi-Fi access is available throughout the premises. $125.
Clarendon Square Inn 198 West Brookline St ☎617/536-2229, ⓦwww.clarendonsquare.com; **Prudential T.** Gorgeous, well-loved bed and breakfast on a pretty South End side street with indulgent perks like heated bathroom tiles, limestone floors, and a 24hr roof-deck hot tub. Rooms range from $125 to $445.
Encore 116 West Newton St ☎617/247-3425 ⓦwww.encorebandb.com; **Back Bay T.** Another well-loved and very lovely B&B with contemporary decor, Wi-Fi, and a sitting area or deck in all three of their rooms. $150.

Kenmore Square and the Fenway

Oasis Guest House 22 Edgerly Rd ☎617/267-2262, ⓦwww.oasisgh.com; **Symphony T.** Sixteen comfortable, very affordable rooms, some with shared baths, in a renovated brownstone near Symphony Hall. $90.

Brookline

Beacon Inn 1087 and 1750 Beacon St ☎617/566-0088 or 1-888/575-0088, ⓦwww.beaconinn.com; **Hawes T.** Fireplaces in the lobbies and original woodwork contribute to the relaxed atmosphere in these two nineteenth-century brownstones, part of the same guest house. The rooms here would be well-suited to a country inn, with their patterned wallpaper, hardwood floors, and window sconces; some have working fireplaces. $100.
Beacon Townhouse Inns 1047 Beacon St ☎1-800/872-7211; **1023 Beacon St** ☎1-888-714-7779, ⓦwww.beacontownhouseinn.com; **Saint Mary T.** Two National Register historic brownstones within walking distance of the Fenway and Boston University; the rooms are perfectly ordinary, but come with private bath and cable TV; some have kitchenettes. $90.
Brookline Manor Inn 32 Centre St ☎617/232-0003 or 1-800/535-5325, ⓦwww.brooklinemanorinn.com; **Coolidge Corner T.** This small guest house, with private and shared baths, is located on a pleasant stretch off Beacon Street, just a short subway ride from Kenmore Square. The same management also runs the *Beacon Townhouse Inns*. $100.
Taylor House 50 Burroughs St, Jamaica Plain ☎617/888/228-2956, ⓦwww.taylorhouse.com; **Green Street T.** This delightful B&B, with two beautiful golden-retriever mascots, is a bit out of the way, but its three charming rooms, tucked away on the second floor of an 1855 Italianate house, feature queen-sized beds and Internet access. Complimentary continental breakfast, which includes fresh baked bread, is served daily. $165.

Cambridge

A Cambridge B&B 1657 Cambridge St ☎617/868-7082 or 1-877/994-0844, ⓦwww.cambridgebnb.com; **Harvard T.** This homely colonial revival house has three pleasant rooms outfitted with canopy beds, and a common room furnished with over stuffed chairs and plenty of lace. Shared bath. $75.
A Cambridge House 2218 Massachusetts Ave ☎617/491-6300 or 1-800/232-9989, ⓦwww.acambridgehouse.com; **Davis T.** Though a bit far out from any points of interest, this classy B&B with gorgeous rooms decked out in canopy beds and period pieces is worth the trek for its full breakfasts plus evening wine-and-cheese in the parlor. Rooms ranging from $110 to $230.

A Friendly Inn 1673 Cambridge St ☎617/547-7851, ⊛www.afinow.com; Harvard **T**.
A good deal, and just a few minutes' walk from Harvard Square. The rooms won't wow you, but the price is right and there are private baths, Wi-Fi, cable TV, and laundry. $100.

Harding House 288 Harvard St ☎617/876-2888, ⊛www.cambridginns .com; Harvard **T**. This cozy Victorian home has fourteen bright rooms with hardwood floors, throw rugs, TV, and a/c; includes a tasty breakfast. Shared or private bath. Free parking. $85.

Irving House 24 Irving St ☎617/547-4600, ⊛www.cambridginns.com; Harvard **T**. A quaint option near Harvard Square sharing the same management as the *Harding House*, with laundry and kitchen facilities; both shared and private baths are available. $75.

Mary Prentiss Inn 6 Prentiss St ☎617/661-2929, ⊛www.maryprentissinn.com; Harvard **T**. Eighteen clean, comfortable rooms in an impressively refurbished mid-nineteenth-century Greek Revival building. Full breakfast and snacks are served in the living room, or, weather permitting, on a pleasant outdoor deck. $150.

Prospect Place 112 Prospect St ☎617/864-7500 or 1-800/769-5303, ⊛www.prospectpl.com; Central **T**. This Italianate edifice holds a restored parlor, along with nineteenth-century period antiques – including two grand pianos – and floral-decor rooms. $110.

Hostels

There are a fairly limited number of **hostel** accommodations in Boston, and if you want to stay in one, you should definitely book ahead, especially in the summertime.

Beantown Hostel 234 Friend St ☎617/723-0800, ⊛www.hostelz.com; North Station **T**. The tone of the place is set by the *Hooters* sports bar a few doors down – not the classiest, cleanest, or happiest establishment, but the price is decent. Curfew 2.15am. $35/dorm bed.

Berkeley Residence YWCA 40 Berkeley St ☎617/375-2524, ⊛www.ywcaboston.org/ berkeley; Back Bay **T**. Clean and simple rooms next door to a police station. All rates include breakfast; dinner is an additional $8. Singles are $60, doubles $90, and triples $105, plus a $2 membership fee.

Greater Boston YMCA 316 Huntington Ave ☎617/927-8040, ⊛www.ymcaboston.org/central; Symphony **T**. Good budget rooms, and access to the Y's health facilities (including a pool and weight room). Singles are $46–66, but you can get a four-person room for $96. Co-ed facilities are available from late June until early September; the rest of the year it's men only. Ten days maximum stay.

HI–Boston 12 Hemenway St ☎617/536-1027, ⊛www.bostonhostel.org; Hynes **T**. Around the Back Bay–Fenway border, this hostel features standard dorm accommodation, but stands out for its fun management, Internet access, and pancake breakfasts on Sunday. $32–39.

HI–Fenway Summer Hostel 575 Commonwealth Ave ☎617/267-8599, ⊛www.bostonhostel.org; Kenmore **T**. A converted Boston University residence with private rooms and a handful of three-bed dorms with en-suite baths and a/c; there's also laundry and Internet access on-site. Open mid-May to late Aug. $36.

⓫

Eating

Historically, weather-beaten Yankees have tended to favor hearty meals made from native ingredients without a lot of fuss. Today, though, while outsiders may see menu items like broiled scrod, clam chowder, and Yankee pot roast as quintessentially New England, most Bostonians take pride in their city's contemporary, diverse palate (while retaining a certain nostalgia for the classic dishes as comfort food). The city's dining scene mirrors the increasing diversity of Boston's population itself, with innovative restaurants taking root everywhere – particularly in the South End, where French and fusion cuisine (in a fashionable setting, of course) are the catch of the day. Happily, too, there is no shortage of places to eat in Boston: the city is packed with bars and pubs that double as restaurants, cafés that serve affordable meals, plus plenty of higher-end, dinner-only options.

As for Boston's culinary landscape, there are ever-popular Italian restaurants – both traditional southern and fancier northern – that cluster in the North End, mainly on Hanover and Salem streets. The city's tiny Chinatown packs in not only a fair number of Chinese spots, but Japanese, Vietnamese, and Malaysian, too. Dim sum, where you choose selections from carts wheeled past your table, is especially big for Sunday brunch. On the other end of the spectrum, Boston's trendiest restaurants, many serving voguish New American fusion cuisine, tend to cluster in Back Bay and the South End. Meanwhile, across the Charles, Cambridge's eating options, mostly laid out along Massachusetts Avenue between Central, Harvard, and Porter squares, run the gamut from budget Indian and Mexican eateries to high-end American cuisine. Funky (if slightly out-of-the-way) Inman Square, just below Cambridge's border with Somerville, has a few good spots as well, many of them specializing in contemporary twists on New England classics.

To keep things manageable, we've broken down the listings within this chapter into two categories: **coffeehouses** and **restaurants**. While many coffeehouses offer filling food alongside their caffeinated wares, for the sake of simplicity we've grouped cafés that have extensive food menus under "restaurants."

Coffeehouses

Boston's status as a university town is reflected in its well-established **café** scene. The toniest spots are those that line Back Bay's **Newbury Street**, where you pay as much for the fancy environs as for the quality of the coffee. Value is much better in the **North End**, where Italian cafés serve excellent

Eating and drinking maps

We've keyed the eating and drinking establishments found in this chapter – as well as Chapter 12, "Drinking" – within the neighborhoods portion of the Guide. These maps can be found on the following pages:

beverages and desserts, plus provide the liveliest atmosphere in town. The most laid-back cafés are across the river in **Cambridge**, catering to the large student population.

Downtown

Flat Black Coffee Company 50 Broad St ⊤617/951-1440; State **T**. While the *Starbucks* invasion has done some real damage to Downtown's coffee culture, this Australian-inspired newcomer (in Australianese, a "flat white" is a particularly blended mix of steamed milk and espresso) offers up free-trade coffee to happy financial district patrons. Tasty pastries on offer as well as free Wi-Fi.

The North End

Caffé dello Sport 308 Hanover St ⊤617/523-5063; Haymarket **T**. A continuous stream of Rai Uno soccer matches is broadcast from the ceiling-mounted TV sets, making for an agreeable din amongst a very local crowd. Along with espresso, beer, wine, and sambuca are served.
Caffé Paradiso 255 Hanover St ⊤617/742-1768; Haymarket **T**. A simple but still great little neighborhood hangout with rugby and soccer matches on the TV. Drink options include espresso, wine, and cocktails, but come for the tasty pastries and wickedly good gelato.
Caffé Vittoria 296 Hanover St ⊤617/227-7606; Haymarket **T**. A Boston institution, the *Vittoria* is one of the city's most authentic Italian cafés. Its dark wood paneling, pressed tin ceilings, murals of the Old Country, and Sinatra-blaring Wurlitzer are all vintage North End. The café is only open at night, though a street-level addition next door is open by day for excellent cappuccinos.

Beacon Hill

Caffe Bella Vita 30 Charles St ⊤617/720-4505; Charles **T**. A casual café with fine cups of joe, tasty pastries, good gelato and free Wi-Fi. Also doubles as a great lunch or casual dinner spot, making this affable Italian spot a good place to linger over low-key salads and soups.

Back Bay

L'Aroma Café 85 Newbury St ⊤617/424-0951; Copley **T**. This amiable spot has a friendly staff, good paninis, and tasty cappuccinos for refueling while shopping at the boutiques and trendy shops on Newbury Street.
Tealuxe 108 Newbury St ⊤617/927-0400; Copley **T**. A sister shop to the Harvard Square original (see p.165), this charming little tea spot has endless varieties of hot, iced, and bubble teas to satisfy your pick-me-up needs.

The South End

Francesca's Espresso Bar 565 Tremont St ⊤617/482-9026; Back Bay **T**. A great place to check out the Tremont Street crowd passing by the plate-glass windows. The coffee shop gets packed in the evenings before the clubs open, with a largely gay clientele caffeinating itself for a night out.
Uptown Espresso 563 Columbus Ave ⊤617/236-8535; Ruggles **T**. Often voted "best of Boston," this lovely little spot in a South End brownstone features free Wi-Fi, tasty sandwiches and pastries, and of course, fabulous espresso drinks, best lingered over in their sunroom or serene outdoor patio.

Kenmore Square and the Fenway

Espresso Royale Caffe 736 Commonwealth Ave ☏617/277-8737; Kenmore **T**. Kenmore's a little thin on coffeeshops, but this funky little chain will do. Alongside traditional cups of java, original blends like a zesty orange cappuccino are served; the cheerful decor is enhanced by abstract wall paintings and cozy seats.

Brookline

KooKoo 7 Station St, Brookline ☏617/730-5525; Brookline Village **T**. Adorable neighborhood café with local pastries, tasty espresso drinks,

and sandwiches made with love. Grab an iced coffee and a falafel roll-up for exploring the whimsical shops of Station Street.

Jamaica Plain

Coffee Cantata 605 Center St, Jamaica Plain ☏617/522-2223; Green St **T**. Inviting local café with good coffee and delicious cupcakes, complemented by more substantial offerings like frittatas and asparagus ravioli.

Canto 6 3346 Washington St, Jamaica Plain ☏617/983-8688; Green St **T**. Tasty espresso drinks and life-changing pastries like the "bostok," a brioche with orange

Sweet ice cream dreams

There's a rumor floating around Boston that the town scoops up more **ice cream** than any other US city. While that statistic remains unconfirmed, there's no question that Bostonians love their cones, and they're blessed with a fabulous local set of ice-cream purveyors. The following seven rise above the rest and are Boston's best spots for getting your sweet on.

Brigham's Incorporated 109 High St ☏617/338-7315; State **T**. During the Great Depression, Brigham's let patrons pay for their ice cream with IOUs (some $25,000 in scoops was owed at one point). After 90 years of business (they're now a local chain) these guys are still serving up some of the best ice cream in town.

Christina's 1255 Cambridge St, Inman Square, Cambridge ☏617/492-7021; Central **T**. Inspiring well-deserved devotion amongst a legion of fans, Christina's is the kind of place people brace rush hour traffic over just to get their hands on a scoop of the Adzuki bean, burnt sugar, or honey lavender – procured from the owner's spice shop right next door.

Emack & Bolio's 255 State St ☏617/367-0220; Aquarium **T**. 290 Newbury St ☏617/247-8772; Copley **T**. Though this pint-sized parlor with a rocker past has grown into a national purveyor, Boston is still very much its home. Try a scoop each of Chocolate Moose and Vanilla Bean Speck in a chocolate-dipped waffle cone to get hooked. Also well known for frothy smoothies.

Gelateria 272 Hanover St ☏617/720-4243; Haymarket **T**. Lighter yet more flavorful than your regular ice cream, this sleek gelato joint has tempting flavors like hazelnut and fresh grapefruit.

Herrell's Ice Cream 15 Dunster St, Cambridge ☏617/497-2179; Harvard **T**. A collection of "Best of Boston" awards adorning the walls attest to the well-deserved popularity of this local ice-cream parlor. The chocolate pudding flavor is a particular delight, as is the lemon mousse milkshake. Famed for its signature "smoosh-ins" – crushed up candy or cookie bits that are mixed in scoop by scoop.

JP Licks 659 Center St, Jamaica Plain ☏617/524-6740; Heath St **T**; 352 Newbury St ☏617/236-1666; Hynes **T**. A beloved institution that's named for its original Jamaica Plain location, this funky, Jersey cow-themed café has home-made hot fudge sauce as well as tempting flavors like coconut almond chip.

Toscanini's 1310 Massachusetts Ave, Cambridge ☏617/354-9350; Harvard **T**; 899 Main St, Cambridge ☏617/491-5877; Central **T**. The New York Times has called it "the best ice cream in the world." Their inventive, ever-changing ice-cream list includes original flavors like Khulfee – a concoction of pistachios, almonds, and cardamom.

blossom cream, or the "sleepy hollow," a roll filled with egg and gruyere and baked to crispy perfection.

Cambridge

1369 Coffee House 757 Massachusetts Ave ☎617/576-4600; **Central T.** The *1369* mixes earnest thirty-something leftists with youthful hipsters in a relaxed environment. Your best bets are the standard array of caffeinated beverages and particularly exquisite desserts. There's a second and similarly snug location at 1369 Cambridge St (☎617/576-1369; #69 bus).

Algiers 40 Brattle St ☎617/492-1557; **Harvard T.** A fashionable North African café

▲ Algiers café

popular with the artsy set. The cozy nooks are usually populated by Harvard bookworms taking advantage of the restorative powers of the signature mint coffee. Free Wi-Fi.

Bookcellar Café 1971 Massachusetts Ave ☎617/864-9625; **Porter T.** A relaxed basement coffeehouse, with a few old sofas and some folding chairs scattered across the concrete floor. The java is good (and cheap) and you can peruse the wide range of magazines and used books while you sip.

Café Pamplona 12 Bow St ☎617/547-2763; **Harvard T.** Spanish-style basement café and patio that hasn't budged since 1959. Drop in for a *media noche* (ham, pork, and muenster on a mini French roll) and linger over a fluffy cappuccino.

Tealuxe 0 Brattle St ☎617/441-0077; **Harvard T.** The original location of a new local chain and still a great place to hunt down. The place is smaller than a teacup, but they manage to stock over a hundred varieties of tea including crème de la Earl Grey, reported to taste like birthday cake. Good bubble teas, too.

Somerville

Diesel Café 257 Elm St ☎617/629-8717; **Davis T.** They take their caffeine seriously at this trendy, garage-like coffee shop where patrons get revved on High Octane (double shots). Best is the photo booth where you can document your transformation from morning slob into caffeinated go-getter.

True Grounds 717 Broadway ☎617/591-9559; **Davis T.** Well-loved neighborhood café with free Wi-Fi, cozy quarters, seriously good sandwiches, and espresso drinks born out of love and knowledge. They also stock *Christina's* ice cream (see box opposite).

Restaurants

There is no shortage of places to **eat** in Boston, and the city has price ranges and cuisines to please every palate. Head to Boston's **North End** for tasty **Italian** food served amidst authentic and romantic environs. Or pop by the gay-savvy **South End**, the city's foodie district and Boston's best spot for contemporary New American fare. **Chinatown** has a number of tasty Asian-inspired eateries; it also stays open late and manages to get up early enough to serve dim sum brunch. **Kenmore Square** has a number of late-night hangouts to please its student and club-going population; the block where Boylston Street meets up with Mass Ave (technically in **Back Bay**) is also popular for after-hours pizza slices and the like. **Downtown** and the **Waterfront** are good for seafood, and the former has a lot of tasty, quick lunch options for feeding its workday regulars. Rounding out the Boston food tour, **Back Bay** has a great café culture that encourages outdoor seating and people watching. Across the river, laidback, liveable **Cambridge** and **Somerville** have an impressive collection of low-key Indian and Mexican eateries, as well as contemporary fusion fare that easily rivals Boston's.

Downtown

Defining "downtown" Boston can be a little nebulous (some say it's strictly the Financial District and Government Center, while others expand it to include everything from the Financial District down to the Theater District). To keep things simple, we've sub-divided the Downtown restaurants section into smaller sub-headings, so that no matter where you are, you're always near good food.

Boston Common and Downtown Crossing

Chacarero 26 Province St ☏617/367-1167, ⓦwww.chacarero.com; Downtown Crossing **T**. Fabulous and fresh, the *chacarero* is a Chilean sandwich built upon warm, soft bread and filled with avocado, chicken, green beans, muenster cheese, and hot sauce. It's the gold standard of Downtown lunch fare, with good veggie options as well. Closed weekends, cash only. There's a second option nearby at 426 Washington St (☏617/542-0392; both Downtown Crossing **T**).

Falafel King 48 Winter St ☏617/338-8355; Downtown Crossing **T**. You'll know you've found this hidden gem, nestled with an unappealing, semisketchy food court, when you come across a long line of gleeful regulars. Quick, cheap, and tasty, the *Falafel King* offers up traditional shawarma sandwiches ($5.50) made better with pickles, baba ghanoosh (eggplant) salad ($5.75), and, if the *King* deems you worthy, free samples of his well-loved falafel. Closed weekends, cash only.

Locke-Ober 3 Winter Place ☏617/542-1340; Park **T**. A Boston legend, this blue-blooded institution consists of traditional fancy fare like steak tartare and oysters on the half shell. Old-school and lovingly indulgent, patrons should dress to impress and prepare to spend a wad of cash. Reservations required.

No. 9 Park 9 Park St ☏617/742-9991, ⓦwww.no9park.com; Park St **T**. Well-loved Boston landmark with serene green walls and plates busy with southern French and Italian entrees ranging from Peking duck with smoked melon ($37) to butter poached lobster ($45). A seven-course tasting menu ($90; with wine, $150) allows you to try almost everything.

Sam La Grassa's 44 Province St ☏617/357-6861; Downtown Crossing **T**. Quite possibly Boston's best deli, complete with home-made pickles and tasty, bulging sandwiches such as the "fresh from the pot" corned beef ($8). Only open during weekday lunch hours (11am–3.30pm).

Scollay Square 21 Beacon St ☏617/742-4900, ⓦwww.scollaysquare.com; Park St T. *Scollay Square* is named after a section of downtown Boston that was famed for its burlesque acts in 1940s. While this *Square* isn't quite so racy (it's a white tablecloth kind of a place) there is nostalgic feel to its environs, with dark mahogany woods, inlaid mirrors, vintage photographs and classic American fare like upscale macaroni and cheese ($16) and seared sea scallops with chive oil ($24). Sip a mojito ($9) with the businessmen at the bar, or linger on the sunny outdoor patio.

Silvertone 69 Bromfield St ☏617/338-7887; Park Street **T**. Nostalgia runs high at this bustling basement bar and eatery with standout comfort foods like mashed potatoes and meatloaf and a super-cheesy mac and cheese. Rightly popular with the afterwork crowd, *Silvertone* also has cocktails, and good selection of beers on tap. Closed Sun.

Faneuil Hall and around

Durgin-Park 340 Faneuil Hall Marketplace ☏617/227-2038, ⓦwww.durgin-park.com; Government Center **T**. A Boston landmark in operation since 1827 (their slogan is "established before you were born"), *Durgin-Park* has a no-frills Yankee atmosphere and a waitstaff known for their surly charm. It's a good place to go for iconic New England foods like roast beef, baked beans, and warm Indian pudding. The downstairs bar is cheaper and livelier.

Quincy Market Faneuil Hall Marketplace ⊤617/338-2323; **Haymarket T**. The *doyenne* of Faneuil Hall marketplace, *Quincy Market* houses a better-than-normal food court on its first floor, packed with tempting stalls serving everything from seafood and Italian pastries to sushi and Greek food.

Union Oyster House 41 Union St ⊤617/227-2750, ⓦ www.unionoysterhouse.com; **Haymarket or State T**. The oldest continuously operating restaurant in America has two big claims to fame: King Louis-Philippe lived over the tavern during his youth, and, perhaps apocryphally, the toothpick was first used here. The food is decent, too: the seafood dishes are fresh and well-prepared, but the real draw here is the raw bar – six oysters will set you back around $12.

Wagamama Quincy Market in Faneuil Hall Marketplace ⊤617/742-9242, ⓦ www .wagamama.com; **Haymarket or State T**. A reliable option in a touristy setting, this British noodle joint has cheap and filling ramen fare like the *moyashi soba* in a vegetable soup with squash, snow peas, and bean sprouts ($10).

Walrus and the Oyster 200 Faneuil Hall Market-place ⊤617/742-1530; **Haymarket or State T**. For such a touristy spot (it's in Quincy Market) the Wellfleet oysters and fresh lobster here are a surprising treat.

The Financial District and around

Milk Street Café 50 Milk St ⊤617/542-3663; **State T**. Kosher and quick are the key words at this Downtown eatery, popular with business folks and vegetarians for the large designer sandwiches and salads. Their second location is set within lovely Post Office Square Park (⊤617/350-7275; **Downtown Crossing T**).

Mr Dooley's Boston Tavern 77 Broad St ⊤617/338-5656; **State T**. One of the many Irish pubs downtown, though with a quieter, more laid-back feel than the rest. Known for both its live music acts and Traditional Irish Breakfast Sundays (bacon, eggs, black pudding, and baked beans), the latter a particularly useful bit of know-how as finding anything open around here on Sun can be a challenge.

Pressed Sandwiches 2 Oliver St ⊤617/482-9700; **State T**. It's all in the name – savory, pressed sandwiches, served hot with tasty fillings like prosciutto and mozzerela or hummus and veggies. There's another Downtown option at 85 Bedford St (⊤617/357-5400; **Downtown Crossing T**).

Sultan's Kitchen 116 State St ⊤617/560-9009; **State T**. The best Turkish food in Boston, this lunch spot is favored by businessmen who line up for the agreeably spicy Ottoman classics. Take a table in the casual upstairs room and you'll feel miles away from nearby tourist-laden Quincy Market.

The Theater District

Finale Desserterie 1 Columbus Ave ⊤617/423-3184; **Boylston or Arlington T**. Devilishly good desserts are the mainstay at this extremely cushy sweet-tooth emporium; the top-notch wines and cordials that go with them are a treat, too. There's another location in Harvard Square, Cambridge at 30 Dunster St (⊤617/441-9797; **Harvard T**).

Jacob Wirth 31 Stuart St ⊤617/338-8586; **Boylston T**. A German-themed Boston landmark, around since 1868. Even if you don't like bratwurst washed down with a hearty lager, something is sure to please. There are sing-alongs on Fri.

Montien Thai 63 Stuart St ⊤617/338-5600; **Boylston T**. Situated on the cusp of the Theater District next to Chinatown, *Montien* is a pleasant merging of the two neighborhoods. Great for a quiet before-show meal, the menu is authentic Thai (think *Massaman* curry with coconut milk for $12) pleasing locals and visitors alike. There is also a Cambridge location at Inman Square, 1287 Cambridge St (⊤617/868-1240; **Central T**).

Pigalle 75 Charles St S ⊤617/423-4944; **Boylston T**. Breeze into one of *Pigalle's* chocolate-colored booths and settle yourself in for a romantic evening of indulgent French fare. For a perfect conclusion to a night at the theater, try their roasted beet rolls with mint and horseradish cream ($12) or go for the classic steak *frites* ($29).

🏃 **Teatro 117 Tremont St** ⊤617/778-6841; **Boylston T**. A gorgeous space with high arched ceilings and serene blue lighting, *Teatro* bustles with patrons enjoying pre- and post-show Italian fare, or simply indulgent antipasti ($8–24) and drinks. Be sure to order the calamari with lemon aioli ($14), considered to be some of the best squid in town; the rigatoni with bolognese sauce ($19) is another standout. Although noisy, it's still a great date spot.

Chinatown

Dongh Khanh 83 Harrison Ave ☎617/426-9410; Chinatown **T**. During the summer, people line up to get their hands on Dongh Khanh's bubble tea, made from fresh fruit and tasty fixings (the avocado is to die for). Their traditional Vietnamese dishes are pretty good as well.

Hei La Moon 88 Beach St ☎617/338-8813, **Chinatown T**. Just outside of Chinatown proper, *Hei La Moon* is a local favorite for dim sum brunch, with authentic dishes like shrimp *shumai* and barbecued pork buns offered alongside more adventurous fare like chicken feet. Expect a long wait on Sun, so try to arrive on the early side.

Peach Farm 4 Tyler Street ☎617/482-3332; **Chinatown T**. A Chinatown seafood standby with unfashionable digs but fresh seafood fare that you'll see swimming in tanks moments before it arrives on your plate. Go for the oysters in black bean sauce ($13) or the pea leaf sprouts with garlic ($8). Open late.

Pho Pasteur 682 Washington St and 8 Kneeland St ☎617/482-7467; **Chinatown T**. Both branches of this restaurant offer numerous variations on *pho*, a Vietnamese noodle dish. The Kneeland location serves only *pho*, while the one on Washington has other Vietnamese specialties as well. Regardless of what you order, it's all incredibly cheap.

Shabu-Zen 16 Tyler St ☎617/292-8828; **Chinatown T**. This fun and healthy spot lets you cook your own thinly sliced meats and veggies via a tableside, hot broth soup. Entrees include rice or noodles, a side of raw veggies, and dessert; the chicken platter is $11.

Taiwan Café 34 Oxford St ☎617/426-8181; **Chinatown T**. Local foodies swoon over this busy, authentic Taiwanese eatery which serves up mustard greens with edamame ($7.95), clams with spicy black bean sauce, and steamed pork buns ($5.95) done just right. Cash only and open until midnight.

The Leather District and around

Les Zygomates 129 South St ☎617/542-5108, ⊛www.leszygomates.com; **South Station T**. Busy French bistro with good wine selections (more than a hundred inter-national varieties) and gourmet *frites* a few blocks away from South Station. Try the lamb with beet coulis ($30) for dinner, and for dessert indulge in wine with the almond plum crumble. Good lunches, too. Live jazz nightly, beginning at 8pm.

O Ya 9 East St ☎617/654-9900; **South Station T**. The portions are petite and the sushi prices sky high, but patrons swoon over *O Ya*'s exquisite wild bluefin tuna *tataki* and roasted beet sashimi. One of Boston's greatest foodie hangouts, in a sleek, intimate space.

Miel 510 Atlantic Ave in the Intercontinental Hotel Boston ☎617/217-5151; **South Station T**. It's pricey (entrees $20–35), but there's something fantastic about being able to walk two blocks from a late-night South Station train and be rewarded with *Miel*'s luxurious French fare. Open 24hrs a day, the warm, lemony interior is comple-mented with outlandish *brasserie* inspired

cuisine such as tuna tartare with basil ice cream and sauteed scallops with arugula.

Sorriso Trattoria 107 South St ☎617/259-1560; **South Station T**. Exposed brick and lofty ceilings complement the tasty Italian fare at this hip trattoria convenient to South Station. Entrees ($17–25) are prepared with local ingredients when available, such as the arugula and Vermont goat cheese ravioli ($18); lunch is less expensive and just as good.

South Street Diner 178 Kneeland St ☎617/350-0028; **South Station T**. The stools at the counter have been spinning since 1947 when this cheap and tasty Boston landmark opened its doors for local factory workers. Now known as more of a late-night hangout with burgers, sandwiches, and the like, they're open 24 hours on the weekend (5pm–5am weekdays). There's also a jukebox and beers on tap.

Waterfront and the Seaport District

The Barking Crab 88 Sleeper St (at the Northern Avenue Bridge) ☎617/426-CRAB; **South Station T**. This endearing, touristy seafood shack aims to please with its homey atmosphere (it looks like a circus tent), friendly service, and unpretentious menu. Pretty much anything that can be pulled from the sea is served, including their standout "barking crab" cakes ($10) and fish and chips ($12); it's prime waterfront location attracts quite a crowd in the warmer months.

Flour Bakery + Café 12 Farnsworth St ☎617/338-4333; **South Station T**. An offshoot of the well-loved South End institution (see p.175), this low-key eatery is tucked inside a meandering brick warehouse space. Positively bursting with fantastic pastries, sandwiches, and salads, they're best known for their life-changing BLTs and house-made raspberry seltzer. Top it off with a homemade peanut butter Oreo cookie.

LTK Bar & Kitchen 225 Northern Avenue ☎617/330-7430; **South Station T**. This snazzy space on the waterfront is *Legal Seafoods*' contemporary little sister (LTK stands for "Legal Test Kitchen"), with table-side ipod docks, funky mood lighting, and orders taken via Wi-Fi. The food isn't mind-blowing (an international blend ranging from clam chowder to Kung Pao shrimp to Cubano sandwiches), but the buzzing after-work rendezvous vibe makes for good times.

Milk Bottle 300 Congress St ℡617/426-8855; South Station **T**. This Boston landmark in front of the Children's Museum dishes out bagels with cream cheese, salads, and coffee from its tiny kiosk window; patrons lounge contentedly at nearby picnic tables.

No Name Restaurant 15 1/2 Fish Pier ℡617/423-2705; South Station **T**. *No Name* earned its moniker from an inconspicuous start serving fisherman back in its early days (it's been around since 1917). The eatery has gotten considerably better known since then, with touristy lines on the weekend. Still, it's a Boston landmark, with frill-free fried fish on paper plates (boiled lobster $25, broiled scallops $14), accompanied by water views.

Salvatore's 225 Northern Ave ℡617/737-5454; South Station **T**. While it lacks the North End's charming environs, *Salvatore's* is a fabulous find for Italian fare and a welcome edition to the up-and-coming Seaport District. Known for their signature pizza, locals also rave about the chicken *valdostana* ($18) with a gorgonzola cream sauce.

🏃 **Sel de la Terre** 255 State St ℡617/720-1300; Aquarium **T**. *Sel de la Terre* honors its name (salt of the earth) with rustic Provençal fare like hearty bouillabaisse, lamb and eggplant, and perhaps the best french fries in Boston. Conveniently, you can acquire the fixings for a waterfront picnic here, too, by calling ahead to order ($11 per person), and picking it up on your way to the ferry.

The North End

Bacco 107 Salem St ℡617/624-0454, ℅www .baccoboston.com; Haymarket **T**. Restaurateur Patrick Buben's (also the co-owner of *Tapeo* in Back Bay) addition to the North End scene serves contemporary Italian fare in a laid-back atmosphere with modern furnishings. Try the lemon swordfish with the pasta of the day ($22).

Bricco 241 Hanover St ℡617/248-6800, ℅www.bricco.com; Haymarket **T**. With more of a contemporary vibe than much of the North End, and a swish wine bar to match, *Bricco* offers up sophisticated Italian fare like the gnocchi *ripieni* with *mozzarella di bufala* ($24) and brick oven pizza at the bar until 2am.

Carmen 33 North Sq ℡617/742-6421; Haymarket **T**. With its intimate size and pretty, exposed brick walls, *Carmen* is

perhaps the North End's most romantic spot. No dessert, but their signature small plates such as the roasted red beets with mint and ricotta ($6) or entrees like the *crespelle bolognese* ($20) make sure you don't leave hungry.

The Daily Catch 323 Hanover St ℡617/523-0567; Haymarket T; 261 Northern Ave ℡617/338-3093; South Station **T**. Ocean-fresh seafood – notably calamari and shellfish (Sicilian-style, with mega doses of garlic) – draws big lines to this tiny storefront restaurant. The Seaport District location offers a solid alternative to touristy Yankee scrod-and-chips platters.

🏃 **Galleria Umberto** 289 Hanover St ℡617/227-5709; Haymarket **T**. This is North End nirvana. There are fewer than a dozen items on the menu, but the lines are consistently to the door for Umberto's perfect pizza slices and savory *arancini* (fried and stuffed rice balls). Lunch only, and get there early as they always sell out.

Hot Tomatoes 261 North St ℡617/557-0033; Haymarket **T**. Created by the people that own *Carmen* (see above), this welcome North End newbie offers fantastic salad and sandwich fare like the "Green Monster" (fresh mozzarella, arugula, artichokes, grilled eggplant, yellow squash and pesto; $8.50).

Lulu's Bake Shoppe 227 Hanover St ℡617/720-2200; Haymarket **T**. A cutie-pie vintage cupcake shop with baked goods just like mom used to make (and retro pink interior to match). Head straight for the chocolate ones filled with peanut butter ($1.75).

Mare 135 Richmond St ℡617/723-6273; Haymarket **T**. *Mare* features first-rate seasonal seafood dishes amidst contemporary decor: flat-screen TVs mysteriously broadcast images of swimming fish, so you can ponder the life of your food before you eat it. Known for their their organic, pared-down menu, the salmon crudo with apple salad ($14) or the truffle crusted skate ($24) are both sure to please.

🏃 **Maria's Pastry** 46 Cross St ℡617/523-1196; Haymarket **T**. The place doesn't look like much, and there isn't the standard line out front, but Maria's truly has some of the best pastries in the North End – her chocolate cannoli with fresh ricotta filling is the mandatory first choice.

Mike's Pastry 300 Hanover St ☎617/742-3050; **Haymarket T**. Iconic and bustling with tourists yet still attended by locals, in many ways Mike's is the North End. Love it or hate it, lining up for one of their twine-wrapped boxes of heavenly pastries is a quintessential Boston experience.

Modern Pastry 257 Hanover St ☎617/523-3783; **Haymarket T**. You can't miss *Modern's* glorious vintage sign out front, nor would you want to – inside is fresh *torrone, cannoli* and little marzipan fruits. Family-owned for seventy years.

Monica's Tratorria 67 Prince St ☎617/720-5472; **Haymarket T**. Some of the most intensely flavored Italian fare around, prepared and served by Monica's three sons, one of whom drew the cartoons plastered over the walls. They do a brisk takeout (sandwiches and such) at lunch, though the best dishes are reserved for dinner. Monica herself has a gourmet shop around the corner, at 130 Salem St.

🏃 **Neptune Oyster 63 Salem St** ☎617/742-3474; **Haymarket T**. Snazzy little raw bar filled with devoted fans who swear by the fantastic shucked shellfish and best-in-town lobster rolls (served hot with butter or cold with mayo). Closed Mon and Tues.

Pizzeria Regina 11 1/2 Thatcher St ☎617/227-0765, ⊛www.polcaris.com; **Haymarket T**. This North End legend is a great spot for tasty, cheap pizza, served in a neighborhood feed station, where the wooden booths haven't budged since the 1940s. Don't be fooled by chains bearing the *Regina* label in other parts of town, this is the original, vastly superior location. Cash only.

Prezza 24 Fleet St ☎617/227-1577; **Haymarket T**. Named for the chef's grand-mother's hometown in Italy, this well-recommended, minimalist hotspot offers decadent dishes like sweet rock shrimp and risotto with shaved black truffles. *Prezza* is also known for its lovingly prepared wine list; there are over 500 bottles on the menu, with many wines available by the glass or half bottle. A two-course meal will cost around $50.

Taranta 210 Hanover St ☎617/720-0052, ⊛www.tarantarist.com; **Haymarket T**. *Taranta* is a mix of Italian and Peruvian flavors, which translates into pork chops with sugar cane and giant Peruvian corn ($30) and lobster ravioli with mascarpone cherry

tomato sauce ($25). Although it's on bustling Hanover St, *Taranta* remains a bit of secret among locals, but the folks who go once uaually wind up becoming regulars.

Charlestown

Figs 67 Main St ☎617/242-2229, ⊛toddenglish .com; **Community College T**. This noisy, popular offshoot of *Olives* has excellent thin-crust pizzas, topped with such savory items as figs and prosciutto or caramelized onions and arugula. Another location is at **42 Charles St in Beacon Hill** (t617/242-3447; **Charles T**).

Olives 10 City Square ☎617/242-1999, ⊛toddenglish.com; **Community College T**. *Olives* is consistently rated among Boston's best restaurants, and justifiably so. Chef Todd English turns out very expensive New Mediterranean food, such as pork Milanese with an apple, sausage, and cheddar calzonette, of unforgettable flavor in sizable portions. Around $150 per couple, with drinks. Closed Sun and Mon.

▲ Olives

Sorelle Bakery and Café 1 Monument Ave ☎617/242-2125. Enjoy phenomenal muffins, cookies, and orange and poppy scones ($1.50 each), plus pasta salads and other lunch fare on *Sorelle's* delightful hidden patio.

🏃 **Tangierino 83 Main St** ☎617/242-6009, ⊛www.tangierino.com; **Community College T**. Super-romantic Moroccan restaurant with authentic entrees like *ka'dra* lamb with figs and cheese-filled eggplant ($27). Next door, patrons puff contentedly on hookahs and ogle the belly dancers at their glorious *Casbah Lounge*.

Warren Tavern 2 Pleasant St ☎617/241-8142; **Community College T**. Paul Revere and George Washington were both regulars here, and the oldest standing structure in Charlestown is still decent for a drink and good tavern food; burgers run at about $8.

Beacon Hill and the West End

Beacon Hill Bistro 25 Charles St (in the Beacon Hill Hotel) ☎617/723-1133; Charles **T**. Sleek New American and French bistro with an upscale feel. Short ribs with prunes ($9) share counter space with cod with capers and tomatoes ($18.50); breakfast is trad-itional American.

Flat Iron Tapas Bar & Lounge *Bulfinch Hotel*, 119 Merrimac St ☎617/778-2900; North Station **T**. Amidst a pretty tiled interior, this sleek West End newcomer has fabulous hot and cold tapas like tuna tartar with coconut and lime ($8) and pork belly confit with apple ($10). Be sure to order the cheesecake lollipop tree for dessert ($14 for the table).

Harvard Gardens 316 Cambridge St ☎617/523-2727, ⊛www.harvardgardens.com; Charles **T**. Candle-lit romance is on the menu here, with Italian-inspired fare such as brandied lobster and asparagus macaroni ($16) and a happening singles' scene in the bar area. A great spot for brunch, too, where the pastrami hash is a self-described hangover cure ($10).

The Hungry I 71 Charles St ☎617/227-3524; Charles **T**. Pricey but very romantic, the food here is delectable and features a changing menu of classic American fare with creative twists. If you come on a night when the signature venison with *poivre noir* is served, prepare for food heaven.

🏃 **Lala Rokh** 97 Mount Vernon St ☎617/720-5511, ⊛www.lalarokh.com; Charles **T**. Have the waitstaff help you with the inscrutable menu at this exotically plush Azerbaijani restaurant, where you can fill up on the appetizers (such as roasted eggplant *kashk-e-bademjan*) and *torshi* (condiments) alone; locals rave about the *morgh pollo* (saffron chicken with cumin and rose petals). Main courses are $15–22.

Osteria Rustico 85 Canal St ☎617/742-8770; North Station **T**. An inexpensive hole-in-the-wall lunch spot that makes for a welcome break in an area that's mainly sports bars. *Osteria's* regulars rave about the gnocchi with fresh tomatoes and basil, the *tonno* (tuna) salad, and anything made with their addictive tomato cream sauce.

Panificio 144 Charles St ☎617/227-4340; Charles **T**. A fixture on Beacon Hill, this beloved café is a good place to grab a quick sandwich or salad; they also have a good brunch menu.

Paramount 44 Charles St ☎617/720-1152; Charles **T**. The Hill's neighborhood diner serves Belgian waffles and frittatas to the brunch regulars by day, and American standards like hamburgers and meat loaf by night. Expect long waits on weekends.

The Spotted Apron 326 Cambridge St ☎617/624-9700; Charles **T**. Extremely cute cupcake café, with offerings in red velvet ($3.35) or chocolate buttermilk ($2.85) all spotted with their signature polka dots. Salads and panini served, too. Free Wi-Fi.

Upper Crust 20 Charles St ☎617/723-9600; Charles **T**. A popular pizza joint with fresh and tasty offerings; there's generally a slice of the day (such as spinach with pesto and tomato; $3). Another location is at 225 Newbury St ☎617/262-0090; Copley **T**.

Back Bay

Aujourd'hui *Four Seasons*, 200 Boylston St ☎617/338-4400 or 1-800/332-3442; Arlington **T**. Near the top of everyone's list of Boston's best restaurants, this is a good place to splurge. Tuck into roasted Maine lobster (at market price) – accompanied by crabmeat wontons, pineapple compote, and fenugreek broth – served on antique china while enjoying the view of the Public Garden.

🏃 **Café Jaffa** 48 Gloucester St ☎617/536-0230; Hynes **T**. Boston's best falafel and other Middle Eastern staples are served in this cool, inviting space with polished wood floors.

Croma 269 Newbury St ☎617/247-3200, ⊛www.cromaboston; Hynes **T**. Much of *Croma's* menu is standard Italian fare. Avoid the salads, which are average, and stick with the stone-oven baked pizzas ($12) with a twist, such as the Peking Duck, Greek (olives, feta, red onion, and peppers) and Inglese (bacon, egg, and imported sausage). Good place to see and be seen.

Grill 23 161 Berkeley St ☎617/542-2225, ⊛www.grill23.com; Arlington **T**. This carnivore-fest is as clubby as Boston gets: the steaks are aged in-house, the fish are from exotic locales, and it's all accompanied by myriad wines. As with most big city steakhouses, be prepared to drop some serious dough.

India Samraat 51A Massachusetts Ave ☎617/247-0718, ⊛www.indiasamraat.com; Hynes **T**. Casual Indian outpost that has been serving up aromatic *rogan josh* (lamb cubes cooked with yogurt and almonds; $13) and other tasty mainstays to Back Bay patrons for close to two decades.

Kashmir 279 Newbury St ☎617/536-1695, Hynes T. A great Indian spot, the food and décor are equally inviting at *Kashmir,* Newbury Street's only Indian restaurant, and one of Boston's best. The lunch buffet is wonderful and a steal at only $10 (weekends $13).

Legal Seafoods *Park Plaza Hotel*, 27 Park Square ☎617/426-4444, ⊛www.legalseafoods .com; Arlington T; 255 State St ☎617/227-3115; Aquarium T; 100 Huntington Ave, Level Two, Copley Place ☎617/266-7775; Copley T; 800 Boylston St, Prudential Center ☎617/266-6800; Prudential T; 5 Cambridge Center ☎617/864-3400; Kendall T; 20 University Rd ☎617/491-9400; Harvard T. The *Starbucks* of the sea: it seems you can't turn a corner in Boston without encountering one of these ubiquitous eateries. As they claim, the seafood is fresh, and their clam chowder is loved by many, but the chain feel of the place may put a dark cloud over your meal.

The Other Side Cosmic Café 407 Newbury St ☎617/536-9477; Hynes T. This ultracasual hipster hangout on "the other side" of Newbury Street (it's across Mass Ave), cut off from the trendy part of Newbury Street, offers gourmet sandwiches, creative green salads, and fresh juices. They also have pitchers of quality beer. Open late.

Parish Café & Bar 361 Boylston St ☎617/247-4777, Arlington T. The ambience isn't much, but who cares when you're eating one of the best sandwiches in Boston? *Parish Café* formed when a number of local and celebrity chefs from Boston's best restaurants created a fancy rotating sandwich selection, such as the "Blue Ginger" (rare tuna with teriyaki glaze and avocado wasabi aioli; $13).

Skipjack's 199 Clarendon St ☎617/536-3500, ⊛www.skipjacks.com; Arlington T. Cool, South Beach-style decor and a bold menu distinguish this seafood spot from its rival, the always-busy *Legal Seafoods*. Look for the gingered sea bass ($25) or fried scrod with tartar sauce ($17). The Sunday jazz brunch is popular.

Sonsie 327 Newbury St ☎617/351-2500, ⊛www .sonsieboston.com; Hynes T. This Newbury Street staple is good for contemporary bistro fare, particularly swanky sandwiches,

pastries, and a killer chocolate bread pudding. In the summertime, aim for their Sunday brunch when the restaurant opens onto the street, jazz filters lazily through the air, and the filling food is fabulous.

Stephanie's on Newbury 190 Newbury St ☎617/236-0990, ⊛www.stephaniesonnewbury .com; Copley T. Though they pride themselves on their yellowfin tuna salad, what sets *Stephanie's* apart is the sidewalk dining in the prime people-watching territory of Newbury Street. Open until midnight.

Summer Shack 50 Dalton St ☎617/867-9995; Hynes T. Spacious seafood locale with kitschy maritime decor and lots of seating. The raw bar is tops (around $1.75 per clam), and the grilled fish (market price hovers around $20) is also quite good. Plus if you're feeling downmarket, you can always choose the corn dog ($5.50).

Tapeo 266 Newbury St ☎617/267-4799, ⊛www.tapeo.com; Copley T. An authentic Spanish addition to the Newbury Street dining scene, *Tapeo* has a cool vibe and great tapas such as boneless pheasant with mushrooms and sausage with fig sauce. Dishes start at $5.

Trident Booksellers & Café 338 Newbury St ☎617/267-8688; Copley T. Great little neighborhood café featuring a "perpetual breakfast" and tasty, vegetarian-friendly lunch and dinners. Set inside one of Boston's best independent bookstores, plates include a breakfast burrito with mushrooms and avocado ($8.25) and pan-seared salmon over sweet potato hash ($13). Pick up an obscure magazine and read it while gazing out onto Newbury Street. Open until midnight.

The South End

Addis Red Sea 544 Tremont St ☎617/426-8727; Back Bay T. A lovely, intimate Ethiopian eatery where you sit on carved wooden stools and eat *injera* (a warm, spongy bread) and *gomen wat* (collard greens with onions and garlic; $8) over a petite, communal table.

Aquitaine 569 Tremont St ☎617/424-8577; Back Bay T. This swanky French *brasserie* is the place to be and be seen; settle into a marvelous leather banquette, gape at the astonishing array of wines, and feast on the best steak *frites* ($26) and foie gras in town. They also have a more affordable brunch (the prix fixe option is $10).

Yankee cooking (and drinking)

Despite strides made by creative chefs and trendy eateries, traditional cuisine remains strong in Boston, built on the unfussiness of the Puritan ethic and the city's proximity to the Atlantic Ocean. Pot roast, seafood chowder, and cream pies are the foundations upon which Boston's cuisine is built. This distinctive brand of Yankee cooking – few other places think baked beans is an appropriate side dish for lobster, for example – can be as comforting as comfort food gets. Pair your meal with a local brew for entry into Yankee food paradise.

Lobster, chowder, and pisser clams

Boston's greatest culinary tradition is, without a doubt, **seafood**. In the eighteenth and nineteenth centuries, cod fishing was a cornerstone of the regional economy, and the city's connection to the sea continues to this day, showing up everywhere from menu items to fluffy stuffed animals. So strong is Boston's love for fish that a wooden "Sacred Cod" hangs in the Massachusetts State House as testament to the fishing industry's importance – when Harvard pranksters stole the emblem in the 1930s, the House refused to reconvene until it was recovered.

New England offers a stellar variety of maritime morsels. Perhaps the most iconic is **lobster**, served via a lobster roll that is prepared by stuffing sweet lobster meat, mayo, salt, and pepper into a buttered and toasted hot dog bun. Boiled lobster is easy enough to make (you just stick it in boiling water), but eating it is a labor of love, requiring nutcrackers, a nerdy-looking bib, and lots of napkins – it helps if you bring an experienced lobster aficionado with you for your first go-around. **Clams** are another staple, showing up in creamy chowders or on their own steamed (also called "steamers" or "pisser clams") and eaten straight from the shell or fried to a crispy perfection. Other shellfish specialties include **scallops**, baked with a butter-crumb topping, and **raw oysters**, splayed on the half-shell and served on a bed of ice with lemon juice, horseradish, and hot sauce.

Bob's Southern Bistro 604 Columbus Ave, Roxbury ☎617/536-6204; Mass Ave **T**. The best soul food in New England, with good chitlins, black-eyed peas, and collard greens; don't miss the "glori-fried chicken," it's the house specialty. There's also a wonderful, waist-expanding Sunday brunch buffet ($20), accompanied by live Jazz.

B&G Oysters 550 Tremont St ☎617/423-0550; Back Bay **T**. If you can manage to get a table at this tiny restaurant, you're in luck. The oysters (from $2.25 each) are simply the best Boston has to offer.

Butcher Shop 552 Tremont St ☎617/423-4840; Back Bay **T**. Not your grandpa's butcher shop, this sleek offspring of the Barbara Lynch empire (the woman behind *B&G Oysters* and *No. 9 Park*) offers small plates set with seasonal fruits and fancy meat cuts in addition to a swanky wine bar and some of the best hot dogs in town.

Charlie's Sandwich Shoppe 429 Columbus Ave ☎617/536-7669; Back Bay **T**. A little diner-style hole-in-the-wall offering some of the best breakfasts in the entire city. Standouts include the decadent banana and pecan griddlecakes and their justly famous turkey hash. Closed Sundays, cash only, and beware – no customer toilets.

Delux Café & Lounge 100 Chandler St ☎617/338-5258; Back Bay **T**. This retro hideaway has all the fixings of a great dive: fantastic, kitschy decor, constant cartoon viewing, and a Christmas-lit Elvis shrine. The menu is funky American fusion with old standbys like grilled cheese sandwiches and split pea soup. Cash only; good bar, too.

Flour Bakery + Café 1595 Washington St ☎617/267-4300; Back Bay **T**. Quite possibly the best café in town, this stylish South End spot has a drool-worthy array of brioche au chocolat, old-fashioned sour cream coffee

▲ Flour Bakery + Café

cake, gooey caramel nut tarts, rich cakes, savory sandwiches, home made breads, and thirst-quenching drinks. Choosing just one can be torture. There's also a new location in the Seaport District (see p.170).

Franklin Café 278 Shawmut Ave ☎617/350-0010; Back Bay **T**. New American cuisine at very reasonable prices, enjoyed by a hip, unpretentious clientele. There are only eleven tables, so be prepared to wait at the bar for at least two martinis.

Hamersley's Bistro 553 Tremont St ☎617/423-2700, Ⓦwww.hamersleysbistro.com; Back Bay **T**. *Hamersley's* is widely regarded as one of the best restaurants in Boston, and with good cause. Every night star chef (and owner) Gordon Hamersley dons a baseball cap and takes to the open kitchen, where he dishes out unusual – and unforgettable – French-American fare that changes with the season, such as pan-roasted lobster with leeks, roasted chestnuts, and black truffles ($38).

Metropolis Café 584 Tremont St ☎617/247-2931; Back Bay **T**. Presided over by star-shaped lanterns, this cozy spot (a former ice-cream parlor) has a loosely mediterranean menu by night (think roasted chestnut soup or sardines over garlicky escarole), but they're best known for their tasty Sunday brunch featuring the likes of mimosas with fresh strawberries and grilled blueberry muffins.

Mike's City Diner 1714 Washington St ☎617/267-9393; Back Bay **T**. Classic diner breakfasts and lunches – both greasy but good – in an out-of-the-way setting. Look out for the two eggs, two pancakes, choice of meat, home fries and toast called "The Emergency Room."

Pho Republique 1415 Washington St ☎617/262-0005, Ⓦwww.phorepublique.net; Back Bay **T**. Funky Vietnamese restaurant that attracts a young, stylish clientele who dine on hearty servings of pho ($15) and sip divine lychee martinis ($9) under ambience-diffusing seashell chandeliers.

Pops 560 Tremont St ☎617/695-1250; Back Bay **T**. Founded on the premise that "great food doesn't have to be exclusive or expensive" this South End newcomer has welcoming paisley rooms, striped seating, a serene outdoor porch, and sophisticated comfort foods such as a crispy shrimp po'boy ($10).

Rachel's Kitchen 12 Church St ☎617/423-3447; NE Medical Center **T**. A darling little brunch and lunch spot, *Rachel's* feel's like your favorite aunt's kitchen complete with fresh OJ, egg sandwiches, and cinnamon toast made better with brioche.

South End Buttery 314 Shawmut Ave ☎617/482-1015; **Back Bay T**. Impossible to resist, this adorable neighborhood café offers egg sandwiches on homemade biscuits, housemade soups and sandwiches, foamy cappuccinos, and terrific cupcakes named for the owner's dogs.

Stella 1525 Washington St ☎617/247-7747; **Back Bay T**. Fantastic Italian fare, such as mouthwatering parmesan *arancini* balls ($8) and homemade gnocchi ($19), served in a beautiful white interior. Nice outdoor seating in summer, and you can catch the equally good bar menu from 11–1:30am.

Toro 1704 Washington St ☎617/536-4300; **Back Bay T**. A hip and lively tapas bar brimming with sassafras mojitos ($10) and inventive tapas plates such as the octopus ceviche ($9) and salt cod fritters with lemon ($9), all thanks to the work of local celebrity chef Ken Oringer (the man behind *Clio* p.176 and *La Verdad Taqueria* p.176). Plates range from $5–12.

Tremont 647 647 Tremont St ☎617/266-4600; **Back Bay T**. Adventurous American cuisine by night (think sea bass in banana leaves), *Tremont 647* is best loved for their Sunday "pajama brunch" when locals and servers roll up in their Sunday morning finest.

Union Bar and Grille 1357 Washington St ☎617/423-0555; **NE Medical Center T**. This elegant eatery has tremendously good food and deep, black leather banquettes situated amongst exposed wooden beams. Many locals also go for the pomegranate or aloe martini ($10) at the bar (the latter was voted "best drink in Boston" by *Boston Magazine*). Dinners begin with a pitch-perfect skillet of cornbread, followed by way-better-than-mom's American food such as the pan roasted chicken with chorizo stuffing ($19). While the weekend brunch is very inexpensive, expect to spend $25 an entree for dinner.

Kenmore Square and the Fenway

Anna's Taqueria 1412 Beacon St ☎617/739-7300; **Coolidge Corner T**. Exceptional tacos, burritos, and quesadillas are the only things on the menu at this bright and cheap Mexican eatery. But they're so good that branches had to be opened around the

corner at 446 Harvard St (☎617/ 277-7111; **Coolidge Corner T**), and in Cambridge at 8222 Somerville Ave (☎617/661-8500; **Porter T**), to accommodate the legions of devotees.

Audubon Circle 838 Beacon St ☎617/421-1910; **Kenmore T**. The seemingly endless bar may grab your attention first, but it's the food that's worth staying for. Any of the appetizers are good bets, as are the grilled items – from burgers with chipotle ketchup to tuna steak with banana salsa and *fufu* (fried plantains mashed with coconut milk). Expect to pay around $8 per dish. There's a limited selection of homemade desserts, as well.

Brown Sugar 129 Jersey St ☎617/266-2928; **Kenmore T**. Charming neighborhood restaur-ant near the Museum of Fine Arts, serving some of Boston's best Thai food. Everything here is wonderfully fresh, and some things, like the basil chicken, are superbly spicy. There are ample vegetarian options, too.

Clio 370 Commonwealth Ave ☎617/536-7200; **Hynes T**. Local celebrity chef Ken Oringer shines with his stylish *Clio*, a French-inspired affair boasting a constantly rotating menu. Dishes include the likes of foie gras with bitter strawberry ($20) and sauteed diver scallops with butternut squash ($36), all served within warmly-lit surroundings.

Eastern Standard 528 Commonwealth Ave ☎617/532-9100; **Kenmore T**. A relaxed bistro serving up fairly fancy, pre-Red Sox game fare. The menu can be a bit hit or miss, so go for the spaghetti carbonara or veal schnitzel – or just to watch a game in their lofty, atmospheric bar.

El Pelon Taqueria 92 Peterborough St ☎617/262-9090; **Museum T**. Boston has plenty of trustworthy burrito spots, but *El Pelon's calabacitas* burrito (with butternut squash, zucchini, beans, rice, and jack cheese; $5) should be at the top of everyone's list. There's also a wonderful array of cheap tacos, platos, and tortas.

Great Bay Hotel Commonwealth, 500 Commonwealth Ave ☎617/532-5300 ⓦwww .gbayrestaurant.com; **Kenmore T**. This stellar seafood restaurant more than lives up to its five-year reputation. The pancetta-wrapped swordfish ($27) and wolffish with artichoke ragout ($26) are both sublime, and the clam chowder is considered the best of the best

Five superb seafood spots

If you're new to seafood, these fish-flavored eateries are sure to get you hooked.

B & G Oysters p.174.
Fancy South End foodie spot with some of the best (and priciest) fish fare in town.

The Barking Crab p.170.
The *Crab's* waterfront location and accompaniments (paper plates and greasy French fries) keeps this seafood shack buzzing throughout summer.

Daily Catch p.171.
Smaller than a barnacle, they still manage to pack people into this endearing Sicilian-inspired restaurant.

Neptune Oyster p.170.
Sleek and petite, it's where top Boston chefs (and everyday laymen) sate their lobster roll fix. A must-do.

Summer Shack p.174.
Kitschy and kid-friendly, this spacious spot is part clam shack, part raw bar heaven.

▲ Lobster roll, B & G Oysters

Sweet teeth

If no meal is truly complete without dessert, then Boston is a fine place to be, home to everything from kid-fueled candy shops to sit-down dessert spots. The North End rules for after-dinner delights as it's laced with incredible late-night **Italian pastry joints** offering espresso and sambuca alongside crisp cannoli and custard-filled éclairs. *Gelato* is scooped in the neighborhood as well, though the entire city is truly crazy about **ice cream**. Fine ice cream parlors are all over town, but *Christina's* (p.164), across the river in Cambridge, churns out the stuff of legend with flavors like ginger, adzuki bean, and green tea, freshly-crafted in their adjoining spice shop. That said, the city's most historic dessert, delicious **Boston cream pie** (really a custard-filled cake with chocolate glaze on top) has been served in the *Omni Parker House Hotel's* dining room since 1855. The dessert came full circle when Dunkin' Donuts reinvented it as a popular **doughnut** in the 1950s.

◄ Another satisfied customer

Bottoms up

While Boston isn't exactly a party town, you certainly won't have any trouble getting a quality beer here: the city is credited with jump-starting the country's **microbrew** industry (whereby beer is crafted and sold on a small scale). Local revolutionary **Sam Adams**, the self-proclaimed original microbrewery and a Boston original since 1985, was started when fifth-generation brewer Jim Koch deemed the nation ready for "better beer." His instincts were astute: the label is currently the largest of the regional beers and is well-known throughout the country. Better yet, the success of Sam Adams served as a catalyst for other small-time **New England brewers** like Magic Hat, Smuttynose, and Geary's, varieties of which can be found on tap in Boston bars.

If you can only sample a pint of one local brew, head to **Boston Beer Works**, the original of which opened up across from Fenway Park in 1992; its success prompted a West End location and a spacious new haunt in Salem, MA. The brewpub is praised for its extensive beer offerings – some 50 ales, lagers, porters, and stouts are brewed on-site annually – including the seasonal "Victory Red," a ruby-colored ale first brewed in Boston on October 27, 2004 "in anticipation of the greatest day in baseball history."

▲ A pint of Sam Adams

◀ Row of taps at Boston Beer Works

($11). Entrees are complemented by soft, colorful lighting and whimsical wood-panelling reminiscent of the hull of a ship.

La Verdad Taqueria 1 Lansdowne St ☏617/351-2580; Kenmore T. Situated alongside Fenway Park and the bumping clubs of Lansdowne Street, this Ken Oringer hotspot (see *Clio* above and *Toro* on p.175) is perfect for watching a Red Sox game or for just setting up your own big night out with a taco, a beer, and a shot ($5 special).

Petit Robert Bistro 468 Commonwealth Ave ☏617/375-0699; Kenmore T. This sweet and petite French bistro boasts a chalkboard menu that's been priced for the little guy; entrees, such as the chicken *coq au vin* with buttered noodles, run $14–20. There's also another location in the South End at 480 Columbus Ave (☏617/867-0600; Back Bay T).

Rod Dee 129 Jersey St ☏617/266-2928; Museum T. Good deals abound at this student-savvy Thai place, situated on a strip brimming with cheap eats (including *El Pelon*, see above). The *pad thai* standby is only $6.25, with more adventurous fare on hand as well.

Allston-Brighton and Brookline

Fugakyu 1280 Beacon St, Brookline ☏617/734-1268, ⓦwww.fugakyu.net; Coolidge Corner T. Fun and highly regarded sushi joint where your food arrives on mini-sushi boats via a miniature water canal.

Matt Murphy's 14 Harvard St, Brookline ☏617/232-0188, ⓦwww.mattmurphyspub.com; Brookline Village T. Authentic Irish comfort food such as potato and leek soup with warm brown bread and shepherd's pie with a crispy potato crust. The place is tiny, but the waits are well worth it.They also have occasional live music. No credit cards.

Party Favors 1356 Beacon St, Brookline ☏617/566-3330, ⓦwww.partyfavorsbrookline.com; Coolidge Corner T. Entering *Party Favors* immediately triggers a mouthwatering Pavlovian response – you can smell the cupcakes, but you can't see them. Hidden amongst the birthday balloons and party favors lies a secret treasure trove of Boston's best cupcakes.

Rangoli 129 Brighton Ave, Allston-Brighton ☏617/562-0200, ⓦwww.rangoliboston.com; Harvard Ave T. Inexpensive southern Indian fare, favoring spicy vegetarian selections. Be sure to try the *dosa*: sourdough pancakes

rolled like giant cannoli around a variety of savory fillings (from $6.50).

Washington Square Tavern 714 Washington St, Brookline ☏617/232-8989, ⓦwww.washingtonsquaretavern.com; Washington Square T. Cozy, off-the-beaten-path restaurant/bar with an eclectic menu that turns out inventive meals like pork tenderloin with fig glaze and sweet potatoes ($18). Just hanging out and absorbing the vibe at the bar is worthwhile, too.

Zaftig's 335 Harvard St, Brookline ☏617/975-0075; Coolidge Corner T. Justly famous Jewish deli with a lengthy menu and excellent reuben and pastrami sandwiches. *Zaftig's* is best-known for their Sunday brunch, and rightly so – the banana stuffed French toast in a bourbon vanilla batter ($9) is extraordinary.

South Boston

Amrheins 80 W Broadway, South Boston ☏617/268-6189; Broadway T. A Southie landmark and a favorite of local politicians for generations. The good-ole' American comfort food won't dazzle your palate, but it's reasonably priced and you get plenty of it.

Jamaica Plain

Bella Luna 405 Centre St, Jamaica Plain ☏617/524-6060; Green St T. Nouvelle pizza with a funky array of fresh toppings. You can order from their list of combinations or design your own; prices start from $5. Downstairs is the fabulous *Milky Way* bar, complete with karaoke nights and even a bowling alley.

Centre Street Café 669A Centre St, Jamaica Plain ☏617/524-9217; Green St T. At weekend brunch time, the line stretches down the street in front of this lovely, laidback, local institution. Lunch and dinner are less of a big deal and are just as good; expect inventive American fare such as the potatoes Santa Cruz with fresh veggies or sesame noodles with coconut-peanut sauce (both $10).

Ten Tables 597 Centre St, Jamaica Plain ☏617/524-8810; Green St T. This inviting little spot with exposed brick walls was designed to feel like an intimate dinner party – there really are only ten tables. The French and American fare (entrees $15–20), made from local ingredients, is sure to please. While the menu changes seasonally, locals rave about the four-course vegetarian tasting menu ($25, every night except Wed), an item that's here to stay.

Cambridge – Harvard Square and around

Bartley's Burger Cottage 1246 Massachusetts Ave ℡617/354-6559; **Harvard T.** A must-visit in Cambridge. Boston's best burgers can be washed down with raspberry lime rickeys while sitting amongst Americana-festooned environs as the waitstaff shouts your order out. Good veggie burgers, too. Cash only, and funky hours, but that's all part of the appeal.

Boca Grande 1728 Massachusetts Ave ℡617/354-7400; **Porter T.** Halfway between a restaurant and a taco stand, crowded *Boca* features delectable, if not quite authentic, Mexican fare at low prices (no entree is above $5). The overstuffed burritos are excellent meals in themselves. Two more branches are at 149 First St, Cambridge (℡617/354-5550; Kendall **T**) and 1294 Beacon St, Brookline (℡617/739-3900; Washington St **T**).

Charlie's Kitchen 10 Eliot St ℡617/492-9646; **Harvard T.** Marvelously atmospheric local hangout in the heart of Harvard Square, with red vinyl booths, sassy waitresses with hipster hairdos, and great cheeseburger specials. The upstairs bar is equally cool, particularly during Tuesday night karaoke.

Chez Henri 1 Shepard St ℡617/354-8980; **Harvard or Porter T.** Fantastic French fare with a strong Cuban accent, which translates into crispy duck with a tamarind-rum glaze ($15) and adds up to some of Cambridge's best cuisine. Most folks (looking to spend less cash) head straight to the adjacent bar for the amazing Cuban pressed sandwich ($13).

Darwin's Ltd 148 Mt Auburn St ℡617/354-5233; **Harvard T.** The rough-hewn exterior conceals a delightful deli serving the best sandwiches on Harvard Square – wonderfully inventive combinations include roast beef, sprouts, and apple slices served on freshly baked bread. No credit cards. There's another location at 1629 Cambridge St (℡617/491-2999; Harvard **T**).

Harvest 44 Brattle St ℡617/868-2255; **Harvard T.** Upscale, white-tableclothed Harvard Square institution with an oft-changing menu of rich New American cuisine; the outdoor courtyard is another fine feature. Go for the fish of the day (market price) or the tuna bolognese with fresh tomatoes and gnocchi ($16).

Henrietta's Table Charles Hotel, 1 Bennett St ℡617/661-5005; **Harvard T.** One of the few restaurants in Cambridge serving classic New England fare. Rich entrees such as roasted duck ($15) or pork chops ($16) work well with side dishes of wilted greens or mashed potatoes. Some would say a trip to *Henrietta's* is wasted if it's not for their famous brunch, served every Sunday from noon to 3pm; it costs $42 per person but allows unlimited access to a cornucopia of farm-fresh treats from around New England.

Hi-Rise Bread Co. 56 Brattle St ℡617/492-3003; **Harvard T.** A good place to linger on a summer's day, this leisurely café is tops for their homemade granola and bulging sandwiches such as the "Mr and Mrs Snob Sandwich" (turkey with grilled asparagus and avocado; $10).

LA Burdick's 52D Brattle St ℡617/491-4340; **Harvard T.** Simply breathing in the aromas at this fabulous *chocolaterie* is an exercise in indulgence: iced chocolate, chocolate mousse cake, and little chocolate mice and penguins, all waiting to be consumed.

Pho Pasteur 35 Dunster St ℡617/864-4100; **Harvard T.** Located in The Garage, the Harvard Square take on the mini-mall filled with hipster and hippie-inspired stores. A more upscale incarnation of the successful Chinatown string of Vietnamese joints, *Pho Pasteur* serves a variety of filling and delicious pho noodle soups beginning at $6. The spring rolls ($4) are another treat.

Tamarind Bay 75 Winthrop St ℡617/491-4552; **Harvard T.** This bright basement eatery serves up what is perhaps the area's best Indian food. The banana dumplings and *lalla mussal dal* (black lentils simmered in spices; $13.50) will make you want to stand up and clap.

Upstairs on the Square 91 Winthrop St ℡617/864-1933, ⊚www.upstairsonthesquare .com; **Harvard T.** With a whimsical decor of animal-striped carpet patterns, glorious green walls, and winged light bulbs, it's no surprise that *Upstairs on the Square* serves inventive food, falling somewhere between New American and Old Colonial, with entrees like Nantucket sea scallops

EATING | Restaurants

with porcini marmalade and tarragon ($37). They also have a carved pink bar where they mix up fanciful cocktails accented with gummi sharks. Reservations recommended.

Cambridge – Central Square and around

Baraka Café 80 1/2 Cambridge St ☎617/868-3951; Central T. A hidden jewel, this North African eatery just off Central Square is loved by local residents. Known for its signature lemonade (boosted with rose water and orange essence), *Baraka Café* offers small plates like *bedenjal mechoui* (smoky eggplant with garlic) as well as entrees like *m'satel* (lamb chops served with almond tartlet and saffron shallots; $16). Cash only.

Central Kitchen 567 Massachusetts Ave ☎617/491-5599; Central T. Hip Central Square bistro with a chalkboard menu offering delightful European classics (*moules frites* for $12) and contemporary American twists (mushroom ragout with ricotta dumplings for $17) in an intimate, stylish setting.

Cuchi Cuchi 795 Main St ☎617/864-2929; Central Square T. Start by lingering over fantastic cocktails at the bar to soak in *Cuchi Cuchi's* Gatsby-esque fabulousness. The waitresses are decked out in vintage flapper dresses, and gilded mirrors and painted lampshades abound. The international menu reflects a similar attention to detail; the savory cornets with tuna tartar and avocado (five for $20) are lovingly prepared, as is the beef stroganoff with shallot and mushroom sauce ($12).

Koreana 154 Prospect St ☎617/576-8661, ⓦwww.koreanaboston.com; Central Square T. Tables here have a built-in grill, allowing you to barbecue your own tasty food (prices start from $16). The sushi bar (from $3 per piece) is also pretty good.

Rendezvous 502 Massachusetts Ave ☎617/576-1900; Central T. A welcome addition to Central Square, *Rendezvous* serves Mediterranean-inspired fare with a locally-grown flavor in an affable, airy dining room. Although the dishes rotate, sample plates include swiss chard dolmas with cucumber-purslane salad ($20) and roast chicken with Moroccan spices ($23). The Sunday prix fixe menu ($35) is highly recommended.

Cambridge – Kendall Square and around

Emma's 40 Hampshire St ☎617/864-8534; Kendall T. This tasty, local pizzeria has signature thin pies and slices featuring fun toppings like roasted sweet potatoes and ricotta. Consistently listed at or near the top of "best in Boston" lists.

Blue Room 1 Kendall Sq ☎617/494-9034, ⓦwww.theblueroom.net; Kendall T. Unpretentious restaurant with superlative grilled fusion cuisine; pan-seared skate ($21) and braised lamb ($23) are common, but what accompanies them – cumin and basmati yogurt or tomatillos – isn't. The menu changes with what ingredients are available, so the food is always fresh and innovative.

Cambridge – Inman Square and around

All Star Sandwich Bar 1245 Cambridge St ☎617/868-3065, ⓦwww.allstarsandwichbar .com; Central Square T. Who can resist a sandwich shop that lets you "hop up your rod" by adding in potato chips? This tasty little spot does a mean meat loaf sandwich ($9) as well as good chili ($3.50) and fries "from hell" ($4.50).

East Coast Grill 1271 Cambridge St ☎617 /491-6568, ⓦwww.eastcoastgrill.net; Harvard or Central Square T. A bright and funky atmosphere in which to enjoy fresh seafood and Caribbean side dishes such as grilled avocado, pineapple salsa, and fried plantains. The Sunday serve-yourself Bloody Mary bar is reason enough to visit, and there is a raw bar tucked into one corner.

Midwest Grill 1122 Cambridge St ☎617/354-7536; Central T. It's hard to stop yourself from gorging to beyond full at this tempting Brazilian *churrascuria* where waiters come around to your table with hot skewers of meat that are sliced and then dropped onto your plate; $24 for dinner, which includes a tempting, all-you-can-eat buffet.

Olé Mexican Grill 11 Springfield St ☎617/492-4495; Central T. Widely-regarded as one of Boston's best Mexican eateries, this pricier-than-a-taqueria-spot is worth it for the *tacos de atún asado* (rare tuna steak in handmade tortillas for $19), jicama salad ($8.75), and guacamole ($9).

Oleana 134 Hampshire St ☎617/661-0505; **Central T**. If you can, secure a table here on the blissful, wisteria-laden patio, where you can linger over Mediterranean-fused lamb steak with fava bean moussaka ($25) and Armenian bean and walnut paté with homemade string cheese ($4). Be sure to save room for their stellar Baked Alaska, served with coconut ice cream and passion fruit-caramel sauce ($14).

Punjabi Dhaba 225 Hampshire St ☎617/547-8272; **Central T**. This unassuming Indian eatery inspires almost maniacal devotion among its fans, who trek across Cambridge for quick and cheap *palak paneer* and chicken *tikka masala*.

Somerville

Dalí 415 Washington St ☎617/661-3254, ⓦwww.dalirestaurant.com; **Harvard T**. An upscale tapas restaurant featuring energetic Spanish music, occasional flamenco, excellent sangria, and most importantly superlative tapas (from $4.50). Start with the Spanish white asparagus, farm trout with red wine sauce, and braised rabbit in sweet-and-sour sauce.

Diva 246 Elm St ☎617/629-4963, ⓦwww .divabistro.com; **Davis T**. This trendy Davis Square spot isn't your typical Indian restaurant: the space is stylishly modern and cushy (complete with a lounge next door), the entrees relatively pricey ($11–17), and the northern and southern dishes unusually mild, spice-wise.

EVOO 118 Beacon St ☎617/661-3866, ⓦwww .evoorestaurant.com; **Harvard T**. New American cuisine with very locally-minded ingredients; they own part of a nearby farm. The hip clientele happily munches on the likes of seared sea scallops ($26) and pear and goat cheese salads ($9).

Gargoyles on the Square 215 Elm St ☎617/776-5300, ⓦgargoylesonthesquare.com; **Davis T**. The classiest joint in Davis Square combines contemporary American fare with a touch of French; look for the homemade ravioli with apple and brie ($9). There's a $20 minimum on Fri and Sat.

▲ Redbones

Redbones 55 Chester St ☎617/628-2200, ⓦwww.redbones.com; **Davis T**. A variety of American barbecue ($10–19) is represented in huge portions, accompanied by delectable sides such as collard greens and Cajun "dirty rice." In the unlikely case that you have room for dessert, the pecan pie is top-notch. Long lines form at dinner, so arrive early. No credit cards.

Soundbites 708 Broadway ☎617/623-8888; **Davis T**. The staff will hustle you in and out of this local breakfast eatery, but in between you'll savor challah French toast loaded with fresh fruit ($5), as well as some of the best pancakes in town. Be prepared for a wait, although you can grab a cup of joe while still in line. No credit cards.

Drinking

D espite – or, perhaps, because of – the lingering Puritan ethic that pervades Boston, people here tend to **drink** more than they do in the rest of the country, with the consequence that few American cities offer as many bars per capita in which to knock back a few beers. Before you start planning a big night out, however, it's worth pointing out that drinking in Boston is not without its headaches – and we don't just mean the morning after.

While the number of watering holes in Boston is high, the range of options is not, and most **stop serving alcohol at 2am**. Another sticking point is that the city's university culture means the US **drinking-age minimum of 21** is strictly enforced; even if you're obviously of-age, you'll still be required to show at least one form of valid photo **identification**, either in the form of a driver's license or passport, to gain entrance to any place serving drinks. Smokers will find themselves marginalized thanks to the **smoking ban**, which prohibits smoking even on outdoor patios. If you must smoke indoors, there are a handful of cigar lounges in town; your best bet is Cigar Masters (745 Boylston St; ☎617/266-4400, ⓦwww. cigarmasters.com; Copley **T**), where patrons can puff contentedly while relaxing in leather armchairs; cigar prices range from $3-30. And finally, as the **T** shuts down at 12.30am, it can be difficult to find a taxi due to the mass exodus of drinkers when the bars let out.

As for types of places, it's not surprising that, given the city's Irish heritage, **pubs** make up the majority of Boston's drinking establishments. Especially high concentrations of these are found in the **West End**, **Cambridge**, and **Downtown** around Quincy Market; many are unextraordinary, but several are the real deal, drawing as many Irish expats as they do Irish-American locals.

More upscale are the **bars** and **lounges** of **Back Bay**, especially those along Newbury and Boylston streets, which offer as much scenester attitude as

Eating and drinking maps

We've keyed the eating and drinking establishments found in this chapter – as well as Chapter 11, "Eating" – within the neighborhoods portion of the Guide. These maps can be found on the following pages:

atmosphere. Some of the most popular bars in this area are actually adjuncts of restaurants and hotels; still others cater to the city's gay population, although most of the gay bars can be found in the **South End** (see chapter 15, "Gay Boston," for the best).

The rest of the city's neighborhood bars, pick-up joints, and yuppie hotspots are differentiated by their crowds: **Beacon Hill** tends to be older and stuffier; **Downtown**, mainly around Quincy Market and the Theater District, draws a healthy mix of tourists, business people, and sporty types; in addition to its student-oriented clientele **Kenmore Square** also brims with Red Sox fans of all styles and stripes. Across the river, **Cambridge** is perhaps the most fun, with a let-loose population of creative types and eclectic Ivy Leaguers.

Downtown

Beantown Pub 100 Tremont St ☎617/426-0111; **Park Street T.** This centrally located pub has a touristy clientele, a range of decent beer, a varied jukebox, and is a great place to play pool.

Bell in Hand Tavern 45 Union St ☎617/227-2098; **State or Government Center T.** The oldest continuously operating tavern in Boston, dating from 1795, draws a fairly exuberant mix of tourists and young professionals.

The Black Rose (Roisin Dubh) 160 State St ☎617/742-2286; **State T.** Down-home Irish pub specializing in imported beers from the Emerald Isle: Harp, Murphy's, and – especially – Guinness all flow freely. It's a bit of a lust magnet and things get pretty boisterous on weekends.

Cheers Faneuil Hall Marketplace ☎617/227-0150, Ⓦwww.cheersboston.com; **Haymarket T.** A replica of the NBC set (the original inspiration is on Beacon Street; see p.183), this place is little more than an overpriced tacky tourist trap that's good for a photo-op.

Felt 533 Washington St ☎617/350-5555; **Downtown Crossing T.** *Felt* is an upscale pool hall and dance lounge full of the young and beautiful willing to pay $14 an hour for a table. One of the new places to be seen.

Good Life 28 Kingston St ☎617/451-2622; Ⓦwww.goodlifebar.com **Downtown Crossing T.** This stylish bar generates quite a buzz, owing as much to its inventive martinis as to nights dedicated to the likes of old-school hip-hop and deep house music. Choose between tasty full meals ($12–25), dozens of vodkas, or getting your groove on downstairs.

Green Dragon Tavern 11 Marshall St ☎617/367-0055; **Government Center T.** Another tavern that dates to the colonial era, this was a popular meeting place for patriots during the Revolution. There's a standard selection of tap beers, a raw bar, and a full menu rife with twee historical humor ("One if by land, two if by seafood"). Less of a pick-up joint than some of the other bars in the area.

Houston's 60 State St ☎617/573-9777; **State Street T.** Part of a swanky restaurant chain, *Houston's* doubles as the sleekest bar in Faneuil Hall. In summer, a low deck opens out into the evening air; close enough to feel the energy from Faneuil Hall, but far enough removed so you can swill your martini in peace.

JJ Foley's 21 Kingston St ☎617/695-2529; **Downtown Crossing T.** Attended by bike messengers and businessmen during the day, this little Irish gem plays host to a casual scene of locals and students by night. Friendly and recommended.

Limelight 204 Tremont St ☎617/423-0785; Ⓦwww.limelightboston.com; **Boylston T.** A nearly unbelievable karaoke utopia where you can either opt for the stage ($5 cover) and perform in American Idol-esque environs (you even get to choose your own background imagery), or the studios ($10 an hour) where you and your friends can belt out "Like A Virgin" in privacy.

The Kinsale 2 Center Plaza ☎617/742-5577; **Government Center T.** Shipped brick by brick from Ireland to its current location in the shadow of Government Plaza, this outrageously popular Irish pub is as authentic as it gets; the menu even lists beer-battered fish and hot pastrami on a "bulkie" (Boston slang for a sandwich bun).

▲ Les Zygomates

Les Zygomates 129 South St ⊤617/542-5108; **South Station** T. This elegant wine bar (also reviewed on p.170) has a wide and exceptional selection of varietals. Neophytes might want to get their palates wet at the weekly wine-tasting sessions (Tues 7–8.30pm; $30).

Lucky's 355 Congress St ⊤617/357-5825; **South Station** T. Over the water and quite a walk from the subway, this subterranean lounge bar is one of Boston's best-kept secrets – mainly because it's off the beaten tourist path (the fact that there's no sign out front adds to its in-the-know vibe). Inside is a swinging '50s pad complete with martini-swilling patrons and frequent live jazz; on Sun, Frank Sinatra impersonators get the locals dancing.

Mr Dooley's Boston Tavern 77 Broad St ⊤617/338-5656; **State** T. One of Downtown's many Irish pubs, though with a more laid-back feel than the rest. Known for its live music acts and traditional Irish Breakfast Sundays (bacon, eggs, black pudding, and baked beans).

Weggie's Pub 162 Lincoln St ⊤617/542-7080; **South Station** T. A fun local dive with vinyl seating, pool tables, greasy food, and a low-key crowd in a space that's situated just outside of Chinatown and has been there for over twenty years.

Charlestown

Tangierino 83 Main St ⊤617/242-6009, ⓦwww.tangierino.com; **Community College** T. While couples get romantic next door at *Tangierino's* swanky Turkish restaurant (see p.172), others head to the adjacent, atmospheric *Casbah Lounge* to puff contentedly on hookahs and get entertained by belly dancers.

Tavern On The Water 1 8th St Pier 6, ⊤617/242-8040, ⓦwww.tavernonthewater

.com; **Community College** T. Located right on the water (the USS *Constitution* is anchored nearby), the *Tavern* sports what is possibly Boston's best skyline view. The food is forgettable, so stick with whatever's on tap.

Warren Tavern 2 Pleasant St ⊤617/241-8142; **Community College** T. Paul Revere and George Washington were both regulars here, and the oldest standing structure in Charlestown is still decent for a drink. Also has a generous menu of dependable tavern food.

Beacon Hill and the West End

21st Amendment 150 Bowdoin St ⊤617/227-7100; **Government Center** T. This dimly lit, down-home watering hole, which gets its name from the amendment that repealed Prohibition, is a favorite haunt of legislators from the adjacent State House and students from nearby Suffolk University. You might even run into Senator John Kerry.

Bin 26 Enoteca 26 Charles St ⊤617/723-5939; **Charles** T. Lovingly run by the proprietors of *Lala Rokh* (see p.172), this classy wine bar has up to 250 bottles in its rotation and 50-60 varieties available by the glass. Helpful servers can aid you in matching your drink up with its perfect food counterpart, perhaps a marinated olive plate ($7) or a slice of gorgonzola ($6).

Boston Beer Works 112 Canal St ⊤617/896-BEER; **North Station** T. Originally a Fenway spot, this Boston institution has since opened up new digs out in the West End. With over 15 micro-beers on tap (made on the premises), billiards, and reasonable bar food, it makes for a great spot to kick back and watch the game.

Cheers 84 Beacon St ⊤617/227-9605, ⓦwww.cheersboston.com; **Arlington** T. As the conspicuous banners outside shout out, this is the bar that served as the inspiration for the TV show *Cheers*. If you must go, be warned – it's packed with camera-toting tourists and the inside bears little resemblance to the NBC set. The food, though cutely named (eNORMous burgers), is pricey and mediocre, and it's almost certain that nobody will know your name.

Emmet's Pub and Restaurant 6-B Beacon St ⊤617/742-8565; **Park Street** T. Named after the Irish rebel Robert Emmet, this cozy watering hole tucked in the quieter section of Beacon Street is one of the more relaxed places to have a beer in town; the bulk of its

business comes from government workers from the nearby State House during happy hour. The kitchen serves decent staples, such as fish and chips.

Fours 166 Canal St ☏617/720-4455, ⊛www .thefours.com; North Station **T**. The classiest of the West End's sports bars, with an army of TVs broadcasting games from around the globe, as well as paraphernalia from the Celtics, Bruins, and other local teams.

McGann's 197 Portland St ☏617/227-4059; North Station **T**. An authentic Irish bar, but with a more upmarket, restaurant-like feel. There's a very active world rugby-watching crowd in addition to the usual Red Sox fans.

Sevens Ale House 77 Charles St ☏617/523-9074; Charles **T**. While the tourists pack into nearby *Cheers*, you can drop by this cozy, wood-paneled joint to watch a game or shoot darts in an authentic Boston neighborhood bar. Positives include a wide selection of draft beers, daily specials, and substantial portions.

Back Bay and the South End

The Beehive 541 Tremont St ☏617/423-0069; ⊛www.beehiveboston.com; Back Bay **T**. Snuggled inside the *Boston Center for the Arts* is this spacious newcomer to Boston's bar scene. With chandeliers dripping from the ceiling, a red-curtained stage, and knock-you-down cocktails, the *Beehive* exudes a vaudeville vibe, complete with jazz, cabaret, or burlesque shows playing nearly every night of the week.

Bristol Lounge 200 Boylston St ☏617/351-2053; Arlington **T**. An upmarket lobby-side lounge in the *Four Seasons* where the desserts are as popular as the drinks and a pianist plays smooth jazz that's ideal for the post-theater crowd. Their burgers are particularly good.

Bukowski's Tavern 50 Dalton St ☏617/437-9999; Hynes **T**. Arguably Boston's best dive bar, this parking garage watering hole has views over the Mass Pike and such a vast beer selection that a homemade "wheel of indecision" is spun by waitstaff when patrons can't decide what to drink. Excellent rock 'n' roll jukebox, too. There's a smaller, equally cool location in Inman Square, Cambridge 1281 Cambridge St (☏617/497-7077; Central **T**).

Cactus Club 939 Boylston St ☏617/236-0200; Hynes **T**. Should you be in the mood for loud music, shoulder-to-shoulder crowds,

and techni-colored margaritas, the *Cactus Club* is here for you.

Dillons 955 Boylston ☏617/421-1818; Hynes **T**. Formerly a trendy restaurant and housed in what used to be a police department building, *Dillons* is an upscale Irish bar/ restaurant popular with the post-work crowd.

Excelsior 272 Boylston ☏617/421-1818; Copley **T**. Technically a restaurant offering imaginative modern American cuisine, *Excelsior* is more famous among Bostonians for its posh and happening bar scene and impressive cocktails.

Jacque's Cabaret 79 Broadway ☏617/426-8902; Arlington **T**. *Priscilla, Queen of the Desert* invades New England at this drag dream where past-it divas lip-synch "I Love the Nightlife." There's a nice melting pot of patrons, including frequent bachelorette parties. Showtime is 10.30pm nightly (Tues is Karaoke night), but beware – the festivities end at midnight, Cinderella. Cover $6–10.

Kings Boston 10 Scotia St ☏617/266-2695; Hynes **T**. The sleekest bowling in town: sixteen state-of-the-art lanes, lit up with soft blue lights and augmented by martinis. They also have a nice set of pool tables.

Oak Bar 138 St James Ave in the *Fairmont Copley Plaza* ☏617/267-5300; Copley **T**. Rich wood paneling, high ceilings, and excellent martinis (including the engagement martini, replete with diamond ring and deluxe suite for only $12,750) make this one of the more genteel Back Bay spots to drink.

Match 94 Massachusetts Ave ☏617/247-9922; Hynes **T**. Mini-burgers and martinis –that's the match at this stylish joint. Though the interior has a bit of a formulaic chain vibe, it's hard to pass up late-night food mixed with good drinks.

The Rattlesnake Bar and Grill 382 Boylston St ☏617/859-7772; Arlington **T**. The food is mediocre and the crowd often full of wayward Romeos, but people keep coming back because of the rooftop deck. Come summer, it's absolutely heaving with drinkers.

Saint 90 Exeter St ☏617/236-1134; Copley **T**. Upscale bar/club where the young and beautiful come to dance at weekends. Three modish lounge spaces, including a white leather vodka bar (with swanky flavors like lychee and cardamom) and a red-toned "bordello" room, complete with ample plush furnishings and mirrors for you to check yourself out.

Top of the Hub 800 Boylston St ⊤617/536-1775; **Prudential T.** An atmospheric space on the 52nd floor of the Prudential Center, *Top of the Hub* features a snazzy jazz lounge, swanky cocktails, and fancy food. A great date spot, although you have to go through an unromantic security check first.

Twentyeight Degrees 1 Appleton St ⊤617/728-0728; **Back Bay T.** The food is swanky Italian-inspired fare, but the drinks (like the frozen bellini or blueberry basil martini) are a safer bet at this gay-savvy, candle-lit lounge replete with leather seating, wispy curtains at your table, and the prettiest bathrooms in Boston.

Whiskey's 885 Boylston St ⊤617/262-5551; **Hynes T.** A real-life beer commercial: young guys wearing baseball caps, sports on TV, and a strong smell of booze. For some, that adds up to the perfect place to watch the Sox play a game.

Whiskey Park 64 Arlington St (in the Park Plaza) ⊤617/542-1482; **Arlington T.** Owned by Rande Gerber (aka Mr Cindy Crawford), this lounge's chic chocolate-brown leather-chair design was conceived by Michael Czysz, the guy behind Lenny Kravitz's swinging Miami pad. The prices match the celebrity name-dropping, but there's hardly a better place in town to grab a cocktail.

Kenmore Square and the Fenway

An Tua Nua 835 Beacon St ⊤617/262-2121; **Kenmore T.** Despite its Gaelic name ("the new beginning") this popular Boston University hangout is just as much dance bar as it is Irish pub. Sat dance nights get especially crowded with BU and North-eastern undergrads (ladies, be prepared for youthful oglers); Wed and Sun are salsa nights.

Audubon Circle 838 Beacon St ⊤617/421-1910; **Kenmore T.** Sleek, modern bar, where a well-dressed crowd gathers for cocktails and fancy bar food (see review p.176) before and after games at nearby Fenway Park.

Bill's Bar 5 1/2 Lansdowne St ⊤617/421-9678, ⓦ www.billsbar.com; **Kenmore T.** A fairly relaxed and homey Lansdowne Street spot, with lots of beer, lots of TV screens, and lots of live rock bands – in which case expect a cover charge of $10.

Boston Beer Works 61 Brookline Ave ⊤617/536-2337; **Kenmore T.** A brewery located right by Fenway Park, *Boston Beer Works* is a popular place for the Red Sox

faithful to warm up before games and drown their sorrows after. Their signature ale is the Boston Red, but the seasonal brews are also worth a taste. Decent food, too.

Cask 'n Flagon 62 Brookline Ave ⊤617/536-4840; **Kenmore T.** While some say the recently expanded *Cask* has lost its former low-key greatness, this well-loved sports pub has been an iconic Fenway spot since 1969. With a great location (it's right behind Fenway Park's Green Monster) and landmark stature, there may be no better place to watch the game. Be kind to the moody bouncers, who won't hesitate in barring your entrance if you seem too "drunk" or not to their liking.

Copperfield's 98 Brookline Ave ⊤617/247-8605; **Kenmore T.** Cheap drafts and pool, and frequented by a raucous collegiate crowd there to see the Red Sox game.

🏃 **Eastern Standard 528 Commonwealth Ave** ⊤617/532-9100; **Kenmore T.** Set inside a gorgeous, spacious dining room, this Boston favorite pulls in a nice mix of clientele, both age-wise and style-wise. The knowledgable bartenders are just as quick to mix up a swanky highball as they are to pull you a pint, and there's a pretty patio in the summer.

Foundation Lounge 500 Commonwealth Ave (in the Hotel Commonwealth) ⊤617/532-9100; **Kenmore T.** Large, upscale bar with a hip (but not hipper-than-thou) clientele, as well as a more discreet Red Sox-viewing ambience. Was recently voted "best pickup bar" by *Boston Magazine*.

Game On! 82 Lansdowne St ⊤617/351-7001, ⓦ www.gameonboston.com; **Kenmore T.** Consistently topping "Boston's best sports bar" lists, this expansive bar features an insane 90 televisions on which to watch games, complemented by enthusiastic crowds and bar food that's a step above nachos and chicken strips.

The Lower Depths Taproom 476 Commonwealth Ave ⊤617/266-6662; **Kenmore T.** A welcome newcomer to the ballpark scene, this pub is known for their extensive beer knowledge (16 on tap, plus plenty in bottles) and excellent $1 hot dogs.

Squealing Pig 134 Smith St ⊤617/566-6651; **Longwood T.** A bit further out in the Fenway, this affable spot has a neighborhood pub vibe, complete with friendly bartenders, low-key live music, and tasty comfort food à la their "toasties" sandwiches (chicken, pesto, brie, and tomato all grilled to perfection for $8).

Jamaica Plain

Brendan Behan 378 Centre St, Jamaica Plain ☏617/522-5386; Green St **T**. The godfather of Boston's Irish pubs, this dimly lit institution has the usual friendly staff all week long, as well as live music available on most weekends.

James's Gate 5–11 McBride St, Jamaica Plain ☏617/983-2000; Forest Hills **T**. Beat Boston's harsh winter by sipping Guinness beside the blazing fireplace in this cozy pub, or by trying the hearty fare in the restaurant out back. Pub quiz Mon nights at 8pm.

Cambridge and Allston

B-Side Lounge 92 Hampshire St ☏617/354-0766; Kendall **T**. A trendy but not alienating bar. Lots of live tunes, a great drinks menu, and surprisingly tasty and creative bar food. Well recommended.

▼ B-Side Lounge

The Cellar 991 Massachusetts Ave ☏617/876-2580; Harvard **T**. The two floors here, each with a bar, are regularly filled with a crowd of Harvard faculty members, older students, and other locals imbibing fine beers and killer Long Island iced teas.

Charlie's Kitchen 10 Eliot St ☏617/492-9646; Harvard **T**. While downstairs is a well-loved burger joint (see p.177), upstairs is a buzzing bar, at its rowdiest on Tues karaoke nights. Fifteen beers on tap, a rocking juke box, and a good mix of patrons.

Daedulus 45 1/2 Mount Auburn St ☏617/349-0071; Harvard **T**. While the rest of this restaurant/bar isn't bad-looking (think dark wooden paneling and tables), the real draw is great rooftop deck. Built in a former greenhouse, the pleasant roof comes with lovely neighborhood views and a nicely-dressed twenty- and thirty-something crowd.

Enormous Room 577 Massachusetts Ave ☏617/491-5550; Central **T**. Walking into this tiny lounge tucked above *Central Kitchen* (see p.178) is tantamount to entering a swanky, opium-den-like slumber party. The clientele lounge, sans shoes (these are placed discreetly in cubbies), on a selection of plush couches. Good DJs.

The Field 20 Prospect St ☏617/354-7345; Central **T**. Although *The Field* is located between Harvard and MIT, this Irish pub attracts an eclectic non-college crowd. You can play pool or darts while you sip one of the variety on of beers tap.

Grafton Street 1280 Massachusetts Ave ☏617/497-0400; Harvard **T**. Authentic, cozy Irish pub atmosphere, home to an older, well-dressed set that enjoys smooth drafts and equally good food.

Green Street 280 Green St ☏617/876-1655; Central **T**. Really a restaurant serving dolled-up comfort food, *Green Street* is the kind of spot where discerning drinkers go to savor a Maker's on the rocks. Expect a twenty-and thirty-something, low-key, hip clientele as well as drool-worthy concoctions such as the "Pearl White" (Bombay gin, lillet blanc, fresh lemon, simple syrup, and mint; $7).

Grendel's Den 89 Winthrop St ☏617/491-1160; Harvard **T**. A favorite spot of locals and grad students for quaffing ale. Happy-hour specials includes big plates of appetizers (fried calamari, nachos) for just $1.50 each.

Middlesex Lounge 315 Massachusetts Ave ☏617/868-6739; Central **T**. A slightly hipper-than-thou vibe, but with good reason - the gorgeous space (high ceilings, exposed brick, pretty wood, wood paneling) makes you want to dress to impress. Lush lounge chairs on wheels and minimalist tables you can move around to design your own drinking environs. *Hearthrob*, on the 2nd and 4th Tues of every month, has lines out the door for its scenester electro-retro beat dance heaven.

Miracle of Science 321 Massachusetts Ave ☎617/868-ATOM; Central **T**. Surprisingly hip despite its status as an MIT hangout. There's science-themed decor and a laidback, unpretentious crowd, though the place can get crowded on weekend nights. The bar stools will conjure up memories of high school chemistry class.

Model Café 7 Beacon St N, Allston ☎617/354-0766; Harvard Ave **T**. It's a trek, but if you relish bar hops that end at a well-loved dive, complete with rocking juke box and lots of cheap brews, then *Model* will worm its way into your drunken heart. Cash only.

Muddy Charles Pub 142 Memorial Dr (MIT's Bldg 50) ☎617/253-2086; Kendall **T**. Right on the MIT campus, this popular student pub has incredible waterfront views, cheap pitchers of beer, and a casual, grandfatherly vibe. No food, but patrons are encouraged to use their phone for local restaurant hook-ups.

Noir *Charles Hotel*, 1 Bennett St ☎617/661-8010; Harvard **T**. With its sultry red lighting and tall black leather booths, *Noir* seems the perfect setting to carry on a discreet affair. Most patrons just come for the decadent martinis, however.

People's Republik 880 Massachusetts Ave ☎617/492-8632; Central or Harvard **T**. Smack dab between MIT and Harvard, *People's Republik* attracts a good mix of technocrats and potential world-leaders as a result. It takes its Communist propaganda seriously – with its posters on the walls, anyway; the range of tap offerings is positively democratic.

Phoenix Landing 512 Massachusetts Ave ☎617/576-6260; Central **T**. The *Phoenix* is about the only place in Cambridge you'll still catch European sporting events (shown on the weekends) but it's best known for its fun nightly dance parties.

Plough & Stars 912 Massachusetts Ave ☎617/441-3455, ⊛www.ploughandstars.com; Central or Harvard **T**. Off-the-beaten-path neighborhood hideaway that's very much

worth the hike, whether for its animated cribbage games, pub grub, or its nightly live music.

River Gods 125 Cambridge St ☎617/576-1881; Central **T**. An Irish bar with a twist, as they serve good cocktails alongside Guinness. The grub is great, and DJs spin tunes as patrons lounge in throne-like chairs ogling the suits of armor on display.

Rialto 1 Bennett St ☎617/661-5050; Harvard **T**. The bar adjunct to the posh restaurant of the same name caters to a wealthy crowd that matches the plush atmosphere. Dress semi-formal and be prepared to pay big-time for the drinks and cocktails, which are, admittedly, excellent.

Shay's 58 JFK St ☎617/864-9161; Harvard **T**. Unwind with grad students over wine and quality beer at *Shay's*, a relaxed contrast to the crowded student-oriented bars found elsewhere in Harvard Square.

Temple Bar 1688 Massachusetts Ave ☎617/547-5055, ⊛www.templebarcambridge .com; Harvard or Porter **T**. Cambridge's stand-out scenester bar attracts a chi-chi crowd to its smart digs outfitted with attractive touches like fancy floral arrangements and artsy Martini Rosso advertising posters.

Somerville

Abbey Lounge 3 Beacon St ☎617/441-9631; Central **T**. Just across the Somerville border, this dive bar dream offers up cheap booze, rocking music acts, and a pierced and inked clientele.

The Burren 247 Elm St ☎617/776-6896, ⊛www.burren.com; Davis **T**. Busy student bar whose overflowing crowds, with the expected baseball caps and cargo pants, spill out onto its outdoor terrace, a prime spot for Davis Square people watching.

Thirsty Scholar Pub 70 Beacon St ☎617/497-2294, ⊛www.thirstyscholarpub.com; Harvard **T**. One of the coziest bars around, *Thirsty's* warm red-brick and burnished-wood interior is matched by a smiling waitstaff and down-home comfort food like shepherd's pie and baked beans. Bring a book to read, or listen up while distinguished writers declaim their own at the bar's oft-hosted readings.

Nightlife

I n recent years Boston's **nightlife** has received something of a wake-up call, although for a major American city, its scene still feels small and is geared primarily to a buttoned-down college crowd; you'll find that even at the wildest venues, locals tend to sport the reserved preppy look characteristic of Boston's universities.

Lansdowne Street, adjacent to Fenway Park, remains the queen of the clubbing scene, although a few stylish clubs have sprung up in areas, such as **Downtown Crossing**, that were previously ghost towns by night. Boylston Place – which links Boston Common with the Theater District and is known locally as "The Alley" – is where most of the action is found. Though the city is by no means a 24-hour one, these hotspots have breathed fresh air into a scene that once lived in the shadow of the city's highbrow culture. Elsewhere, the same old clubs reinvent themselves every few years in the hopes of catching up with current trends.

Live music plays a huge role in the city's nightlife arena, with bars and clubs catering to a young crowd, especially in Cambridge around Harvard and Central squares, where you're as likely to hear a squalling rock band as a mellow DJ. Boston has spawned its share of enormous **rock** acts, from the ever-enduring dinosaur rockers Aerosmith to a smattering of post-punk and indie favorites such as the Pixies and Sebadoh. Boston is also home to a number of well-loved **jazz** and **blues** joints; you can usually find something cheap and to your liking almost any day of the week. If you're interested in hearing classical or opera, check Chapter 14, "Performing arts and film".

For **club and music listings**, check Thursday's *Boston Globe* "Calendar," the *Boston Phoenix*, the *Improper Bostonian, Metro, Stuff@night* and *The Weekly Dig*. You'll also find a number of websites helpful for up-to-date listings; for details on media and websites, see p.31 and p.37.

Live music

The strength of Boston's **live music** is in the intimacy of its smaller venues, though superstar acts make the city a regular stop on their world tours as well. Two of the biggest **concert halls** are far out of town: the Tweeter Center, south of the city in Mansfield (☎508/339-2333, Ⓦwww.tweetercenter.com), and the DCU Center, an hour or so west in Worcester (☎508/755-6800, Ⓦwww.centrumcentre.com).

On a more human scale, plenty of **alternative venues** serve up everything from name bands to obscure new acts; if all else fails, there's always street music at "The Pit" in Harvard Square (p.134), where you're bound to hear some free amateur acts – whether you like it or not.

Rock venues

Bank of America Pavilion Fan Pier, Northern Ave ☏617/728-1600, ⊛www.livenation.com; **South Station T.** Concerts by well-known performers from Harry Connick Jr to Deep Purple are held here during the summer under a huge white tent at Boston Harbor's edge.

Bill's Bar 5 1/2 Lansdowne St ☏617/421-9678; **Kenmore T.** This self-titled "dirty rock bar" books a "sleazy" line-up that includes rock, metal, and indie bands as well as reggae Sundays. There are also a number of 18+ shows; cover generally costs around $10.

Great Scott 1222 Commonwealth Ave, Allston ☏617/421-9678; **Harvard Ave T.** Popular with students and older hipsters alike, this well-loved space plays host to local and national (read: national acts you probably haven't have heard of) rock and indie bands. Cheap drinks, and a pleasant patio where you can kick back and play groupie.

Lizard Lounge 1667 Massachusetts Ave, Cambridge ☏617/547-0759; ⊛www .lizardloungeclub.com; **Harvard or Porter T.** The downstairs portion of the *Cambridge Common* restaurant is a favorite among local students. Rock and jazz acts are onstage almost nightly for a fairly nominal cover charge (usually around $8), while every Sun there's a slamming poetry hour.

Middle East 472 Massachusetts Ave, Cambridge ☏617/864-3278, ⊛www.mideastclub.com; **Central T.** Local and regional bands of every sort – salsa to ska and mambo to hardcore – stop in regularly at this Cambridge institution. Bigger acts are hosted downstairs; smaller ones ply their trade in a tiny upstairs space. A third venue, the *Corner*, has shows nightly that are usually free, with belly dancing every Sun. The attached restaurant, *ZuZu*, serves decent Middle Eastern food.

Museum of Fine Arts 465 Huntington Ave ☏617/369-3300, ⊛www.mfa.org; **Museum T.** Better known for their jazz and classical acts, the *MFA* is steadily gaining a strong collection of indie rock fans thanks to their stellar bookings of bands like The Sea and the Cake and Mates of State. Intimate, pared-down performances are held in the Remis Auditorium; tickets run about $20.

Orpheum Theater 1 Hamilton Place ☏617/679-0810; **Park or Downtown Crossing T.** Once an old-school movie house, it's now a vintage venue for big-name bands. The small space ensures you're closer to the action, and its retro environs are a refreshing change from the new, bigger box-styled venues.

Paradise Rock Club 967 Commonwealth Ave ☏617/562-8800, ⊛www.thedise.com; **Pleasant Street T.** One of Boston's classic rock venues. Lots of greats have played here, including Blondie, Elvis Costello, and Tom Waits, to name a few. It's still as happening as it was 25 years ago, only now it has a restaurant-cum-rock lounge next door.

TDBanknorth Garden 50 Causeway St ☏617/624-1000, ⊛www.tdbanknorthgarden .com; **North Station T.** This arena, up in the West End, attracts many of the big-name acts that pass through New England when the Celtics or Bruins aren't playing.

T.T. the Bear's Place 10 Brookline St, Cambridge ☏617/492-BEAR, ⊛www.ttthebears.com; **Central T.** A downmarket version of the *Middle East*: lesser-known bands, but in a space with a grittiness and intimacy its neighbor lacks. All kinds of bands appear, mostly rock and punk.

Jazz, blues, and folk venues

The Beehive 541 Tremont St ☏617/423-0069; ⊛www.beehiveboston.com; **Back Bay T.** A vaudeville-esque space with with jazz, cabaret, or burlesque shows playing nearly every night of the week; see p.184 for a full reivew.

Cantab Lounge 738 Massachusetts Ave, Cambridge ☏617/354-2685, ⊛www .cantab-lounge.com; **Central T.** Although from the outside it looks like the kind of sleazy place your mother wouldn't want you to set foot in, it's actually one of the truly bohemian spots in town, with hopping live jazz and blues.

Club Passim 47 Palmer St, Cambridge ☏617/492-7679, ⊛www.clubpassim.org; **Harvard T.** Folkie hangout in Harvard Square where Joan Baez and Suzanne Vega got their starts. World music and spoken word performances in windowed basement setting.

Johnny D's 17 Holland St, Somerville ☏617/776-2004, ⊛www.johnnyds.com; **Davis T.** A mixed bag with talent ranging from the sublime to the ordinary, and a $10 cover charge for most shows. Acts include garage bands, progressive jazz sextets, traditional blues artists, and some uncategorizables.

NIGHTLIFE | Live music

Regattabar 1 Bennett St, Cambridge ☎617/661-5000, ⊕www.regattabarjazz.com; Harvard **T**. The *Regattabar* draws top national jazz acts, although, as its location in the swish *Charles Hotel* might suggest, the atmosphere and clientele are both decidedly sedate. Dress nicely and prepare to pay at least a \$20 cover.

Ryles 212 Hampshire St, Cambridge ☎617/876-9330, ⊕www.rylesjazz.com; Central **T**. Two levels of live music – swing and salsa upstairs, and smooth jazz and blues downstairs. *Ryles* also does a good jazz brunch on Sun, where a plate of blueberry pancakes and sausage costs \$9.

Scullers 400 Soldiers Field Rd, Cambridge ☎617/783-0090, ⊕www.scullersjazz.com; Harvard **T**. Upscale jazz club in the *DoubleTree Guest Suites* draws five-star

acts, including some of the stars of the contemporary jazz scene. You'll need to hop in a taxi to get here, as the walk along the river at night can be risky. The cover charge varies wildly – anywhere from \$12 to \$55.

Wally's Café 427 Massachusetts Ave, Roxbury ☎617/424-1408, ⊕www.wallyscafe.com; Massachusetts **T**. Founded in 1947, this is one of the oldest jazz clubs around, and some folks think it's one of Boston's best assets.

Western Front 343 Western Ave, Cambridge ☎617/492-7772, ⊕www.thewesternfrontclub.com; Central **T**. The *Front* puts on rollicking jazz, blues, and reggae shows for a dance-crazy audience. Drinks are cheap, and the Jamaican food served on weekends is delectably authentic.

Nightclubs

Boston's **nightclubs** are mostly clustered around "The Alley" (Boylston Place), the Theater District, and Kenmore Square with a few prominent ones in Back Bay and the South End. Many of the venues in those two neighborhoods are **gay clubs**, often the most happening places in town; for a complete listing, see Chapter 15, "Gay Boston."

The music at these clubs changes almost nightly, so to keep apprised of what's on, check the individual club websites, the "Calendar" section in Thursday's *Boston Globe*, or the listings in the weekly *Boston Phoenix* and daily *Metro*. **Cover charges** are generally in the \$5–15 range, though sometimes there's no cover at all. Boston's venues tend to be easily entered – no New York–style selection at the door – though there is a tendency for bouncers to block sneakers and torn jeans. On weekends, clubs can be overrun with suburbanites and yuppies; come on a weeknight if you want to increase your elbow room.

▲ Avalon

Comedy central

Boston's **comedy clubs** can be a pleasant alternative to the club scene, especially when you factor in the lack of dress code and the top-notch comics who often headline as part of a cross-country tour.

Comedy Connection, 245 Quincy Market (☎617/248-9700, ⓦwww.symfonee .com; Government **T**), is a high-caliber venue attracting both local and national acts; Thursday nights are popular with the college crowd as Frank Santos, the "R Rated Hypnotist," takes the stage.

The city's only improv venue, the **Improv Asylum Theater**, 216 Hanover St (☎617/263-6887, ⓦwww.improvasylum.com; Haymarket **T**), often brings the house down with off-the-cuff sketches based on audience cues. Boston's comedy mainstay, **Nick's Comedy Stop**, 100 Warrenton St (☎617/482-0930, ⓦwww .nickscomedystop.com; Boylston **T**), has brought in national acts including the likes of Jay Leno and Jerry Seinfeld during its twenty-five-year tenure. In all cases, book your tickets ($10–40) ahead of time, as shows often sell out.

Downtown, Back Bay, and the South End

Club Europa/Buzz 67 Stuart St ☎617/267-8969, ⓦwww.buzzboston.com; Boylston **T**. On the edge of the Theater District, this is one of Boston's better dance clubs. Most of the action is on the third floor; the second tends to be louder and more crowded. On Sat night the club becomes "Buzz," one of the most plugged-in gay discos in Boston.

Gypsy Bar 116 Boylston St ☎617/417-1333, ⓦwww.gypsybarboston.com; Boylston **T**. Very posh lounge and dance club popular with the European set; you can watch schools of jellyfish pulsing peacefully behind the bar as you order an *Indulgence* cocktail. Prepare to dress snappy – no sneakers or sleeveless tees, as well as (weirdly) no polo shirts. DJ dance beats Fri and Sat, $15 cover after 9.30pm.

Liquor Store 25 Boylston Place ☎617/357-6800, ⓦwww.liquorstoreboston.com; Boylston **T**. Though clubs tend to open and close every six months over here in "The Alley," the *Liquor Store* seems as though it could be here to stay. The young and beautiful steadily party hard here to current hits, R&B, and house while trying their luck on the mechanical bull. No sneakers, expect a cover of around $10.

Ned Devine's Faneuil Hall Marketplace, Quincy Market building ☎617/248-9900, ⓦwww .neddevinesboston.com; Government Center **T**. Irish pub on the first floor with a rowdy nightclub upstairs that's populated by fun-loving tourists and dancing oglers.

No sneakers or hats, expect a cover of around $5.

The Roxyplex 279 Tremont St ☎617/338-7699, ⓦwww.roxyboston.com; Boylston **T**. The Theater District's biggest club has almost taken over the *Tremont House* hotel and now features the *Roxy* and *Matrix* clubs (one cover – either $15 or $20 – gets you into both), the *Caprice Lounge* for cocktails and dining, and *Encore*, a cabaret venue.

Saint 90 Exeter St ☎617/236-1134; Copley **T**. Upscale lounge and club with lush decor and chi-chi drinks – the tables tend to be occupied by people more famous or well-off than you, however. Popular with a swanky thirty-something crowd. Expect a cover of $20.

Sugar Shack One Boylston Place ☎617/351-2510, ⓦwww.alleyboston.com; Boylston **T**. This perennial favorite with the collegiate set features a decor of fake broken windows and drinks with names like Raspberry Truffle. Dance to hip hop, R&B, and Top 40 at this cheesy club, and discover what college guys look like without their baseball caps. There's a $5 cover on Fri, and $8 cover on Sat.

Umbria 295 Franklin St ☎617/338-1000; State **T**. One of the latest additions to the city's bar scene, *Umbria* breaks from the downtown Irish pub mold by dancing to an ultralounge beat – a hybrid of bar, nightclub, and restaurant. Stick by the bar, though, for the fabulous martinis.

Venu 100 Warrenton St ☎617/338-8061, ⓦwww .venuboston.com; Boylston **T**. The city's ultimate hotspot, this slick Theater District club with different theme nights throughout the week gives you opulent eye candy for your hefty ($15) cover charge: Art Deco stylings, beautiful patrons, and a laser-lit dancefloor.

Kenmore Square and the Fenway

An Tua Nua 835 Beacon St ☎617/262-2121; **Kenmore T**. Despite its Gaelic name ("the new beginning"), this popular neighborhood hangout is just as much a dance bar as it is an Irish pub. Thurs hip hop nights get especially crowded with BU and North-eastern undergrads, who sweat it out on the dancefloor or check each other out from the many ringside seats. Wed is salsa night.

Avalon 15 Lansdowne St ☎617/262-2424, ⓦwww.avalonboston.com; **Kenmore T**. *Avalon*'s 1500-person capacity makes it the biggest dance club in Boston, and any weekend night the place is positively jamming, often to the tracks laid down by out-of-town talent like Paul Oakenfold and John Digweed. The cavernous central floor is flanked on either side by bars. Sat is gay night, while mid-week often sees live rock performances. On Fri the $20 cover also gets you into three other clubs: *Axis*, *The Modern*, and *Embassy* (see overleaf).

Axis 13 Lansdowne St ☎617/262-2437; **Kenmore T**. Adjacent to *Avalon*, the *Axis* leans more toward techno and trance. On Fri, the doors between the two clubs open to form a megaclub.

Jillian's 145 Ipswich St ☎617/437-0300, ⓦwww.jilliansboston.com; **Kenmore T**. Clubbing utopia: a massive, three-story entertainment club complex housing a pool hall, a raucous, spacious dance club, and a Lucky Strike bowling alley catering to a dressed-up, twenty-something clientele.

The Modern 36 Lansdowne St ☎617/351-2581; **Kenmore T**. A relaxed lounge filled with plush forest-green velvet chairs, and host to various DJ nights. The upstairs part, called *Embassy*, has a similar but even more laid-back atmosphere.

Jamaica Plain

Milky Way 405 Centre St, Jamaica Plain ☎617/524-3740; **Green Street T**. Hidden beneath *Bella Luna* pizza (see p.177), this lovely retro space features low-key local bands, cheap beer, old-school Galaga and Ms Pac Man games, and (best of all) seven vintage bowling lanes.

Performing arts and film

Boston's **cultural scene** is famously vibrant, and many of the city's artistic institutions are second to none in the US. Foremost among them is the Boston Symphony Orchestra, which gave its first concert on October 22, 1881. In fact, Boston is arguably at its best in the **classical music** department, and there are many smaller but internationally known chamber and choral music groups – from the Boston Symphony Chamber Players to the Handel & Hayden Society – to shore up that reputation. The Boston Ballet is also considered world-class, though it's probably best known regionally for its annual holiday production of *The Nutcracker,* with audience numbers ranking it as the most attended **ballet** production in the world.

The **theater** here is quite active, too, even if it is a shadow of its 1920s heyday, when more than forty playhouses were crammed into the **Theater District** on the edge of downtown. The "big four" theaters – the Colonial, the Wilbur, the Charles, and the Opera House – are operated by Broadway Across America (Ⓦ www.broadwayacrossamerica.com), an organization that brings Broadway hits up north. Many of the other theaters are used as "try-out" venues for shows that will later hit New York. For current productions, check the listings in the *Boston Globe's* Thursday "Calendar" section, the *Boston Phoenix*, or the *Improper Bostonian*.

There is the usual big-city glut of multiplexes showing first-run **films**. For foreign, independent, classic, or cult cinema, you'll have to look mainly to other municipalities – Cambridge is best in this respect, though Brookline and Somerville also have their own art-movie and rerun houses.

Classical music

Boston prides itself on being a sophisticated city of high culture, and nowhere does that show up more than in its proliferation of **orchestras** and **choral groups** and the venues that house them. This is helped in no small part by the presence of four of the premier music academies in the nation: the Peabody Conservatory, the New England Conservatory, the Berklee College of Music, and, across the river in Cambridge, the Longy School of Music.

Most of the companies listed below perform at regular venues, which we've reviewed right after (and those performance spaces do put on additional concerts as well). Check the usual listings sources for concert information, or call the groups directly.

Chamber music ensembles

Alea III and Boston Musica Viva ☏617/353-3340, ⓦwww.aleaiii.com (Alea III) and ☏617/354-6910, ⓦwww.bmv.org (Boston Musica Viva). Two regulars at BU's Tsai Performance Center (see below).

Boston Baroque ☏617/484-9200, ⓦwww.bostonbaroque.org. The first permanent Baroque orchestra in the country (it was founded in 1973) is now a resident ensemble at Jordan Hall and Harvard's Sanders Theatre.

Boston Camerata ☏617/262-2092, ⓦwww.bostoncamerata.com. Regular performances of choral and chamber concerts, from medieval to early American, at various locations in and around Boston.

Boston Chamber Music Society ☏617/349-0086, ⓦwww.bostonchambermusic.org. This society has soloists of international renown who perform twice in Jordan Hall (Fri) and the Sanders Theatre (Sun) as well as in various venues throughout the city.

Boston Symphony Chamber Players ☏617/638-9289 or 1-888/266-1200, ⓦwww.bso.org. The only permanent chamber group sponsored by a major symphony orchestra and made up of its members; they perform at Jordan Hall as well as other venues around Boston.

The Cantata Singers & Ensemble ☏617/868-5885, ⓦwww.cantatasingers.org. Boston's premier choral group, which also performs regularly at Jordan Hall in addition to other venues in the Boston area.

Handel & Hayden Society ☏617/266-3605, ⓦwww.handelandhaydn.org. Performing chamber and choral music since 1815, these distinguished artists can be heard at Symphony Hall, Jordan Hall, and the Cutler Majestic.

Masterworks Chorale ☏617/781/235-6210, ⓦwww.masterworkschorale.org. A state-wide society dedicated to choral performances; concerts are held in Harvard's Sanders Theatre.

Pro Arte Chamber Orchestra ☏617/779-0900, ⓦwww.proarte.org. Co-operatively run chamber orchestra in which musicians have full control. Gives Sun afternoon performances at Harvard's Sanders Theatre.

Performance venues

Berklee Performance Center 136 Massachusetts Ave ☏617/747-8890 for concert information or ☏617/747-2261 for the box office, ⓦwww.berkleebpc.com; Symphony **T**. Berklee College of Music's main performance center, known for its quality contemporary repertoire.

Isabella Stewart Gardner Museum 280 The Fenway ☏617/278-5150, ⓦwww.gardnermuseum.org; Museum **T**. Chamber and classical concerts, including many debuts, are held regularly at 1.30pm on weekends Sept–May in the museum's ornate Tapestry Room; there are also shows on Thurs evenings, including jazz concerts. The $23 ticket (available at the door or online from ⓦwww.ticketweb.com) includes museum admission.

Jordan Hall 30 Gainsborough St ☏617/585-1270, ⓦwww.newenglandconservatory.edu; Symphony **T**. The impressive concert hall of the New England Conservatory, one block west from Symphony Hall, is the venue for many chamber music performances, as well as those by the Boston Philharmonic (☏617/236-0999, ⓦwww.bostonphil.org).

Museum of Fine Arts 465 Huntington Ave ☏617/369-3300 for event information, ☏617/369-3306 for tickets, ⓦwww.mfa.org; Museum **T**. During the summer, the MFA's jazz, folk, and world music "Concerts in the Courtyard" take place each Wed at 7.30pm; a variety of indoor performances – from tango to indie rock to opera recitals – are also scheduled for the rest of the year.

Sanders Theatre 45 Quincy St ☏617/496-4594, ⓦwww.fas.harvard.edu/~memhall/sanders.html; Harvard **T**. Inspired by Christopher Wren's Sheldonian Theatre in Oxford, England, the Sanders is known for its 180-degree design. The Boston Philharmonic, the Boston Chamber Music Society, Masterworks Chorale, and the Boston Baroque all perform here.

Symphony Hall 301 Massachusetts Ave ☏1-888/266-1492 for concert information, ☏1-888/266-1200 for tickets, ⓦwww.bso.org; Symphony **T**. This is the regal, acoustically perfect venue for the Boston Symphony Orchestra, currently under the direction of James Levine; the famous Boston Pops concerts happen in May & June, and in July & August, the BSO retreats to Tanglewood, in the Berkshires.

Tsai Performance Center 685 Commonwealth Ave ☏617/353-TSAI for event information or

☎617/353-8725 for box office, ⓦ www.bu.edu /tsai; **Boston University T**. Improbably tucked into Boston University's School of Management, this mid-sized hall is a frequent venue for chamber music performances, prominent lecturers, and plays; events are often affiliated with BU and thus can be very inexpensive.

Dance

The city's longest-running **dance** company is the world-class **Boston Ballet** (☎617/695-6950 or 1-800/447-7400, ⓦ www.bostonballet.org); their biggest blockbuster, the yearly performance of the *The Nutcracker*, has an audience attendance of more than 140,000. The troupe performs at the Wang Theatre and the Colonial Theatre (see p.196).

In addition, smaller but still prominent troupes, like **World Music** (ⓦ www .worldmusic.org), put on music and dance performances that are a bit less traditional and staid, in venues like the Berklee, the Institute for Contemporary Art, and the Orpheum Theatre. The affable **Big Moves** troupe (ⓦ www.bigmoves .org) has three chub-loving dance companies in town: the *Phat Fly Girls (East),* a hip-hop collective; *Filling The Stage,* a jazz group; and *Caravan of Curves,* the company's bellydancing act. They also offer fun free dance classes like "Putting the Belly back into Belly Dance."

The **Boston Dance Alliance** has an informative website centered on Boston's local dance scene (ⓦ www.bostondancealliance.org).

Theater

It's possible to pay dearly for a night at the **theater**. Tickets to the bigger shows range from $25 to $100 depending on the seat, and there is, of course, the potential of a pre- or post-theater meal (see p.167 for restaurants in the Theater District). Your best option is to pay a visit to **BosTix** (☎617/482-BTIX) – a half-price, day-of-show ticket booth with two outlets: in Copley Square, at the corner of Dartmouth and Boylston streets, and Faneuil Hall, by Abercrombie & Fitch (Mon–Sat 10am–6pm, Sun 11am–4pm; ☎617/482-2849) – tickets go on sale at 11am, and only cash is accepted.

Full-price tickets can be had via **Ticketmaster** (☎617/931-2000, ⓦ www .ticketmaster.com) or by contacting the individual theater directly in advance of the performance. If you have a valid school ID or ISIC card, a number of theatres offer vastly cheaper **student rush** tickets on the day of the performance; call the venue in question for more information. The **smaller venues** tend to showcase more offbeat and affordable productions; shows can be under $10 – though you shouldn't bank on that.

Geared toward local actors and theatre companies, **StageSource**, the Greater Boston theater alliance, has an informative website with information on the Boston scene (☎617/720-6066, ⓦ www.stagesource.org).

Major venues

American Repertory Theatre 64 Brattle St, at the Loeb Drama Center, Cambridge ☎617/547-8300, ⓦ www.amrep.org; **Harvard T**. Excellent, eccentric, fairly avant-garde theater near Harvard Square known for staging plays by big names like Shaw and Wilde as well as postmodern heavyweights like Ionesco and Stoppard. They also have a flexible performance space, Zero Arrow, at the corner of Mass Ave and Arrow Street in Harvard Square.

Boston University Theatre 264 Huntington Ave ☎617/266-0800, ⓦ www.huntingtontheatre.org; **Symphony T**. The largest non-touring

⑭

PERFORMING ARTS AND FILM | Dance • Theater

195

playhouse in Boston, known for their phenomenal sets. Productions here range from the classic to the contemporary, such as Alfred Hitchcock's *The 39 Steps*.

Charles Playhouse 74 Warrenton St ☎617/426-6912, ⒲www.blueman.com; Boylston **T**. The Charles has two stages, one of which is more or less the permanent home of *Shear Madness*, a participatory, comic murder mystery that's become the longest-running non-musical in American theater (ⓦwww.shearmadness.com; $40). The other is currently permanent home to Blue Man Group, the eye-opening, edgy multimedia show performed by three bald and blue-painted men. (ⓦwww.blueman.com; $48–58).

Colonial Theatre 106 Boylston St ☎617/426-9366, ⒲www.broadwayacrossamerica.com; Boylston **T**. Built in 1900 and since refurbished, this is the *grande dame* of Boston theaters, known primarily for its Broadway-scale productions.

Cutler Majestic Theatre 219 Tremont St ☎617/824-8725, ⒲www.maj.org; Boylston **T**. Emerson College, a communications and arts school, took stewardship of this 1903 Beaux Arts beauty in 1983. The lavish venue, with soaring Rococo ceiling and Neoclassical friezes, reopened in 2003 following extensive renovations, and has resumed hosting productions of the Emerson Stage company and the Boston Lyric Opera.

Opera House 539 Washington Street ☎617/259-3400, ⒲www.broadwayacrossamerica.com; Downtown Crossing **T**. Built in 1928, this opulent vaudeville theater recently reopened after a multi-million dollar restoration. It hosts large-scale traveling company productions (such as *Wicked*) as well as the Boston Ballet's Christmas-time production of *The Nutcracker*.

Shubert Theatre 265 Tremont St ☎617/482-9393 or 800/447-7400, ⒲www.citicenter.org; Boylston **T**. Stars from Sir Laurence Olivier to Kathleen Turner have played at the city's "Little Princess," which is one of the two venues at the Wang Center for the Performing Arts. An extensive renovation has restored the 1680-seat theater to its prettier early 1900s appearance, with white walls and gold-leaf accents replacing the previous gaudy brown tones. Along with the Wang Center, the Shubert has been re-branded under the corporate moniker "Citi Performing Arts Center."

Wang Theatre 270 Tremont St ☎617/482-9393 or 800/447-7400, ⒲www.citicenter.org; Boylston **T**. The second theater in the Wang Center for the Performing Arts and Boston's biggest performance center, this venue opened in 1925 as the Metropolitan Theater, a gorgeous movie house of palatial proportions. Its original Italian marble, gold-leaf ornamentation, crystal chandeliers, and 3800 seats all remain. The Boston Ballet has residency here (although the legendary Christmas *Nutcracker* has moved to the Opera House); when their season ends, Broadway musicals often take center stage.

Wilbur Theatre 246 Tremont St ☎617/426-1083, ⒲www.broadwayacrossamerica.com; Boylston **T**. *A Streetcar Named Desire*, starring Marlon Brando and Jessica Tandy, debuted in this small Colonial Revival theater before going to Broadway, and the Wilbur has been working on trying to live up to that production ever since. A beloved Boston landmark, the Wilbur is unfortunately currently on the market, making its future a bit up in the air.

Smaller venues

Boston Center for the Arts 539 Tremont St ☎617/426-2787, ⒲www.bcaonline.org. Back Bay **T**. Several theater troupes – many experimental – stage productions at the BCA, which incorporates a series of small venues on a single South End property. Its major tenant is the Calderwood Pavilion, home of the luxurious Wimberly Theatre, and the Roberts Theatre – a contemporary, black-box, flexible stage set-up.

Hasty Pudding Theatre 12 Holyoke St, Cambridge ☎617/495-5205, ⒲www.hastypudding.org; Harvard **T**. Harvard University's Hasty Pudding Theatricals troupe, dating to 1795, mounts one show per year (usually an eclectic musical comedy with Harvard guys in drag as the centerpiece; Feb & March), then hits the road – after which the Cambridge Theatre Company moves in. That said, the troupe is best known for its priceless "Man and Woman of the Year" awards, in which big-time actors lead a parade through Cambridge, are awarded a pot of pudding, and then get "roasted" by the producers of the Hasty Pudding. Past recipients include Scarlett Johansson, Halle Berry, Ben Stiller, and Richard Gere.

Institute of Contemporary Art Theater 100 Northern Ave ☎617/478-3100, ⒲www

PERFORMING ARTS AND FILM | Theater

.icaboston.org; World Trade Center **T**.
Count on the unconventional at the theater of the ICA, Boston's leading venue for all things postmodern and cutting-edge. The World Music dance troupe performs here regularly.

Lyric Stage 140 Clarendon St ☎617/437-7172, ⓦwww.lyricstage.com; Copley **T**. Both premieres and modern adaptations of classic and lesser-known American plays take place at this intimate theater within the renovated YWCA building.

Film

In Boston, as in any other large American city, it's easy enough to catch general-release **films** – the usual listings sources carry all the details you need. If you're looking for out-of-the-ordinary film fare, however, you'll have to venture out a bit from the center – the best second-run theaters are clustered around Cambridge. Whatever you're going to see, admission will cost you about $10, though matinees before 6pm can be cheaper. You can call ☎617/333-FILM for automated film listings; online listings can be found at ⓦwww.bostonmovietimes.com.

AMC Loews Boston Common 19 175 Tremont St ☎617/423-3499; Park **T**. There are nineteen screens on offer at this plush megaplex right by the Boston Common; the armrests move back so you can hold hands with your honey.

AMC Fenway 13 401 Park Drive ☎617/424-6266; Fenway **T**. Multiplex showing usual blockbuster fare for popcorn munchers with the occasional off-beat flick thrown in. Student discounts on offer.

AMC Loews Harvard Square 10 Church St, Cambridge ☎617/864-4580; Harvard **T**. A nice blend of vintage environs (it opened in 1926) with modern flicks, this petite Loews location also hosted the first live US performance of the Rocky Horror Picture show, a well-loved tradition that continues to this day (Sat at midnight; prepare for a rowdy live cast in addition to the film; ☎617/864-4581, $9.25).

Boston Museum of Science, Mugar Omni Theater ☎617/723-2500, www.mos.org; Science Park **T**. Daytime-only showings of mainly documentaries dealing with the natural world and science, all viewed on a fabulous five-story, wraparound screen. There's also a 3D cinema on offer where you get to wear cool retro glasses.

Brattle Theatre 40 Brattle St, Cambridge ☎617/876-6837, ⓦwww.brattlefilm.org; Harvard **T**. An historic basement indie cinema that pleasantly looks its age. Hosts a thematic film series plus occasional author appearances and readings.

Coolidge Corner Moviehouse 290 Harvard St, Brookline ☎617/734-2500, ⓦwww.coolidge.org; Coolidge Corner **T**. Film buffs flock to this classic theater for foreign and independent

movies. The interior has balconies and is adorned with Art Deco murals.

Harvard Film Archive Carpenter Center, 24 Quincy St, Cambridge ☎617/495-4700, ⓦwww.harvardfilmarchive.org; Harvard **T**. A mixed bag of artsy, foreign, and experimental films are shown here.

Institute of Contemporary Art 100 Northern Ave ☎617/478-3100, ⓦwww.icaboston.org; World Trade Center **T**. Inventive, eclectic and (of course) contemporary, the ICA screens films like Japanese and New England animation as well as bigger-box films like *The Matrix* amongst its gorgeous, glassy environs.

Kendall Square Cinema One Kendall Square, East Cambridge ☎617/499-1996, ⓦwww.landmarktheatres.com; Kendall **T**. All the neon decoration and small screens of your average multiplex, but this well-loved spot has the area's widest selection of first-rate foreign and independent films. It's actually located on Binney Street, near Cardinal Medieros Avenue.

Museum of Fine Arts Theater 465 Huntington Ave ☎617/267-9300, www.mfa.org/film; Museum **T**. Offbeat art films and documentaries, mostly by locals, often accompanied by lectures from the filmmaker. Also hosts several showcases like the Boston Jewish Film Festival and the Boston French Film Festival.

Somerville Theatre 55 Davis Square, Somerville ☎617/625-5700, ⓦwww.somervilletheatreonline.com; Davis **T**. Wacky home for camp, classic, cult, independent, foreign, and first-run pictures. Also doubles as a venue for live music. It's way out there – in more ways than one – past Cambridge, but well worth the trip.

Gay Boston

F or a town with a Puritan heritage and long-entrenched Blue Laws, it may come as some surprise that Boston is one of the more gay-friendly cities on the East Coast. Boston was one of the first cities in the US to endorse same-sex marriage, and in 2007 this sentiment was reaffirmed when state senators and representatives voted against an anti-gay marriage amendment by a landslide.

Much of the action centers around the **South End**, a largely residential area whose gay businesses (primarily restaurants, galleries, and cafés) are concentrated on a short stretch of Tremont Street above Union Park. It's not unusual here to see a gay pride flag flying openly and same-sex couples sitting together on their stoops, enjoying summer nights along with the rest of the neighborhood's diverse community.

Adjacent to the South End, on the other side of Arlington Street, is tiny **Bay Village**, a smaller gay enclave with a couple of good bars and clubs. Largely leftist **Cambridge** is also gay-friendly, with a few established gay nights to show for it, while **Jamaica Plain**, a neighborhood south of Boston proper, is quietly establishing itself as a lesbian-friendly community.

Although the city's **gay nightlife** ranges from leathermen at the *Ramrod* to cocktail-swilling guppies at *Club Café*, it remains small and fairly concentrated; the lesbian club scene, meanwhile, despite gaining more of a foothold in recent years, is still vastly under-represented in comparison.

In the summer, the **Back Bay Fens** and the **Charles River Esplanade**, between Dartmouth and Fairfield streets, at the northern perimeter of Back Bay, is a popular spot for cruising. Footbridges lead from the end of both streets over Storrow Drive to a narrow urban beach alongside the river. You can't swim in the Charles, but it's more than acceptable to sun yourself in a bathing suit here. The area can get a bit dicey at night, though, as can the rest of the Esplanade.

Information and resources

Boston's two free **gay newspapers** are *in newsweekly* (Ⓦ www.innewsweekly .com) and *Bay Windows* (Ⓦ www.baywindows.com). Both are good sources for **club information** – the other being the gay-friendly alternative paper *The Boston Phoenix*. All can be found in various venues and bookstores, notably Calamus and New Words (see p.201). These two noteworthy vestibules also have gay and lesbian community **bulletin boards**, with postings for apartment rentals, club happenings, and so forth.

General resources and support groups

Boston Alliance of Gay, Lesbian, Bisexual, and Transgender Youth (BAGLY) ⓦ www.bagly.org. Hosts events, discussion groups, and much more.

Boston Glass Community Center 93 Massachusetts Ave ⓣ 617/266-3349, ⓦ www.bostonglass .org; Hynes **T**. Drop-in center for people aged 13–25.

Fenway Community Health Center 7 Haviland St ⓣ 617/267-0900 or 1-888/242-0900, ⓦ www .fenwayhealth.org. All manner of health care for the gay community.

Gay and Lesbian Helpline ⓣ 617/267-9001. General information source.

Online

EDGE Boston ⓦ www.edgeboston.com. LGBT local and national news with a good map of local gay clubs and bars.

Gender Crash ⓦ www.gendercrash.com. Local event listings like poetry readings and queer picnics, columns, and more.

Link Pink ⓦ www.linkpink.com. Definitive "pink pages" for businesses, hotels, shops, and services catering to the New England LGBT community.

The List ⓦ www.queeragenda.org. Sign up to receive free weekly emails about upcoming gay and lesbian events in the Boston area.

Out In Boston ⓦ www.outinboston.com. Extensive and fun LGBT website with events listings, local and national news, and "homoscopes."

Sports

Boston Sports Club 560 Harrison Ave ⓣ 617/482-1266. A good gay-friendly gym with pool in the South End.

The Metropolitan Health Club 209 Columbus Ave ⓣ 617/536-3006. One of the most gay-friendly gyms in the city.

Pride Sports Boston ⓦ www.pridesportsboston .com ⓣ 617/937-5858. An alliance of gay- and lesbian-friendly gyms that organizes numerous sporting groups as well as Boston's team in the Gay Games.

Accommodation

All of Boston's **accommodations** are gay-friendly but none endorse a strict gay-only clientele policy. That said, you're likely to find more gay visitors than straight ones sleeping in the city's few gay-run guesthouses and bed and breakfasts. Most are situated in **Back Bay** and the **South End**, putting you within walking distance of the city's best gay bars and cafés; a quieter option in **Jamaica Plain** may appeal to members of the lesbian community, given its proximity to lesbian-friendly spots like the *Midway Café*. The **rates** below refer to the lowest cost of a standard double room throughout most of the year; taxes are not included.

463 Beacon Street Guest House 463 Beacon St ⓣ 617/536-1302, ⓦ www.463beacon.com; Hynes **T**. The good-sized rooms in this renovated brownstone, in the heart of Back Bay, are available by the night, week, and month, and come equipped with kitchenettes, cable TV, and various amenities (though no maid service); some have a/c, hardwood floors, and ornamental fireplaces. Ask for the top-floor room. $90.

Chandler Inn 26 Chandler St ⓣ 617/482-3450 or 1-800/842-3450, ⓦ www.chandlerinn.com; Back Bay **T**. Comfortable, 55-room, European-style hotel above the popular *Fritz* bar (see p.200); perks like satellite TV, in-room wireless Internet, and continental breakfast are included in the rates. $175.

Clarendon Square Inn 198 West Brookline St ⓣ 617/536-2229, ⓦ www.clarendonsquare.com; Prudential **T**. Gorgeous, well-loved bed and breakfast on a pretty South End side street with indulgent perks like heated bathroom tiles, limestone floors, and a 24hr roof-deck hot tub. Rooms starting at $125.

Encore 116 West Newton St ⓣ 617/247-3425 ⓦ www.encorebandb.com; Back Bay **T**. Another well-loved and very lovely B&B with contemporary decor, Wi-Fi, and a sitting area or deck in all three of their rooms. $150.

Oasis Guest House 22 Edgerly Rd ⓣ 617/267-2262, ⓦ www.oasisgh.com; Symphony **T**. Sixteen comfortable, affordable rooms, some with shared baths, in a renovated brownstone near Symphony Hall. $90.

Taylor House 50 Burroughs St, Jamaica Plain ☎617/888/228-2956, ⓦwww.taylorhouse.com; Green Street T. This delightful B&B, with two beautiful golden-retriever mascots, is a bit out of the way, but its three charming rooms, tucked away on the second floor of an 1855 Italianate house, feature queen-sized beds, TVs, and Internet access. Complimentary continental breakfast, which includes fresh baked bread, is served daily. $165.

Bars, clubs, and cafés

In a sense, Boston's **gay scene** is less of a "scene" these days, largely due to the fact that Boston is such a gay-friendly town – LGBT folk should feel welcome all over town. That said, Boston has a good variety of gay bars and clubs, ranging from the sophisticated (*dbar*) to the low-key (*Fritz*) – and of course a number of bumping dance clubs (*Buzz*, Saturday nights at *Avalon*); see Chapter 15, "Nightlife", for further details on these and other venues.

The hottest lesbian ticket around is Thursday night at *Toast Lounge*, in Somerville. For those night owls who haven't gotten their fill of dancing after the clubs close, ask around for an invite to Boston's secretive after-hours private party at *Rise* (306 Stuart St; ☎617/423-7473); the members-only stomping ground for gays and straights only gets going at 2am.

Avalon 15 Lansdowne St ☎617/262-2424, ⓦwww.avalonboston.com; Kenmore T. With a 1500-person capacity, *Avalon* is the biggest dance club in Boston, and any weekend night the place is positively jamming, often to the tracks laid down by out-of-town talent like Paul Oakenfold and Paul Van Dyk. The cavernous central floor is flanked on either side by bars. Sat is the granddaddy of Boston gay nights.

Buzz 51 Stuart St ☎617/267-8669, ⓦwww.buzzboston.com; New England Medical T. Resident DJs Michael Sheehan and MaryAlice lay down dance and house tracks at this two-floor dance club, where the drinks are poured by pumped and shirtless bartenders. $10–15 cover.

Club Café 209 Columbus Ave ☎617/536-0966, ⓦwww.clubcafe.com; Back Bay T. This combination restaurant/video bar popular among South End guppies has two back lounges, *Moonshine* and *Satellite*, showing the latest videos with signature martinis like the Pouty Princess and the Dirty Birdie.

dbar 1236 Dorchester Ave, Dorchester ☎617/265-4490, ⓦwww.dbarboston.com; Savin Hill T. Although Dorchester's *dbar* is a bit out of the way, it's well worth the trip – most locals think it's the best gay bar in town. Set amidst an inlaid mahogany interior, dbar serves fancy fusion fare like seared diver scallops ($19) from 5–10pm; after that it's all about honeysuckle caiparinhas ($8.50) and getting your groove on to Top 40 and house tunes.

Eagle 520 Tremont St ☎617/542-4494; Back Bay T. Generally tends to be the last stop of the night, with a cruise-y, dive-y flavor, and long lines at the boys' bathroom. Prepare for salty bar service.

Francesca's Espresso Bar 565 Tremont St ☎617/482-9026; Back Bay T. A great place to check out the Tremont St crowd passing by the plate-glass windows, this coffee shop gets packed in the evenings before clubs open, with a largely gay clientele caffeinating itself for a night out.

Fritz 26 Chandler St ☎617/482-4428; Back Bay T. This South End sports bar below *Chandler Inn* (see "Accommodation" p.157) is often likened to the gay version of *Cheers* due to its friendly staff and mix of casually attired locals and visitors. Good for Sun brunch.

Jacque's 79 Broadway ☎617/426-8902; Arlington T. *Priscilla, Queen of the Desert*, invades New England at this drag dream where past-it divas lip-synch "I Love the Nightlife." There's a nice melting pot of patrons; it's quite popular for bachelorette parties. Showtime is 10.30pm nightly (Tues is Karaoke night), but beware – the festivities end at midnight, Cinderella. Cover $6–10.

Machine 1254 Boylston St ☎617/266-2986; Kenmore T. A favorite with the gay crowd on Fri & Sat when the club's large dancefloor and top-notch music has the place pumping. The pool tables, video screens, Internet terminals, and bar near the dancefloor let you take a breather and soak up the scene. Cover $6–8.

Boston Pride (June) A nine-day festival that culminates in a parade starting at Boston Common. ⓦ www.bostonpride.org.

Fantasia Fair (Oct) The US's longest running continuous transgender event has been in Provincetown since 1975. ⓦ www.fantasiafair.org.

Out on the Edge (Oct) Held at the Boston Center for Arts, this is one of the world's premier queer theater fests. ⓦ www.thetheateroffensive.org.

Holly Folly (Dec) Provincetown's big gay Yuletide fest draws the crowds back to the Cape Cod seaside town. ⓦ www.hollyfolly.com.

Milky Way 405 Centre St, Jamaica Plain ⓣ 617/524-3740; Green Street **T**. Situated in lesbian-friendly JP, this lovely retro space beneath *Bella Luna* pizza (see p.177) features low-key local bands (think folky-rock), cheap beer, old-school Galaga and Ms Pac Man games, and (best of all) seven vintage bowling lanes.

Midway Café 3496 Washington St, Jamaica Plain, ⓣ 617/524-9038, wwww.midwaycafe .com; Green Street **T**. Neighborhood hangout with a popular Thurs Queeraoke Night; there's free pool 8–10pm, $2 drink specials from 9–10.30pm, and dancing unitl 2am. $5 cover.

Paradise 180 Massachusetts Ave, Cambridge ⓣ 617/494-0700, ⓦ www.paradisecambridge .com; Central **T**. Upstairs, male dancers (almost) bare it all; those who want to keep some clothes on stay downstairs where a smallish dancefloor rocks out to Top 40 tunes. Open till 1am Sun–Thurs and 2am Fri & Sat.

Pure 75 Warranton St ⓣ 617/417-0186, ⓦ www .shuttavac.com; Boylston **T**. Fridays see a bumping lesbian dance night amidst spacious lounge environs; patrons get their groove on to hip hop and top 40 beats. $8–10 cover.

Ramrod 1254 Boylston St ⓣ 617/266-2986, ⓦ www.ramrodboston.com; Kenmore **T**. This Fenway meat market attracts a pretty hungry crowd with its strictly enforced Levi/leather dress code (Fri & Sat) – no shirts or cologne allowed. Not quite as hardcore as it sounds, as it's directly upstairs from the harmless *Machine* (see p.200).

Revive at Club Café 209 Columbus Ave ⓣ 617/536-0966, ⓦ www.dykenight.com; Back Bay **T**. Thurs nights (7–10pm) at Club Café play host to low-key lesbian entertainment aimed at Boston's thirty-plus crowd. Events cover a spectrum of offerings from networking to comedy shows to wine pairing courses.

Toast Lounge 70 Union Sq ⓣ 617/623-9211, ⓦ www.toastlounge.com; Harvard **T**; #86 bus to Union Square. *Toast*'s buzzy atmosphere has become a firm favorite on the lesbian scene, with a popular Fri night dance party.

Twentyeight Degrees 1 Appleton St ⓣ 617/728-0728; Back Bay **T**. The food is swanky Italian-inspired fare, but the drinks (like the frozen bellini or blueberry basil martini) are a safer bet at this gay-savvy, candle-lit lounge replete with leather seating, wispy curtains at your table, and the prettiest bathrooms in Boston.

Bookstores

Calamus Bookstore 92B South St ⓣ 617/338-1931, ⓦ www.calamusbooks.com; South Station **T**. Born from the ashes of the much-lamented Glad Day bookstore, Calamus is owned by former Glad Day manager John Mitzel and is easily recognized by the Rainbow flag outside.

New Words 186 Hampshire St, Cambridge ⓣ 617/876-5310, ⓦ www.centerfornewwords .org; Central Square **T**. This lesbian bookstore caters to all aspects of the literary scene with reading rooms, a host of workshops, and slam poetry events.

15

GAY BOSTON | Bookstores

16

Shopping

T
hough Boston has its share of chain stores and typical mall fare, there are plenty of unusual and funky places to **shop** here. The city is perhaps best loved for its bookstores, having established a reputation as a literary haven and academic center; on a more modern – and fashionable – note, it has also become known for its small, exclusive boutiques that feature the work of local designers.

No matter what you're looking for, Boston is an extremely pleasant place in which to shop for it, with unique, high-quality stores clustered on charming avenues like Beacon Hill's Charles Street and Back Bay's Newbury Street. The former has a dense concentration of **antique shops**, while the latter is an eight-block stretch that starts off trendily, with upscale clothes and boutiques, and then begins to cater to more of a student population as it moves west past Exeter Street; here, **record stores** and **novelty shops** take over, a theme continued out to Kenmore Square. This span also has a handful of good **bookstores** – though the best are clustered in and around Harvard Square, across the Charles River in Cambridge. In recent years, the North End has also become a hotspot for boutique wear, with tempting designer shops clustering in and around Hanover Street; the gay-friendly South End has a number of fashionable clothing and home furnishing stores as well.

The rest of the action takes place in various downtown quarters, first and foremost at **Faneuil Hall Marketplace**. This area has become more commercialized over the years, but its bustling live atmosphere make a trip to this outdoor mall worthwhile, not to mention the many food stalls of **Quincy Market**. To the south, **Downtown Crossing**, at Washington and Summer streets, is centered on **Filene's Basement**, a bargain-hunter's delight for marked-down brand-name clothing. Stores are generally open 9.30 or 10am to 6 or 7pm Monday through Saturday (sometimes later on Tuesday and Wednesday) and on Sunday from noon to 6pm.

Antiques

Cambridge Antique Market 201 Monsignor O'Brien Hwy ⊤617/868-9655, ⊛www .marketantique.com; Lechmere **T**. Slightly off-the-beaten-track, but the 225 dealers at this five-floor co-operative-style market have everything from nineteenth-century furniture to vintage clothing.
Judith Dowling Asian Art 133 Charles St ⊤617/523-5211; Charles **T**. A first-rate selection of Asian pieces from all periods, though at prices that encourage browsing

rather than buying.
Marcoz Antiques 177 Newbury St ⊤617/262-0780; Arlington **T**. Boutique with eighteenth-and nineteenth-century French, English, and American furniture and accessories.
Twentieth Century Limited 73 Charles St ⊤617/742-1031; Charles **T**. A fabulous, sparkling selection of antique jewelry with a focus on earlier twentieth-century pieces; good collection of big names like Chanel and Kenneth Jay Lane, too.

Bookstores

Boston has a rich history as a literary city, enhanced by its numerous universities as well as the many traces of authors and publishing houses that have at one time called the town home. This legacy is well reflected in the quality and diversity of **bookstores** found both in Boston and neighboring Cambridge. For books with a Boston connection, along with a history of literature in nineteenth-century Boston, see "Contexts pp.297–303."

New

Barnes & Noble Downtown Crossing ☎617/426-5502; Downtown Crossing **T**; Prudential Center, 800 Boylston St ☎617/247-6959; Prudential **T**; 660 Beacon St ☎617/267-8484; Kenmore **T**; 325 Harvard St, Brookline ☎617/232-0594; Coolidge Corner **T**. Four large outposts of the national bookstore chain, with decent newsstands and good selections of bargain books and calendars. The one on Beacon Street is topped off by the neon Citgo sign (see p.109).

Brookline Booksmith 279 Harvard St, Brookline ☎617/566-6660, ⓦwww.brooklinebooksmith.com; Coolidge Corner **T**. This cozy shop with hardwood floors doesn't have a particular strength, but its friendly staff makes it perfect for browsing; holds a good author reading series, too.

Calamus Bookstore 92B South St ☎617/338-1931, ⓦwww.calamusbooks.com; South Station **T**. Boston's only gay bookstore, with a good selection of reasonably priced books and cards, plus a vast community bulletin board at the entrance.

Grolier Poetry Bookstore 6 Plympton St, Cambridge ☎617/547-4648; Harvard **T**. With 14,000 volumes of verse, this tiny shop has gained an international following among poets and their fans. Frequent readings.

Harvard Book Store 1256 Massachusetts Ave, Cambridge ☎617/661-1515, ⓦwww.harvard.com; Harvard **T**. Three huge rooms of new books upstairs, with a basement for used volumes and remainders downstairs. Academic and critical work in the humanities and social sciences dominate, with a healthy dose of fiction thrown in.

Harvard Cooperative Society 1400 Massachusetts Ave, Cambridge ☎617/499-2000, ⓦharvard.bkstore.com; Harvard **T**. Founded in 1882 by a group of students, the Coop carries an extensive range of college textbooks, but it's also the best place to buy Harvard and MIT insignia sportswear and clothing.

MIT Press Bookstore 292 Main St, Cambridge ☎617/253-5249, ⓦwww.mitpress.mit.edu/bookstore; Kendall Square **T**. Lots of fascinating science and tech stuff, much of it surprisingly accessible, and racks of discounted and remaindered books as well. Also organizes the authors@MIT series of talks, usually held in the Kirsch Auditorium at the Stata Center (32 Vassar St).

Trident Booksellers & Café 338 Newbury St ☎617/267-8688, www.tridentbookscafe.com; Hynes **T**. One of the last great independent bookstores in Boston. Has a bit of an alternative vibe; buy some funky stationery and write letters home over a cup of coffee in their superb café (see p.174).

Used

Brattle Book Shop 9 West St ☎617/542-0210, ⓦwww.brattlebookshop.com; Park St **T**. One of the oldest antiquarian bookstores in the country. You can buy a book for $1 outside,

▲ Harvard Book Store

or find one for $10,000 inside; they recently sold a first-edition *Walden* for a few grand.

Bryn Mawr Book 373 Huron Ave, Cambridge ☎617/661-1770, ⓦwww.brynmawrbookstore.com; **Harvard T**. This neighborhood bookstore vends titles in a relaxed Cambridge setting. Weather permitting, there are sidewalk displays for pedestrian browsers.

Lorem Ipsum 157 Hampshire St, Cambridge ☎617/497-7669, ⓦwww.loremipsumbooks.com; **Central T**. A magnetic, browse-worthy space, *Lorem Ipsum* is the epitome of the neighborhood bookstore, well-stocked with everything from art and children's lit to pirates and "tiny books." Best is the TV at its entrance on which a taped note decries: "read instead."

Raven Used Books 52-B JFK St, Cambridge ☎617/441-6999, ⓦwww.ravencambridge.com; **Harvard T**. Readers rave about *Raven*, and rightly so. This delightful, well-kept little bookstore stocks scholarly (but not pretentious) reads covering everything from anarchism and gender studies to poetry and film. A great spot for lingering and it's nearly impossible to leave without a book under your arm.

Rodney's 698 Massachusetts Ave, Cambridge ☎617/876-6467, ⓦwww.rodneysbookstore.com; **Central T**. A meandering, time-absorbing space, with two spacious floors brimming with a fun collection of used and eclectic books. Best is the second floor's fabulous art book selection.

Travel

Globe Corner Bookstore 28 Church St, Cambridge ☎617/497-6277, ⓦwww.globecorner.com; **Harvard T**. These travel specialists are well stocked with maps, travel literature, and guidebooks, with an especially strong New England section.
Willowbee & Kent 519 Boylston St ☎617/437-6700; **Copley T**. The first floor of this roomy store has a good range of travel guidebooks

and gear; the second is given over to a travel agency.

Specialty

Kate's Mystery Bookstore 2211 Massachusetts Ave ☎617/491-2660, ⓦwww.katesmysterybooks.com; **Davis T**. Mystery-only bookstore selling both old and new titles; you'll know the place from the faux gravestones in the front yard.
Lucy Parsons Center 549 Columbus Ave ☎617/267-6272, ⓦwww.lucyparsons.org; **Mass Ave T**. The far left lives on in this shrine to socialism, with a particular bent toward women's issues, labor issues, and radical economics. They also have free pamphlets on local demonstrations, plus occasional readings and lectures.
Million-Year Picnic 99 Mt Auburn St, Cambridge ☎617/492-6763; **Harvard T**. For the comic-obsessed. Features Japanese anime, *Superman*, *Tank Girl*, and more, and is stronger on current stuff than older material. The staff has encyclopedic knowledge, and is tolerant of browsers.
New England Comics 14a Eliot St ☎617/354-5352, ⓦwww.newenglandcomics.com; **Harvard T**. Back issues of classic comics, new editions, and graphic novels fill this Cambridge stalwart. There are six other locations in New England, including Allston (131 Harvard Ave ☎617/783-1848; Harvard Ave **T**) and Brookline (316 Harvard St ☎617/566-0115; Coolidge Corner **T**).
Nini's Corner/Out of Town News Harvard Square, Cambridge; Harvard T. Few published magazines cannot be found at one of these two good, old-fashioned newsstands that lie directly across from each other in the heart of Harvard Square.
Schoenhof's 76A Mount Auburn St, Cambridge ☎617/547-8855, ⓦwww.schoenhofs.com; **Harvard T**. Well-stocked foreign language bookstore that's sure to have that volume of Proust you're looking for, as well as any children's books you might want.

Clothes

Boston is a great place for **clothes shopping**, with options running the gamut from dollar-per-pound vintage duds to extravagant boutique and designer threads. The North End has been getting particular attention lately for its up-and-coming boutiques, while the gay-savvy South End has been accruing its own smart selection of clothing and home stores. Cobblestoned Charles Street has perhaps the prettiest shopping environs, with a number of swanky shops to match its upscale address. Newbury Street (Ⓦ www.newbury-st.com) remains the go-to standard for big-name designer stores like Marc Jacobs, Armani, and Chanel, although it also has funky affordable wear with youthful spots like Jasmine/Sola.

Designer stores

Alan Bilzerian 34 Newbury St Ⓣ**617/536-1001; Arlington T.** Tri-level store with international haute couture from Jean-Paul Gaultier and Comme des Garçons alongside the owner's own label. Menswear and accessories occupy the first floor and womenswear the second; clubwear roosts in a small basement section.

Armani 22 Newbury St Ⓣ**617/267-3200, Ⓦ www.emporioarmani.com; Arlington T.** The Italian workaholic's Boston store displays the typical no-fuss classical designs that go down well in this city. Further down is the sportswear-brand Emporio Armani (210–212 Newbury St Ⓣ617/262-7300).

Burberry 2 Newbury St Ⓣ**617/236-1000; Arlington T.** The famously conservative British clothier seems right at home in its four-story Newbury Street digs, across from the *Taj Boston*. Excellent albeit pricey stuff.

Chanel 5 Newbury St Ⓣ**617/859-0055; Arlington T.** A great start to Boston's shopping boulevard, this branch sells every-thing Chanel, from Karl Lagerfeld's ready-to-wear collections to cosmetics.

J. Press 82 Mt Auburn St Ⓣ**617/547-9886; Harvard T.** Old Harvard lives on in J. Press's sober collection of high-quality men's suits; rates are mid-level ($400–1200 per suit) for the store's genteel clientele.

Louis Boston 234 Berkeley St Ⓣ**617/262-6100, Ⓦ www.louisboston .com; Arlington T.** Occupying a stately, freestanding building from 1863 that once housed Boston's Museum of Natural History (which became the Museum of Science), this is the city's classiest and most expensive clothes emporium. Though mostly geared toward men, the top floor is reserved for designer womenswear. A Boston landmark, and still worth a visit, despite the price tags.

Marc Jacobs 81 Newbury St Ⓣ**617/425-0707; Arlington T.** Bustling Marc Jacobs namesake (filled as much with eager college students as fashionistas) downstairs offers the afford-able Marc by Marc Jacobs line, while upstairs is fashion heaven (with equally sky-high prices).

Ralph Lauren 95 Newbury St Ⓣ**617/424-1124; Arlington T.** The Polo brand much loved by preppy Ivy Leaguers sits well in the home of MIT and Harvard.

Riccardi 116 Newbury St Ⓣ**617/266-3158; Copley T.** This, the hippest designer schmatta shop in Boston, could hold its own just fine in Paris or New York. A few of the labels on parade are Dolce & Gabbana, Romeo Gigli, and Jean-Paul Gaultier. Good spot for fancy jeans.

Serenella 134 Newbury St Ⓣ**617/266-5568; Copley T.** High-end women's boutique selling Euro labels like Pucci and Balenciaga to a well-heeled clientele.

Local and boutique stores

Bodega 6 Clearway St Ⓣ**617/421-1550, Ⓦ www.bdgastore.com; Hynes T.** A truly fantastic original. Out front stocks your favorite bodega mainstays (think Cheerios and toilet paper); walk towards the vending machine door to reveal a secret backroom filled with covetous designer sneakers and stylish hip-hop wear.

Dress 221 Newbury St Ⓣ**617/424-7125, Ⓦ www.dressboston.com; Copley T.** A bonafide Boston best. This trendsetting yet friendly boutique has stylish T-shirts (Adam + Eve), jeans (Lofli), separates, and drool-worthy dresses (Vena Cava, Vanessa Bruno) to sate even the most discerning fashion-ista. Ultrachic but very approachable.

House of Culture 585 Columbus Ave Ⓣ**617/236-1090; Massachusetts Ave T.** Local designer Patrick Petty was wardrobe stylist to Mark Wahlberg and Boys II Men, and even if you're not in the market for his creations, nip in to browse and pick up clubbing flyers.

Injeanius 441 Hanover St Ⓣ**617/523-5326, Ⓦ www.injeanius.com; Haymarket T.** A stylish North End boutique that's filled with high-end women's denim like Rock & Republic and Goldsign; best are the helpful employees who magically direct you toward that perfect pair of jeans. They also run a stellar dress boutique, *Twilight,* around the corner at **12 Fleet St (☎617/523-8008).**

Johnny Cupcakes 279 Newbury St ☎617/375-0100, ⓦwww.johnnycupcakes.com; Hynes **T**. Every hipster in town has a Johnny Cupcakes T-shirt, but why shouldn't they when *Johnny* prints each one with smart designs and catchy slogans like "Make Cupcakes Not War"? Endearing with an edge, these locally-made tees and undies are the perfect take-home treat.

Stel's 334 Newbury St ☎617/262-3348, ⓦwww.stelsinc.com; Hynes **T**. Browsing the wares along handcrafted tables and exposed brick walls, this slouchy boutique feels a bit like your grandparents' attic, complete with soft, neutral cardigans and woolen separates. Pricier than your grandparents would like, but *Stel's* is a master of throw-it-together chic.

Stil 170 Newbury St ☎617/859-7845, ⓦwww.stilinc.com; Copley **T**. Another fancy boutique, this one known for its cool Swedish designers and whimsical home decor section (think Jonathan Adler). *Stil* is best loved for its fabulous party dresses.

Twilight 12 Fleet St ☎617/523-8008; Haymarket **T**. Run by the same lovely mastermind behind *Injeanius*, *Twilight* opened up when trendy denim wearers started asking about things to wear for a big night out. Lovingly filled with chi-chi dresses (think Betsey Johnson), heels, and well-priced sparkly jewelry, this smart North End boutique has helpful staffers and makes a great spot for lingering.

Uniform 511 Tremont St ☎617/247-2360, ⓦwww.uniformboston.com; Back Bay **T**. If you know a guy who needs a little style kick, march him directly into *Uniform*, where kindly South End staffers will transform your man into an "after" photo sporting casually chic brands like Penguin and Ben Sherman.

Wish 49 Charles St ☎617/227-4441, ⓦwww.wishstyle.com; Charles **T**. This gem of a boutique offers pretty dresses and ensembles by Nanette Lepore, Theory, and Velvet that'll put you in good stead for either a Nantucket getaway or a Sun stroll on Charles Street.

Chain stores

H & M 100 Newbury St ☎617/859-3192; ⓦwww.hm.com; Copley **T**; 350 Washington St ☎617/482-7001; Downtown Crossing **T**. *H & M*

has won countless fans for its inexpensive yet stylish threads; carries both men and women's fashions.

Jasmine/Sola 344 Newbury St ☎617/867-4636, ⓦwww.jasminesola.com; Hynes **T**; 29 Brattle St, Harvard Square ☎617/576-0031; Harvard **T**; **Prudential Center** ☎617/578-0550; Prudential **T**. Trendy, well-recommended shop retailing streetwear labels like Miss Sixty, Diesel, Juicy Couture, and Bloom, as well as shoes and accessories; menswear shop at the Harvard location.

Lucky 229 Newbury St ☎617/236-0102; ⓦwww.luckybrandjeans.com; Hynes **T**. One of America's hottest jeans brands, thanks to affordable prices and the "Lucky you" message on the inside of the fly.

Patagonia 346 Newbury St ☎617/424-1776; Hynes **T**. Patagonia invented the soft, synthetic fleece called "Synchilla," and there's still no better way to fend off a Boston winter than in a jacket or vest lined with the colorful stuff.

Urban Outfitters 361 Newbury St ☎617/236-0088, ⓦwww.urbanoutfitters.com; Hynes **T**; 11 JFK St, Cambridge ☎617/864-0070; Harvard **T**. Youth fashion labels from Diesel to Stussy, plus funky home furnishings and irreverent gift items.

Used, thrift, and consignment

Bobby from Boston 19 Thayer St ☎617/423-9299; NE Medical or Broadway **T**. Long adored by local rockers and movie wardrobe professionals, Bobby's South End loft is, hands-down, the best place to find men's vintage clothing from the 1920s through the 1960s as well as a great spot for fabulous female finds. Cash or check only.

The Garment District/Dollar-a-Pound 200 Broadway, Cambridge ☎617/876-5230, ⓦwww.garment-district.com; Kendall **T**. Warehouse full of bins crammed with used togs. If you have the time to sift through the leftovers of twentieth-century fashion, you'll upon some great bargains – all at the rate of $1.50 per pound of clothing. And on Fri, it's reduced to 75¢ per pound.

History 1693 Mass Ave, Cambridge ☎617/868-5400; ⓦwww.historyboutique.com; Porter Square **T**. Set amidst fun checkerboard flooring and run by a former history teacher, this vintage haven is well-organized by decade and features a sweet story attached to each item (a slinky '60s babydoll dress reads "this might actually be a *fun* New Year's Eve").

Karma 26 Prince St ⓣ617/723-8338; **Haymarket T.** Not your grandmother's consignment store: a sylish little North End spot carrying vintage designer threads like Prada and Chanel. There's also an inviting array of inexpensive jewelry and a solid sales rack in the back.

Mass Army & Navy Store 328 Newbury St ⓣ617/437-1657; **Hynes T.** You can stock up on camouflage and combat boots at this military surplus store, plus there's a good and inexpensive range of (mostly men's) pants, shirts, and shoes worth inspecting.

Oona's 1210 Massachusetts Ave, Cambridge ⓣ617/491-2654; **Harvard T.** Since 1972, Oona's has been the place to find vintage "experienced clothing" – in this case kimonos, flapper dresses, leather jackets, and various accessories.

Poor Little Rich Girl 255 Elm St, Somerville ⓣ617/684-0157; **Davis T.** A funky little consignment shop with rock star roots (the owner is in a band called "Heavy Stud"), this vintage gem has well-priced goods in a spacious locale.

Velvet Fly 424 Hanover St ⓣ617/557-4359; **Haymarket T.** Dubbed "modern vintage," this cute little North End boutique offers re-worked dresses alongside more contemporary fare as well as handbags, jewelry and other wardrobe staples.

Second Time Around 176 Newbury St ⓣ617/247-3504, ⓦ www.secondtimearound .net; **Arlington T;** 8 Eliot St ⓣ617/491-7185; **Harvard T.** Great prices on barely worn, albeit conservative, clothing, predominantly from Banana Republic, the Gap, Anne Taylor, and Abercrombie & Fitch.

Crafts

Beadworks 167 Newbury St ⓣ617/247-7227, ⓦ www.beadworksboston.com; **Copley T;** 23 Church St, Cambridge ⓣ617/868-9777; **Harvard T.** With so many kinds of beads, it's a good thing the sales staff can assist you in creating a "distinctly personal adornment." Great afternoon activity for older children.

The Cambridge Artists' Cooperative 59 Church St ⓣ617/868-4434, ⓦ www.cambridgeartistscoop .com; **Harvard T.** Three floors fill this Harvard Square shop with all kinds of crafts, from woodcarvings and glass sculptures to wearable art and beaded bags.

Magpie 416 Highland Ave, Somerville ⓣ617/623-3330, ⓦ www.magpie-store.com; **Davis T.** Cute crafts boutique carefully-stocked with hip handmade goods like knitted iPod cases and irreverent needlework. A great way to support your local artist.

Papersource 338 Boylston St ⓣ617/536-3444, ⓦ www.paper-source.com; **Arlington T,** 1810 Massachusetts Ave, Cambridge ⓣ617/497-1077, Porter Square **T,** 1361 Beacon St, Brookline ⓣ617/497-1077, Coolidge Corner **T.** Their motto is "do something creative every day," and at this lovable, spacious stationery store, which brims with fancy paper, eclectic rubber stamps, and creative office stuff, it's easy to do just that.

Rugg Road Paper Co. 105 Charles St ⓣ617/742-0002; **Charles T.** They've got high-end paper products of all kinds, including lovely cards, stationery, and wrapping paper.

Simon Pearce 115 Newbury St ⓣ617/450-8388 or 1-877/452-7763, ⓦ www.simonpearce.com; **Copley T.** Hand-blown glassware from this Irish-born, Vermont-based craftsman.

Food and drink

Look no further than the North End for all manner of tasty pastry; for gourmet-style take-home eats, Cambridge is especially strong in variety.

Bakeries

Bova's Bakery 76 Prince St ⓣ617/523-5601, ⓦ www.northendboston.com/bovabakery; **Haymarket T.** A 24hour bakery in the North End, selling delights like plain and chocolate cannoli, oven-fresh cakes, and whoopie pies; famously cheap, too, with most items around $5.

Choco Choco House 83 Pembroke St Brookline ⓣ617/718-0946, ⓦ www.chocochocohouse .com; **Back Bay T.** Inventive sweets abound at this well-loved South End *chocolaterie* known for its chocolate shoes and handbags as well as its mouthwatering truffles filled with pink champagne and cardamom.

Clear Flour Bread 178 Thorndike St Brookline ☎617/739-0060, ⓦ www.clearflourbread.com; **Packard's Corner T.** Locals line up religiously for what is probably Boston's best artisan breads, brioche, and pear ginger coffee cake. Worth the trek out.

Eldo Bake House 36 Harrison Ave ☎617/350-7977; **Chinatown T.** The best bakery in Chinatown, replete with fluffy mango sponge cakes, tasty egg tarts, and candied ginger and plums.

Maria's Pastry Shop 46 Cross St ☎ 617/523-1196 ⓦ www.northendboston.com/marias; **Haymarket T.** The place doesn't look like much, but *Maria's* has the best Neapolitan treats in town; her custard-filled *sfogliatelle* and *ossa di morti* (bones of the dead) cookies are to die for.

Mike's Pastry 300 Hanover St ☎617/742-3050; **Haymarket T.** The famed North End bakery is one part Italian and two parts American, meaning in addition to cannoli and tiramisu, you'll find counters full of brownies and cookies. The endless array of éclairs is not to be missed – but expect to wait in line for one.

Rosie's Bakery 243 Hampshire St, Cambridge ☎617/491-9488, ⓦ www.rosiesbakery.com; #69 bus; 2 South Station ☎617/239-4684. This bakery offers the richest, most decadent desserts in Cambridge. Their specialty is a fudge brownie called the "Chocolate Orgasm" (though the less provocatively named lemon squares are just as good). A second outlet is in South Station.

Gourmet food and wine shops

Cardullo's 6 Brattle St, Cambridge ☎491-8888, ⓦ www.cardullos.com; **Harvard T.** Gourmet products from just about anywhere are available at this well-stocked Harvard Square store; if nothing else, be sure to stop in for a sample. Depending on the weather, you can sit at one of the sidewalk tables with a fresh sandwich and watch the people go by.

Dairy Fresh Candies 57 Salem St ☎617/742-2639 or 1-800/336-5536, ⓦ www.dairyfreshcandies .com; **Haymarket T.** Mouth-watering array of confections, from chocolates and hard candies to dried fruits and nuts; the perfect pick-me-ups for a Little Italy stroll.

Formaggio Kitchen 244 Huron Ave, Cambridge ☎617/354-4750, ⓦ www.formaggiokitchen .com; **Harvard T**; 268 Shawmut Ave, ☎617/350-6996; **Back Bay T.** One of the best cheese shops in Boston; the gourmet meats, salads, sandwiches, and baked goods are also worth sampling.

Haymarket Blackstone St, no phone; Haymarket T. Although it's not very classy (and certainly not gourmet), Haymarket is a Boston institution, and probably the best place in town to score ridiculously cheap produce. Farm and fish stands are set up all along Blackstone street on Fri and Sat mornings (in warm weather); prepare for lots of heckling and haggling.

Monica's Salumeria 130 Salem St ☎617/742-4101; **Haymarket T.** Lots of imported Italian cheeses, cooked meats, cookies, and pastas.

New Deal Fish Market 622 Cambridge St, Cambridge ☎617/876-8227; **Lechmere T.** Top-notch, sashimi-grade seafood with a wide selection of cuts ranging from the crowd pleasers (crab, lobster, and shrimp) to more specialized fare (maguro tuna and stickle-back). Very fairly priced.

Polcari's Coffee 105 Salem St ☎617/227-0786, ⓦ www.northendboston.com /polcaricoffee; **Haymarket T.** Vintage, well-loved and brimming with coffees, as well as every spice you could think of. Worth going inside for the aroma alone, or just to hear the local gossip from the guys behind the counter.

Salumeria Italiana 151 Richmond St ☎617/523-8743 or 1-800/400-5916, ⓦ www .salumeriaitaliana.com; **Haymarket T.** Arguably the best Italian grocer this side of Rome. Stocks only the finest cheeses, meats, balsamic vinegars, and more.

Savenor's 160 Charles St ☎617/723-6328; **Charles T.** Known for its meats, this small gourmet food shop in Beacon Hill also has a better-than-average produce selection (Julia Child used to shop here), in addition to prepared foods – ideal for taking to the nearby Charles River Esplanade for a picnic.

See Sun Market 19 Harrison St ☎617/426-0954; **Chinatown T.** The most accessible of Chinatown's markets. Has all the basics, like huge bags of rice and a dizzying range of See Sun soy sauces, plus more exotic delicacies like pig's feet and jars of salted ziganid fish.

V. Cirace & Sons 173 North St ☎617/227-3193; Haymarket **T**. A great liquor store, with the expected range of Italian wines – it's in the North End, after all – and much more.

Health food

Nature Food Centers GNC 545 Boylston St ☎617/536-1226; Copley **T**. If you're looking for vitamin-enriched fruit juices, organic produce, and other healthful items, this small store in Copley Square is bound to have it.

Trader Joe's 899 Boylston St ☎617/262-6505; Hynes **T**. Everyone's favorite Hawaiian-themed grocery store, well-stocked with good deals on everyday items like imported cheeses, juice, and baked goods in addition to more eclectic fare like Masala veggie burgers and wasabi mayonnaise. Conveniently located in Back Bay; well-situated for a picnic in the Public Garden.

Whole Foods 181 Cambridge St ☎617/723-0004; Bowdoin **T**. 15 Westland Ave ☎617/375-1010; Symphony **T**. The Boston branches of this pricey, organic-friendly chain have all the alternative foodstuffs you'd expect, plus some of Boston's best salad bars.

Galleries

Dozens of Boston's major **art galleries** can be found on Newbury Street; most are generally browser-friendly. South Street, in downtown's so-called Leather District, tends to feature the most contemporary work, as does the SoWa district in the South End.

Arden Gallery 129 Newbury St ☎617/247-0610, ⓦwww.ardengallery.com; Copley **T**. Arden's focus is on abstractionist contemporary paintings, vivid examples of which are displayed in the oversized second-story bowfront window.

Barbara Krakow Gallery 10 Newbury St, 5th floor ☎617/262-4490, ⓦwww.barbarakrakowgallery .com; Arlington T. This A-list multimedia gallery attracts the hottest artists from New York City and around the globe; Kiki Smith and Annette Lemieux are but two of the stars that have shown here in recent years.

Bernard Toale Gallery 450 Harrison St ☎617/482-2477; Back Bay **T**. Curator Bernard Toale officially sanctified the burgeoning SoWa district when he moved his Newbury Street gallery here in 1998. Painting, photography, drawing, sculpture, video, and prints are all featured.

Fort Point Arts Community 300 Summer St ☎617/423-4299, ⓦwww.fortpointarts.org; South Station **T**. Founded in 1980, this meandering warehouse space is the public front for the Fort Point Arts Community, with contemporary painting and mixed media in its gallery downstairs; upstairs has

historically been workspace heaven for countless local artists. The third weekend in Oct hosts a wildly popular open studios event.

Gallery NAGA 67 Newbury St ☎617/267-9060, ⓦwww.gallerynaga.com; Arlington **T**. Contemporary painting, sculpture, studio furniture, and photography from Boston and New England artists, located in the Gothic Revival Church of the Covenant.

International Poster Gallery 205 Newbury St ☎617/375-0076, ⓦwww.internationalposter .com; Copley **T**. More than 6000 posters on display from 1895 through World War II.

Nielsen Gallery 179 Newbury St ☎617/266-4835, ⓦwww.nielsengallery.com; Copley **T**. Back Bay's oldest gallery puts the accent on contemporary painting and drawing, and, occasionally, sculpture.

The Society of Arts and Crafts 175 Newbury St ☎617/266-1810, ⓦwww.societyofcrafts.org; Copley **T**. The oldest non-profit crafts group in America has two floors here. The first is its commercial outpost, with a wide range of ceramics, glass, and jewelry; the second floor is reserved for themed (and free) special exhibitions.

Malls and department stores

The major **malls** quite obviously cobble together all your needs in one convenient location; none here particularly stand out save perhaps the marketplace at Faneuil Hall, for atmosphere alone. For **department stores**, the idiosyncratic Filene's Basement, in Downtown Crossing, is an institution.

Malls

CambridgeSide Galleria 100 Cambridgeside Place ⊤617/621-8666, ⓌJwww.cambridgesidegalleria .com; Kendall **T**. Not too different from any other large American shopping mall. The haze of neon and packs of teens can be draining, but there's no similarly dense and convenient conglomeration of shops in Cambridge.

Copley Place 100 Huntington Ave ⊤617/379-5000, Ⓦwww.simon.com; Copley **T**. This ambitious, upscale office-retail-residential complex features more than a hundred stores, including Jimmy Choo, Salvatore Ferragamo, and Tiffany & Co., with Barney's and Neiman Marcus as its department store anchors.

Faneuil Hall Marketplace Faneuil Hall ⊤617/523-1300, Ⓦwww .faneuilhallmarketplace.com; Government Center **T**. The city's most famous market, with a hundred or so shops, plus next door's Quincy Market. It's a bit tourist-oriented, but still worth a trip.

The Heritage on the Garden 300 Boylston St ⊤617/423-0002; Arlington **T**. Not so much a mall as a very upscale mixed-use complex across from the Public Garden, consisting of condos, restaurants, and boutiques.

The Shops at Prudential Center 800 Boylston St ⊤617/236-3060; Prudential **T**. This conglomeration of a hundred or so mid-market shops is heavily patronized by local residents and conventioneers from the adjacent Hynes Convention Center, who seem to genuinely enjoy buying commemorative T-shirts and ties from the center-atrium pushcarts.

Department stores

Barneys New York 100 Huntington Ave, in Copley Place ⊤617/385-3300, Ⓦwww.barneys .com; Copley **T**. Bostonians get tired of being compared with New York. But when this luxe Manhattan landmark opened in 2006, there were cries of shopping joy heard round the city. Barneys' lavish two-story space is worth a look just for its whimsical decor; they're best-loved for their women's shoes and accessories department.

Filene's 426 Washington St ⊤617/357-2100, Ⓦwww.filenes.com; Downtown Crossing **T**. The merchandise inside downtown Boston's oldest department store is standard issue; the stunning 1912 Beaux Arts facade is not. You'll have better luck downstairs in Filene's Basement.

Filene's Basement 426 Washington St ⊤617/542-2011, Ⓦwww.filenesbasement .com; Downtown Crossing **T**. Established in 1908, Filene's Basement is a separate business from Filene's; the discounted merchandise comes here not only from upstairs, but from other big-name department stores and a few Boston boutiques. The markdown system works like this: after 14 days, merchandise is discounted 25 percent, after 21 days, 50 percent, and after 28 days, 75 percent. Anything that lasts more than 35 days goes to charity. Be warned: dressing rooms are communal.

Lord & Taylor 760 Boylston St ⊤617/262-6000, Ⓦwww.lordandtaylor.com; Copley **T**. Excellent place to stock up on high-end basics, from sweaters and suits to jewelry and cosmetics.

Macy's East 450 Washington St ⊤617/357-3000, Ⓦwww.macys.com; Downtown Crossing **T**. Much the generic urban department store, with all the basics covered, including a better-than-average cosmetics section and a men's department that outshines that of next-door neighbor Filene's.

Neiman Marcus 5 Copley Place ⊤617/536-3660, Ⓦwww.neimanmarcus.com; Copley **T**. Along with nearby Barneys, this is Boston's most luxurious department store, with prices to match. Three levels, with an impressive menswear collection on the first.

Saks Fifth Avenue 786 Boylston St ⊤617/262-8500, Ⓦwww.saksfifthavenue.com; Copley **T**. Another Back Bay beauty, with plenty of upscale clothes, shoes, and accessories (including Boston's best selection of sunglasses) to please every style maven.

Music

In Your Ear Records 957 Commonwealth Ave, Allston ☎617/787-9755; Pleasant Street **T**, 72A Mount Auburn St, Cambridge ☎617/481-5035; Harvard **T** Indulge in their massive collection of used CDs, records, and other agreeable esoterica to sate your vintage music cravings. The Cambridge location is smaller but equally appealing.

Looney Tunes 1106 Boylston St ☎617/247-2238; Hynes **T**; 1001 Massachusetts Ave ☎617/876-5624; Harvard **T**. The way a record store should be – walls bedecked with vintage jazz records, a great selection of CDs, and a hip staff that's not snooty.

Newbury Comics 332 Newbury St ☎617/236-4930, ⊛www.newbury.com; Hynes **T**. Boston's biggest alternative record store carries lots of independent labels you won't find at the national chains, along with a substantial array of vinyl, posters, zines, and kitschy t-shirts. It's also a good place to pick up flyers on local club happenings. There's a branch in Cambridge at the Garage mall, **36 JFK St** ☎617/491-0337, Harvard **T**.

Nuggets 486 Commonwealth Ave ☎617/536-0679, ⊛www.nuggetsrecords.com; Kenmore **T**. American jazz, rock, and R&B are the strong suits at this venerable new and used record store.

Planet Records 54B JFK St, Cambridge ☎617/492-0693, ⊛www.planet-records.com; Harvard **T**. Unpretentious and well-priced with a good selection of used CDs. It doesn't get more rock 'n' roll than the charred guitar they have hanging by the register – a remnant from the fire that gutted their Kenmore Square location.

Skippy White's 1971 Columbus Ave, Roxbury ☎617/524-4500; Jackson Square **T**. Excellent collection of jazz, blues, R&B, gospel, funk, and hip hop. Hum a few bars and the knowledgeable salesfolk will guide you to the right section.

Stereo Jack's 1686 Massachusetts Ave, Cambridge ☎617/497-9447, ⊛www .stereojacks.com; Porter **T**. Jazz and blues specialists selling mostly used, but some new stuff, too. CDs, tapes, and vinyl.

Twisted Village 12 Eliot St, Cambridge ☎617/354-6898, ⊛www.twistedvillage.com; Harvard **T**. A really weird and really fun mix of fringe styles, among them beat, acid folk, psychedelic prog rock, and "people: real and exotic."

Underground Hip Hop 234 Huntington Ave ☎617/262-0200, ⊛www.undergroundhiphop .com; Symphony **T**. One of the best selections of hip hop here or anywhere. It's well-organized too – sit on a comfy stool, listen all you want to the tunes on their extensive website, and then they'll grab what you want from the back.

Specialty shops

Abodeon 1731 Massachusetts Ave, Cambridge ☎617/497-0137; Porter **T**. A terrific trove of classic twentieth-century design, with furniture by top modern designers as well as assorted new bric-a-brac. Pretty expensive, but most things are cheaper than they would be in New York or LA.

Aunt Sadie's 18 Union Park St ☎617/357-7117; Back Bay **T**. General store-themed South End shop with delightfully campy items like vintage Hawaiian postcards and fun, scented candles with original odors like beach (coconut oil) and amusement park (popcorn).

Black Ink 101 Charles St ☎617/723-3883; Charles **T**; 5 Brattle St, Cambridge ☎617/497-1221; Harvard **T**. Eclectic assortment of things you don't really need but are cool anyway: rubber stamps, a smattering of clothes, amusing refrigerator magnets, and a wide assortment of vintage postcards. They also run The Museum of Useful Things, full of whimsical yet useful things, around the corner from their Cambridge location (49B Brattle St, Cambridge ☎617/576-3322; Harvard T).

Boutique Fabulous 1309 Cambridge St, Cambridge ☎617/864-0656; Central **T**. Fun, retro-flavored Inman Square boutique with assorted vintage housewares and clothing, antiques, and quirky gifts.

Buckaroo's Mercantile 1297 Cambridge St, Cambridge ☎617/492-4792, ⊛www .buckmerc.com; Central **T**. Their website says it perfectly: "howdy and welcome to the land of everything you want and nothing you need." Fabulous retro-inspired wares and tchotchkes like pirate bathmats, Bettie Page *objets*, and leopard print flasks.

Condom World 332 Newbury St ☎617/267-7233; **Hynes T**. Every style, shape, and flavor of condom you can imagine.

Fresh 121 Newbury St ☎617/421-1212; **Copley T**. Pear Chocolate and Fig Apricot are only two varieties of the several sweet-sounding soaps you'll find in this chic bath and body store. They carry over three hundred varieties of French milled soaps, lotions, oils, and makeup, packaged so exquisitely you won't want to open them.

Fresh Eggs 58 Clarendon St ☎617/247-8150; **Back Bay T**. Small boutique featuring exceptionally stylish home furnishings and tchotchkes, from pillow cases to bookends; conveniently, most of it is small enough to carry home in your bag.

Good 88 Charles St ☎617/722-9200, ⓦwww.shopatgood.com; **Charles T**. Within this airy, white-walled gift boutique *Good's* countless pretty *objets* take on a found treasure quality, with gorgeous seashells, vibrant gemstone necklaces, summery totes, and framed nautical prints to dazzle even the most discerning browser.

Hudson 312 Shawmut Ave ☎617/292-0900, ⓦwww.hudsonboston.com; **Back Bay T**. A hip South End home store with a bit of a summer cottage vibe – think glamorous mirrors bordered with pearlescent seashells and white sofas with silkscreened fish pillows.

Koo de Kir 65 Chestnut St ☎617/723-8111, ⓦwww.koodekir.com; **Charles T**. The goal at this stylish, modern spot is to make even the most everyday objects artistic and beautiful. For a pretty penny, you can buy such beautified home furnishings and accessories here.

Leavitt and Pierce 1316 Massachusetts Ave, Cambridge ☎617/547-0576; **Harvard T**. Old-school tobacconists that have been around almost as long as Harvard. An outstanding selection of cigars, imported cigarettes, and

smoking paraphernalia (lighters, rolling papers, ashtrays), plus an upstairs chess parlor right out of the carefree past.

The London Harness Company 60 Franklin St ☎617/542-9234, ⓦwww.londonharness.com; **Downtown Crossing T**. Chiefly known for its high-quality luggage, this place reeks of traditional Boston – indeed, Ben Franklin used to shop here. They also sell items like chess sets, clocks, candlesticks, and inlaid decorative boxes.

Marquis 92 South St ☎617/426-2120; **South Station T**. Proffering a wide range of leather items and hardcore sexual paraphernalia, *Marquis* leaves little to the imagination.

Matsu 259 Newbury St ☎617/266-9707; **Hynes T**. A hip little shop featuring a medium-sized range of sleek Japanese clothing, knickknacks (desk clocks, stationery, funky pens), and contemporary home decor items.

The Original Tremont Tearoom 48–50 Winter St ☎617/338-8100; **Park St T**. An unusual way to spend an afternoon, the country's oldest "psychic salon" offers tea leaf, palm, and Tarot readings as well as mediumship – conversations with "the other side." A thirty minute Tarot reading will set you back $50; there are specials on Sun.

Polka Dog Bakery 256 Shawmut Ave ☎617/338-5155, ⓦwww.polkadog.com; **Back Bay T**. Terrific gourmet dog food shop. Stop in for a gift for the furry one you left back home, or bring your pet with you to nosh on free samples.

Shake the Tree 95 Salem St ☎617/742-0484, ⓦwww.shakethetreeboston.com; **Haymarket T**. A good spot for a little retail therapy, with a collection that includes bright, chunky gemstone necklaces, funky sock monkeys, and aromatic candles.

Sugar Heaven 218 Newbury St ☎617/266-6969, ⓦwww.sugarheaven.us; **Hynes T**. Pick up a bucket on your way in and fill it to the brim with candy from all over the world, including ones you may have thought were extinct.

Sports and outdoor activities

Bostonians have an acute love-hate relationship with their professional **sports** teams, obsessing over the four major franchises – baseball's Red Sox, football's Patriots, basketball's Celtics, and hockey's Bruins – with evangelical fervor. After years of watching their teams narrowly miss championship bids, all their Christmases came at once with the Red Sox finally ending 86 years of hurt by taking the 2004 World Series and the Patriots earning their third title in four seasons just a few months later. At the time of writing, both teams continued to be at the top of their games, with the Patriots winning another Super Bowl in 2005 and the Red Sox winning another World Series in 2007.

Local sports fans have an admirable tenacity, following their teams closely through good seasons and bad; indeed, supporters seem to love bemoaning their teams' woes nearly as much as they do celebrating their victories. This lively, vocal fan base makes attending a game a great way to get a feel for the city, though fans of an opposing team who might be inclined to root against Boston, be warned: you're in store for censure from the local faithful.

While the Patriots' **Gillette Stadium** is located out of town and has little to recommend it, the **TD Banknorth Garden**, where the Celtics and Bruins play, is at least conveniently accessible by **T**, even if it lacks the history of the classic Boston Garden that it replaced (the Garden was demolished in 1997). For fans of baseball, there is no more essential pilgrimage than the one to the Red Sox' idiosyncratic Fenway Park, accessed by the Green Line's Kenmore **T**.

Boston isn't a city where **participatory sports** thrive particularly well, due mostly to the area's often dreary weather. There are, however, more than a number of good areas for jogging, biking, rollerblading, and the like, especially around the Esplanade, not to mention the possibility of getting out on the water that surrounds the city. The **Department of Conservation and Recreation** (**DCR**), 251 Causeway Street (ⓣ617/626-1250, ⓦwww.mass.gov/dcr), oversees most facilities.

Baseball

The Boston **Red Sox** finally stopped tormenting fans when they won the 2004 World Series against the St Louis Cardinals, breaking the infamous "Curse of the Bambino" (see p.112). The ongoing rivalry between the Sox and Yankees is legendary, though Boston's need to define themselves relative to the Yankees' success has eased a bit thanks to recent breakthroughs. Due in part to having one of the largest payrolls in the business – including paying a staggering $51 million in 2006 just for the rights to negotiate a contract with Japanese pitcher Daisuke Matsuzaka – the team should stay competitive for years to come.

Venue and tickets

Even if the Red Sox aren't performing so well, it's worth going to a game just to see **Fenway Park**, at 24 Yawkey Way, one of America's sports treasures. Dating from 1912, it's the oldest professional baseball stadium in the country, much more intimate than most, and one of bizarre dimensions, best represented by the abnormally tall (37-foot) left-field wall, dubbed the "Green Monster." Tickets can cost upwards of $300 for the finest seats, but bleacher seats start from $12 and put you amid the raucous fans; there are few better ways to spend a Sunday summer afternoon in Boston. The stadium is near the Kenmore **T** stop; for ticket infor-mation, call ☎617/482-4SOX or ☎1-877/RED-SOXX or visit Ⓦwww.redsox.com.

The **season** runs from April through September, with playoffs in October. Tickets for the regular season are sold in two increments – once in December, and then again at a larger sale in January. Playoff tickets are acquired via a random drawing in mid-September; check Ⓦwww.redsox.com for exact sale dates. Even though tickets sell out extremely fast, don't give up hope; if you're desperate to see a game, check local Sox blogs or Ⓦboston.craigslist.org to see if any locals have tickets (be sure to meet the seller in person and ensure that they have paper tickets – not just an online printout). Fenway Park also sells a small number of one-per-person tickets at Gate E on game day; be sure to get there five hours early, follow all the rules (no leaving the line, no saving a place for your friends, etc.) and hope to get lucky.

Basketball

While Boston's other sports franchises once had a reputation for falling short of victory, basketball's **Celtics** have won sixteen NBA championships – more than any other US professional sports teams except baseball's New York Yankees and hockey's Montréal Canadiens. But while they enjoyed dynastic success in the 1960s and 1980s, when they played on the buckling parquet floors of the beloved Boston Garden, the Celts fell on hard times in the 1990s, and have not won a title since 1986. The team did make three consecutive playoff spots in 2002–04, and with a superstar-rich roster it's hoped that a new victorious era may be just around the corner.

Venue and tickets

The Celtics play in the sleek if soulless **TD Banknorth Garden**, 150 Causeway St (☎617/624-1000, Ⓦwww.nba.com/celtics), located at the North Station **T** stop in the West End. Most tickets are pricey –

good seats run $50–200 – but you can sometimes snag a set in the rafters for as little as $10; for those, show up in front of the stadium on game day and hope for the best. The season begins in late October and continues all the way through June, playoffs included.

Football

For years, the New England **Patriots** were saddled with the nickname "Patsies," and generally considered to be a laughing stock. Not any longer. Now the pre-eminent team in the NFL, their championship dynasty includes Super Bowl wins in 2002, 2004, and 2005. Led by quarterback Tom Brady and the top coach in the business, Bill Belichick, the team completed a 21-game winning streak from 2003 to 2004, setting an all-time standard.

Venue and tickets

Even before they won all those Super Bowls, going to a game wasn't a reasonable goal unless you had connections or were willing to pay a scalper upwards of $100 – tickets sell out far in advance. If you can get your hands on a pair the old-fashioned way, expect to pay $50–125 a head. The stadium is located in distant Foxborough, just north of the Massachusetts–Rhode Island border (for information, call ☎1-800/543-1776; for tickets, dial ☎617/931-2222 or visit Ⓦwww.patriots.com). Better to drop by a sports bar on a Sunday afternoon during the fall season (Sept–Dec); the best ones are located in the West End and Kenmore Square (see Chapter 12, "Drinking").

Ice hockey

Until a decade ago, ice hockey's Boston **Bruins** were a consistently successful franchise, at one point running up a streak of 26 straight winning seasons – the longest in professional sports, including appearances in the Stanley Cup finals on two occasions, 1988 and 1990, both of which they narrowly lost. A series of retirements, injuries, and bad luck turned things around and by the mid-90s they were posting the worst records in the National Hockey League. Though the team has made the playoffs in recent years, they sit in the middle of the pack and remain far removed from their glory days.

An equally entertaining, and cheaper, alternative to the Bruins is **college hockey**. The biggest event is the "Beanpot" (Ⓦwww.beanpothockey.com), an annual competition that takes place on the first two Mondays in February, in which the four big local teams – **Boston University Terriers**, **Harvard Crimson**, **Boston College Eagles**, and **Northeastern Huskies** – compete for city bragging rights.

Venues and tickets

You can catch the Bruins at the **TD Banknorth Garden**, 150 Causeway St (North Station **T**; ☎617/624-1000, Ⓦwww.bostonbruins.com), where tickets can be expensive ($17–300), especially if a good opponent is in town. The long regular season begins in October and continues, with playoffs, into June.

Meanwhile, BU plays at Agganis Arena, 925 Commonwealth Ave (☎617/353-7000, Ⓦgoterriers.cstv.com); Harvard at Bright Hockey Center, N Harvard St, Allston (☎617/495-2211 or 1-877/GO-HARVARD, Ⓦwww.fas.harvard.edu/~athletic); BC at the Conte Forum, Chestnut Hill (☎617/552-GoBC, Ⓦbceagles.cstv.com); and Northeastern at Matthews Arena, St Botolph St (☎617/373-GoNU, Ⓦwww.gonu.com). Beanpot tickets ($26–38; ☎617/931-2000, also available from team websites) are hard to come by, but regular-season seats go for around $20 and the games are generally a good time.

Running, rollerblading, and cycling

On the rare days that Boston is visited by pleasant weather, residents take full advantage of it, turning up in droves to engage in **outdoor activities**. The most popular of these are **running**, **rollerblading**, and **cycling**, and they all pretty much take place along the banks of the Charles River, where the Esplanade provides eighteen miles of well-kept, picturesque trails stretching from the Museum of Science all the way down to Watertown and Newton.

On the Cambridge side of the Charles is Memorial Drive, closed off to traffic between Western Avenue and Eliot Bridge (May to mid-Nov Sun 11am–7pm); it's a prime place for blading and tanning.

Two of the most popular **bike trails** in the area are the Dr Paul Dudley White Bike Path (really just another name for the Esplanade loop) and the Minuteman Bikeway, which runs 10.5 miles from Alewife **T** station on the Red Line in Cambridge through Lexington to Bedford.

You can take your bike on the **T**'s Red, Orange, and Blue lines (Mon–Fri 10am–4pm & 7pm–close, Sat & Sun all day), except on Patriots' Day, St Patrick's Day, Independence Day, and at 8.30–11pm whenever there's a Red Sox game or an event at the TD Banknorth Garden. While the Green and Silver Lines do not allow bicycles on board at any time, the MBTA has recently installed bike racks onto 330 of their buses; check ⓦ www.mbta.com to see if your bus route is bike-ready. When taking your bicycle on the subway, always follow the conductor's directions.

Rental shops

Blade rentals generally start at around $15/day; bike rentals around $25/day.
Ace Wheelworks 145 Elm St ☎617/776-2100, ⓦ www.wheelworks.com; Porter **T**.
Back Bay Bicycles 333 Newbury St ☎617/247-2336, ⓦ www.backbaybicycles.com; Hynes **T**.
Beacon Hill Skate Shop 135 S Charles St ☎617/482-7400; Charles **T**.
Community Bicycle Supply 496 Tremont St ☎617/542-8623, ⓦ www.communitybicycle.com; Copley **T**.
Wheelworks Bicycle Workshop 259 Massachusetts Ave, Cambridge ☎617/876-6555; Central **T**.

Information and tours

The DCR (see p.213) has information about bike trails as well.
Boaton Bike Tours ☎617/308-5902, ⓦ www.bostonbiketours.com. Tours of Boston, Cambridge, and surrounds, departing from Boston Common. May-Oct Sat & Sun 11am; $24–30, including equipment rental and map.
Charles River Wheelmen ☎617/332-8546 or 325-BIKE, ⓦ www.crw.org. Organizes regular, and usually free, bike tours on weekends from April through Nov.

InLine Club of Boston ⓦ www.sk8net.com. Organizes community skates and other in-line events.
Massachusetts Bicycle Coalition, 171 Milk St, suite 33 ☎617/542-BIKE, ⓦ www.massbike.org. Information about bike trails, and sells a Boston bike map ($6).

▲ The Boston Marathon

Ice skating

The DCR operates several **ice-skating rinks** in the Boston area between mid-November and mid-March, of which the best-kept and most convenient to downtown is the **Steriti Memorial Rink**, 550 Commercial St (☏617/523-9327) in the North End. When it's cold enough, the lagoon in the Public Garden offers free (unmonitored) skating, while the **Frog Pond** in Boston Common (Mon 10am–5pm, Tues–Thurs & Sun 10am 9pm, Fri–Sat 10am–10pm; $3; ☏617/635-4505; Park St **T**) charges for the sport but also rents skates on-site (adults $4, children under 13 free; rentals are $8 adults, $5 children). The Larz Anderson skating rink in Brookline has gorgeous digs set amidst the Anderson family's sprawling former estate; there are rentals on offer as well as lovely city views (23 Newton Street; Tues 10am–noon, Thurs 10am–noon, Fri 7.30pm–9.30pm, Sat & Sun noon-5pm; $7 non-resident adults, $4 children; ☏617/739-7518). To find out dates and times and keep tabs on skating conditions throughout the city, visit the DCR website (see p.213).

Water sports

The image of white sails dotting the Charles River Basin and Boston Harbor may be inviting; alas, you'll be stuck watching them from shore unless you have recognized **sailing** credentials or are willing to take a class. Should you have the former, present them to the Boston Harbor Sailing Club on Rowes Wharf (☏617/720-0049, ⓦwww.bostonharborsailing.com; Aquarium **T**) and you can rent yourself a variety of boats from a daysailer ($75/day) to a cruiser ($417/day).

Classes are available through a number of outfits, the best being Community Boating (April–Oct; learn to sail class $75; ☏617/523-1038, ⓦwww .community-boating.org) and Piers Park Sailing Center, 95 Marginal St (April–Oct; ☏617/561-6677, ⓦwww.piersparksailing.org; Maverick **T**), which does a 21-hour course for $635. Children sailors get the best deal of all, though, through Community Boating (see Chapter 20, "Kids' Boston").

Possibly an easier way to get on the water is renting a **canoe** or **kayak** from the Charles River Canoe and Kayak Center, Sailor's Road (May–Oct Fri 1pm–dusk, Sat–Sun 10am–dusk; ☏617/462-2513, ⓦwww.ski-paddle.com; Harvard **T**), which maintains a green-roofed kiosk 200 yards from the Eliot Bridge on the Boston side of the Charles. Equipment is rented by the day or hour (canoes and kayaks $14–60); lessons are also available, but certainly not required.

Fitness centers

If you're staying at a hotel without a gym and are in need of a workout, a number of **health clubs** and **fitness centers** offer one-time daily memberships for out-of-towners. The Beacon Hill Athletic Clubs (ⓦwww.beaconhillathleticclubs .com), with locations at 261 Friend St (☏617/720-2422; North Station **T**), 3 Hancock St (☏617/367-2422; Park St **T**), and 85 Atlantic Ave (☏617/742-0055; State St **T**), offers $15 walk-in day passes. Revolution Fitness, at 209 Columbus Ave (☏617/536-3006; ⓦwww.revfitboston.com; Back Bay **T**), offers day passes for $15 with proof of hotel stay, $20 without. The Boston Athletic Club, 653 Summer St (☏617/269-4300, ⓦwww.bostonathleticclub.com;

Among all the miscellaneous forms of sports-like entertainment in the city, perhaps the oddest (and most fun, if you're into this type of thing) is **paintball** – a kind of simulated warfare where you shoot paintballs (and they do sting) at members of the opposing team, all while scampering around an area full of bunkers and obstacles. The proceedings take place in Somerville at Boston Paintball, 43 Foley St (reservations ☎617/941-0123, ⓦwww.bostonpaintball.com; $30; Sullivan Sq **T**).

Downtown Crossing **T**), charges $25 a day for full use of their facilities, which include a sauna and pool, on presentation of your hotel key.

Otherwise, women can pay $15 to take advantage of Women's Fitness of Boston, 27 School St (☎617/227-1221; Government Center **T**), a gym with a relaxed female-only environment. Both sexes can practice their downward dogs at the drop-in power **yoga** classes led by Baron Baptiste Power Yoga Institute (☎617/661-YOGA, ⓦwww.baronbaptiste.com); its two locations, at 25 Harvard St, Brookline ($14 per class; Brookline Village **T**), and 2000 Massachusetts Ave, Cambridge ($14; Porter **T**), also rent mats ($2).

Bowling

Massachusetts's variation on tenpin bowling is **candlepin bowling**, in which the ball is smaller, the pins narrower and lighter, and you have three rather than two chances to knock the pins down. It's somewhat of a local institution that is sadly on the wane in the city itself. The best places to find it in the Greater Boston area are Lanes and Games, 195 Concord Turnpike, Somerville (daily 9am–midnight; ☎617/876-5533, ⓦwww.lanesgames.com; Alewife **T**) and Milky Way, 403–405 Centre St, Jamaica Plain (Mon–Thurs 6pm–midnight, Fri–Sat 6pm–12.45am, Sun 6–11pm; ☎617/524-3740, ⓦwww.milkywayjp.com; Stony Brook **T**). Suburban and regional venues still abound; visit ⓦwww.masscandlepin.com for a list of venues.

The local demise of candlepin bowling has been countered by a renaissance of the more conventional form of the game. Kings at 50 Dalton St in Back Bay (Mon–Wed 5pm–2am, Thurs–Sun 11.30am–2am, ☎617/266-BOWL, ⓦwww.backbaykings.com; Hynes **T**) is an upscale 16-lane bowling alley/bar usually packed to the rafters.

Pool

There are plenty of places to shoot **pool** in the Boston area, and not just of the dive-y variety you'll invariably find in some of the city's more down-and-out bars. One of the best is *Boston Billiard Club*, 126 Brookline Ave (☎617/536-7665, ⓦwww.bostonbilliardclub.com; Kenmore **T**), a classy and serious pool hall that also has a nice bar. *Flat Top Johnny's*, at One Kendall Square in Cambridge (☎617/494-9565, ⓦwww.flattopjohnnys.com; Kendall **T**), draws a diverse young clientele to its low-key environment. *Felt* at 533 Washington St (☎617/350-5555; Downtown Crossing **T**) draws well-heeled yuppies and ardent pool players. The best pub to play is the *Beantown Pub*, 100 Tremont St (☎617/426-0111; Park Street **T**).

18

Kids' Boston

One of the best aspects of **traveling with kids** in Boston is the feeling that you're conducting an ongoing history lesson. While that may grow a bit tiresome for teens, younger children tend to eat up the colonial-period costumes, cannons, and the like. Various points on the Freedom Trail are, of course, best for this, though getting out of the city to Lexington and Concord (see Chapter 20, "Around Boston") will lead you along a similar path.

The city's **parks**, notably Boston Common, Franklin Park, and the Public Garden – where you can ride the Swan Boats in the lagoon during summer or climb on the sculpture *Mrs Mallard and Her Eight Ducklings* – make nice settings for an afternoon with the children, too. The Boston Common in particular is known for its fabulous playground, complete with swings, an expansive jungle gym, and kid-sized fountain. Wisteria-laden Christopher Columbus Park, over in the North End, is another good bet, with pretty waterfront views and a splashy little fountain where kids can beat the heat on summer days. The best outdoor option, however, may be a Red Sox game at Fenway Park, as the country's oldest baseball stadium is easily reached by the **T** and games here are relatively affordable – if you can get tickets. **Harbor cruises** are also a fairly popular and unique way to see Boston, as is ascending to the top of one of the city's skyscrapers. There are, as well, a number of **museums** aimed at the younger set, most of them located along one waterfront or another.

For general resources geared toward Boston families, check out the wonderfully informative ⓦwww.bostoncentral.com, with listings on everything from arts and crafts to zoos and aquariums; *The Boston Globe's* website at ⓦwww.boston.com is the local go-to site for area listings and events.

Museums and sights

Though kids might not have **historical attractions** at the top of their list of favorite places, most of Boston's major **museums** manage to make the city's history palatable to youngsters. This is true at the USS *Constitution*, the old warship moored in the Charlestown Navy Yard (see p.76), and the **USS Constitution Museum**, where a video game on the top floor allows kids to test their battle skills.

The **Children's Museum**, the **Museum of Science**, the **MIT Museum,** and the **Harvard Museum of Natural History** (p.61, p.89, p.149, & p.143 respectively) are four other places to let the little ones loose for a while; all provide a lot of interactive fun that's as easy for adults to get lost in as it is kids, plus the Children's Museum sits behind the 40-foot **Hood Milk Bottle**, a food stand that serves bagels, sandwiches, and the like. For animal sightings, the **Franklin Park Zoo** and the **New England Aquarium** (p.128 & p.60), respectively) can't be beat. Finally, views from the dizzying heights of the Back Bay's **Prudential Tower** (p.100) are always sure to thrill.

Activities

For a different kind of education, America's oldest public boating set-up, Community Boating, 21 Embankment Rd (℡617/523-1038, Ⓦwww .community-boating.org), between the Hatch Shell and Longfellow Bridge, offers youngsters aged 10 to 18 who can swim 75 yards the cheapest **sailing lessons** around, for just $1. The fee also allows summer-long access to the boathouse and entry to a number of one- to five-day classes, including kayaking and windsurfing.

If that seems like too much work, your children can learn things sitting down at the Museum of Science's **Charles Hayden Planetarium** and **Mugar Omni Theater** (adults $9, kids $7; ℡617/723-2500, Ⓦwww.mos.org; Science Park **T**), which feature IMAX movies, laser shows set to the music of various rock and pop bands, and documentaries about the solar system. Afterwards, the kids can check out the **Gilliland Observatory**, which, weather permitting, opens its roof and points its telescopes heavenwards on Friday nights (8.30–10pm; free; ℡617/589-0267; Science Park **T**).

Another event that makes learning fun is the Museum of Fine Arts' free "Family Place" (Sun 11am–4pm, ℡617/267-9300, Ⓦwww.mfa.org; Museum **T**), which offers family-oriented **drawing** activities and **readings** in a number of galleries. Check the website or call the museum directly for additional goings-on throughout the year. The last Saturday of each month is "Playdate" at the Institute of Contemporary Art (free to up to two adults accompanied by children 12 and under, ℡617/478-3100, Ⓦwww.icaboston.org; World Trade Center **T**), when children hang out with artists, immerse themselves in creative play such as painting, designing, or sketching, and then let loose at an interactive performance on the ICA's phenomenal stage.

Shops

If and when the history starts to wear thin, there's always the failsafe of Boston's **malls** to divert the kids' attention (see p.209). To combine history with your shopping, you could head to Faneuil Hall and Quincy Market, which are both hundreds of years old. Faneuil Hall also plays host to *Build-A-Bear Workshop and Friends 2B Made* (℡617/227-2478; Government Center **T**), where kids get to pick out a teddy or doll, give it a heart and a name, and then take it home in its own Cub Condo carrying case.

Red pops, warheads, and other delightful **candies** can be had at Irving's Toy and Candy Shop, 371 Harvard St, Brookline (℡617/566-9327; Coolidge Crossing **T**), while candy from all over the world can be bought at Newbury Street's Sugar Heaven (see p.212). If the kids are screaming for **ice cream**, load them up with homemade scoops of maple cream and cookie dough at *Herrell's*, 15 Dunster St (℡617/497-2179; Harvard **T**), while you indulge in boozy flavors like peach schnapps and Kentucky bourbon (there are a number of other good ice cream spots around town as well, see p.164 for listings).

▲ Hood Milk Bottle at the Children's Museum

Few kids (or adults, for that matter) can resist the whimsical Stella Bella (1360 Cambridge St, Inman Square (☎617/491-6290; Harvard **T**; and 1967 Massachusetts Ave, Porter Square ☎617/864-6290; Porter **T**; ⓦwww.stellabellatoys.com), one of the best **toy stores** in the area. Children are encouraged to sample the merchandise in a toy-strewn play space, while parents can kick back at the new parent's coffee hour on Fridays at 10.30am; Mondays have sing-along time at 11am. Another worthy toy store is Henry Bear's Park, whose extensive array of toys, games, and picture books has been pleasing families for over thirty years (361 Huron Ave, Cambridge ☎617/547-8424, Porter **T**; and 16 Harvard St, Brookline Village ☎781/646-9400; Brookline Village **T**; ⓦwww.henrybear.com).

Pixie Stix' petite boutique (131 Charles St ☎617/523-3211, Charles **T**) is a stylish godsend for girls in their tween years, with cute clothes striking a balance between cool-enough-for-school and parent-approved. The best maternity store in town is 9 Months (286 Newbury St ☎617/236-5523, Hynes **T**; ⓦwww.9monthsinc.com) with chic clothes for the mom-to-be and coo-worthy stuffed animals and knit sweaters for the little ones.

There's no shortage of **bookstores** catering for children in Boston either; the Children's Book Shop, 237 Washington St, Brookline (☎617/734-7323, ⓦusers.erols.com/childrensbookshop; Brookline Village **T**), Curious George Goes to Wordsworth, 1 JFK St (☎617/498-0062 or 1-800/899-2202, ⓦwww.curiousg.com; Harvard **T**), and Barefoot Books, 1771 Massachusetts Ave (☎617/349-1610, ⓦwww.barefootbooks.com; Porter **T**), are sure to have the latest titles, and others you didn't know existed. Near the latter is an excellent **novelty** store, Animal, Vegetable, Mineral, at 2400 Massachusetts Ave (☎617/547-2404; Davis **T**), with goldfish bowls full of plastic dinosaurs, rubber eyeballs, and the like.

Theater and puppet shows

If you want to get the tots some (kindergarten) culture, try the Boston Children's Theatre, 321 Columbus Ave (☎617/424-6634, ⓦwww.bostonchildrenstheatre.org), whose productions of kids' classics are performed at the C. Walsh Theater, on the Beacon Hill campus of Suffolk University, and the McCormack Theatre, at UMASS Boston. Otherwise, head out to Brookline for the Puppet Showplace Theatre, 32 Station St (Wed and Thurs 10.30am, Sat & Sun 1pm and 3pm; ☎617/731-6400, ⓦwww.puppetshowplace.org); tickets are $9.50 a head – big or small.

Festivals and events

t's always good to know ahead of time what **festivals** or **annual events** are scheduled to coincide with your trip to Boston – though even if you don't plan it, there's likely to be some sort of parade, public celebration, or seasonal shindig going on. For detailed information, call the Boston Convention and Visitors Bureau (☎1-888/SEE-BOSTON, ⓦwww.bostonusa .com) or check out the *Boston Globe*'s helpful website (ⓦwww.boston.com); for a look at public holidays in Boston, see the "Opening hours, public holidays, and festivals" section in Basics.

The schedule below picks out some of the more fun and notable events happening throughout the year, and is not meant to be exhaustive. If you are looking for specific **highlights**, note that a few nationwide events more or less reach their apotheosis here, such as St Patrick's Day (March) and Independence Day (July); tops in Boston-only happenings include the Boston Marathon (April), the Head of the Charles Regatta (Oct), and the Boston Tea Party Re-enactment (Dec).

January

First Night The New Year's celebration begins on New Year's Eve but carries into the first few days of the year; see events under Dec, below.
Chinese New Year Usually late month

☎1-888/SEE-BOSTON Dragon parades and firecrackers punctuate the festivities throughout Chinatown. The New Year can fall in Feb, too, depending on the Chinese lunar calendar.

February

The Beanpot First two Mon ⓦwww .beanpothockey.com Popular college hockey tournament, between Boston University,

Harvard, Boston College, and North-eastern. Visit individual colleges' websites for more information.

March

St Patrick's Day Parade and Festival Sun closest to **March 17** ☎1-888/SEE-BOSTON Boston's substantial Irish-American community, along with much of the rest of the city, turns out for this parade through South Boston (see Chapter 8, The

southern districts) and brims with Irish folk music, dance, and food. March 17 also happens to be "Evacuation Day," or the anniversary of the day that George Washington drove the British out of Boston during the Revolutionary War, which gives

Bostonians another historical excuse to tie one on.

New England Spring Flower Show Second or third week in March ☎ 617/933-4984, Ⓦ www.masshort.org Winter-weary Bostonians turn out in droves to gawk at hothouse greenery in this week-long horticultural fest, which takes place in Dorchester's Bayside Expo Center. Tickets cost $20.

April

Boston Marathon Third Mon ☎ 617/236-1652, Ⓦ www.bostonmarathon.org Runners from all over the world gather for this 26.2-mile affair, one of America's premier athletic events. It crosses all over the Boston area, ending in Back Bay's Copley Square.

Patriots' Day Third Mon ☎ 1-888/SEE-BOSTON A celebration and re-creation of Paul Revere's and William Dawes's famous ride from the North End to Lexington that alerted locals that the British army had been deployed to confiscate rebel armaments.

May

Lilac Sunday Third Sun ☎ 617/524-1718, Ⓦ www.arboretum.harvard.edu/plants /lilac_sunday.html You can view more than three hundred lilac varieties in full bloom at the Arnold Arboretum during this early summer event – a Boston institution.

June

Jimmy Fund Scooper Bowl First week ☎ 1-888/SEE-BOSTON For a modest donation of around $7, you're allowed unlimited samples of the city's best ice creams.

Boston Pride Festival First week in June ☎ 617/262-9405, Ⓦ www.bostonpride.org A celebratory affair, Pride Boston spans a

week and kicks off with a rainbow flag-raising at City Hall, culminating a week later with a gay pride parade, festival, and block parties.

Dragon Boat Festival Variable weekend in early June ☎ 617/426-6500 ext 778, Ⓦ www .bostondragonboat.org A colorful Chinese festival whose highlight, dragon boat racing on the Charles River, is accompanied by the thundering sound of Taiko drums.

Bunker Hill Weekend Sun nearest June 17 ☎ 617/242-5601 The highlight of this three-day festival in Charlestown is the parade celebrating the Battle of Bunker Hill (even though the bout was lost by the Americans).

Cambridge River Festival Third week in June ☎ 617/349-4380, Ⓦ www .cambridgema.gov/~CAC/ Memorial Drive is closed off from JFK St to Western Avenue for music shows, dancing, and eclectic food offerings, all along the Charles River.

Boston Early Music Festival Every odd-numbered year ☎ 617/661-1812, Ⓦ www.bemf.org This huge, week-long Renaissance fair with a strong music theme includes concerts and exhibitions throughout town.

▲ Pride Boston

July

Harborfest Late June–weekend nearest July 4
☎617/227-1528, ⓦwww.bostonharborfest.com
Includes a series of concerts on the waterfront (mostly jazz, blues, and rock), and the
highly competitive "Chowderfest," where
area restaurants compete for the "Boston's
Best Chowder" crown.

Boston Pops Concert and Fireworks July 4
☎1-888-4th-POPS, ⓦwww.july4th.org The
Boston Pops' wildly popular annual
evening concert in the Oval area, in front of
the Hatch Shell, is followed by thirty
minutes of flashy pyrotechnics; people

sometimes line up at dawn in order to get
good seats.

Reading of the Declaration of Independence July 4
☎1-888/SEE-BOSTON Pretend it's July 4th,
1776, by attending the annual reading of the
nation's founding document from the balcony
of Old State House, the party then continues
on with speeches over at Faneuil Hall.

USS Constitution Turn-Around July 4 Old
Ironsides pulls up anchor and sails out
(briefly) into Boston Harbor in this annual
event that's a salute to the country's
independence (and the ship's vitality).

August

August Moon Festival Near the end of the
month ☎1-888/SEE-BOSTON During this
festival, Chinatown's merchants and
restaurateurs hawk their wares on the
street amid dragon parades and
firecrackers.

Italian Festas Throughout July and August
☎1-888/SEE-BOSTON Features music,
dancing, and games throughout the North
End; during the parades, locals pin dollar
bills to the floats and statues of patron
saints that are borne through the streets.

September

Arts Festival of Boston Around Labor Day
weekend ☎617/451-ARTS, ⓦwww
.cityofboston.gov/arts Boston is transformed
into a giant gallery, with five days of
exhibits, arts and crafts pavilions, fashion
shows, evening galas, receptions, and
outdoor musical performances at various
locations.

Beantown Jazz Festival Third week in Sept
☎617/451-ARTS, ⓦwww
.beantownjazz.org. Run by the outstanding
Berklee College of Music, the festival kicks-
off with a big names concert at Symphony
Hall (tickets $40–100), followed by free
shows the next day in venues around the
South End.

Boston Film Festival Two weeks in early to mid-
Sept ☎617/523-8388 Centered on the AMC
Loews Boston Common, the festival
screens flashy major releases alongside
independent shorts and documentaries,
with frequent discussions by directors and
screenwriters.

Boston Blues Festival Late Sept ⓦwww
.bluestrust.com This festival brings blues to
the shores of the Charles River for two cool,
"my-baby-done-left-me" days.

Boston NEMO Festival Late Sept ⓦwww
.nemoboston.com Taking place over three
days, with over 300 bands and over thirty
venues, this festival bands together rocker
boys and girls to the tunes of indie-rock.

Open studios

Each fall, the **Boston Open Studios Coalition** arranges for local artists to showcase
their paintings, pottery, photographs, and other works of art to the public, on a neigh-
borhood-by-neighborhood basis. Exhibitors include the United South End Artists
(☎617/267-8862), the Jamaica Plain Artists (☎617/524-3816), ACT Roxbury
(☎617/445-1061 extension 222), the Mission Hill Art Association (☎617/427-7399),
and the Fort Point Channel Arts Community (☎617/423-4299). Check ⓦwww
.bostonopenstudios.org for listings.

October

Oktoberfest Early Oct ☎617/491-3434, ⊛www.harvardsquare.com The usual beer, sauerkraut, and live entertainment in Harvard Square, done Boston style – meaning the hops-fueled shenanigans end at 6pm.

Columbus Day Parade Second Mon ☎1-888/SEE-BOSTON Kicked off by a ceremony at City Hall at 1pm, the raucous, Italian-flavored parade continues into the heart of the North End.

Boston Fashion Week Mid-Oct ⊛www.bostonfashion.com Nothing on London, Paris, New York, or Milan, but there are some fun events celebrating local designers.

Head of the Charles Regatta Next-to-last weekend ☎617/868-6200, ⊛www.hocr.org Hordes of locals and college students descend on the banks of the Charles River between Central and Harvard squares, ostensibly to watch the crew races, but really more to pal around and get loaded.

Pumpkin Festival Third Sat in Oct ☎617/635-4505 ⊛www.lifeisgood.com The happy T-shirt company "Life is Good" rallies locals to carve for a cause – Camp Sunshine – while seeing if they can beat their own mind-boggling record of lit up jack-o-lanterns (30,128).

Salem Haunted Happenings/Halloween ☎1-800/777-6848, ⊛www.salemweb.com Throughout Oct, Salem features autumnal, Halloween, and witch-themed events up to and including the 31st, featuring séances and the like and ending with Halloween celebrations. A great day trip from Boston.

November

Annual Lighting Ceremony Late Nov ☎1-888/SEE-BOSTON Faneuil Hall Market-place kick-starts the holiday season with the annual lighting of some 300,000 festive bulbs.

Thanksgiving Last Thurs ☎1-800/USA-1620, ⊛www.visit-plymouth.com In Plymouth, Massachusetts, the first Thanksgiving ever is commemorated with tours of old houses and traditional feasts.

December

Boston Tea Party Re-enactment Sun nearest Dec 16 ☎617/482-6439 or 1-888/SEE-BOSTON A lusty re-enactment of the march from Old South Meeting House to the harbor, and the subsequent tea-dumping that helped spark the American Revolution.

First Night Dec 31–Jan 2 ☎617/542-1399, ⊛www.firstnight.org A family-friendly festival to ring in the New Year, featuring parades, ice sculptures, art shows, plays, and music throughout Downtown and Back Bay; culminates in a spectacular fireworks display over Boston Harbor. A button, granting admission to all events, tends to run around $20.

Out of the City

Out of the City

20

Around Boston

While there's enough of interest in Boston itself to keep you going for several days at the very least, the city lies at the center of a region concentrated with historic sights, and there's plenty to see and do within a relatively short distance, though most of it merits little more than a half-day visit. Perhaps the best inland day trip you (or history buffs, at least) can make within a 25-mile radius of Boston is to the revolutionary battlegrounds of **Lexington** and **Concord**, but the city also makes an excellent base for visiting the numerous quaint and historic towns that line the North Shore of the Massachusetts coast. With its gruesome witch trials, **Salem**, around thirty minutes by train from North Station, is often travelers' first place of interest, and there's much more there besides, notably sights highlighting its prosperous days as a major port. Nearby **Marblehead** is pretty enough to merit a wander, too, if lacking any real must-sees; after a short stop there, you can continue on to the more rustic **Gloucester**, the setting of Sebastian Junger's book *The Perfect Storm*, and **Rockport**, worthwhile if you have the time and are captivated by the faded glories of the New England fishing trade. Route 1 is the quickest way up the coast, though coastal Route 1A is more scenic. **Buses** run up this direction as well, operated both by the MBTA and by independent tour companies (see p.29) as does the MBTA commuter rail, with **trains** leaving regularly from Boston's North Station, on the Orange and Green lines.

On the South Shore, the 1627 Pilgrim village of **Plymouth** is the main tourist draw, though it has little to offer other than recreations of Pilgrim settlements and the vessel that brought them here, the *Mayflower II*. Further south, the famous old whaling port of **New Bedford** served as inspiration for Herman Melville's *Moby Dick*; today, the town docks ferries headed for Martha's Vineyard, and its salty docks and cobblestoned streets continue to be worthy of a visit.

More removed from the greater Boston area, the sea-breezy peninsula of **Cape Cod** and its two sandy sisters, the islands of **Nantucket** and **Martha's Vineyard**, are too far out for day-tripping; Chapters 21, 22, and 23 are devoted to Boston's well-loved region of sun and sand.

Lexington and Concord

The serene New England towns of **Lexington** and **Concord**, almost always mentioned in the same breath, trade on their notoriety as the locations of the first armed confrontation with the British at the start of the American Revolution. Lexington is mostly suburban, while Concord, five miles west, is even sleepier, with more of a country feel. Most of the towns' historical quarters have been incorporated into the **Minute Man National Park**, which takes in the Lexington Battle Green, North Bridge, and much of Battle Road, the route the British followed on their retreat from Concord to Boston. These famous battles are evoked in a piecemeal but enthusiastic fashion throughout the park, with scale models, remnant musketry, and the odd preserved bullet hole, all set amidst the area's pretty leafy environs. It's worth noting that, although beautiful at all times of the year, New England winters can put a damper on a trip out to the Lexington-Concord region – most of its major historical sites are closed for the snowy season.

Just beyond the park's boundaries lies another literary sight, **Walden Pond**, transcendental stomping ground for Henry David Thoreau, and now a beloved swimming hole for locals. The whimsical **DeCordova Museum and Sculpture Park**, just over the town border in Lincoln, is very much worth a visit. It's worth noting that, despite being accessible from Boston by train, a car or a tour bus is really necessary to visit the two towns, due to the distances between sites and the lack of decent public transport. The best way to get around is via the Liberty Ride (daily May–Oct: 10.30am–4.30pm; $20; ⓣ781/862-0500 ext.2, ⓦwww.libertyride.us), a hop-on, hop-off trolley tour led by affable and well-informed tour guides. While its route technically begins at the National Heritage Museum in Lexington, it's possible to take the commuter rail from North Station into Concord Station ($6.25 one-way), and pick up the trolley over by Concord center.

Some history

On April 19, 1775, the first battle of the **American Revolution** began here when British troops marched to Concord to seize American munitions. The British plans to attack were hardly a secret; the American "Minute Men" were so called because they were prepared to fight at a moment's notice. When the British set out from Boston Common, Paul Revere and William Dawes set out on separate routes to sound the alarm. Within minutes, church bells were clanging and cannons roaring throughout the countryside signaling the rebels to head for Lexington Green; hundreds more converged around the North Bridge area of Concord. Revere managed to give the final alarm to a sleeping John Hancock and Samuel Adams (who were in town to attend a provincial congress) at the Hancock-Clarke House.

John Parker, the colonial captain, was down the street at the Buckman Tavern, when he received word that the British were closing in on the Green. "Don't fire unless fired upon," he ordered the men, "but if they mean to have a war, let it begin here." With only 77 Americans pitted against 700 British regulars, it was more a show of resolve than a hope for victory. Who fired the first shot remains a mystery, but in the fracas that followed, eight Americans were killed, including Parker (the soldiers who died here are buried in a particularly affecting memorial at the southeast end of the Green). One wounded soldier crawled across the road to his home, only to die at his wife's feet – the still-standing house, on the corner of Harrington and Bedford streets, displays a commemorative plaque. The British suffered no casualties, and marched three miles west to Concord.

By the time they arrived, it was already after sunrise on April 19, and hundreds more Minute Men had amassed on a farm behind North Bridge near where the lion's share of munitions were stored. When a British officer accidentally set fire to a building, the Americans believed that the town was going up in smoke. They fired on the British guarding the other side of the bridge – the "shots heard round the world," as history books have it. The British were now outnumbered four to one, and suffered heavily in the ensuing battle, which continued all the way back to Boston.

Lexington

The main thing to see in **Lexington** is the wide-open space called **Battle Green**. The land serves as the town's common and is fronted by Henry Kitson's iconic *Minute Man* statue. This imposing bronze figure (popularly assumed to be that of Captain John Parker) is depicted bearing a musket, was built in 1900,

▲ Lexington's Battle Green

and stands on boulders dislodged from the stone walls behind which the colonial militia fired at their British opponents on April 19, 1775.

On the eastern periphery of the green, the **visitor's center** (daily: April–Nov 10am–5pm; Dec–March 9am–4pm, free; ☎781/862-1450, ⓦwww.lexingtonchamber.org) has a diorama that shows the detail of the battle and a helpful staff that can help orient you historically and geographically. Facing the green, the **Buckman Tavern** (April to mid-Nov Mon–Sat 10am–5pm, Sun noon–5pm; 30–45min guided tour; $5; ☎781/862-5598, ⓦwww.lexingtonhistory.org/buckman_2002), an eighteenth-century bar and hostelry that served as the Minute Men's headquarters while awaiting news of British incursion, looks like a typical pub, right down to its seven-foot-wide fireplace and lengthy tap bar on the first floor; the only bonafide vestige of revolutionary activity is the hole from a British bullet that's been preserved in an inner door near the taproom.

A couple of blocks north, at 36 Hancock St, a plaque affixed to the brown, two-story **Hancock-Clarke House** (mid-March to late Oct Mon–Sat 11.30am–4.30pm, Sun 1–4.30pm; 30–45min guided tour $5; ☎781/862-1703) solemnly reminds us that this is where "Samuel Adams and John Hancock were sleeping when aroused by Paul Revere"; the latter was the grandson of Reverend John Hancock, the man for whom the house was built in 1698. Exhibits on the free-admission museum floor include the drum on which William Diamond beat the signal for the Minute Men to converge and the pistols that British Major John Pitcairn lost on the retreat from Concord. Less interesting is the small wooden **Munroe Tavern**, somewhat removed from the town center at 1332 Massachusetts Ave (April–late Oct Mon–Sat 11.30am–4.30pm, Sun 1–4.30pm; 30–45min guided tour; $5; ☎781/862-2016), which served as a field hospital for British soldiers, though for a mere hour and a half only. If you intend to visit all three sights, you'll save a bit by getting a combination ticket ($12), available at any of the three.

Just outside of Lexington town, a contemporary brick-and-glass building houses the **National Heritage Museum**, 33 Marrett Rd (Mon–Sat 10am–5pm, Sun noon–5pm; free; ⓦwww.monh.org), which tries to be just that, with rotating displays on all facets of American history, daily life, and culture, plus a permanent exhibit on the battle events of Lexington.

If you're looking to have a **meal**, try *Via Lago*, 1845 Massachusetts Ave (☎781/861-6174), a casual counter-service spot that's good for fresh, tasty pastas, sandwiches, and salads; or you can head to *Khushboo*, 1709 Massachusetts Ave (☎781/863-2900), where the decor isn't much but the savory Indian food is sure to wow you. If you're looking to **stay** in town, *Morgan's Rest Bed & Breakfast* at 205 Follen Rd (☎781/652-8018, ⓦwww.morgansrestbandb.com; $105) is a cozy and well-loved B&B.

Concord

One of the few sizable inland towns of New England at the time of the Revolution, **Concord**, a fifteen-minute drive on Route 2A west of Lexington, and a forty-minute train ride ($6.25 one way) from Boston's North Station, retains a pleasant country atmosphere. Trains arrive at Concord Station, about half a mile from the city center, and within walking distance of the rambling **Colonial Inn** (☎1-800/370-9200, ⓦwww.concordscolonialinn.com; $200), near the corner of Main and Monument streets. After a morning spent denouncing eighteenth-century British rule, it's customary to indulge in a quintessential British activity here – high tea – in its historic digs (reservations recommended for tea; $10–25). The inn also has a traditional dining room and a tavern that served as a makeshift revolutionary hospital during the war.

From the top of **Hill Burying Ground** to the west, you can survey Concord, as did Major Pitcairn when the Americans amassed on the far side of North Bridge. A few blocks behind it on Route 62 is **Sleepy Hollow Cemetery** – though not the one of headless horsemen fame, which is located far from here in the Hudson River Valley. You will, however, find eminent Concord literati Emerson, Hawthorne, Thoreau, and Louisa May Alcott buried atop the graveyard's "Author's Ridge," as signs clearly indicate. Fun fact: although the stones state that Sophia and Una Hawthorne are buried in Kensal Green, England, they were actually re-interred here in 2006 after their gravestones were, in a grand twist of fate, ruined by a Hawthorne tree.

Minute Man Historical Park and Old Manse

The best way get your Revolutionary War bearings in the area is to begin at the **Minute Man Visitor Center**, where Route 2A intersects with Airport Road (April to late-Oct daily 9am–4pm; free; ☎978/369-6993, ⓦwww.nps.gov /mima). Helpful rangers here will fill you in with a 24-minute film, and lead you to facts and maps directing you further down the five-mile "Battle Road Scenic Byway" (the April 19, 1775 route upon which 3500 British Regulars fought 1700 colonial militiamen; the Brits were later forced to retreat back to Boston on this same path). One highlight of the trail, just a bit west on Route 2A from the visitor's center, is the **Paul Revere Capture Site**, where, amidst a humble circle of stones a solemn plaque decrees "April 19, 1775, 1.30 am: at this point on the Old Concord road ended the midnight ride of Paul Revere." Revere's horse was taken from him, and as he walked into Lexington he was just in time to hear the first shots of the American Revolution. It's worth stopping by **Hartwell Tavern** (west on Route 2A) which still has its original 1733 brick and floorboards, for a chat with informative park rangers and the chance to witness a real-live musket firing demonstration (April to late-Oct daily 11.15am, 2.15pm, 3.15pm, 4.15pm; free); costumed rangers fire off a ¾ inch lead ball with help from their trusty seventeenth-century Brown Bess musket. The Minute Man Park culminates at the most hyped spot in Concord – **North Bridge** – the site of the first effective armed resistance to British rule in America. If you take the traditional approach from Monument Street, you'll be following the route the British took. Just before crossing the bridge, an inscription on the mass grave of some British regulars reads, "They came 3000 miles and died to keep the past upon its throne." The bridge itself, however, looks a bit too well-preserved to provoke much sentiment, and no wonder – it's actually the fifth replica of yet another replica of the original structure.

A stone's throw from North Bridge, the gray-clapboard **Old Manse**, at 269 Monument St (mid-April to Oct Mon–Sat 10am–5pm, Sun noon–5pm; $8; ☎978/369-3909, ⓦwww.oldmanse.org), was built for Ralph Waldo Emerson's grandfather, the Reverend William Emerson, in 1770. The younger Emerson lived here on and off, and, in 1834, penned *Nature* here, the book that signaled the beginning of the Transcendentalist movement. Of the numerous rooms in the house, all with period furnishings intact, the most interesting is the small upstairs study, where Nathaniel Hawthorne, a resident of the house in the early 1840s, wrote *Mosses from an Old Manse*, a rather obscure essay that gave the place its name. Hawthorne passed three happy years here (although later getting evicted for non-payment of rent) shortly after getting married to his wife, Sophia, who, following a miscarriage, used her diamond wedding ring to etch the words "Man's accidents are God's purposes" into a window pane in the study. Another point of interest can be found on the first floor, where there's a framed swath of original English-made wallpaper with the British "paper tax" mark stamped on the back.

The Wayside and Concord Museum

Another literary landmark, **The Wayside**, is east of the town center at 455 Lexington Rd (April–Oct Sat & Sun tours at 11am, 1pm, 3pm, 4.30pm; $5; ⊤978/318-7825, ⓦwww.nps.gov/mima/wayside). The 300-year-old yellow wooden house was once home to both the Alcotts and the Hawthornes, though at different times. Louisa May Alcott's girlhood experiences here formed the basis for *Little Women* (though she actually penned the novel next door at the Orchard House, where the family lived from 1858 to 1867 and her father, Bronson, founded his School of Philosophy; there are tours here from April to late-Oct Mon–Sat 10am–4:30pm and Sun 1–4:30pm, Nov to late-March Mon–Fri 11am–3pm, Sat 10am–4.30pm and Sun 1–4:30pm; $8; ⊤978/369-4118, ⓦwww.louisamayalcott.org). Among the antique furnishings, the most unusual is the slanted writing desk at which Hawthorne toiled standing up, in the fourth-floor "tower" he added on for that purpose. If you don't feel like taking a guided tour, the small but well-presented **museum** (free) at the admissions area provides a brief overview of the home.

Just down the road at no. 200 (with its entrance on the Cambridge Turnpike) stands the excellent **Concord Museum** (Jan–March Mon–Sat 11am–4pm, Sun 1–4pm; April–Dec Mon–Sat 9am–5pm, Sun noon–5pm; $10; ⊤978/369-9763, ⓦwww.concordmuseum.org). Located on the site of Emerson's apple orchard, it has more than a dozen galleries displaying period furnishings from eighteenth- and nineteenth-century Concord, including a sizable collection of Thoreau's personal effects, such as the bed from his Walden Pond house. More interesting, however, are the Revolutionary War artifacts throughout, such as one of the signal lanterns hung from the Old North Church in Boston, to warn of the British march.

When hunger strikes, you can try the *Cheese Shop*, 29 Walden St (⊤978/369-5778), a great place to stop for deluxe picnic fixings from pâté and jellies to all manner of cheeses. If you've got a hankering for old school comfort food, head to *Helen's*, 17 Main St (⊤978/369-9885; cash only), for grilled cheese and tomato sandwiches ($6) topped off with a root beer float ($4).

Walden Pond and DeCordova Museum

Though the tranquility that Thoreau sought and savored at **Walden Pond**, just two miles south of Concord proper off Route 126 (daily dawn–dusk; $5 parking; ⊤978/369-3254, ⓦwww.mass.gov/dcr/parks/northeast/wldn.htm), is for the most part gone – thanks mainly to the happy sunbathers and hikers who pour in to retrace his footsteps – the place itself has remained much the same since the author's famed two-year exercise in self-sufficiency began in 1845. "I did not feel crowded or confined in the least," he wrote of his life in the simple log cabin; and, though his semi-fictionalized account of the experience might have you believing otherwise, Thoreau hardly roughed it, taking regular walks into town to stock up on amenities and receiving frequent visitors at his single-room house.

The reconstructed **cabin**, complete with a journal open on its rustic desk, is situated near the parking lot (you'll have to content yourself with peering through the windows), while the site of the original structure, closer to the shores of the pond, is commemorated with stones placed there by visitors. The pond itself, which spans about a quarter-mile across (and is only half a mile long), is a popular swimming hole. The water looks best at dawn, when the pond still "throws off its nightly clothing of mist"; late-risers should bring a swimsuit and comfortable shoes to maximize their transcendental experience of it all. Also, as is the case with most everything in New England, Walden Pond is particularly stunning during the Fall months (Sept–Nov).

Though technically a part of the town of Lincoln, the **DeCordova Museum and Sculpture Park**, 51 Sandy Pond Rd (Tues–Sun 11am–5pm; $9, sculpture park free when museum is closed; ℡781/259-8355, Ⓦwww.decordova.org), is only a few miles south of downtown Concord and very much worth a visit. All manner of contemporary sculpture peppers the museum's expansive grounds, but most fascinating are the bigger works, like John Buck's *Dream World* and Paul Matisse's *Musical Fence*, which look like they've burst through the walls of a museum and tumbled into their present positions; Matisse's piece is interactive – tap it with a wooden stick like you would a xylophone. Most of the sculptures are by American (and in particular New England) artists, and are sufficiently impressive to make the **garden** overshadow the small on-site museum, whose rotating special exhibits are often just as eye-catching, with an emphasis on contemporary multimedia art.

Salem

Historic **Salem**, easily accessed from Boston by both the North Station commuter rail North Station ($5.25 one-way) and by a 45min ferry from Central Wharf (by the Aquarium; ℡978/941-0220, Ⓦwww.salemferry.com; $12 one-way), is a great afternoon excursion from the city. Just sixteen miles from Boston on 128N, it's a quaint little town with an unusual history that's worth discovering on an overnight stay. This is where Puritan self-righteousness reached

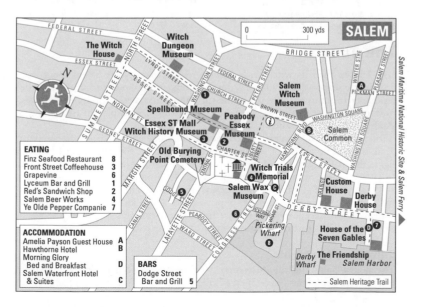

its apogee in the horrific **witch trials** of 1692, and the place uses the stigma to its advantage by hyping up the correlating spookiness, especially around **Halloween**, which, despite some of the cheesiness on offer, is a great time to visit. Around the holiday, sites are open longer, myriad special events, talks, and walking tours are held, and you get the chance to do some leaf-peeping during New England's spectacular fall season (Ⓦ www.hauntedhappenings.org).

To gather **information**, head to the helpful Salem National Visitor's Center, at 2 New Liberty St (daily 9am–5pm; ☎ 978/740-1650, Ⓦ www.salemweb .com), which also serves as the Salem Heritage Trail's unofficial starting point; they also have public bathrooms.

Accommodation

Salem is full of small **B&Bs** – some with no more than three rooms – in old historic houses with steep staircases. It is perhaps the only town in America where **hotels** are booked for Halloween months in advance; if you plan on coming any time in October, beware of high prices and full houses.

Amelia Payson House 16 Winter St ☎ 978/744-8304, Ⓦ www.ameliapaysonhouse .com. A sweet little B&B in a restored 1845 Greek Revival house run by friendly and accommodating owners. The rooms are clean and not too frilly, with Wi-Fi and snacks available. You'll eat a tasty breakfast in the morning off of pretty floral china. Rates start at $95 a night.

Hawthorne Hotel 18 Washington Square W ☎ 978/744-4080, Ⓦ www.hawthornehotel.com. Built in 1920, this restored hotel, furnished with eighteenth-century reproduction furnishings, is *the* place to stay in Salem. Rooms are smart and comfortable, and wireless Internet access is available. An adjoining B&B is also on the property. Rates start from $104 per night.

Morning Glory Bed and Breakfast 22 Hardy St ☎ 978/741-1703, Ⓦ www.morningglorybb .com. This three-room B&B down by the water (and the House of Seven Gables) has a friendly owner and a roof deck with water views. Rates from $125.

Salem Waterfront Hotel & Suites 225 Derby St ☎ 978/740-8788, Ⓦ www.salemwaterfronthotel .com. This Best Western newcomer adds 86 much-needed rooms to the center of town near the water. Standard large hotel fare, with minimalist design, heated indoor pool, free Wi-Fi, and prices to match. Rooms run about $175.

The Town

Less known than its witch trials past were the many years Salem spent as a flourishing seaport (in 1790 it was the sixth biggest city in the country), and the remnants from this era only add to the unsettling aura, with abandoned wharves, rows of stately sea captains' homes, and an astounding display of riches at the **Peabody Essex Museum**.

Today, the 1.7-mile **Salem Heritage Trail** (modeled after Boston's Freedom Trail, marked by a strip of red paint and all) links the town's principal historic sights, the majority of which are tied to the town's gruesome witch-hanging days. In an even more ironic twist of history, a sizable (around 5000 at the last count) and highly visible contingent of **Wiccans** now live proudly in modern Salem, as well as (more expectedly) a large population of Goth kids. The latter are more than willing to accept modest fees for their fortune-telling services; keep in mind they're as much a part of the tourist industry as everything else in Salem.

Salem's witch sights

The hokey **Salem Witch Museum**, 19½ Washington Square (daily: July–Aug 10am–7pm; Sept–June 10am–5pm; $7.50; ☎ 978/744-1692 or 1-800/544-1692,

@www.salemwitchmuseum.com), provides some entertainment, if kitschy, orientation on the witch trials. Its self-billing as a multimedia sound-and-light show makes it sound grander than it actually is: wax figures are used to depict the hysteria, a Darth Vader-esque voice is used to narrate the show, and thanks to the museum's circular seating arrangement, there are significant portions of the performance where you can't actually see what's happening. Nonetheless, that it's housed in a suitably spooky former Romanesque church enhances the atmosphere, and it's still better and more official than the other "witch museums" in town – you'll learn that before the hysteria subsided nineteen were hanged, one man was pressed to death, and hundreds of New England residents sent to jail where they had to pay for the food they ate; Salem citizen Rebecca Nurse was even charged for the chains she wore. In front of the museum is the imposing statue of a caped **Roger Conant**, founder of the town's original 1626 Puritan settlement, which was called Naumkeag after the eponymous river; the name was changed to Salem – a bastardization of "shalom" (meaning peace) – in 1629.

Salem's downtown thoroughfare, the car-free Essex Street Pedestrian Mall, is full of museums and boutiques selling witch-related paraphernalia with varying degrees of tact and taste. The **Spellbound Museum**, 190 Essex St (April–Nov 10am–5pm; Dec–March call for hours; $10; T978/745-0138, @www .spellboundtours.com), is one of the best museums in town and displays a range of curios from around the world, like shrunken heads, vampire killing kits, and tools used by practitioners of voodoo. The museum also hosts an entertaining evening ghost-hunting tour (daily at 8pm; $13) around the town's supposedly haunted sights; visitors are encouraged to take as many pictures as possible in the hope of capturing light anomalies called "orbs" – supposedly the first manifesta- tions of spirits – on camera. At the **Witch History Museum**, 197–201 Essex St (daily 10am–5pm; $7; T978/741-7770, @www.witchhistorymuseum.com), you can catch an impressive live presentation of the witch trials and tour a slightly hokey recreation of "Old Salem" village. On the west side of town, the **Witch Dungeon Museum**, 16 Lynde St (April–Nov daily 10am–5pm; $7; T978/741- 3570, @www.witchdungeon.com), occupies a nineteenth-century clapboard church and treats visitors to farcical re-enactments of key witch trial-related events. Upstairs, it's the trial of Sarah Good – a pipe-smoking beggar woman falsely accused of witchcraft – based on actual court transcripts; after the show, actors escort you below ground to a re-created "dungeon" where you see that some of the prison cells were no bigger than a telephone booth.

On a less sensationalistic note, two blocks further west, at 310 Essex, is Salem's only surviving house with an actual link to the trials. The misleadingly named **Witch House** (May–Nov 10am–5pm; $6; T978/744-8815, @www .salemweb.com/witchhouse) is the former home of judge Jonathan Corwin. Furnished with antiques, the museum focuses more on Puritan life and architecture than on the trials themselves, which are only mentioned toward the end of the half-hour tour.

A pleasant respite from all the hysteria is the simple and moving **Witch Trials Memorial** at Charter and Liberty streets, a series of stone blocks etched with the names of the hanged. The memorial is wedged into a corner of the **Old Burying Point Cemetery**, where one witch judge, John Hathorne, forebear of Salem's most famous son, Nathaniel Hawthorne, is buried, as well as Captain Richard More, a passenger on the *Mayflower*.

The Peabody Essex Museum

Worth the trip to Salem alone is the newly renovated **Peabody Essex Museum**, at East India Square (daily 10am–5pm; $13; T978/745-9500,

ⓦ www.pem.org), the oldest continuously operating museum in the US. The museum's vast, modern space incorporates more than thirty galleries displaying art and artifacts from around the world that illustrate Salem's past importance as a major point of interaction and trade between the East and West. Founded by ship captains in 1799 to display their exotic items obtained while overseas, the museum also boasts the biggest collection of nautical paintings in the world. Other galleries hold Chinese and Japanese export art, Asian, Oceanic, and American decorative arts, and, in a preserved house that the museum administers, court documents from the Salem Witch Trials.

On the ground level, creatively curated whaling exhibits include Ambrose Garneray's gruesome 1835 painting, *Attacking the Right Whale* (which depicts five sailors killing a whale, blood and all), as well as a fabulous scrimshaw collection that features a nineteenth-century pie crimper and an 1829 etched sperm whale tooth that reads "Death to the living/long life to the killers/success to sailors wives & greasy luck to whalers." A cavernous central gallery on the second floor features fanciful figureheads from now-demolished Salem ships hung from the walls, plus the reconstructed interior salon from America's first yacht, *Cleopatra's Barge*, which took to the seas in 1816. More contemporary exhibitions are found on the second floor, including the museum's stellar Asian collection.

The museum's prize possession, however, is **Yin Yu Tang**, a sixteen-room Qing dynasty house that the museum purchased, dismantled, and brought to Salem to foster awareness and appreciation of Chinese culture. This serene space features elaborately wrought scrollwork windows and two small fish ponds filled with Koi; keep an eye out for the little pink radio box high on the reception room wall – installed in millions of Chinese village homes in the 1960s, the radios played news, music, and political announcements for twenty years, and could not be turned down or off. Though the house has been open to the public since 2003, it's still a hot ticket: admission is included with a museum ticket, but you still must reserve a time at the front desk to see it.

The Salem Maritime National Historic Site

Little of Salem's original waterfront remains, although the 2000-foot-long **Derby Wharf** is still standing, fronted by the imposing Federalist-style **Custom House** at its head. These two, and ten other mainly residential buildings once belonging to sea captains and craftsmen, make up the **Salem Maritime National Historic Site**, which maintains a **visitor's center** at 174 Derby St and 2 New Liberty St (daily 9am–5pm; ☎978/740-1650, ⓦ www.nps.gov /sama). The Custom House is where Nathaniel Hawthorne worked as a surveyor for three years, a stint which he later described as "slavery." The office-like interior is rather bland, as is the warehouse in the rear, with displays of tea chests and such. Park rangers also give tours of the adjacent **Derby House** (daily 9am–5pm; $5), whose millionaire owner, Elias Derby, received it as a wedding gift from his father; it overlooked the harbor to better allow him to monitor his shipping empire. Next door, the **West India Goods Store** emulates a nineteenth-century supply shop by peddling nautical accoutrements like fishhooks and ropes, as well as supplies like molasses candy and "gunpowder tea," a tightly rolled, high-grade Chinese green tea. On the water you'll find the **Friendship**, a reconstruction of a 171-foot, three-masted Salem East Indiaman that was built in 1797 and has been moored here since 1998. Daily self-guided tours are available from 9am to 5pm; if a ranger isn't around then you can sign up for a tour slot. Rangers also lead intriguing "privateering" tours ($5), where you can tour maritime grounds and hear how Salem ships captured 458 vessels (cargo and sailors included) during eighteenth century wartime.

The House of the Seven Gables

The most famous sight in the waterfront area is undoubtedly the **House of the Seven Gables**, 54 Turner St (daily: Jan–June and Nov–Dec 10am–5pm; July–Oct 10am–7pm; $12; ☎978/744-0991, ⓦwww.7gables.org), a rambling old mansion by the sea that served as inspiration for Hawthorne's novel of that name. Forever the "rusty wooden house with seven acutely peaked gables" that Hawthorne described, this 1668 three-story dwelling has some other notable features, such as the bricked-off "Secret Stairway" that leads to the chimney and a small room. The house was inhabited in the 1840s by Susanna Ingersoll, a cousin of Hawthorne whom he often visited. The author's birthplace, a small, barn-red house built before 1750, has been moved here from its original location on Union Street; the pretty grounds also feature a wishing well amidst lovely surrounding gardens.

As you're leaving, pop into Ye Olde Pepper Companie, just across the way at 122 Derby St (☎978/745-2744, ⓦwww.yeoldepeppercandy.com) to sample their peppermint and lemon "gibralters," the first candies to be made and sold commercially in the US (dating to 1806).

Eating and drinking

Salem has a good selection of pub grub and casual American fare on offer; the fancier eateries lurk by the waterfront.

Dodge Street Bar and Grill 7 Dodge St ☎978/745-0139. A great little dive bar known for its live music scene that's complemented by area Berklee School of Music professors. If you can make it, try to hit up a Tues night Fats Hammond show, characterized by its jazzy riffs and killer organ player.

Finz 76 Wharf St ☎978/744-8485. A spacious, snazzy seafood eatery (think pan seared scallops with a dirty martini, $30 for both) on a wharf overlooking the harbor.

Front Street Coffeehouse 20 Front St ☎978/740-6697. Endearing little coffee shop with sandwiches freshly made to order, big salads, low-key outdoor tables, and free Wi-Fi.

Grapevine 26 Congress St ☎978/745-9335. Top-notch bistro featuring exotic dishes like Cambodian mussels and roasted red snapper with Thai sauce, plus good vegetarian options.

Lyceum Bar and Grill 43 Church St ☎978/745-7665. Popular spot for Yankee cooking with modern updates like dill-infused clam chowder and lobster stuffed with shrimp, scallions, ginger, and breadcrumbs.

Red's Sandwich Shop 15 Central St ☎978/745-3527. This well-loved local spot serves hearty breakfast and brunch fare with bigger-than-your-plate pancakes, egg sandwiches, and low-key lunches in a little red house built in 1698. Cash only.

Salem Beer Works 278 Derby St ☎978/745-2337. You can try innovative microbrews (there are 15 on tap) such as Black Bat Stout, or choose from their extensive pub grub menu with savory fare like steak tips ($14) and burgers ($9).

Marblehead

Adjacent to Salem, the maritime town of **Marblehead**, about a thirty-minute drive on Route 128 northeast of Boston, is filled with winding streets made up of small but well-preserved private sea captains' homes that lead down to the harbor. Once the domain of Revolutionary War heroes – it was Marblehead boatmen who rowed Washington's assault force across the Delaware River to attack Trenton – it's now a pleasant mix of Boston commuters and long-time residents. One thing that hasn't changed over the years is the town's dramatic setting on a series of rocky ledges overlooking the wide natural harbor, which makes it one of the East Coast's biggest **yachting centers**. The annual Race Week, the highlight of the Marblehead regatta established in 1889, takes place at the end of July.

Settled in 1629, Marblehead has largely escaped commercialism thanks to its occupants' affluence and, oddly, a severe shortage of parking. The latter should not deter you from visiting, however, as this is one of the most picturesque ports in New England. You can get a good look at it from **Fort Sewall**, which juts into the harbor at the end of Front Street; these are the remnants of fortifications the British originally built in 1644, which later protected the USS *Constitution* (on view in the Charlestown Navy Yard; see p.76) in the War of 1812. Closer to the center of town is **Old Burial Hill**, which holds the graves of more than six hundred Revolutionary War soldiers and has similarly sweeping views. **Abbot Hall**, on Washington Street (Mon, Tues, Thurs, & Fri 8am–5pm, Wed 7.30am–7pm, Sat 9am–6pm, Sun 11am–6pm), an attractive 1876 town hall which can be seen from far out at sea, houses Archibald Willard's famous patriotic painting *The Spirit of '76*, created for the Philadelphia Centennial Exposition of 1876, and the 1684 town deed signed by Nanapashemet Indians.

Given Marblehead's waterfront location, seafood headlines the town's dining options. If you're looking for a **snack** (or just to get out on the water) try *Lime Rickey's*, on Devereaux Beach (☎781/631-6700; summers only), for inexpensive burgers and the like. Alternatively, *Three Cod Tavern*, 141 Pleasant St (☎781/639-3262, ⓦwww.threecodtavern.com), serves straightforward seafood and pub grub amidst a sleek mahogany interior. Some would say that local institution *Maddie's Sail Loft*, 15 State St (☎781/631-9824), *is* Marblehead – head over here for a brew once you've finished your meal. The best place to **stay** in town is the spacious *Marblehead Inn*, 264 Pleasant Street (☎781/639-9999, ⓦwww.threecodtavern.com; $160), equipped with stove tops, dishwashers, and hot tubs in most rooms set amidst an 1872 Victorian estate; *One Kimball at Marblehead Light*, 1 Kimball Street on Marblehead Neck (☎781/631-0010, ⓦwww.onekimball.com; $200), has two gorgeous, contemporary rooms overlooking the ocean and Marblehead Lighthouse.

Gloucester

Founded in 1623, **Gloucester**, just forty miles north of Boston up Route 1 to 127, is the oldest fishing and trading port in Massachusetts – though years of overfishing the once cod-rich waters have robbed the town of any aura of affluence it may have had in the past. Indeed, what little fame remains stems from the tragedy of the *Andrea Gale*, a local fishing boat caught, and lost, in the worst storm in recorded history, when three simultaneous storms merged off the coast in October 1991 and produced 100-foot-high waves; its story is told in Sebastian Junger's *The Perfect Storm* (see "Books", p.299). The fate of all the sailors (some 100,000 total) who have perished offshore over the centuries is commemorated by a 1923 bronze statue, *Man at the Wheel*, overlooking the harbor. To learn a bit more about the port's fishing past, head to the excellent **Cape Ann Historical Museum**, near the docks at 27 Pleasant St (Tues–Sat

10am–5pm; $6.50; ☎978/283-0455, ⓦwww.capeannhistoricalmuseum.org), where the history of the region is well documented through old photographs, fishing and quarrying implements, and paintings of mostly local scenes by a variety of artists including Winslow Homer, Milton Avery, Augustus Buhler, and Gloucester-born marine artist Fitz Hugh Lane.

Another lovely way to spend the day is to head east on East Main Street to the famed **Rocky Neck Art Colony**. While the Colony's quality of art varies widely, there are always a handful of standout galleries, and the area's endearing flower gardens and pretty harbor views make for a pleasant (and free) meander.

Over in East Gloucester, at Eastern Point off Route 127A, lies the magical **Beauport** (tours hourly: mid-May to mid-Sept Mon–Fri 10am–4pm, mid-Sept to mid-Oct Mon–Sat 10am–4pm; $10; ☎978/283-0800), a 45-room mansion perched on the rocks overlooking Gloucester Harbor. Started in 1907 as a simple summer retreat for the collector and interior designer Henry Davis Sleeper (who designed Hollywood homes for Joan Crawford and Johnny Mack Brown), the house evolved over the following 27 years into a gabled, turreted villa filled with vast collections of European, American, and Asian *objets*. The house is a fanciful hodgepodge of styles and themes, each room strikingly different from the next; keep an eye out for the room crafted to feel like the stern of a ship (replete with ocean views out to Boston), hand-painted wallpaper that has no repetitions, and a red and gold "octagonal" room, where there are eight side rugs, eight-piece game boards, and even an eight-pointed table.

Another compelling attraction is found a short drive south along the rocky coast of Route 127: the imposing **Hammond Castle Museum**, 80 Hesperus Ave (June–Aug daily 10am–4pm; Sept–May Sat & Sun 10am–4pm; $8; ☎978/283-7673, ⓦwww.hammondcastle.org), whose builder, the eccentric financier and amateur inventor John Hays Hammond Jr, wanted to bring medieval European relics to the US. The austere fortress, which overlooks the ocean from the spot that inspired Longfellow's poem *The Wreck of the Hesperus*, is loaded with treasures, from armor and tapestries to, strangely enough, an elaborately carved wooden facade of a fifteenth-century French bakery, and the partially crushed skull of one of Columbus's shipmates. The ultimate flight-of-fancy, however, is the 30,000-gallon pool whose contents can be changed from fresh to salt water at the switch of a lever – Hammond allegedly liked to dive into it from his balcony.

Practicalities

If you're looking to get out on the water, the **visitors' center**, located just past the wistful *Fishermen's Wives Memorial* at Stage Fort Park, Route 127 (June to mid-Oct daily 9am–5pm; ☎978/281-8865), can give you a map detailing area beaches; best is the lounge-worthy Good Harbor Beach off Witham Street ($20 for parking). There is also ample information on **whale watches**, for which the region is known.

To **stay** in Gloucester, try the *Atlantis Oceanfront Motor Inn*, 125 Atlantic Rd (☎978/283-0014, ⓦwww.atlantismotorinn.com; $90), with clean rooms and a waterfront location. For a **meal**, stop by *Duckworth's Bistrot*, en route to Rocky Neck at 197 E. Main St (☎978/282-1919, closed Mon), for swanky fusion fare, or sip martinis at the fabulous *Franklin Café*, 118 Main St (☎978/283-7888), sister restaurant of Boston's beloved South End bistro of the same name (see p.175). *Virgilio's*, 29 Main St (☎978/283-5295), has incredible Italian sandwiches, while *Passport's*, 110 Main St (☎978/

281-3680), is good for casual soups, salads, and seafood. For local **nightlife**, head to *The Crows Nest*, 334 Main St (☎978/281-2965), long the salty fisherman's hangout.

Rockport and around

Five miles north of Gloucester, scenically situated **Rockport** is the more lively and social of the two towns, with children filling its many ice-cream shops and young couples crowding the bars and clamshacks. Its main drag is a thin peninsula called **Bearskin Neck**, lined with old salt-box fishermen's cottages transformed into restaurants and art galleries (a red lobster shed near the harbor's edge has been christened "Motif #1" because it's been painted so many times). The Neck rises as it reaches the sea, and there's a nice view of the rocky harbor from the end of it. **Dock Square**, at the town's center, makes for pleasant shopping and meandering.

One of the best reasons for visiting Rockport is its access to the sea. One good way to get out on the waves is the schooner **Appledore III** (daily departures from Tuna Wharf on Bearskin Neck: 1pm, 3pm, and 5pm, sunset cruise at 7pm; ☎978/546-7540; $30, $33 for sunset cruise), offering majestic sailing via its 62-foot traditional topsail schooner; North Shore Kayak Outdoor Center, 9 Tuna Wharf (☎978/546-5050), offers kayaking and bike tours (around $35) led by affable guides.

As few miles north of town in the small residential neighborhood of Pigeon Cove sits the aptly named **Paper House** (daily April–Oct 10am–5pm; ☎978/546-2629, $1.50). Everything inside is made of paper, from chairs and a piano (keys excepted) to a desk made from copies of the *Christian Science Monitor*. It's the lovely end result of a twenty-year project started in 1922 by a local mechanical engineer who "always resented the daily waste of newspaper." Just a bit further north on Route 127, **Halibut Point State Park** (daily late-May to late-Sept 8am–8pm; suggested donation) is a fantastic place to spend the afternoon. Formerly a nineteenth-century granite quarry, it's now a breath-taking rocky outcrop offering fabulous views and craggy coastal access to the ocean (many a marriage proposal has taken place at the park's unruly shoreline). On your way back into town, stop by the *Lobster Pool Restaurant*, on Folly Cove via Route 127S (☎978/546-7808), for fresh lobster rolls eaten via picnic tables that overlook Ipswich Bay.

Practicalities

If you **stay** the night at the *Bearskin Neck Motor Lodge,* 64 Bearskin Neck (☎978/546-6677, ⓦwww.rockportusa.com/bearskin, $160), you'll wake up to lobstermen hauling in their buoys just outside your oceanfront porch. The pretty Victorian *Pleasant Street Inn*, 17 Pleasant St (☎978/546-3915, ⓦwww .pleasantstreetinn.net, $105), offers clean and friendly bed and breakfast accommodation, full breakfasts in the morning, and an in-town location. For such a small space, Rockport offers a stellar array of **restaurants**. The casual ambience at the *Beach Street Bistro*, 18 Beach Street (☎978/546-0055), belies its fabulous fusion fare, with dishes like Greek-style lamb chops ($23) and bananas foster. At breakfast time, head over to *The Coffee Shop*, 27 Main St (☎978/546-9443), where locals swill coffee in mugs brought from home; be sure to sample one of their home-made donuts.

One minor practicality: **parking** in Rockport can be tough; unless you're staying in town, it's best to park and ride ($1 one-way) by the Chamber of Commerce (☎978/546-6575), on Route 127 at 3 Whistlestop Mall.

Plymouth

While most day-trippers from Boston head north first, Boston's South Shore, sweeping the coast from suburban Quincy to the former whaling port of New Bedford, has its own fair share of worthwhile destinations. It's best known for tiny **Plymouth**, America's so-called "hometown," forty miles south of Boston. The town is mostly given over to commemorating the landing of the 102 Pilgrims here in December of 1620 and need only be visited by people with a real interest in the story.

The famous **Plymouth Rock**, where the Pilgrims are said to have touched land, is enclosed by a solemn, pseudo-Greek temple by the sea. As is typical with most sites of this ilk, the rock is of symbolic importance only – the Pilgrims had already spent several weeks on Cape Cod before landing here, and no one can be sure where they actually did land. On the hill behind the venerable stone, the **Plymouth National Wax Museum**, 15 Carver St (daily: March–May & Oct–Nov 9am–7pm; June–Sept 9am–9pm; closed Dec–Feb; $6; ☎508/746-6468), has a kitschy sound-and-light tableau of the early days of settlement. Down the street is the equally unconvincing **Pilgrim Hall Museum**, 75 Court St (Feb–Dec daily 9.30am–4.30pm; $6; ☎508/746-1620, ⓦwww.pilgrimhall.org), where you enter a room filled with furniture that may or may not have come over on the *Mayflower*, along with numerous pairs of shoes that the Pilgrims may or may not have worn.

A more authentic attraction, and a better way to spend your time, is the replica of the *Mayflower*, called the **Mayflower II** (April–Nov daily 9am–5pm; $8; ☎508/746-1622, ⓦwww.plimoth.org), which was restored in 2000. The ship is berthed on the State Pier in Plymouth Harbor, but before entering the ship you'll encounter a tacky display of cardboard cutouts telling the story of America's forbears. Built in Britain by English craftsmen following the historically accurate plans of an American naval architect at MIT, the *Mayflower II* was ceremoniously docked in Plymouth in 1957 and given to America as a gesture of goodwill. You're free to wander the ship at leisure, and there are trained staff members – in contemporary clothing – available to answer any questions. Others in period costume will put on a well-presented pretence of ignorance of current events.

Similar in approach and authenticity is the **Plimoth Plantation**, three miles south of town off Route 3 (April–Nov daily 9am–5pm; $21; ☎508/746-1622, ⓦwww.plimoth.org). Everything you see in the plantation, such as the Pilgrim Village of 1627 and the Wampanoag Indian Settlement, has been created using traditional techniques; even the farm animals were "backbred" to resemble their seventeenth-century counterparts. Again, actors dressed in period garb try to bring you back in time; depending on your level of resistance, it can be quite enjoyable. If you intend to see both the Plantation and the *Mayflower II*, you'd do better to buy a combo ticket ($25) from the admissions desk.

Practicalities

Plymouth's **visitor center** is on the waterfront at 130 Water St (☎508/747-7525, ⓦwww.visit-plymouth.com). Plymouth & Brockton provides a regular **bus**

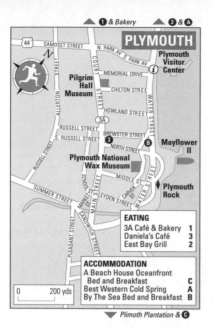

PLYMOUTH

Plymouth
Visitor
Center

Pilgrim
Hall
Museum

Mayflower
II

Plymouth National
Wax Museum

Plymouth
Rock

EATING
3A Café & Bakery   1
Daniela's Café   3
East Bay Grill   2

ACCOMMODATION
A Beach House Oceanfront
Bed and Breakfast   C
Best Western Cold Spring   A
By The Sea Bed and Breakfast   B

0   200 yds

▼ *Plimoth Plantation &* ❹

service to and from Boston ($12 one-way, $22 round-trip; ☎508/746-0378, ⓦwww.p-b.com). Once in Plymouth, a daily express **ferry** heads to Provincetown throughout the summer season (June–Sept daily 10am; $36; ☎508/747-2400 or ☎1-800/678-8667, ⓦwww.provincetownferry.com).

Should you need to overnight in town, a good standard **motel** is the clean and comfortable *Best Western Cold Spring,* 188 Court St (☎508/746-2222; $90). For a more homey choice try *By the Sea*, 22 Winslow St (☎508/830-9643, ⓦwww.bytheseabedandbreakfast.com; $150), a harborfront B&B with two spacious suites and private bath. America's hometown has a few favorable **food** options. Just north of downtown the wonderful *3A Café & Bakery*, 295 Court St (☎508/747-3740), serves tasty Greek food for breakfast and lunch. The waterfront *East Bay Grill* (☎508/746-9751) is the best of the seafood spots, while *Daniela's Café,* 23 Court St (☎508/746-0707), is the best restaurant in town, with crab cakes ($9) and pesto and mozzarella sandwiches at lunchtime ($7) and sleeker bistro dinner fare like smoked, bacon-wrapped pork tenderloin ($22).

New Bedford and around

The famous old whaling port of **New Bedford**, 60 miles due south of Boston, is still home to one of the nation's most prosperous fishing fleets: every year, they haul in the largest catch on the East Coast. New Bedford has aged well, too. Recent preservation efforts, with an eye to the town's whaling heritage, have only served to heighten its aesthetic appeal.

The **downtown** area is now called the New Bedford Whaling National Historic Park, a collection of old buildings, art galleries, and antique stores, the centerpiece of which is the remarkable **New Bedford Whaling Museum**, 18 Johnny Cake Hill (daily 9am–5pm, Thurs in summer to 9pm; $10; ⓦwww.whalingmuseum.org). Housed in a former church and presided over by a 66-foot blue whale skeleton, the museum features the world's largest ship model and an evocative half-scale version of the whaling vessel *Lagoda*, as well as collections of scrimshaw, harpoons, and artifacts retrieved by whalers from the Arctic and the Pacific.

More affecting is the **Seamen's Bethel**, directly opposite the museum, the famous "Whaleman's Chapel" that was built in 1832 and conjured up in Herman Melville's *Moby Dick* (May–Oct daily 10am–4pm, mid-Oct to April

Mon–Fri 11am–1pm, Sat 10am–5pm, Sun 1–5pm; call ahead, though, as often closed on weekends and for private events; donation requested; ☎508/992-3295). The chapel features the ship-shaped pulpit described in Melville's tale, but this one is a replica built after a fire in 1866. More evocative are the memorials lining the walls for those who died at sea, a custom for lost sailors that is continued to this day. The park **visitor center**, 33 William St (daily 9am–5pm; ☎508/996-4095), has interesting guides to local history – the Underground Railroad went through here – as well as maps of the park, waterfront, and nearby **mansions**, remnants of the town's whale-derived wealth. Chief among these are the old Federalist and Victorian houses around **County Street**, of which Melville commented:

Had it not been for us whalemen, that tract of land would this day perhaps have been in as howling condition as the coast of Labrador . . . all these brave houses and flowery gardens came up from the Atlantic, Pacific, and Indian oceans. One and all, they were harpooned and dragged hither from the bottom of the sea.

The Greek Revival **Rotch-Jones-Duff House & Garden Museum**, 396 County St (Mon–Sat 10am–4pm, Sun noon–4pm; $5; ☎508/997-1401, ⓦwww.rjdmuseum.org), built by a Quaker whaling captain in 1834, retains many of its original decorations and furnishings and is festooned with decadent marble fireplace mantles and Oriental rugs. The formal gardens, laid out in their original style, with boxwood hedges, roses, and wildflowers, occupy an entire city block. On many Friday nights here in the summer you can hear low-key live music (as well as at the Whaling Museum); check the website for a calendar. Neighboring **Madison**, **Maple**, and **Orchard streets** also contain a number of fanciful, brightly repainted mansions. It's worth driving by – about all you can do, as they're all private – before heading out of town.

Practicalities

If you want to **stay** in New Bedford, the *Orchard Street Manor*, 139 Orchard St (☎508/984-3475, ⓦwww.the-orchard-street-manor.com; $125), is an atmospheric B&B replete with pool table, Moroccan accoutrements, and great breakfasts, all set in a nineteenth century former whaling captain's home. Across the street from the visitors' center, *Freestone's*, 41 Williams St (☎508/993-7477), serves excellent chowder and microbrews in a restored 1877 bank. For more local flavor, try the authentic Portuguese dishes at *Antonio's*, 267 Coggeshall St (☎508 /990-3636). For a little **nightlife**, the Zeiterion Theatre (☎508/994-2900, ⓦwww.zeiterion.org) hosts fantastic dance, theater, and music performances in a glorious vintage vaudeville space.

In recent years, New Bedford's pretty environs and traffic-less drive from Boston has increased its popularity as a docking point for **ferries** to **Martha's Vineyard**; for more information see p.275.

21

Cape Cod

APE COD, whose base is a mere hour's drive from Boston without traffic, is one of the most celebrated slices of real estate in America, boasting a consistently stunning quality of light that shines over some of New England's best beaches. The slender, crooked Cape gives Massachusetts an extra three hundred miles of coastline, access to much of which is hampered by shore-hugging upper-middle-class homes. Those parts of the Cape that haven't fallen prey to suburban overdevelopment have been preserved as the snug villages they were a hundred or more years ago, replete with town green, white steeple church, and the odd lighthouse. Only **Provincetown**, at the very tip, manages to successfully mesh the past with the present; its unique art galleries, shops, and restaurants make it far and away the destination of choice here. It's also perched on the best stretch of the extensive **Cape Cod National Seashore**, so there's no overwhelming need to go elsewhere, though tiny upscale towns like **Sandwich**, **Brewster**, and **Chatham** make for scenic stops along the way. In recent years local chambers of commerce have been trying to lure tourists in the off season by touting the region's "historical attractions," but the reality is that for most the beach reigns supreme.

Some history

In all the hype about Plymouth and its associations with the Pilgrims, it's often forgotten that they first set foot on North American soil at Provincetown, where there's an enormous monument commemorating the event. The Cape got its name a bit earlier, though, when the area was visited in 1602 by explorer **Bartholomew Gosnold**, the first European to visit southeastern New England, who dubbed it "Cape Cod" on account of the profusion of cod in the local waters. Immigration to the Cape up to 1700 was almost exclusively made up of homesick Englishmen who crossed the Atlantic to take advantage of the burgeoning markets of the New World, and who named the places after towns back home, such as Sandwich, Falmouth, and Barnstable. Indeed, during the Revolutionary War many Cape Codders sided with the Crown; how much of this was genuine affection for British rule and how much was prompted by their vulnerability to British naval strength is debatable. By the early 1800s, **whaling** had become the Cape's primary industry, the ports of Provincetown, Barnstable, Wellfleet, and Truro doing particularly well, while other Cape Codders were employed in the fishing and agricultural industries, including the harvesting of **cranberries**. By the time of the Civil War, with the whaling industry in serious decline, Cape Cod inhabitants began to look to the burgeoning railways for salvation.

Cape Cod's rise as a **tourist destination** is mainly attributable to the development of the motor car and the railway. Wealthy Bostonians and New Yorkers were, for the first time, able to get to the Cape with relative ease, many purchasing

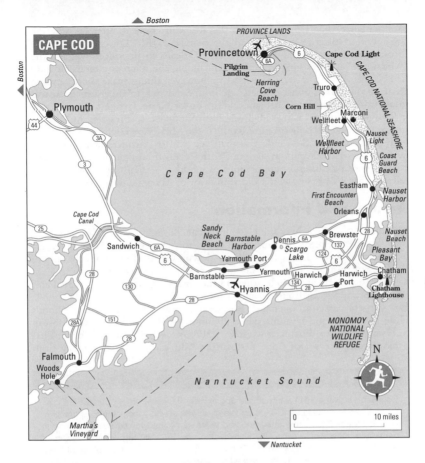

land to build summer homes and returning to live on the Cape permanently upon retirement. Today, the year-round population more than doubles in the summer, when some 80,000 cars a day cross the **Cape Cod Canal**.

But nature is the real arbiter of the Cape's fate. After the last Ice Age, glaciers deposited huge amounts of debris as they began to melt and retreat, forming Cape Cod, the islands of Martha's Vineyard and Nantucket, and Long Island in the process. Because it lacks the solidity of other sections of the New England coast, and due to rising sea levels, Cape Cod is particularly vulnerable to **erosion**. Between Wellfleet and Provincetown the land is scarcely one mile wide, and narrowing all the time. The one benefit of the adverse environmental situation is that it keeps development in check, especially in the vicinity of the protected **National Seashore**. Even highly developed areas are interspersed with pockets of meadowland and seagrass, lending the Cape at least the illusion of wide-open spaces.

The shape of the Cape

The Cape is shaped like a **flexed arm**, with Sandwich at the shoulder, Chatham at the elbow, and Provincetown the clenched fist at the very end. According to local parlance, the "Upper Cape" is the area you come to after crossing the Sagamore or Bourne bridges from the mainland, the "Lower Cape" is the forearm that stretches approximately from Orleans to Provincetown, and the "Mid-Cape" is everything in between, including the main commercial center of Hyannis. From a traveler's perspective, however, things make more sense in terms of the **north coast** of the Cape from Sandwich to Brewster, the **south coast** from Falmouth to Chatham, and the **outer Cape**. The best plan of attack is Route 6A, the Old King's Highway, from Sandwich to Brewster. At Orleans, just past Brewster, Route 6A joins Route 6, the Mid-Cape Highway, an exceedingly dull road that does little else than get you to Provincetown in a hurry. With a very few exceptions, Route 28, the main thoroughfare on the south coast, wends past baleful outcroppings of suburbia – even Cape Codders will tell you that it's a byway best avoided in favor of its scenic northern cousin.

Arrival and information

The main way of reaching the Cape is by **car**, though if you're heading there on a summer weekend, you may well regret this choice. On a fairly quiet day it takes under two hours to get from downtown Boston to the Sagamore Bridge, but this can double on summer weekends and holidays – try to leave as early in the day as possible, to avoid the rush to get over the bridge. Peter Pan (one-way $15 to Bourne, slightly more to elsewhere; ☎1-800/343-9999, ⓦwww.peterpan.com) operates a **bus** service from Boston to Bourne, Woods Hole, Falmouth, and Hyannis, while Plymouth & Brockton (one-way Boston to Hyannis $17, to Provincetown $27; ☎508/746-0378, ⓦwww.p-b.com) has a more complete set of Cape destinations. You can also take a **ferry** from

The Cape Cod Canal

Between 1909 and 1914 a **canal** was dug across the westernmost portion of Cape Cod, effectively making the Cape an island. It was an old idea – the Pilgrims who landed on the Cape some three hundred years earlier had talked about building a canal as a means of avoiding the shipwreck-prone 135-mile trip around the Cape, thus facilitating trade between the Plymouth colony and the Dutch colony of New Amsterdam (New York), but they lacked the manpower to get the work done. Later on, George Washington, contemplating the advantages a canal would have in protecting naval ships and commercial vessels during war, resurrected the idea, but it was not until 1880 that work finally began. The Cape Cod Canal Company employed more than five hundred immigrant workers to begin the laborious process – they used hand shovels and carted debris away in wheelbarrows. In 1899 wealthy New York businessman Augustus Belmont took over the project; ten years later, state-of-the-art earthmoving equipment was introduced, and the canal was completed in 1914, though at the time it was too shallow and narrow to allow anything but one-way traffic. In 1928 the federal government purchased the canal, and during the Great Depression employed 1400 men to complete it. By 1940 the finished canal was the widest in the world. Hundreds of boats now use the canal every day, many of them leisure craft that have to contend with dramatic shifts in water currents and tides. You can join them on a **boat trip** with Hy-Line Cruises ($10–15; ☎508/295-3883, ⓦwww.hy-linecruises.com), which runs a variety of trips ranging from straightforward tours to three-hour jazz outings from Onset Bay Town Pier off routes 6 and 28. Still, you don't have to be on the water to enjoy it; the view of the canal and its verdant shores from the Sagamore and Bourne bridges is one of the most dramatic on the East Coast. There is also a **bike trail** on either side of the canal.

Boston to Provincetown: Bay State Cruise Company (☎617/748-1428, ⓦwww.baystatecruisecompany.com) runs two boats daily in the summer from Boston's Commonwealth Pier (90min express round-trip $71, 3hr standard ferry round-trip $33, while Boston Harbor Cruises (☎617/227-4320, ⓦwww.bostonharborcruises.com), does two express services a day from Long Wharf to Provincetown (90min; $70). A Plymouth to Provincetown ferry is run by Captain John's Boats (90min round-trip $36; ☎508/747-2400 or 1-800/242-2469, ⓦwww.provincetownferry.com). Finally, a number of **airlines** fly direct to Cape Cod, including US Airways (☎1-800/428-4322, ⓦwww.usairways.com), which goes to Hyannis from Boston, and Cape Air (☎1-800/352-0714, ⓦwww.capeair.com), which heads to Hyannis and Provincetown from Boston several times a day, even in winter.

The main Cape Cod **visitors' center**, situated at the junction of routes 6 and 132 in Hyannis (Mon–Fri 8.30am–5pm, summer weekends also 10am–4pm; ☎1-888-332-2732), has information about all the towns on the Cape. You can also research the area and make reservations online before you go at the Cape Cod Chamber of Commerce's website, ⓦwww.capecodchamber.org.

Getting around

Once on the Cape, a **car** is the best way to get around. Rentals are available through: *Thrifty*, in Orleans (☎508/255-2234); *Enterprise*, 332 Iyannough Rd, Hyannis (☎508/778-8293); or *Hertz,* 223 Stevens St, Hyannis (☎508/778-8293). Alternatively, the Cape Cod Regional Transit Authority (☎1-800/352-7155, ⓦwww.thebreeze.info) runs frequent public **buses** (6.30am–7pm) along routes 28 and 132 connecting the Cape's outlying towns; simply flag them down on the side of the road and cough up $1.50–3.50. The Cape also has plentiful and scenic **bike** paths; you can rent at *Bike Zone* ($20/day; ☎508/775-3299), which has locations in Hyannis, East Falmouth, Mashpee, and South Yarmouth. A more touristy option, from Hyannis anyway, is the **Cape Cod Scenic Railroad** (late-May to Oct; $18; ☎508/771-3800, ⓦwww.capetrain.com), which runs once a day from Center Street along a meandering two-hour circuit west through cranberry bogs to the Cape Cod Canal and Sandwich.

Cape Cod's south coast

Route 28, which hugs the Nantucket Sound coast of the Cape until it merges with routes 6 and 6A at Orleans, is certainly not the most attractive or scenic route on the Cape; much of it is lined with motels and commercial buildings, and it can get seriously clogged with traffic during the summer. Nonetheless, it runs through a number of important hubs along the south coast, notably **Falmouth** and **Hyannis**. At its end are the two best reasons for hitting this path, the quiet town of **Chatham** and the even quieter **Monomoy National Wildlife Refuge**.

Falmouth and Woods Hole

FALMOUTH boasts more coastline than any other Cape Cod town and no fewer than fourteen harbors among its eight villages, at the center of which is **Falmouth Village**, with its prim, picket-fence-encircled central green

With over 300 miles of coastline, Cape Cod certainly doesn't lack **sand**. What it does lack is parking and facilities at its beachfront locations; what few have the full gamut of services (restrooms, lifeguards, and snack bars) are, not surprisingly, usually busiest. The island's southern stretches, facing Nantucket Sound, tend to be calmer and warmer than its northern options, making this coast more family-oriented than its Atlantic side, where the water tends to be chillier and rougher, but also good for riding waves on boogie boards. **Parking** across the Cape is a bit of a crapshoot: some counties allow daily non-permit beach parking (usually between $10 and $20/day), whereas others limit beach parking to residents. Your best bet, if you're planning on hitting the beach a good deal during your stay, is to visit the local town hall and inquire about non-resident parking permits (which can range from $30 for three days to $60 a week). These town beaches are most often bay or pond, whereas the best ocean beaches are pay as you go – so don't rush to buy a pass until you have an idea of where you'd like to swim.

Around Hyannis

Craigville Beach off Craigville Beach Road in Centerville, just west of Hyannis. Well-oiled and toned sun-worshippers flock to this broad expanse of sand nicknamed "Muscle Beach."

Kalmus Beach off Gosnold Street in central Hyannis. A big windsurfing destination at the mouth of the busy harbor, with full facilities but an urban feel.

Eastham

Coast Guard Beach off Ocean View Drive. Pristine and picturesque Cape Cod National Seashore beach with views for miles, as well as lifeguards and restrooms; you can catch a shuttle bus from Salt Pond or the Eastham High School.

Nauset Light off Ocean View Drive. Scenic Atlantic-facing beach connected to Coast Guard Beach by shuttle bus and also part of the Cape Cod National Seashore; serviced by lifeguards and with restrooms.

Falmouth

Old-Silver Beach off Route 28-A in North Falmouth. Popular, calm beach with great sunsets; college kids and young families gather here, the latter drawn to its natural wading pool.

Surf Drive Beach off Shore Street. Another family favorite; a shallow tidal pool between jetties is known as "the kiddie pool."

surrounded by Colonial, Federal, and Greek Revival homes. Typical of New England, a number of these old sea captains' houses are now B&Bs, and are complemented by a touristy mixture of clothing shops, ice-cream parlors, and real estate agents. The 1794 **Conant House**, 55–65 Palmer Ave (mid-June to mid-Sept Mon–Fri 10am–4pm, Sat 10am–1pm; $5; ☎508/548-4857, ⓦwww .falmouthhistoricalsociety.org), run by the Falmouth Historical Society, contains scrimshaw, rare glass and china, and sailors' memorabilia. There's also a room dedicated to local girl **Katherine Lee Bates**, who composed the song **America the Beautiful**; she was born in 1859 down the road at 16 Main St. The Historical Society also maintains the **Julia Wood House**, next door to the Conant House (same hours and price), an early nineteenth-century doctor's home, one room of which is set up as a clinic, with a horrifying display of primitive dental utensils.

The salty drop of a town that is **WOODS HOLE** owes its name to the water passage, or "hole," between Penzance Point and Nonamesset Island, linking

Orleans

Nauset Beach East Orleans. Arguably the Cape's biggest beach scene, this 10-mile-long barrier beach has terrific facilities (and regular sunset concerts), plus prime windsurfing and boogie-boarding conditions.

Skaket Beach off Skaket Beach Road. Calm bay beach ideal for families; when the tide goes out, kids take to the pools left behind.

Provincetown

Long Point Beach A blissfully quiet beach at the end of a trail lined with scented wild roses and beach plums; you can get there on foot (it's a *long* walk on the jetty) or by frequent shuttle from MacMillan Wharf.

Herring Cove Beach off Route 6. Easily reached by bike or through the dunes, and famous for sunset-watching, this beach is actually more crowded than those nearer town, though never unbearably so.

Province Lands off Race Point Road. Beautiful vast, sweeping moors, and bushy dunes are buffeted by crashing surf.

Race Point Beach off Race Point Road. Abutting Province Lands, this wide swath of white sand is backed by beautiful, tall dunes – the archetypal Cape Cod beach.

Sandwich

Sandy Neck Beach off Sandy Neck Road, East Sandwich. Six-mile-long barrier beach loaded with low dunes favored by off-roaders; the paths are shut down in summer to encourage the local bird population's hatching season.

Town Neck Beach off Town Neck Road. Narrow and rocky beach 1.5 miles out of town with pretty views of passing ships and decent facilities.

Wakeby Pond Ryder Conservation Area, John Ewer Road. The Cape's largest fresh-water pond has a life-guarded beach and full facilities.

Wellfleet

Cahoon Hollow Beach off Ocean View Drive. Good surfing and full facilities make this town-run beach popular with the thirty-something set. Don't miss the famous *Beachcomber* shack for delicious oysters.

Marconi Beach off Marconi Beach Road. Dramatic cliff-framed beach best hit in the morning before the sun falls behind the bluffs. Good facilities.

White Crest off Ocean View Drive. The main distinction between White Crest and neighboring Cahoon is the clientele – here, it's a predominantly young college crowd.

Vineyard Sound and Buzzards Bay. It's little more than a clump of casual restaurants and convenience stores clustered around the harbor and the **Woods Hole Oceanographic Institute**, 15 School St (late May to early Sept Mon–Sat 10am–4.30pm, Sun noon–4.30pm; early Sept to Oct Tues–Sat 10am–4.30pm, Sun noon–4.30pm; Nov–Dec Tues–Fri 10am–4.30pm; April Fri & Sat 10am–4.30pm, Sun noon–4.30pm; closed Jan–March; $2; ☏508/457-2034, ⊛www.whoi.edu). The latter houses an exhibit on the rediscovery of the *Titanic* in 1986, a project the institute spearheaded, and some neat submarine capsules that children will enjoy, but little else besides. During the summer the Institute offers **tours** once a day (reserve in advance) where you get to walk through some of their otherwise off-limits labs. Also worthwhile are the informative, hands-on cruises run from the harbor by **OceanQuest**: lobster and scallop traps are pulled up for inspection and those on board are encouraged to handle the sealife (July–Aug Mon–Fri 10am, noon, 2pm & 4pm, more sporadically on summer weekends and in September; $20; ☏1-800-37-OCEAN, ⊛www.oceanquestonline.org).

Back on land, much of the sealife that lurks off the Cape's shores is kept behind glass at the National Marine Fisheries Service, at the corner of Albatross and Water streets (mid-June to early Sept daily 10am–4pm, early Sept to mid-June Mon–Fri 10am–4pm; free; ☎508/495-2001, ⓦwww.nefsc.noaa.gov), which maintains America's oldest **aquarium**. With a mission to preserve local marine life, its displays are mostly limited to the likes of codfish, lobster, and other piscine creatures that are more appealing on a plate; the exception, the institute's pet seals, Coco and Sandy, give visitors a thrill at feeding time (daily 11am & 4pm).

Accommodation

Despite having little in the way of in-town diversions, Falmouth has some lovely **accommodation** options that make a good base for exploring the Cape and catching the **ferry** from Woods Hole to Martha's Vineyard.

Mostly Hall 27 Main St, Falmouth ☎508/548-3786 or 1-800/682-0565, ⓦwww.mostlyhall.com. An amiably run 1849 mansion with queen-sized canopy beds in each of the six rooms. Closed Jan to mid-Feb. Rooms range $125–200.
Woods Hole Passage 186 Woods Hole Rd, Falmouth ☎508/548-9575, ⓦwww.woodsholepassage.com. Brightly painted chambers in a refurbished red-shingled carriage house set on spacious grounds. This is the place to go to save some money in the area. Rooms from $120, with single beds available.

Eating and drinking

Betsy's Diner 457 Main St, Falmouth ☎508/540-0060. A worthwhile stop for an authentic 1950s diner serving no-nonsense fare that beckons you to "Eat Heavy."
The Clam Shack 227 Clinton Ave, Falmouth ☎508/540-7758. A local institution which serves up heaping plates of fried seafood (and obviously clams) on outside picnic tables and a smashing rooftop deck with prime waterfront views.
Fishmonger's Cafe 56 Water St, Woods Hole ☎508/540-5376. Laid-back natural-foods eatery with a surprising number of vegetarian dishes in addition to seafood standards; try the fine fisherman's stew loaded with shrimp, scallops, and mussels ($20).

Hyannis

HYANNIS is primarily a transportation and commercial hub – it's home to the Cape's largest airport, as well as the main ferry service to Nantucket – and while traveling through it may be necessary, it's not the Cape's most scenic destination. Much of the city has an industrial feel, although there have been a number of flowery revitalization efforts downtown, and there are some pleasant public beaches and quaint B&Bs for those who need to stay. The town still derives a bit of glamour from its association with the **Kennedy Compound**, the family's best-known summer home, located in **Hyannisport**, a private, upscale residential section of town a couple of miles southwest of Hyannis proper. Visitors who come here expecting to take a guided tour will be disappointed: this group of houses is concealed by tall fences, and it's best glimpsed, if you must, from the water: Hy-Line Cruises, at the Ocean Street Docks, runs hour-long cruises that peek in on the compound (mid-April to late Oct; $14; ☎1-800/492-8082, ⓦwww.hy-linecruises.com).

If it's Kennedy-ana you've come to see, the best place to start is the **John F. Kennedy Hyannis Museum**, 397 Main St (mid-May to Oct Mon–Sat

10am–5pm, Sun noon–5pm; Nov to mid–Dec Wed–Sat 10am–4pm; $5; ☎508/790-3077), which displays the expected nostalgia, mainly in the form of old black-and-white photographs. It's not a comprehensive history, and instead focuses on Kennedy's relationship with Cape Cod. For a welcome non-presidential diversion, you might take a free tour of the **Cape Cod Potato Chip Factory**, on Breed's Hill Road near the Cape Cod Mall (Mon–Fri 9am–5pm; free; ☎508/775-7253, ⓦwww.capecodchips.com). The tasty chips, once a local phenomenon but now found almost everywhere, are made with natural ingredients hand-cooked in kettles; it's hard to resist the free samples, in any case.

Practicalities

The local Chamber of Commerce maintains an **information center** at 1481 Route 132 (Mon–Sat 9am–5pm, summer also Sun 9am–5pm; ☎1-877-HYANNIS, ⓦwww.hyannis.com), not to be confused with the Cape Cod Visitor Center just up the road. If you have a boat to catch and need to **stay** in Hyannis, options include the family-oriented *Sea Beach Inn*, 388 Sea St (☎508/775-4612, ⓦcapecodtravel.com/seabeach; $90), with small, neat, affordable rooms, and the wood-shingled *Sea Breeze Inn*, 270 Ocean Ave (☎508/771-7213, ⓦwww .seabreezeinn.com; $100), which has ten frilly queen-bedded rooms, some with shared bath. Both inns are a short walk from the beach. The *Simmons Homestead Inn*, 288 Scudder Ave (☎508/778-4999 or 1-800/637-1649, ⓦwww.simmons homesteadinn.com; $180), is a great B&B in Hyannisport, a pet-friendly spot with thirteen creatively themed rooms in an 1820 sea captain's home.

Many of Hyannis's **restaurants** are on Main Street, which is unfortunately not all that near the hotels – and so, as public transport stops at 7pm, it's helpful to have a car. Be sure to indulge in the full *rodizio* at the well-loved *Brazilian Grill*, 680 Main St (☎508/771-0109), with mouth-watering meats delivered straight from the skewer and onto your plate. For more of local flavor, *Spanky's Clam Shack*, right by the ferry at 138 Ocean St (☎508/771-2770), features fresh broiled and fried seafood. *Collucci Brothers Diner*, 50 Sea St (☎508/771-6896), is a great spot for big breakfasts, while *Four Seas*, in Centerville at 360S Main St (☎508/775-1394), has been serving up enormously fantastic ice-cream cones by Craigville beach since 1934.

Chatham

The next town worth visiting on the South Shore is genteel **CHATHAM**, a long 21 miles west on Route 28, whose quiet and posh small-town atmosphere is largely attributable to some strictly enforced zoning laws, which have prevented the kind of indiscriminate attract-tourists-at-all-costs mentality evident in other Cape communities. The focal point here is **Chatham Village**, whose **Main Street** is home to a variety of upscale boutiques, provisions stores, and some sophisticated restaurants and charming inns.

A few minutes' drive outside the village, the 1877 **Chatham Light** stands guard over a windswept bluff beyond which many a ship met its doom on the "Chatham Bars," a series of sandbars that served to protect the town from the worst of the Atlantic storms – until in January 1987, when a fierce Nor'easter broke through the barrier beach to form the **Chatham Break**, leaving Chatham exposed to the vagaries of the ocean. Right below the lighthouse is a nice beach, but with parking limited to half an hour you're better off biking there from town. A mile north on Route 28, the **Fish Pier** on Shore Road provides a spot to wait for the fleet to come in mid-afternoon. From here you can also take a water taxi to Monomoy Island, a 2700-acre wildlife refuge (see box overleaf).

Monomoy National Wildlife Reserve

Stretching out to sea for nine miles south of Chatham, desolate **Monomoy National Wildlife Refuge** is a fragile barrier beach that was attached to the mainland until breached by a storm in 1958. A subsequent storm in 1978 divided the island in half, and today the islands are accessible only by boat – when weather conditions permit. The refuge spreads across 2750 acres of sand and dunes, tidal flats and marshes, with no roads, no electricity, and, best of all, no human residents, though a small fishing community once existed here. Indeed, the only man-made buildings on the islands are the South Monomoy Lighthouse and lightkeeper's house.

It's a perfect stopover point along the North Atlantic Flyway for almost three hundred species of shorebirds and migratory **waterfowl**, including many varieties of gull and the endangered piping plovers. In addition, the islands are home to white-tailed deer, and harbor and gray seals are frequent visitors in summer. Several organizations conduct island **tours**, among them the Cape Cod Museum of Natural History (℡508/349-2615, ⓦ www.ccmnh.org) and private carriers like the Monomoy Island Ferry, a small boat run by Keith Lincoln (℡508/945-5450, ⓦ www.monomoyislandferry.com); rates are around $20, depending, among other things, on the number of people in your group. In any case, if there are six or more of you, you'll need to get a special **permit** from the headquarters of the Wildlife Refuge, located on Morris Island (℡508/945-0594), which also has a **visitors' center** offering leaflets on Monomoy. Morris Island is accessible from Morris Island Road, south of the Chatham Light.

Accommodation

Chatham is well endowed with tasteful **accommodation**, and the **B&Bs** here are a bit more upscale than those found elsewhere on the Cape. Despite the ample selection, reservations are strongly advised, even outside of high season.

The Captain's House Inn 369–371 Old Harbor Rd ℡508/945-0127 or 1-800/315-0728, ⓦ www .captainshouseinn.com. Easy elegance prevails at this sumptuously renovated 1839 Greek Revival whaling captain's home; most rooms have fireplaces, and prices include delicious breakfasts and afternoon tea with freshly baked scones. $275.
The Carriage House Inn 407 Old Harbor Rd ℡508/945-4688, ⓦ www.thecarriagehouseinn .com. This year-round B&B with young,

friendly owners provides seven modern but welcoming rooms and slightly lower prices than the surrounding inns. $220.
Pleasant Bay Village Resort Motel 1191 Orleans Rd ℡508/945-1133, ⓦ www .pleasantbayvillage.com. Some of the more affordable digs in town, with spacious, private, clean motel rooms (suites available), pool and hot-tub, breakfast in the morning, and unbelievably beautiful gardens. $185.

Eating

Not surprisingly, given its status as one of the more sophisticated destinations on Cape Cod, Chatham abounds in upmarket **restaurants**, as well as the more casual eateries typical in these parts.

Carmine's Pizza 595 Main St ℡508/945-5300. Casual checked-tablecloth joint serving inexpensive and tasty pizzas with an accent on spice – the Pizza from Hell combines garlic, red pepper, jalapeños, and pineapple slices.
Chatham Bars Inn 297 Shore Rd ℡508/945-0096 or 1-800/527-4884. The Gatsby-esque hotel's

formal dining room offers expensive New England cuisine with wonderful ocean views.
Chatham Squire 487 Main St ℡508/945-0945. This informal and affordable spot has a raw bar, an eclectic menu that sometimes incorporates elements of Mexican and Asian cuisine, and often live acoustic bands at night. Kid-friendly.

Christian's 443 Main St ☎ 508/945-3362. The movie posters upstairs are fitting, considering that the menu items are named after films; hard to go wrong with the well-priced Roman Holiday (Caesar salad) followed by A Fish Called Wanda (salmon sautéed with mushrooms).

Marion's Pie Shop 2022 Rte 20 ☎ 500/432-9439. Popular with locals and tourists alike for delicious sweet apple pies, savory chicken pies, and chewy breakfast cinnamon rolls. A Chatham must-do.

Vining's Bistro 595 Main St ☎ 508/945-5033. Imaginative offerings at this appealing dinner spot range from Thai Street Vendor's Beef Salad to a warm lobster taco.

Cape Cod's north coast

The meandering stretch of highway that parallels the Cape Cod Bay shoreline between Sandwich and Orleans is among the most scenic in New England, affording glimpses of the Cape Cod of popular imagination: salt marshes, crystal-clear ponds, ocean views, and tiny villages. What began as a Native American pathway from Plymouth to Provincetown became the Cape's main road in the seventeenth and eighteenth centuries. There are hundreds of historic buildings along the 34-mile stretch, a large number of which have been turned into antiques shops or B&Bs. The towns that hold these are pleasant enough, though **Sandwich** and Brewster have the highest concentration of well-preserved historical homes. Even if you're traveling by car, it's worth it to temporarily ditch the wheels in favor of a bike to take the **Cape Cod Rail Trail**, a totally flat but popular bike path on the site of the former Old Colony Railroad track, running from Dennis, about fifteen miles past Sandwich, through Brewster to **Wellfleet**, a distance of twenty miles up the Cape.

Sandwich

Overlooked **SANDWICH** kicks off Route 6A with little of the commercialization common to so many Cape towns, thanks in part to its position so close to the mainland. The first permanent settlement on Cape Cod, Sandwich traces its roots to Pilgrim traders in the late 1620s who appreciated its proximity to the **Manomet Trading Post**, where they could barter goods and knowledge with the local Native Americans. The salt marshes in the area also provided an abundant supply of hay for their animals. Unsurprisingly, agriculture was Sandwich's main industry until the 1820s, when Bostonian Deming Jarves established a glassmaking factory here. Though the dense woodlands supplied plenty of fuel for the furnaces, by the 1880s the Sandwich factory was no longer able to compete with the coal-fired glassworks of the Midwest.

A stroll around Sandwich's old **village center** gives you a good taste of things to come along Route 6A: a little village green, white steepled church, a smattering of bed and breakfasts, antiques shops, and a general store. Near Main and River streets, the **Shawme Duck Pond** and adjacent **Dexter Grist Mill**, a replica of one built in 1654, make for a pleasant, peaceful stop, especially if you want to hear about (and maybe even see it in progress) the milling process (mid-June to mid-Sept daily 10am–4pm; $3; no phone). Close to the shore, at 129 Main St, the **Sandwich Glass Museum** (April–Dec daily 9.30am–5pm, Feb–March Wed–Sun 9.30am–4pm, closed Jan; $4.50; ☎ 508/888-0251, Ⓦ www.sandwichglassmuseum.org) contains fourteen galleries that house artifacts from the Boston & Sandwich Glass Company, which set up shop here in 1825. Besides thousands of functional and decorative pieces, the museum has a working glassblowing studio, with presentations every hour.

Sandwich's attractions also include several miles of **beach** on Cape Cod Bay. The water here (like all the Cape's bayside beaches) is several degrees cooler than over on the Nantucket Sound side. It will cost you $10 to park at **Town Neck Beach**, on Town Neck Rd off Route 6A.

Practicalities

The place to **stay** in Sandwich is the *Dan'l Webster Inn & Spa*, 149 Main St (℡508/888-3622 or 1-800/444-3566, Ⓦ www.danlwebsterinn.com; rooms starting at $209 in summer), a rambling Colonial-style hostelry modeled on an earlier building that was a haunt of Revolutionary patriots, with commercial hotel-style rooms and charming courtyards. The hotel also does some of the best **meals** in town: top-notch, classic American dishes are served, for a price, every evening, but it's worth it for the compelling opportunity to nibble edible flowers (among other things) from the inn's aquafarm; they also serve breakfast and lunch in a sunlit conservatory.

Eastham

Largely undiscovered **EASTHAM**, up Route 6 past Orleans as the Cape begins to curve toward Provincetown, is home to fewer than five thousand residents, most of whom are quite content to sit and watch the summer traffic pass by on its way north. Though the sum of Eastham's commercial facilities is little more than a small strip of shopping malls and gas stations along Route 6, if you veer off the highway in either direction you will capture some authentic Cape flavor.

The first detour is the **Fort Hill** area, part of the Cape Cod National Seashore, with a scenic overlook for sweeping views of **Nauset Marsh**, a former bay that became a marsh when **Coast Guard Beach** was formed ($20 parking; free shuttle buses to the beach). North of here, at the corner of Ocean View Drive and Cable Road, is the red-and-white **Nauset Light**, originally

▲ Cape Cod's shore

The protected **Cape Cod National Seashore**, which President Kennedy saved from development because of his fondness for it, extends along much of the Cape's Atlantic side, stretching forty miles from Chatham north to Provincetown. It's a fragile environment: three feet of the lower Cape is washed away each year, and much of it ends up as extra sand on the beach before the sea takes that away, too. Environmentalists are hoping that an extensive program of grass-planting will help prevent further erosion.

It was on these shifting sands of the outer Cape that the **Pilgrims** made their first home in the New World. They obtained their water from Pilgrim Spring near Truro, and at Corn Hill Beach they uncovered a cache of corn buried by the Wampanoag Indians who had been living on the Cape for centuries – a discovery which kept them alive their first winter, before moving on to Plymouth.

Displays and films at the **Salt Pond Visitor Center**, on Route 6 just north of Eastham (daily 9am–4.30pm; ☎508/255-3421, ⓦwww.nps.gov/caco), trace the geology and history of the Cape. A pretty road and hiking/cycling trail head east to the sands of **Coast Guard Beach** and **Nauset Light Beach**, both of which offer excellent swimming. You can also catch a free shuttle ride there from the visitors' center in summer. Another fine beach is **Head of the Meadow**, halfway between Truro and Provincetown. In several areas parking is restricted to residents only, but you can often park by the road and strike off across the dunes to the shore.

㉑

located in Chatham, but installed here in 1923 and moved back 350ft a decade ago when it was in danger of crumbling into the sea. In 1838, this spot was home to no fewer than three brick lighthouses, known as the "Three Sisters," built 150ft apart. In 1892, serious erosion necessitated their replacement by three wooden towers; two were eventually moved away in 1918 and the third five years later. Having been acquired by the National Park service, they now stand in the woods well away from today's coastline.

On Eastham's bayside, **First Encounter Beach**, off Samoset Road, refers to the first meeting of Pilgrims and Native Americans in 1620. It was hardly a cordial rendezvous; with the *Mayflower* anchored in Provincetown, an exploration party led by Myles Standish came ashore only to meet a barrage of arrows. Things settled down after a few gunshots were returned, and since then the beach has been utterly tranquil. A plaque set back in the dunes describes the encounter in detail.

Practicalities

The place to **stay** in Eastham is the *Whalewalk Inn*, 220 Bridge Rd (☎508/255-0617 or 1-800/440-1281, ⓦwww.whalewalkinn.com; $220), where immaculate guest rooms, spa services, and tasty breakfasts are the big draws; the cottages are more spacious than the rooms in the main inn building. There's also a **hostel**, *Mid-Cape American Youth Hostel*, 75 Goody Hallet Drive (☎508/255-2785, ⓔmidcape@usahostels.org; $27 non-members; open mid-May to mid-Sept), in a collection of woodsy cabins, although there is a chance they'll be closing for renovations – call ahead to double check. People are obsessed with the onion rings at *Arnold's Lobster & Clam Bar*, 3580 Route 6 (☎508/255-2575), a popular seafood **restaurant** and beer garden, while *Sam's Deli*, 100 Brackett Rd (☎508/255-9340), is the place to go for bulging beach sandwiches. Just north on Route 6, the fish market and seafood snack bar *Friendly Fisherman* in N. Eastham (☎508/255-2575) has some of the best lobster rolls on the Cape, while in Orleans the romantic and Mediterranean-inspired *Abba*, 89 Old Colony

Way (℡508/255-8144), is one of the best restaurants in the area, with the likes of lobster in a yellow curry sauce with butternut jasmine rice ($29).

Wellfleet

WELLFLEET, with a year-round population of just 2500, is, like Eastham eight miles to the south, one of the least developed towns on the Cape. Once the focus of a thriving oyster-fishing industry, today it is a favorite haunt of writers and artists who come to seek inspiration from the unsullied landscapes and the heaving ocean. Despite the fact that a number of art galleries have surfaced – most of them along **Main** or **Commercial streets** – the town remains a remarkably unpretentious place, with many of the galleries themselves resembling fishing shacks and selling highly distinctive original work aimed at the serious collector, alongside mass-market souvenirs. The Art Gallery Association produces a guide to the galleries which can be picked up at the **information booth** at the corner of Route 6 and LeCount Hollow Rd (℡508/349-2510). The **Wellfleet Historical Society Museum**, 266 Main St (late June to early Sept Tues & Fri 10am–4pm, Wed, Thurs & Sat 1–4pm; free; ⓦwww.wellfleethistoricalsociety.com), has an interesting collection of furniture, items salvaged from shipwrecks, nautical artifacts, and photographs as well as exhibits on the local oyster industry.

The most scenic part of town is actually outside the center, at the bluff-lined **Marconi Beach**, east off Route 6 in South Wellfleet, where Guglielmo Marconi issued the first transatlantic radio signal on January 18, 1903, and announced greetings from President Roosevelt to King Edward VII. Nothing remains of the tall radio towers built for this purpose, but there are some scale models beneath a gazebo-type structure overlooking the ocean. A short trail up the cliffside leads to a vantage point from which you can see horizontally across the entire Cape – just a mile wide at this point. Marconi is a good spot for a beach day, too: there are lifeguards, public restrooms and showers, and parking ($20) that rarely fills to capacity.

Practicalities

If you want to **stay** the night in Wellfleet, try the indulgent *Stone Lion Inn*, 130 Commercial St (℡508/349-9565, ⓦwww.stonelioncapecod.com; $155), an 1871 sea captain's home with luxury linens and outstanding breakfasts; or the charming *Blue Heron Cove B&B*, 260 Blue Heron Rd (℡508/349-0021, ⓦwww .blueheroncove.net; $275), a cozy country inn situated beside a wildlife sanctuary and overlooking Cape Cod Bay. For a more budget conscious option, there is a **hostel** further east in nearby Truro; the *HI-Truro*, on Route 6 at 111 N.

Oyster shucking

No visit to Wellfleet would be complete without a taste of the town's famous oysters. In fact, the little mollusks are so abundant here that the French explorer Samuel de Champlain named the town "Port aux Huitres" (or oyster port) when he disembarked in 1606. The current name of Wellfleet, given by the English in 1763, also has an oyster heritage – it's a nod to England's own Wellfleet oyster beds. One of the best places to dive into a plate of the raw variety is the rowdy *Beachcomber*, on Cahoon Hollow Beach (℡508/349-6055), a fun beach shack with incredible waterfront views. You can also attend the Wellfleet **Oyster Weekend** (mid- to late Oct; ⓦwww .wellfleetoysterfest.org), complete with raw bars and shucking contests.

Pamet Rd (☎508/349-3889, 🌐www.capecodhostels.org; $35 non-members; open mid-May to mid-Sept), is housed in a breezy former Coast Guard Station right on the dunes. Tiny though Wellfleet is, there are a number of casual seafood **restaurants** worth checking out, such as *Moby Dick's*, on Route 6 across from Gull Pond Road (☎508/349-9795), which offers family seafood dining; *Mac's* (☎508/349-0404) has both a "glorified clam shack" and an upscale seafood eatery in two spots right on the Wellfleet Pier. For nightlife, the old-school Wellfleet Drive-In Theatre, 51 Route 6 (☎508/349-7176; 🌐www .wellfleetdrivein.com), has outdoor movies and music in summer, replete with burgers and mini-golf; on weekends it doubles as a fun flea market.

Provincetown

"Far from being out of the way, Provincetown is directly in the way of the navigator... It is situated on one of the highways of commerce, and men from all parts of the globe touch there in the course of a year."

from Cape Cod by Henry David Thoreau

The compact fishing town of **PROVINCETOWN**, at the very tip of Cape Cod, is a popular summer destination for bohemians, artists, and fun-seekers lured by the excellent beaches, art galleries, and welcoming atmosphere. It is known most famously as a **gay** resort destination, complete with frequent festivals and theme weekends. Now that same-sex marriage is legal in Massachusetts, the town sells itself as a home for destination weddings. P-town – as this coastal community of five thousand year-round inhabitants is commonly known – also has a drop of **Portuguese** culture to embellish it, after a smallish population of fishermen began settling here starting in the mid-1800s; their legacy is now celebrated in an annual June festival filled with music and Portuguese soup-tasting competitions. Throughout the summer, P-town's population swells into the tens of thousands, and there's often a carnival atmosphere in the bustling streets. The appealing hamlet should not be missed, especially as it's just a few hours' ferry ride from Boston.

Some history

Provincetown has a number of **Pilgrim**-related monuments – after all, they landed here before heading to Plymouth – but they were not the first European visitors to arrive. Way back in 1004, many believe Leif Erikson's brother, **Thorvald**, disembarked here to repair the broken keel of his ship and named the place "Cape of the Keel"; it was later dubbed Cape Cod by Bartholomew Gosnold in 1602. The Pilgrims came ashore here and stayed for five weeks in 1620, signing the **Mayflower Compact**, one long and rather vaguely worded sentence espousing a democratic form of self-government, before sailing across Cape Cod Bay.

Provincetown was incorporated in 1727, and soon became a thriving fishing, salt-processing, and whaling port; indeed, by 1880, the town was the richest per capita in Massachusetts. Fishing retains its importance here, but the town's destiny to become one of the East Coast's leading **art colonies** was assured in 1899, when painter Charles W. Hawthorne founded the **Cape Cod School of Art**, which encouraged artists to explore the outdoors and exploit the Mediterranean-like quality of the light. So many of his friends came to investigate the place that it became known as the "Greenwich Village of the North." By the early 1900s, many painters had begun to ply their trade in abandoned "dune shacks" by the sea, and by 1916 there were no fewer than six art schools here. The natural beauty and laid-back atmosphere also began to seduce rebellious young writers like Mary Heaton Vorse, who established the **Provincetown Players** theater group in 1915. **Eugene O'Neill** joined the company in 1916, premiering his *Bound East for Cardiff* in a waterfront fish house done up as a theater. **Tennessee Williams** was another frequent visitor, and more recently, **Michael Cunningham** wrote part of *The Hours* here.

As much of an impact as its colorful residents have had, equally important in Provincetown's history has been its **geography**. The entire Cape is a glacial deposit on a crooked sliver of bedrock, but due to its position at the very tip, Provincetown is particularly susceptible to the vagaries of wind and water, the fragile environment lending a certain legitimacy to the strict **zoning laws** that have kept major development at bay and, consequently, continue to preserve the flavor of the old town. There's also evidence that the shifting dunes of this part of the Cape Cod National Seashore, including the barren but beautiful **Province Lands**, were once covered with topsoil and trees that were cut for fuel, thus hastening the process of erosion – a further example of the need for conservation.

Arrival and information

Two companies make the ninety-minute trip across Massachusetts Bay from Boston to Provincetown: **Boston Harbor Cruises** departs from **Long Wharf**

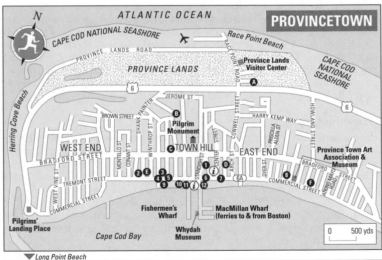

ACCOMMODATION		EATING			
Carpe Diem	D	Bubala's by the Bay	4	Portuguese Bakery	11
Carriage House		Café Edwige	6	Spiritus Pizza	3
Provincetown	E	Café Heaven	5	**BARS & CLUBS**	
Crowne Pointe		Ciro & Sal's	8	Atlantic House	10
Historic Inn & Spa	C	Karoo Kafe	7	Boatslip	2
Dune's Edge Campground	A	Lobster Pot	12	The Pied	9
Outermost Hostel	B	Napi's	1		
White Horse Inn	F				

(daily late May to mid-June leaving 9am, returning 4pm; late June to early Oct Mon–Wed leaving 9am, returning 4pm, Thurs leaving 9am & 6.30pm, returning 4pm & 8.30pm, Fri–Sun leaving 9am, 2pm & 6.30pm, returning 11am, 4pm & 8.30pm; $70 round-trip; ⊕617/227-4321, ⓦwww.bostonharborcruises.com), while **Bay State Cruises** leaves, somewhat inconveniently, from the **Common-wealth Pier** by Boston's World Trade Center (daily late May to early Oct leaving 8am & 5.30pm, returning 10am & 7.30pm; daily late June to early Oct leaving 8am, 1pm & 5.30pm, returning 10am, 3pm & 7.30pm; $71 round-trip; ⊕617/748-1428, ⓦwww.boston-ptown.com). The latter has an excellent **excursion fare** for weekend day-tripping, too: $29 round-trip will get you to P-town and back with a three-hour window to tool around in – but keep in mind that these slower boats take three hours each way (late May to early Sept Fri–Sun leaving 9.30am, returning 3.30pm). A Plymouth to Provincetown ferry is run by Captain John's Boats (90min round-trip $36; ⊕508/747-2400 or 1-800/242-2469, ⓦwww.provincetownferry.com).

Provincetown is at the end of **Route 6**, the Cape's main highway, and **buses** regularly trawl this stretch from Boston and all the major Cape towns; Bonanza Bus Lines (⊕401/751-8800 or 1-888/751-8800, ⓦwww.bonanzabus.com) and Plymouth & Brockton buses (⊕508/746-0378, ⓦwww.p-b.com) are the ones to call. Buses stop right in the middle of town near MacMillan Wharf. There is a **visitors' center** right by the bus stop, 307 Commercial St (⊕508/487-3424), where you can pick up all sorts of information. You can get online information before you go at ⓦwww.provincetown.com; gays and lesbians may also want to check ⓦwww.gayprovincetown.com.

Getting around

Provincetown is a very **walkable** place; **bicycles** can come in handy, though, especially if you want to venture a bit further afield. For rentals, Arnold's, 329 Commercial St (⊕508/487-0844), right in the center of town, is open from mid-April to mid-Oct, as is Nelson's Bike Shop, 43 Race Point Rd (⊕508/487-8849), located close to the **bike trails** that meander through the Province Lands. Bikes at both places go for about $20 per day. Provincetown also claims the title of first **whale–watching** spot on the East Coast; the best company is the Dolphin Fleet (June–Oct; $30; ⊕508/349-1900 or 1-800/826-9300, ⓦwww.whalewatch.com), with cruises leaving frequently from MacMillan Wharf.

If you want to take a **boat ride**, Provincetown Harbor Cruises, MacMillan Wharf (⊕508/487-4330), runs an hour-long sightseeing trip round the bay in season ($14), while Flyer's Boat Rentals, 131A Commercial St (⊕508/487-0898 or 1-800/750-0898, ⓦwww.flyersrentals.com), provides a range of rental boats, from kayaks to powerboats. Alternatively, take their **shuttle** across Cape Cod Bay to Long Point Beach (mid-June to mid-Sept; $10 one-way, $15 round-trip).

Accommodation

Many of the most picturesque cottages in town are **guesthouses**, some with spectacular views over Cape Cod Bay. The best place to be is the quiet West End, though anything on Bradford Street will also be removed from the summertime racket. Prices are generally very reasonable until mid-June, and off-season you can find real bargains. In addition, there are a few **motels**, mostly confined to the outskirts of town, towards the Truro line. The gay-oriented

Intown Reservations (☎508/487-1883 or 1-800/67P-TOWN) can usually rustle up lodging at busy times. The welcoming Dune's Edge Campground, on Route 6 just east of the central stoplights (☎508/487-9815, ⓦwww .dunes-edge.com), charges $35 for use of one of its wooded sites.

Carpe Diem 12 Johnson St ☎1-800/487-0132, ⓦwww.carpediemguesthouse.com. Friendly, accommodating innkeepers, beautifully-appointed rooms, horseback riding, and a wine and cheese hour in the afternoon at this lovely B&B on a quiet side street. $205.

Carriage House Provincetown 7 Central St ☎1-800/309-0248, ⓦwww.thecarriagehse.com. A gorgeous space with lots of attention to detail, a steam room and hot tub, and fantastic breakfasts. $225.

Crowne Pointe Historic Inn & Spa 7 Winthrop St ☎1-877/276-963, ⓦwww.crownepointe.com.

Provincetown's most luxurious digs: gorgeous rooms, a fancy restaurant, and unbelievable spa treatments. $330.

Outermost Hostel 28 Winslow St ☎508/487-4378. Hostel with thirty $35 beds in five woodsy dorm cabins; includes kitchen access and parking.

White Horse Inn 500 Commercial St ☎508/487-1790. A whimsical, colorful, art-strewn space; some rooms have shared baths. There are also family-sized apartments with kitchens. Beach access, and a beatnik vibe. $125.

The town and around

The town center is essentially two three-mile-long streets, **Commercial** and **Bradford**, connected by about forty tiny lanes of no more than two short blocks each. Though much diluted by tourism, the beatnik spirit is still in evidence, most pronounced in regular Friday-night expositions in the many art galleries along Commercial Street. On summer evenings the narrow street fills with hordes of sightseers, locals, and, amazingly, cars, even though they can do little more than crawl along. **Fisherman's Wharf**, and the more touristy **MacMillan Wharf**, busy with whale-watching boats, yachts, and colorful old Portuguese fishing vessels, split the town in half. Macmillan Wharf also houses the **Whydah Museum**, 16 Macmillan Wharf (June–Aug daily 10am–7pm, April–May & Sept–Oct daily 10am–4pm; $8; ☎508/487-8899, ⓦwww .whydah.com), which displays some of the bounty from a famous pirate shipwreck off the coast of Wellfleet in 1717. The lifelong quest of native Cape Codder Barry Clifford to recover the treasure from the one-time slave ship *Whydah* – repository of loot from more than fifty ships when it sank – paid off royally with his discovery of the ship in the summer of 1983. Thousands of coins, gold bars, pieces of jewelry, and weapons were retrieved, ranging from odds and ends like silver shoe buckles and flintlock pistols to rare African gold jewelry. The most evocative display in the museum, glimmering gold coins notwithstanding, is the ship's **bell**, a little rusty but not so corroded that you can't read "The Whydah Galley – 1716" clear as day.

Two blocks north of the piers, atop aptly named Town Hill, is the 252ft granite tower of the **Pilgrim Monument** (daily: July–Aug 9am–6.15pm; May–June & Sept–Nov 9am–4.15pm; $7; ☎508/487-1310, ⓦwww.pilgrim -monument.org), modeled after a bell tower in Siena, Italy. It commemorates the Pilgrims' landing and their signing of the Mayflower Compact. From the observation deck you can see all the way to Boston on a clear day. At the bottom of the hill on **Bradford Street** is another bas-relief monument to the Mayflower Compact. Back on the main drag, the delightful **Province-town Art Association and Museum**, 460 Commercial St (July–Aug daily noon–5pm & 8–10pm; mid-May to June & Sept daily noon–5pm, Sat & Sun noon–5pm & 8–10pm; Oct–April Sat & Sun noon–4pm; April to mid-May Sat & Sun noon–5pm; $5, free Fridays after 5pm; ☎508/487-1750,

▲ Commercial Street in Provincetown

Ⓦ www.paam.org), rotates works from its 2000-strong collection, with equal prominence given to local and established artists. Friday night is best (and free), when openings by new artists frequently take place.

On the other side of the wharves is the quieter and slightly less cramped **West End**, where many of the weathered clapboard houses are cheerfully decorated with colorful blinds, white picket fences, and wildflowers spilling out of every possible orifice. At Commercial Street's western end, the Pilgrim **landing place** is marked by a modest bronze plaque on a boulder. Nearby, just past the *Provincetown Inn*, is the **Breakwater Trail**, a mile-long **jetty** leading to Long Point Beach, a great place to watch the sun set.

A little ways beyond the town's narrow strip of sand, a string of **undeveloped beaches** is marked only by dunes and a few shabby huts. The Province Lands **visitors' center**, in the middle of the dunes off Race Point Rd (late May to early Sept daily 9am–5pm; early Sept to late-Oct & April to late May daily 9am–4.30pm; ☎508/487-1256), has an observation deck from which you might spot a whale – or even, when the tide is right, the ruins of the **HMS Somerset**, a sunken British battleship from the Revolutionary War. Province Lands is also home to the best **bike path** on Cape Cod, roaming through the dunes without a building in sight.

Eating

Great **food** options abound in Provincetown – look out in particular for the **Portuguese** restaurants that can be found throughout town. Whenever possible, especially in the few restaurants where it's possible to eat al fresco (mosquitoes can be a big problem), arrive early or call ahead to make a reservation; many restaurants are packed in season. Most eateries **close** in the winter, though some remain open on weekends only.

Bubala's By the Bay 138 Commercial St ⊤ 508/487-0773. Perhaps the freshest seafood in P-Town, served within a fun hangout right on the water; good non-fish fare as well and open all day.

Café Edwige 333 Commercial St ⊤ 508/487-2008. Breakfast's the thing at this popular second-floor spot; try the home-made Danish pastries and fresh fruit pancakes. Creative bistro fare at dinnertime.

Café Heaven 336 Commercial St ⊤ 508/487-2808. Breakfast nirvana – white walls bedecked with bright, contemporary paintings, eggs Benedict with home-made English muffins, and fresh-squeezed juice; great salads, sandwiches, and dinner options, too. Just like heaven, there's usually a line to get in.

Ciro & Sal's 4 Kiley Court ⊤ 508/487-6444. Traditional Northern Italian cooking with plenty of veal and seafood; a bit on the pricey side, but worth it.

Karoo Kafe 338 Commercial St ⊤ 508/487-6630. Tasty, low-key South African fare. Order the Cape Malay stew (curry, coconut milk, and veggies over rice) at the counter and enjoy it amongst sunny, zebra-striped seating.

Lobster Pot 321 Commercial St ⊤ 508/487-0842. Its landmark neon sign is like a welcome mat for those who come from far and wide for the ultra-fresh crustaceans. Affordable and family-oriented.

Napi's 7 Freeman St ⊤ 508/487-1145. Popular dishes at this art-strewn spot include pastas and seafood items, notably a thick Portuguese fish stew. They have a less expensive menu on weeknights.

Portuguese Bakery 299 Commercial St ⊤ 508/487-1803. This old standby is the place to come for cheap baked goods, particularly the tasty fried *rabanada*, akin to portable French toast.

Nightlife and entertainment

Provincetown loves to party. Each in-season weekend, boatloads of revelers seek out P-town's notoriously wild **nightlife**. Heavily geared towards a **gay** clientele, resulting in ubiquitous tea dances, drag shows, and video bars, some establishments have terrific waterfront locations and terraces to match, making them ideal spots to sit out with a drink at sunset. After the clubs close, party-goers assemble around late-night *Spiritus Pizza*, 190 Commercial St (⊤ 508/487-2808) to figure out the next big thing.

Atlantic House 6 Masonic Place, behind Commercial St ⊤ 508/487-3821. The "A-House" – a dark drinking hole that was a favorite of Tennessee Williams and Eugene O'Neill – is now a trendy gay dance club and bar; everyone ends up here around 12.30am.

Boatslip 161 Commercial St ⊤ 508/487-1669, ⓦ www.boatslipresort.com. The Sunday tea dances at this resort are legendary; you can either dance away on a long wooden deck overlooking the water, or cruise inside under a disco ball and flashing lights; afterwards, people usually head to *The Pied*.

The Pied 193 Commercial St ⊤ 508/487-1527. Though largely a lesbian club (it's the oldest in the country), the outdoor deck and inside dance floor at this trendy waterfront space attract a good dose of men, too, for their longstanding After Tea T-Dance (Sun 6.30–9pm).

22

Nantucket

The thirty-mile, two-hour sea crossing to **NANTUCKET** from Cape Cod may not be an ocean-going odyssey, but it does set the "Little Gray Lady" apart from her larger, shore-hugging sister, Martha. Just halfway out from Hyannis, neither mainland nor island is in sight, and you realize why the Native Americans dubbed it "distant land." Once you've landed, you can avert your eyes from the smart-money double-deck cruisers with names like *Pier Pressure* and *Loan Star* and let the place remind you that it hasn't always been a rich folks' playground. Indeed, despite the formidable prowess of its seamen, survival for settlers on the island's barren soil was always a struggle. The tiny, cobbled carriageways of **Nantucket Town** itself, once one of the largest cities in Massachusetts, were frozen in time by economic decline 150 years ago. Today, this area of delightful old restored houses – the town has more buildings on the National Register of Historic Places than Boston – is very much the island hub, while seven flat, easily cycled miles to the east the rose-covered cottages of **Siasconset** (always abbreviated to 'Sconset) give another glimpse of days gone by. However appealing the island's man-made attractions are, it's Nantucket's gentle natural beauty that's the real draw, with heaths and moorlands, mile after mile of fabulous beaches, and a network of bicycle paths that connect the many spots maintained by conservation trusts.

Arrival and information

Most likely you'll arrive in Nantucket by **ferry**. Both the Steamship Authority (☎508/447-8600, ⓦwww.islandferry.com) and Hy-Line (☎508/778-2600 or 1-800/492-8082, ⓦwww.hy-linecruises.com) run year-round passenger services to the island from Hyannis, but only the Steamship Authority's boats take cars. Both have fast ferries that charge from $30 to $38 each way for passengers; the Steamship Authority's car ferry (mid-May to mid-Oct, $205 per vehicle) allows passengers only at $15. Island-hoppers can take Hy-Line's inter-island ferry ($73.50 round-trip), which runs once daily June–Sept between Hyannis, Martha's Vineyard's Oak Bluffs, and Nantucket. A much quicker way to get to the island is by **air**: Island Airlines (☎1-800/248-7779, ⓦwww.islandair.net) and Cape Air (☎1-800/352-0714, ⓦwww.flycapeair.com) run year-round daily services from Hyannis to Nantucket; Cape Air also offers daily services to and from Boston, New Bedford, Providence, and Martha's Vineyard. The **airport** (☎508/325-5300, ⓦwww.nantucketairport.com) is about three miles southeast of Nantucket Town; flights average $150 round-trip.

Visitor information is available from the **Chamber of Commerce**, 48 Main St (Mon–Fri 9am–5pm; ☎508/228-1700, ⓦwww.nantucketchamber.org), who can also assist you in finding a room on the island, or from the helpful **Nantucket Information Bureau**, 25 Federal St (April–Dec 9am–6pm; rest of

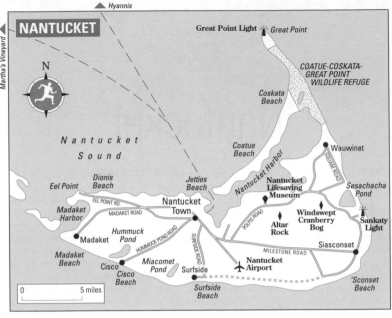

year Mon–Sat 9am–5.30pm; ☎508/228-0925, ⊛www.nantucket.net). The **Nantucket Historical Association**, 15 Broad St (Mon–Fri 9am–5pm; ☎508/228-1894, ⊛www.nha.org), which maintains twenty historical properties on the island, offers an $18 **combination ticket** for entrance to all its buildings, including the Whaling Museum ($6 for only the historic sites).

Getting around

Once you've arrived, **getting around** should pose no problem. From the moment you get off the ferry you're surrounded by **bike** rental places and tour companies. Try Young's Bicycle Shop (☎508/228-1151, ⊛www .youngsbicycleshop.com), conveniently located on Steamboat Wharf; it should cost $30 per day for a standard mountain bike. Driving a **car** makes little sense here, especially in peak season, when island arteries can easily get clogged, and it won't endear you to the locals. If you didn't bring one with you on the ferry, there is an expensive and limited on-island supply available from Young's Bicycle Shop, as well as at Windmill (☎508/228-1227 or 1-800/228-1227, ⊛www.nantucketautorental.com) and one airport outlet, Hertz (☎508/228-9421, ⊛www.hertz.com).

A better way to get around is by **bus**: five shuttle routes on the island are operated between May and September by the Nantucket Regional Transit Authority (daily 7.30am–11.30pm; ☎508/228-7025, ⊛www.shuttlenantucket .com), with fares starting at $1 (exact change) per journey for in-town travel; you can get unlimited travel for three days ($12), a week ($20), or a month ($50). Barrett's Tours (☎508/228-0174 or 1-800/773-0174; $20) runs ninety-minute narrated bus tours around the island, stopping in 'Sconset, the historic windmill, beaches, and a cranberry bog. You probably won't need the aid of **taxis** while

here, but they are usually available at the airport or by the ferry terminal; A-1
(☎508/228-3330) and Chief Cab (☎508/284-8497) are both reliable.

Accommodation

But for the youth hostel, **accommodation** on Nantucket can be expensive,
although there is quite a range of options available; in Nantucket Town,
you'll find everything from resorts with pools, health clubs, and sophisticated
restaurants to cozy inns and B&Bs; further afield, you can rent private homes
by the week – though it's not easy to find a room for under $175 in high
season, and most doubles cost over $200. Try ⓦwww.summerhome.com
/Nantucket.htm for reliable rental listings posted by local residents. The
following rates are all for the summer; you can expect deep discounts
throughout the rest of the year.

Centerboard 8 Chester St ☎508/228-9696,
ⓦ www.centerboardguesthouse.com. A pretty,
well-situated B&B with flat-screen TVs and
three spacious, neutral-toned rooms that
are kid-friendly. $225.
Cliff Lodge 9 Cliff Rd ☎508/228-9480, ⓦwww
.clifflodgenantucket.com. Quiet B&B in a
residential area with some low-priced
singles in the off-season; owned by the
same lovely proprietors as the *Martin
House Inn*. $145.
Hawthorn House 2 Chestnut St ☎508/228-
1468, ⓦwww.hawthornhouse.com. Central,
well-appointed guesthouse with a helpful,

friendly staff and ten handsome rooms
outfitted with tapestries and antique furnishings; Wi-Fi throughout. $170.
HI-Nantucket Surfside Beach ☎508/228-
0433, ⓦwww.capecodhostels.org. Dorm beds
in a former lifesaving station, a stone's throw
from Surfside Beach, and just over three
miles south of Nantucket Town (it's right by
a shuttle stop). Rates range $27–37 per
night, curfew 11pm (but they'll give you the
code to get back in). Free Internet. Open
only mid-May to Sept.
Martin House Inn 61 Center St ☎508/228-
0678, ⓦwww.martinhouseinn.com. Thirteen

The whalers of Nantucket

Scores of anonymous Captains have sailed out of Nantucket, that were as
great, and greater than your Cook...for in their succorless empty-handedness,
they, in the heathenish sharked waters, and by the beaches of unrecorded,
javelin islands, battled with virgin wonders and terrors that Cook with all this
marines and muskets would not willingly have dared.

From *Moby Dick*, by Herman Melville

The whalers of Nantucket drew the attention of many with their skill and resultant
domination of a notably treacherous trade. The early chronicler Crèvecoeur provided
an extensive account of Nantucket as it was in 1782 in his *Letters from an American
Farmer*. Although perturbed by the islanders' universal habit of taking a dose of opium
every morning, he held them up as a model of diligence and good self-government.
Whaling was a disciplined profession, unmarred by the stereotyped debauchery of
sailors elsewhere, and to feed themselves and equip their ships the islanders kept up
a shrewd and extensive trade with the mainland. The whalemen were not paid; instead
each had a share (a "lay") of the final proceeds of the voyage. And what a voyage it
was – the common occurrence when a harpooned whale would speed away, dragging
a ship helter-skelter behind it for endless terrifying hours, was known as a "Nantucket
Sleighride." You can read more about the whalers in Herman Melville's *Moby Dick*, a
valediction of sorts since by the time it was published in 1851, Nantucket's fortunes had
gone into an abrupt decline. As a magazine article of 1873 reported, "Let no traveler
visit Nantucket with the expectation of witnessing the marks of a flourishing trade ... of
the great fleet of ships which dotted every sea, scarcely a vestige remains."

lovely rooms offer good value in this romantic 1803 seaman's house; close to shops and ferries. $115.

The Nesbitt Inn 21 Broad St ☎508/228-0156. The central location, friendly innkeepers, and affordable rooms, most with original furniture, compensate for the shared baths (three for thirteen rooms) in this 1872 Victorian inn. Singles from $105.

Sherburne Inn 10 Gay St ☎1-888/577-4425, ⓦwww.sherburneinn.com. A lovely, well-appointed B&B with cozy, elegant rooms, free Wi-Fi, pretty grounds, and afternoon tea and sherry. $250.

Union Street Inn 7 Union St ☎508/228-9222, ⓦwww.unioninn.com. Luxurious, well-loved B&B with all the trimmings: beautiful rooms, cozy bathrobes and fancy soaps, and fresh afternoon pastries. $345.

The White House 48 Center St ☎508/228-8114, ⓦwww.nantucketwhitehouse.com. Four well-appointed, child-friendly rooms in an historic B&B right in the center of town. There is also a delightful outdoor patio, fridge access, and every day breakfast vouchers for restaurants around Nantucket. $195.

Nantucket Town

Very much the center of activity on the island, the cobbled walkways of **NANTUCKET TOWN** boast a delightful array of eighteenth- and nineteenth-century homes, most of them concentrated around **Main Street**. Before you hit town, though, you can get the salty feel of the half-dozen wharves around Nantucket's harbor when arriving on the ferry, which docks at **Steamboat Wharf**. A number of private summer homes are perched on Old North Wharf just south of that, while lively **Straight Wharf**, which dates to 1723, contains souvenir shops, restaurants, and the restored red-brick building of the **Museum of Nantucket History** (hours vary; free; ☎508/228-1700), originally a warehouse for whaling supplies. Exhibits include early fire fighting apparatus, vintage photographs, and a diorama depicting the waterfront's busy goings-on before the **fire** of 1846, which tragically destroyed most of the harbor and a third of the town.

The excellent **Whaling Museum**, 13 Broad St (☎508/228-1894, ⓦwww .nha.org; late May to mid-Oct Sun–Sat 10am–5pm, late Oct to mid-Dec Thurs 11am–4pm, Sun noon–5pm; $15; $18 site pass includes Oldest House, Quaker Meeting House, and Old Mill), houses an outstanding collection of seafaring exotica in an old candle-making factory built just before the big fire. Highlights include a gorgeous gallery of scrimshaws delicately engraved by strong-armed nineteenth-century sailors; there is also a luminous fresnel lens, formerly housed in the Sankaty Head Lighthouse. A gigantic sperm whale skeleton presides over the entrance; look for the rotted tooth on its jaw – officials believe a tooth infection brought on the whale's demise.

Polpis Road

Polpis Road, an indirect and arcing track from Nantucket Town to 'Sconset, holds a number of natural attractions both on and off its main course. Your first stop should be the less wild **Nantucket Life Saving Museum**, off the northern side of the road at no. 158 (mid-June to mid-Oct daily 9.30am–4pm; $5; ☎508/228-1885, ⓦwww.nantucketlifesavingmuseum.com), whose lifesaving motto was "you have to go out, but you don't have to come back;" the museum is filled with an evocative collection of early lifesaving surfboats, buoys, rescue equipment, photographs, and artifacts from the *Andrea Doria*, which sunk off Nantucket forty years ago. Further on, an unmarked track leads south to **Altar Rock**, the island's highest point, where you'll want to walk around for views of the surrounding bogs. One of these, the 200–acre **Windswept Cranberry Bog**, east on Polpis Road, is a feast of color at most

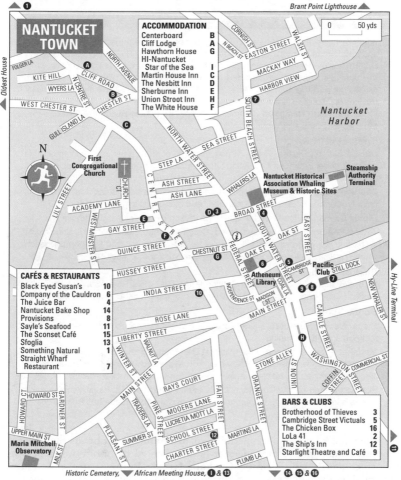

NANTUCKET TOWN

ACCOMMODATION

Centerboard	B
Cliff Lodge	A
Hawthorn House	G
HI-Nantucket	
Star of the Sea	I
Martin House Inn	C
The Nesbitt Inn	D
Sherburne Inn	E
Union Stroot Inn	H
The White House	F

Brant Point Lighthouse ▲

0   50 yds

Nantucket Harbor

Steamship Authority Terminal

Nantucket Historical Association Whaling Museum & Historic Sites

First Congregational Church

Pacific Club   STILL DOCK

Atheneum Library

CAFÉS & RESTAURANTS

Black Eyed Susan's	10
Company of the Cauldron	6
The Juice Bar	4
Nantucket Bake Shop	14
Provisions	8
Sayle's Seafood	11
The Sconset Café	15
Sfoglia	13
Something Natural	1
Straight Wharf Restaurant	7

BARS & CLUBS

Brotherhood of Thieves	3
Cambridge Street Victuals	5
The Chicken Box	16
LoLa 41	2
The Ship's Inn	12
Starlight Theatre and Café	9

Maria Mitchell Observatory

Historic Cemetery, ▼ African Meeting House, ❶ & ⓭   ▼ ⓮ ⓯ & ⓰

22

times of the year, especially so in mid-October, when the ripened berries, loosened from the plants by machines, float to the top of the water.

Siasconset, Great Point, and Coatue

Seven flat miles east of Nantucket Town, the village of **SIASCONSET**, or 'Sconset as it's universally known, is filled with venerable cottages literally encrusted with salt and covered over with roses. Once solely a fishing village, it began to attract visitors eager to get away from the foul smells of Nantucket Town's whale-oil refineries, and in the late 1800s, enough writers and actors came from big cities to give 'Sconset some modicum of artistic renown. There's not too much to see, other than the houses themselves along Broadway and Center streets – certainly picturesque enough – and the year-round population of 150 only supports a few commercial establishments, all close to one another in the center of town.

With fifty miles of **beaches**, most of which are open to the public, Nantucket is more accessible than Martha's Vineyard for ocean enthusiasts. The island's southern and eastern flanks, where the water tends to have rougher surf, is ideal for surfers, while the more sheltered northern beaches are good for swimming. With extremely limited, albeit free, **parking**, it makes sense to walk or cycle to all but the most far-flung of the strands. You can rent **watersports equipment** (kayaks, windsurfers, and the like, for $15–65) from Nantucket Community Sailing, on Jetties Beach (☎508/228-5358, ⓦwww.nantucketsailing.com).

Nantucket Town
Brant Point off Easton Street. Strong currents at the harbor entrance mean this beach is better equipped for tanning and watching the comings and goings of boats in the harbor, rather than swimming.

Children's Beach off South Beach Street. Just minutes from Steamboat Wharf, this calm harbor beach is perfect for children, and has a full range of facilities.

Dionis Beach Eel Point Road. A quiet beach with high dunes and calm waters.

Jetties Beach off Bathing Beach Road. Catch the shuttle bus that runs along North Water and South Beach streets in the center of town, or leg it to this popular beach whose facilities include lifeguards, changing rooms, and a snack bar.

East of Town
'Sconset Beach (known also as Codfish Park). Off Polpis Road. Sandy beach with moderate surf and a full range of facilities. Just a short walk to several eating places.

South Shore
Cisco Beach Hummock Point Road. Long, sandy beach with lifeguards and restrooms; ideal for surfing.

Madaket Beach at the end of the Madaket Bike Path. Another long beach with strong surf and gorgeous sunsets over the water. Portable restrooms (not for the squeamish), lifeguards, and shuttle bus (leaves from Broad Street in Nantucket Town).

Surfside Beach off Surfside Road. Wide sands attract a youthful crowd of surfers; there's a large parking lot, but you'd do better to take the shuttle bus from town.

A few miles north, the peppermint-striped **Sankaty Light**, an 1849 lighthouse, stands on a picturesque 90ft bluff, accented by unruly waves below. Further north still, **Coatue–Coskata–Great Point**, a five-mile-long, razor-thin slice of sand, takes in three separate wildlife refuges, and is accessible by four-wheel-drive (for which you'll need a special $125 permit; ☎508/228-5646, ⓦwww.thetrustees.org); it's free if you're on foot. If you don't feel like walking (the sand is very soft and taxing on the feet), you could take one of the tours offered by the Trustees of Reservations, leaving from the Wauwinet Gatehouse (2.5hrs; $30; ☎508/228-6799, ⓦwww .thetrustees.org). In the Coskata section, the wider beaches are backed by salt marshes and some trees: with binoculars, you may catch sight of plovers, egrets, oystercatchers, terns, and even osprey. The beach narrows again as you approach the **Great Point Light**, at the end of the spit, put up in 1986 after an earlier light was destroyed during a 1984 storm. This new lighthouse is solar-powered, and is said to be able to withstand 240mph winds and 20ft waves. Unsurprisingly, this is not the safest place to swim, even on a calm day. Coatue, the last leg of the journey, is the narrow stretch that separates Nantucket Harbor from the ocean; so narrow, in fact, that stormy seas frequently crash over it, turning Great Point into an island.

Madaket and the South Shore

At the western tip of Nantucket, rural **MADAKET** is the small settlement located on the spot where Thomas Macy landed in 1659. There's little in the way of visitor attractions, but the area's peacefulness and natural beauty makes up for that. Unspoiled **Eel Point**, a couple of miles north, sits on a spit of sand covered with all manner of wild plants and flowers, including wild roses and bayberries, which attract an array of birds, including the graceful egrets which can be seen in late spring and summer stalking the shallow offshore sandbars. **Maps** and **self-guided tours** are available for $4 from the Nantucket Conservation Foundation, 118 Cliff Rd (℡508/228-2884, ⊛www.nantucketconservation.com). East of Madaket, and only about three miles from Nantucket Town, **Cisco**'s windswept beach faces water popular with surfers, though erosion due to windy blasts here has resulted in several houses being lost. Two miles east of Cisco, freshwater **Miacomet Pond**, surrounded by reeds and grasses, and a favorite haunt of swans and ducks, is a prime spot for a picnic.

Eating and drinking

The early chronicler Crèvecoeur, in an extensive account on Nantucket published in 1782, stated that on Nantucket "music, singing and dancing are holden in equal detestation." Thankfully, eating is not: the island abounds in first-rate **restaurants**, most of them located in Nantucket Town and specializing in seafood. Be prepared, however, for the shock of the bill: it's often Manhattan prices, and then some. As far as **drinking** goes, many of the restaurants have bars attached to them, though there are also a few pubby places to get boozed up. All of the establishments below, unless otherwise indicated, are in Nantucket Town.

Black Eyed Susan's 10 India St ℡508/325-0308. Beloved little brunch spot with inventive egg scrambles and cheery buttermilk pancakes. Worth the wait in line; cash only.

Company of the Cauldron 5 India St ℡508/228-4016. A romantic, vine-covered, candlelit haven with live harp music thrice weekly. Both seatings of a shifting prix fixe menu ($56) sell out quickly, so make reservations.

The Juice Bar 12 Broad St ℡508/228-5799. The best ice-cream spot on the island, it's packed with patrons eager for hand-rolled cones and cups filled up with inventive flavors like chocolate peanut butter cookie dough and classics like mint oreo.

Nantucket Bake Shop 79 Orange St ℡508/228-2797. A local landmark, the *Bake Shop* opens at 6.30am so that morning folks can get their hands on warm scones and fresh blueberry muffins; there are also tons of tasty cookies such as the beloved "chocolate chunker."

Provisions 3 Harbor Square ℡508/228-3258. Great variety of bulging, gourmet sandwiches with names like the "Turkey Terrific" and the "Yacht Club" (smoked salmon, lemon caper cream cheese, and cucumbers).

Sayle's Seafood 99 Washington St Extension ℡508/228-4599. Breezy, very casual seafood shack where you choose your own lobster. There's also a phenomenal, all-encompassing "clambake" option ($35/person in-store, $60/person at your house).

The Sconset Café End of Milestone Rd, Siasconset ℡508/257-4008. This endearing little institution is like a flavorful oasis after the 7-mile bike ride out to 'Sconset. You'll find inexpensive salads and sandwiches at lunchtime, fresh muffins, and baked goods throughout the day, and candlelit, New American fare at dinner with rotating menu items like halibut with coconut curry sauce ($25) and crab cakes remoulade ($10). Cash or check only.

Sfoglia 130 Pleasant St ℡508/325-4500. Just outside of town, this romantic spot serves seasonal Italian fare like *pappardelle alla Bolognese* ($14) with local mussels ($13) and chicken *al mattone* ($26) amidst gloriously mismatched tables in an artful, candlelit space. Reservations recommended.

Something Natural 50 Cliff Rd ☎508/228-0504. The place to go for sandwiches to take to the beach; fabulously fresh creations like avocado, cheddar and chutney ($8.75) on home-made bread are best washed down with Nantucket Nectar's "Matt Fee Tea" – named for the owner. No seating per se, but there are picnic blankets and tables on offer.

Straight Wharf Restaurant 6 Harbor Square ☎508/228-4499. Lovely New American spot with smoked bluefish pate and watermelon salad in an airy, art-strewn space overlooking the harbor. The bar goes from seafood eatery to more of a fun-loving *Animal House* vibe after dark; they also do a mean weekend brunch.

Nightlife and entertainment

For such a teensy island, Nantucket has a nice spectrum of **nightlife** offerings, ranging from martini bars and down and dirty local pubs to clambakes and impromptu beach get-togethers. One good spot to see a **movie** is the Starlight Theater and Café, 1 N Union St (☎508/228-4435), for more arty flicks year-round. Also in Nantucket Town, the Theater Workshop of Nantucket puts on **plays** and musicals at Bennett Hall, next to the First Congressional Church at 62 Center St (☎508/228-4305, ⓦwww.theatreworkshop.com), while Actors Theater of Nantucket (☎508/228-6325, ⓦwww.nantuckettheatre.com) produces Broadway-type plays, comedy nights, and children's matinees at the Methodist Church, 2 Center St. Additionally, the Nantucket Musical Arts Society stages **classical concerts** with renowned musicians through July and August, also in the First Congregational Church. For a romantic evening with the stars, head over to the Maria Mitchell observation tower, 4 Vestal St (☎508/228-9273, ⓦwww.mmo.org; $10 adults, $6 kids; Mon, Wed, & Fri nights at 9pm in summer; rest of year, Fri only), which has been open since 1847 when its namesake skyrocketed to fame with the discovery of a telescopic comet.

Brotherhood of Thieves 23 Broad St ☎508/228-2551. This basement bar is a Nantucket institution and the place to go for live folk music, year-round.

Cambridge Street Victuals 12 Cambridge St ☎508/228-7109. A fun after-work type of bar with a deep blue interior, a good mix of folks, and Guinness, Stella, and microbrews on tap.

The Chicken Box 14 Dave St ☎508/228-9717. Every summer night, people of all stripes pack into "The Box" for great live shows and low-key drinking environs. Shuffleboard and pool tables, too. Cash only; an ATM is inside.

LoLa 41 15 South Beach St ☎508/325-4001. The place to go dolled up in Lilly Pulitzer fashion for a $15 martini.

Ship's Inn 13 Fair St ☎508/228-1101. Also doubling as a lovely French fusion restaurant and B&B, the *Ship's Inn* houses a low-key, sophisticated bar in the basement of its 1831 whaling captain's mansion.

㉓

Martha's Vineyard

T he largest offshore island in New England, twenty-mile-long **MARTHA'S VINEYARD** offers enough fantastic beach fare, local history, and standout clam shacks to win over even the surliest New Englander. It encompasses more physical variety (and has more of a laidback attitude) than Nantucket, with hills and pasturelands providing scenic counterpoints to the beaches and wild, windswept moors on the separate island of **Chappaquiddick**. Roads throughout the Vineyard are framed by knotty oak trees, which lend a romantic aura to an already pretty landscape. The most genteel town on the island is **Edgartown**, all prim and proper with its freshly painted, white-clapboard Colonial homes and manicured gardens. The other main town, **Vineyard Haven**, has a more commercial atmosphere, not surprising considering that it is one of the main places where the ferries call in. **Oak Bluffs**, in between the two, is more sizeable than Vineyard Haven (and the other docking point for ferries), and is known for its array of wooden gingerbread cottages and inviting eateries. Regardless of where you visit, watch out for the terminology: heading "Up-Island" takes you, improbably, southwest to the cliffs at **Aquinnah** (formerly known as Gay Head); conversely, "Down-Island" refers to triumvirate of easterly towns mentioned above.

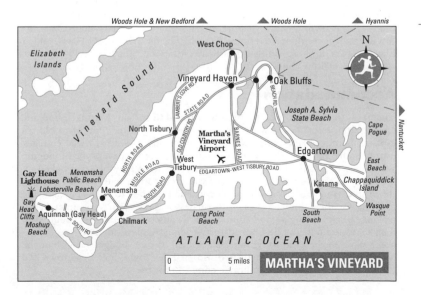

Arrival and information

Most people come to Martha's Vineyard by **ferry**, arriving at either Oak Bluffs or Vineyard Haven, usually from Woods Hole on Cape Cod (see box opposite for schedules and fares). You can also **fly** via Cape Air (℡508/771-6944 or 1-800/352-0714, Ⓦwww.flycapeair.com) from Boston (from which there's an hourly shuttle in the summer), Hyannis, Nantucket, or New Bedford. The Vineyard's **airport** (℡508/693-7022) is in West Tisbury. **Taxis** greet all arriving ferries and flights; all companies use the same fare sheets, and some share phone numbers. Try Martha's Vineyard Taxi (℡508/693-8660), All Island (℡508/693-2929), or AdamCab (℡508/627-4462).

Tourist **information** is available at the Chamber of Commerce in Vineyard Haven or at the post office in Edgartown, both of which stock the requisite pamphlets and island maps.

Getting around

Martha's Vineyard has an increasingly frequent and reliable **bus** system that connects the main towns from around 7am to 12.45am daily (℡508/639-9440, Ⓦwww.vineyardtransit.com); tickets cost $1 per town, including the town of origin, or $6 per day. Getting a day pass and a map is the best way to get around without a car, but there are also 3hr narrated **tours** run by Martha's Vineyard Sightseeing ($23; ℡508/627-TOUR, Ⓦwww.mvtour.com); the trolleys run from spring to fall from all ferry arrival points. Another option is to **bike**; in Vineyard Haven you can rent from Martha's Bike Rentals at the Five Corners, just a block from the ferry (℡1-800/559-0312, Ⓦwww.marthasvineyardbikes .com); in Oak Bluffs from Anderson Bike Rentals on Circuit Ave (℡508/693-9346); or in Edgartown from R.W. Cutler Bikes at 1 Main St (℡1-800/627-2763, Ⓦwww.edgartownbikerentals.com). A basic mountain bike generally starts at $20/day, no matter the company.

Bringing a **car** over on the ferry is an expensive option, and often impossible on summer weekends without reserving months in advance. If you just can't do without a car, you can rent one from Budget, in Vineyard Haven, Oak Bluffs, Edgartown, or the airport (℡508/693-1911 or 1-800/527-0700, Ⓦwww.budget.com), or Adventure Rentals/Thrifty in Vineyard Haven and at Islandhoppers in Oak Bluffs (℡508/693-1959 or 508/696-9147, Ⓦwww .adventurerentalsmv.com).

Accommodation

There's a tremendous variety of **accommodation** on Martha's Vineyard, ranging from resort hotels with every conceivable creature comfort to old sea captains' homes oozing with charm and personality, as well as rental cottages, usually booked on a weekly basis. Keep in mind that whatever type of lodging you decide on, summer accommodation in Martha's Vineyard gets booked up very early, so reserve well in advance. If you do get stuck with nowhere to stay, the main Chamber of Commerce office will do their best to help. The following rates are for the summer season, and off-season prices can vary dramatically, making fall and spring a good time to call for discounted rates – though even then the weekends may be booked for weddings. Unless otherwise noted, the hotels close in the dead of winter (Jan & Feb). If on a budget, check out the Martha's Vineyard Family **Campground** in Edgartown, 569 Edgartown Rd (℡508/693-3772, Ⓦwww.campmvfc.com; $46 for two).

The most frequent ferries – and the only ones that can take cars – run year-round from **Woods Hole** on Cape Cod. In addition, the Woods Hole ferry is one of the few reliable ways to get to the island in the **winter**, when ferries run solely to Vineyard Haven. In the summer, however, leaving from somewhere else can be more convenient. **Falmouth** and **Hyannis** have day-boats, though only the Hyannis boats runs in the winter. In order to avoid weekend Cape Cod traffic, the ferries from **New Bedford** and **Quanset Point** in Rhode Island have become popular options; for New Yorkers, there is also a ferry that leaves from **Montauk**. Unless otherwise specified, the ferries listed below run several times daily in the peak mid-June to mid-September holiday periods. Most have fewer services from mid-May to mid-June and from mid-September to October. **Parking** at the ferries is usually $10 per day, and most charge extra for bikes (up to $6 per). **Prices** listed below are for a round-trip. Be sure to reserve ahead as rides do sell out.

From Cape Cod

Falmouth to Oak Bluffs (about 35min). Passengers only. The *Island Queen* ($12; ☎508/548-4800, ⊛www.islandqueen.com).

Falmouth to Edgartown (1hr). Passengers only. A small boat, so call ahead for reservations Fri–Sun. Falmouth Ferry Service ($30; ☎508/548-9400, ⊛www.falmouthferry.com).

Woods Hole to both Vineyard Haven and Oak Bluffs (45min). Car ferry, year-round. Reservations required to bring a car on summer weekends and holidays – you can bring a car standby all other times, though the wait can be long. Steamship Authority ($120 high season or $70 low season per car, not including passengers, who must pay $5.50 each way; ☎508/477-8600, ⊛www.steamshipauthority.com).

Hyannis to Oak Bluffs (about 1hr 40min; fast ferry about 50min). Passengers only. Hy-Line ($31, $59 fast ferry; ☎508/778-2600 or 1-888/778-1132, ⊛www.hy-linecruises.com).

From elsewhere in Massachusetts, Rhode Island, and New York

New Bedford to Vineyard Haven or Oak Bluffs (1hr). Passengers only. A great way to avoid Cape traffic, particularly if you're coming from Rhode Island or New York. ($58; ☎1-866/453-6800, ⊛www.nefastferry.com).

Quanset Point, Rhode Island, to Oak Bluffs (1.5hr). Passengers only. Good for those traveling from Connecticut or New York; Quonset is south of Providence and Warwick. Viking Ferry ($69; ☎401/295-4040, ⊛www.vineyardfastferry.com).

Montauk, Long Island to Oak Bluffs (6hr). Pedestrians only; Tues and Thurs in summer only. Great for New Yorkers, although it's no short trip. Viking Ferry ($120; ☎631/668-5700, ⊛www.vikingfleet.com).

From June through September, the Hy-Line ferry company also runs a **connecting service** which runs once daily between Oak Bluffs, Martha's Vineyard's, and Nantucket (one departure daily; pedestrians only; $28 one-way, ☎508/778-2600).

The Clark House Inn 20 Edgartown Rd, Vineyard Haven ☎508/693-6550, ⊛www.clarkhouseinn.com. A friendly, well-loved B&B that's a short ride to the ferry and has clean, cozy rooms, great breakfasts, fresh lemonade and home-made cookies. $150.

Crocker House Inn 12 Crocker Ave, Vineyard Haven ☎1-800/772-0206, ⊛www.crockerhouseinn.com. Elegant and accommodating, the *Crocker House* features pretty rooms, free Wi-Fi, good proximity to shops, and lots of home-made goodies. $185.

HI-Martha's Vineyard Edgartown–West Tisbury Rd ☎508/693-2665 or 1-800/901-2087, ⊛www.capecodhostels.org. In an appealing setting at the forest's edge and away from town; near the island's main bike path, and right on the bus route. Free Wi-Fi. 72 beds in dormitory accommodation, with shared bath and a full kitchen. April to mid-Nov only; dorm beds $27–35/night.

Menemsha Inn & Cottages and Beach Plum Inn North Rd, Menemsha ☎508/645-9454, ⊛www.menemshainn.com and ⊛www.beachpluminn.com. These adjacent properties are both beautifully maintained and managed. Within walking distance of the Menemsha beach, they also include access to private town beaches on the south shore. The *Beach Plum Inn* is better for younger adults, while the cottages at *Menemsha* are better for families. Open May–Nov; book early. Rooms from $240; cottages starting at $2200/week.

Nashua House B&B 30 Kennebec Ave, Oak Bluffs ☎508/693-0043, ⊛www.nashuahouse.com. Small rooms, some with shared baths, but this very central hotel is an easy walk from the ferry. It can get loud at night, but with rates starting from $100 in high season it's one of the less expensive choices for a friendly inn.

Oak Bluffs Inn Circuit Ave, Oak Bluffs ☎1-800/955-6235, ⊛www.oakbluffsinn.com. Guests rave about the gorgeous wraparound porch, the clean and cozy rooms (many of which are kid-friendly), the fantastic innkeepers, and proximity to ferries, beaches, and restaurants. $215.

Pequot Hotel 19 Pequot Ave, Oak Bluffs ☎1-800/947-8704, ⊛www.pequothotel.com. Friendly, mid-sized hotel in the gingerbread cottage neighborhood with rocking chairs on the porch, Wi-Fi and TVs in every room, and a quick walk to town. $200.

Victorian Inn 24 South Water St, Edgartown ☎508/627-4784, ⊛www.thevic.com. This historic B&B, set in a vintage whaling captain's home, features bright, stately rooms, with a quiet location just off Main Street that's accessible to restaurants, shops, and the harbor. $225.

Wesley Hotel 1 Lake Ave, Oak Bluffs ☎508/693-6611 or 1-800/638-9027, ⊛www.wesleyhotel.com. The last of Oak Bluff's grand hotels, though it's quite commercial now, with small, dimly lit rooms. Overpriced in high season, but with 95 rooms it may have availability when others don't. $205.

Winnetu Inn & Resort South Beach, Edgartown ☎508/627-4747, ⊛www.winnetu.com. This family-friendly resort hotel is just a short walk from a private stretch of South Beach; very well-appointed rooms, many with kitchenettes. In high season expect 2- to 3-night minimum stays. $295.

The island

The Vineyard is basically divided into two sections, the far busier of which is "**Down-Island**," which includes the ferry terminals of **Vineyard Haven** and **Oak Bluffs**, and smart **Edgartown**. The largely undeveloped western half of the island, known as "**Up-Island**," comprises woods, agricultural land, ponds, and nature reserves, with a smattering of tiny villages thrown in, including **West Tisbury**, **Chilmark**, and **Aquinnah** (Gay Head). Although there are plenty of trails to explore, much of the land belongs to private estates and as such is out of bounds to the public.

Vineyard Haven

Most visitors by boat arrive at **VINEYARD HAVEN** (officially named **Tisbury**), at the northern tip of the island. Founded by islanders from Edgartown disillusioned with the iron-fist Puritan rule of the Mayhew family, Vineyard Haven supplanted Edgartown as the island's main commercial center in the mid-1800s, because ferries preferred the shorter run to the mainland; today, the town, which may well be the least attractive on the island, retains its distinctively business-like ambience, its late-Victorian main street lined with a mix of shops, banks, law and real estate offices, and ice-cream parlors.

The brand-new **bus terminal**, visible as you get off the ferry, is also home to a small **visitors' kiosk**, but for more detailed information and help in finding accommodation, walk up Beach Road to the **Chamber of Commerce**,

24 Beach Rd (late May to early Sept daily 9am–5pm, early Sept to late May Mon–Fri 9am–5pm; ☎508/693-0085, ⓦ www.mvy.com).

Oak Bluffs

OAK BLUFFS, just across Lagoon Pond from Vineyard Haven, is the newest of the island's six towns. It was a quiet farming community until the Methodists established their campground, known as "Wesleyan Grove," here in the 1850s. This section of Oak Bluffs remains a relatively tranquil haven filled with the brightly colored "carpenter Gothic" or "**gingerbread**" cottages they built. During the summer, family-oriented events, Sunday-morning church services, and secular Saturday evening concerts are still held in the iron and wood-constructed **tabernacle**. The best-known event that takes place here is **Illumination Night** (third Wed in Aug; free), when all the cottages put up Japanese lanterns collected over the years, accompanied by band music at the tabernacle. At one end of Wesleyan Grove, the sweet 1867 **Cottage Museum**, 1 Trinity Park (mid-June to Sept Mon–Sat 10am–4pm; $3 donation), offers a charming collection of photographs, old Bibles, and other artifacts from the campground's history.

In a frenzy of post-Civil War construction, speculators built up the area near the waterfront with dance halls, a skating rink, a railway linking "Cottage City" to Edgartown, and resort hotels, of which only the 1879 **Wesley Hotel**, on Lake Avenue, survives. Most of the current action focuses on **Circuit Avenue**, where the shops and bars attract a predominantly young crowd. The restored **Flying Horses Carousel**, at Circuit and Lake avenues (mid-April to mid-Oct daily 10am–10pm; $2 per ride), is the oldest operating carousel in the country; hand-carved in 1876, the 22 horses on parade here have bona fide horsehair manes.

Oak Bluffs also has a few beaches worth checking out, though the **town beach**, on Sea View Avenue, can get very noisy and crowded in season. Further south, the **Joseph A. Sylvia State Beach**, a sandy six-mile stretch of shore, is more appealing, and it parallels an undemanding pedestrian/cycle path that leads all the way to Edgartown, with pleasant views to accompany you.

Edgartown

Six miles southeast of Oak Bluffs, **EDGARTOWN**, originally known as Great Harbor, is the oldest and swankiest settlement on the island. It has been extravagantly dolled up for visitors, with elegant Colonial residences glistening white and surrounded by exquisitely maintained gardens and trimmed hedges. It doesn't end there, of course: downtown brims with upmarket boutiques, smart restaurants, and artsy galleries.

Once you've got your bearings at the seasonal **visitors' center** on Church Street (late May to early Sept daily 9am–5pm) – basically just public restrooms, a bus stop, and a place to pick up brochures – it's a short walk to the **Vineyard Museum**, at the corner of Cooke and School streets (mid-June to mid-Oct Tues–Sat 10am–5pm; rest of year Wed–Fri 1–4pm, Sat 10am–4pm; $7; ☎508/627-4441, ⓦwww.marthasvineyardhistory.org), a complex of buildings maintained by the Martha's Vineyard Historical Society. One of them, the 1845 **Captain Frances Pease House**, is full of whaling relics and native arrowheads and, best of all, an Oral History Center, which traces the history of the island through more than 250 recorded narratives of older locals.

A short walk along North Water Street leads past charming sea captains' homes to the white cast-iron **Edgartown Lighthouse** – it's a replacement of the 1828 original, destroyed in the hurricane of 1938. Take the bus from the visitor's center to **South Beach** in Katama, three miles south of town, for some of the best public access to the Atlantic Ocean on-island.

Chappaquiddick

Chappaquiddick (aka "Chappy") is a strikingly beautiful and sparsely populated little island, just yards away from Edgartown's shores. Unfortunately, it's name will always be associated with scandal: Edward (Ted) Kennedy ruined his chances for the presidency in the summer of 1969 when 28-year-old Mary Jo Kopechne drowned in his car at **Dike Bridge**, under circumstances that conspiracy theorists still debate. The island is an easy 5min jaunt from Edgartown via the *On Time* ferry (so called because it has no regular schedule and is thus always "on time"; $3 per person, $10 for a car and one driver; ☎508/627-9427), which departs frequently from a ramp at the corner of Dock and Daggett streets. There are no stores, restaurants, or hotels on Chappy, just private residences and hundreds of acres of dunes, salt marshes, ponds, scrubland, and barrier beach. The island is easy to get around on a bike, though too large to walk comfortably.

The Trustees of Reservations' small Japanese garden **Mytoi**, on Dike Road (open dawn-dusk; free), is worth stopping by for a few minutes – it's unusual to see the typical rounded bridges and groomed trees in a pine forest. The Trustees are also the caretakers of **Wasque**, a windswept stretch of beach that is a continuation of South Beach in Edgartown, but much less crowded. On Chappy's far east side you'll find the five-hundred acre **Cape Poge Wildlife Refuge**, an important habitat and migration stopover for thousands of birds. Half the state's scallops are harvested here, too. The best way to see it is to take one of the 3hr **natural history tours** that involve walking and kayaking that depart from the Mytoi parking area, on Dike Road (late May to mid-Oct; $30; ☎508/627-7689).

West Tisbury

In 1999, **WEST TISBURY** joined Chappaquiddick in the lore of the Kennedy curse, when **John Kennedy, Jr.**'s plane crashed in the water less than twenty miles from the landing field. Most of West Tisbury's history has been considerably more peaceful, and the village, the largest of the up-island communities, also has some of the best culture on the island. West Tisbury was founded in the 1670s by settlers from Edgartown, who happened upon a fast-flowing stream here. As the community developed, sheep farming became the main industry and residents continue to dote on their town's rural atmosphere; there are several flourishing horse and agricultural produce farms, some of which you can see if you drive or bike down the scenic **Middle Road**. West Tisbury is also home to the only operating vineyard on the island, **Chicama Vineyards**, on Stoney Hill Road off of State Road (mid-May to Oct Mon–Sat 11am–5pm, Sun 1–5pm; early May and Oct–Dec Mon–Sat 1–4pm; Jan–April Sat 1–4pm, ☎508/693-0309, ⓦwww .chicamavineyards.com), which has been producing Massachusetts quality (read: sub-par) wines since 1971. It's a pretty spot, and tastings are free.

The **Farmers' Market**, held at the 1859 **Old Agricultural Hall** on South Road every Saturday morning (and sometimes Wed mornings in the summer), attracts visitors from all over the island for its colorful displays of locally grown produce. Recently an additional Agricultural Hall was built, to be used as a setting for shows, dances, pot-luck suppers, and an annual **agricultural fair** that takes place for three days at the end of August. Across the street from the old hall is the **Field Gallery**, 1050 State Rd (☎508/693-5595), locally famous for Tom Maley's larger-than-life sculptures of ladies dancing on the grass. Also on State Road next to the Old Ag Hall is **Alley's General Store** (☎508/693-0088), an island institution since 1858, selling everything from cans of baked beans to mini *ouija* boards, and with a wide front porch where locals often meet for a chat. There's a place behind the store, appropriately enough named *Back Alley's*, to get good sandwiches. Nearby, at 636 Old County Rd, is the picturesque **Granary Gallery** (open dawn–dusk; free), featuring Ella Tulin's sculpture of a woman with a small torso and seven-foot-high thighs sitting in front, and a variety of notable Vineyard and New England artists' work within.

West Tisbury has a bountiful supply of conservation areas, including the 216-acre **Cedar Tree Neck Wildlife Sanctuary** on Indian Hill Road (daily sunrise–sunset; free), in which bayberry bushes, swamp azaleas, tupelos, and pygmy beech trees all grow. Three main trails lead to a pretty but stony beach and a bluff with views to Aquinnah (Gay Head) and the Elizabeth Islands. Meanwhile, the **Sepiessa Point Reservation**, on New Lane off West Tisbury Road (daily dawn–dusk; free), surrounds West Tisbury Pond with trails ideal for bird-watching.

Chilmark

Five miles west of Tisbury, unspoiled **CHILMARK**, with just over 800 year-round residents, is the land that time almost forgot, full of pastures separated by stone walls, dense woodlands, and rugged roads. That's not to say that the twenty-first century hasn't arrived: **Beetlebung Corner**, where Middle, State, South, and Menemsha Cross roads meet, and which is named for the wooden mallets (aka "beetles") and stoppers ("bungs") once made from the nearby tupelo trees, is the village's center, heralded by a small grocery-deli, a boutique, and some other modern commercial concerns, though there's also an old schoolhouse, the last one-room version on the island.

The island's **beaches** vary from calm, shallow waters, predominantly on the northern and eastern sides, to long stretches of pounding surf on the southern side, where the water also tends to be a bit warmer. Unfortunately, many of the best beaches are private, or are only open in the summer to residents, but there are some notable exceptions. All of the beaches listed below have lifeguards in at least some areas during summer days.

Aquinnah (Gay Head)

Lobsterville Beach Lobsterville Road. Two miles of prime Vineyard Sound beach backed by dunes. Parking on Lobsterville Road is prohibited, so bike or get here by taking the ferry from Menemsha.

Moshup Beach (Gay Head Public Beach) State Road/Moshup Drive. Gorgeous setting at the foot of Gay Head Cliffs, best reached by bicycle, shuttle bus, or taxi. Parking costs $20 a day in season.

Chappaquiddick

Cape Poge Wildlife Refuge at the end of Dike Road. This sandy beach is less crowded than Wasque at the far east end of the island. $3 per person for non-members.

Wasque at the end of Wasque Road south of School Road. Wide-open South Shore beach. $3 per person and $3 per vehicle.

Chilmark

Lucy Vincent Beach off South Road. Sandy beach with access to some of the island's clay cliffs (note that bathing in the clay puddles is restricted) through the end of September to residents and visitors with passes.

Menemsha Public Beach next to Menemsha Harbor. The only Chilmark beach open to the public, with sparkling waters and a picturesque setting. It becomes *very* crowded around sunset, since it is one of the few places to see the sun go down over a beach on the East Coast (the north shore of Cape Cod bay is another exception).

Squibnocket off State Road at the end of Squibnocket Road. This narrow, rocky beach is less attractive than the other Chilmark beaches, but the waves break further

On South Road the tranquil **Chilmark Cemetery** is the final resting place of writer Lillian Hellman and comedian John Belushi, who claimed that the island was the only place in the world where he could get a good night's sleep. Near the entrance, a boulder engraved with the comedian's name – a decoy to prevent fans from finding his actual unmarked grave – is often blessed with rather unceremonious "offerings," like beer cans and condoms. Nearby, a dirt track leads to **Lucy Vincent Beach**, named after the town's prim and proper librarian, who saw it as her mission to protect Chilmark residents from corruption by cutting out from her library books all pictures she deemed to be immoral. Rather ironically, the beach, which is open only to residents and their guests in the summer, today doubles as a **nudist** spot in its less crowded areas. Off North Road, pick up a map at the trailhead of **Waskosim's Rock Reservation** for a fascinating three-mile hike through a variety of habitats including wetlands and black gum and oak woods.

In the northern part of Chilmark, another tiny island community, **Menemsha**, is a picturesque but hodgepodge collection of gray-shingled fishing shacks with a man-made harbor used for location shots in the making of *Jaws*. The harbor also serves as an important commercial and sports-fishing port, much of the catch ending up at restaurants all over the island. Stroll past the fish markets of offshore, making it the best island spot for **surfing**. It's a town beach, which means it's off-limits during summer days, but anyone can show up after 5pm and in September – one of the best times to catch the waves.

Vineyard Haven
Lake Tashmoo Town Beach Herring Creek Road. Swim in the warm, brackish water of the lake, or in the cooler Vineyard Sound.

Owen Park Beach off Main Street. A harbor beach close to the center of town. Not much of a swimming hole, or a beach, but it's a walkable distance from downtown.

Oak Bluffs
Joseph A. Sylvia State Beach along Beach Road between Oak Bluffs and Edgartown. A narrow six-mile strand of sandy beach with clear, gentle waters and plenty of roadside parking.

Oak Bluffs Town Beach between the Steamship Authority Dock and the State Beach. Narrow sliver of beach on Vineyard Sound that gets very crowded in season.

Edgartown
Bend-in-the-Road Beach Beach Road. Really an extension of the Joseph A. Sylvia State Beach, with similar facilities and access.

Katama Beach (South Beach) end of Katama Road. Beautiful barrier beach backed by protected salt pond. Strong surf and currents – known for its "good waves and good bodies."

Lighthouse Beach Starbuck's Neck, off North Water Street. Close to town, this harbor beach can get a bit too mucked with seaweed.

West Tisbury
Lambert's Cove Beach Lambert's Cove Road. One of the island's prettiest, but open only to residents during high season.

Long Point Wildlife Refuge Beach off South Road. The perfect Vineyard beach: long and wide, with a freshwater pond just behind. Get there early for a parking space, on the south side of the street near the airport.

Dutcher's Dock for a real sense of the island's maritime heritage, or bring an early-evening picnic to pebbly **Menemsha Beach** to enjoy the spectacular sunsets. The **Menemsha Hills Reservation**, off North Road a couple of miles toward West Tisbury, is also well worth a visit, its mile-long rocky shoreline and sand bluffs along Vineyard Sound peaking at **Prospect Hill**, the highest point on the Vineyard, with wonderful views of the Elizabeth Islands.

Aquinnah (Gay Head)
In 1997, the people of **Aquinnah** voted to revert the town's name back to its original Wampanoag Indian name from its more familiar title – Gay Head – the culmination of a ten-year-plus court battle in which the Wampanoags won guardianship of 420 acres of land, to be held in perpetuity by the federal government and known as the **Gay Head Native American Reservation**. Most people come to this part of the island (its westernmost point) to see the multicolored clay **Gay Head Cliffs**, whose brilliant hues are the result of millions of years of geological work. When the oceans were high, and the Vineyard underwater, small creatures died and left their shells behind to form the white layers. At other times, the area was a rainforest and vegetation compressed to form the darker colors. The weight of the glaciers thrust the

many layers of stone up at an angle to create the cliffs, dubbed "Gay Head" by passing English sailors in the seventeenth century on account of their bright colors. The clay was once the main source of paint for the island's houses, but now anyone removing any (unless you're a Wampanoag Indian) faces a substantial fine; in any case, the cliffs are eroding so fast that it's not safe to approach them too closely anyway.

A short path lined with seafood shacks and craft stalls leads the way from the parking lot to the **overlook**, which affords stunning views to the Elizabeth Islands, and, on a clear day, as far as the entrance to Rhode Island's Narragansett Bay. The imposing red-brick **Gay Head Lighthouse** (mid-June to mid-Sept Fri–Sun evenings; $3), built in 1854 to replace a wooden structure that dated from 1799, is well situated for sunset views. Below the lighthouse, though not accessible from it, a **public beach** provides an equally impressive view of the cliffs from a different angle. To reach it, take the wooden boardwalk from the **Moshup Beach** parking lot to the shore, then walk round towards the lighthouse.

Eating, drinking, and nightlife

It's easy enough to find something to **eat** on Martha's Vineyard; the ports in particular have rows of places to tempt tourists who've just disembarked the ferries. Four of the island's six towns are **dry**, meaning you can only purchase alcohol in Oak Bluffs and Edgartown. Note, though, that you can bring wine or beer purchased there to restaurants in the other towns.

Much of the Vineyard's evening **entertainment** comes in the form of private dinner parties, but that doesn't mean there's nothing to do if you're not invited to one. First-run **movies** can be seen at Capawok, an Art Deco theater on Main Street in Vineyard Haven (☎508/696-9200), or in Edgartown at Entertainment Cinemas, 65 Main St (☎508/627-8008). For current **listings** information, check the *Vineyard Gazette* (🌐www.mvgazette.com), good for cultural events, and the weekly *Martha's Vineyard Times* (🌐www.mvtimes.com), better for nightlife listings.

ArtCliff Diner 39 Beach Rd, Vineyard Haven
☎508/693-1224. Perfect for a pre-ferry send-off breakfast, with the likes of almond-crusted French toast and chorizo, egg, and pepperjack sandwiches. Cash only, closed Wed.

The Bite 29 Basin Rd, Menemsha ☎508/645-9239. Roadside/seaside nirvana. Fried clams, scallops, and zucchini, served in paper bags from a tiny seaside shack. Good chowder, too. Cash only.

The Black Dog Bakery and Tavern 11 Water St, Vineyard Haven ☎508/693-4786. Though you'll see these T-shirts all over the island and the mainland, the original restaurant and bakery serve fare as tasty as the spot is touristy. The (dry) tavern serves full and "light" (less expensive) seafood dinners, while you can stock up on muffins or bagels at the next-door bakery for the return ferry ride.

Chilmark Chocolates 19 State Rd, Chilmark
☎508/645-3013. People line up and rally for *Chilmark's* island-grown berries dipped in unbelievably-good organic chocolate. Closed Mon–Wed.

David Ryan's 11 N Water St, Edgartown
☎508/627-4100. Loud two-story bar with a chi-chi martini lounge upstairs and raucous dancing to rock 'n' roll downstairs – usually on the tables.

Détente 3 Winter St, Edgartown ☎508/627-8810. A good place for a romantic splurge, *Détente's* petite dining room, dark-wood paneling, and well-paired New American mains (think roasted venison with thyme spaetzle, $32) make for some of the island's most memorable meals. Reservations recommended.

Larsen's Fish Market Mason Rd, Menemsha
☎508/645-2680. For about $15 you can pick out your very own lobster and then eat it on

low-key flats overlooking the harbor. Good steamers too, as well as raw fish take-home options.

Le Grenier Main St, Vineyard Haven ☎508/693-4906. Don't mind the fussy ambience and weird murals; this fancy French spot serves up some of the tastiest dinner fare on the island (roasted duck à l'orange, $29).

Lola's Southern Seafood *Island Inn*, **Beach Rd, Oak Bluffs** ☎508/693-5007, ⊛www .lolasssouthernseafood.com. Trendy thirty-something disco with a Top-40 dance floor and nightly live acts during the summer; weekends only rest of the year.

🏃 **Offshore Ale Company 30 Kennebec Ave, Oak Bluffs** ☎508/693-2626. Friendly local brewpub with wooden booths, a peanut shell strewn floor, and live shows almost nightly in season. If you're there at night, be sure to stop by *Back Door Donuts* (in the Reliable Market Parking lot, ☎508/693-4786; 9:30pm–12.28am) for a life-changing apple fritter – it's an island must-do.

The Net Result 79 Beach Rd, Vineyard Haven ☎508/693-6071. The *Net Result* claims to sell "fish so fresh they'll make you blush."

Along with being one of the best fish markets in New England, they also sell rave-worthy sushi rolls and stellar takeout items like their bulging lobster roll (a steal at $10).

The Newes from America 23 Kelley St, Edgartown ☎508/627-4397. Swill five hundred beers in this atmospheric pub (not necessarily all in the same night) and they'll name a stool after you. Decent and filling affordable pub grub, too.

Ritz Café 1 Circuit Ave, Oak Bluffs ☎508/693-9851. This cupboard-sized bar is anything but ritzy, but its pool tables and live music acts (nightly in summer; weekends only rest of the year) make a nice escape from the scene.

Slice of Life 50 Circuit Ave, Oak Bluffs ☎508/693-3838. Great New American spot, particularly for lunch. Order the fried green tomato BLT and ogle the tourists from the sunny, enclosed patio.

Zapotec 10 Kennebec Ave, Oak Bluffs ☎508/693-6800. Moderately priced seafood variations on Mexican cuisine, like swordfish fajitas, served in a cute and colorful house behind Oak Bluff's main drag.

㉓

MARTHA'S VINEYARD | Eating, drinking, and nightlife

Contexts

Contexts

History

Boston has been an important city since its colonial days. Numerous crucial and decisive events, especially as they related to America's struggle for independence, have taken place here; it's also been fertile ground for various intellectual, literary, and religious movements throughout the years. What follows is a very short overview of the city's development, with an emphasis on the key happenings and figures behind them; for a more in-depth look, check out some of the volumes listed in "Books", p.299.

Early exploration and founding

The first indications of explorers "discovering" the Boston area are the journal entries of Giovanni da Verrazano and Estevan Gomez, who – in 1524 and 1525, respectively – passed by Massachusetts Bay while traveling the coast of North America. The first permanent European settlement in the Boston area was undertaken by a group of 102 British colonists, around half of them Separatists – better known now as **Pilgrims** – chased out of England for having disassociated themselves entirely from the Anglican Church. They had tried to settle in Holland, but the Dutch wouldn't let them become citizens, so they boarded the Mayflower ship to try the forbidding, rugged coast of North America, where they landed in 1620 near Plymouth Bay – after a short stopover at the tip of Cape Cod – and founded Plimoth Plantation. Within the first decade, one of them, a disillusioned scholarly loner by the name of **William Blackstone**, began searching for land on which to make a new start; he found it on a peninsula at the mouth of the Charles River known as Shawmut by the local Indians. Blackstone thus became Boston's first white settler, living at the foot of modern-day Beacon Hill with a few hundred books and a Brahma bull.

In 1630, close to one thousand Puritans, led by **John Winthrop**, settled just across the river to create Charlestown, named after the king of England. Unlike the Pilgrims, the Puritans didn't necessarily plan to disconnect themselves completely from the Anglican Church, but merely hoped to purify themselves by avoiding what they considered to be its showy excesses. Blackstone eventually lured them to his side of the river with the promise of a better water supply, and then sold them the entire Shawmut Peninsula, keeping only six acres for himself. The Puritans subsequently renamed the area after the town in England from which many of their company hailed: **Boston**.

The colonial period

Early Bostonians enjoyed almost total political autonomy from England and created a remarkably democratic system of government, whose primary body was the town meeting, in which white male church members debated over and voted on all kind of matters. This liberal approach was counterbalanced, however, by religious intolerance: four Quakers and Baptists were hanged for their non-Puritan beliefs between 1649 and 1651.

Also, during these times Boston and neighboring **Cambridge** were making great strides in culture and education: Boston Latin, the (not yet) nation's first secondary school, was established in 1635; **Harvard**, its first university, a year later; and the first printing press in America was set up in Cambridge in 1639, where the Bay Psalm Book, New England Primer, and freeman's oath of loyalty to Massachusetts were among the first published works.

With the restoration of the British monarchy in 1660, the crown tried to exert more control over the increasingly prosperous and freethinking Massachusetts Bay Colony, appointing a series of governors, notably the despotic **Sir Edmund Andros**, who was chased from the colony by locals in 1689, only to be reinstalled by the monarchy the following year. Britain's relentless mercantilist policies, designed to increase the nation's monopolistic hold on the new colonies, resulted in a decrease in trade that both plunged Boston into a depression and fanned the anti-British resentment which would eventually reach a boiling point during the mid-1700s. The Molasses Act of 1733, for example, taxed all sugar purchased outside the British Empire, dealing a stiff economic blow to the colonies, who were dependent upon foreign sources for their sugar supply.

The American Revolution

At the outset of the 1760s, governor Francis Bernard informed the colonists that their success was a result of "their subjugation to Great Britain," before green-lighting the **Writs of Assistance**, which gave British soldiers the right to enter colonists' shops and homes to search for evidence of their avoiding duties. The colonists reacted with outrage at this violation of their civil liberties, and a young Boston lawyer named James Otis argued in front of a panel of judges headed by lieutenant governor Thomas Hutchinson to repeal the acts. After listening to his four-hour oration, many were convinced that revolution was justified, including future US president John Adams, who wrote of Otis's speech: "Then and there the child Liberty was born."

Nevertheless, in 1765 the British introduced the **Stamp Act**, which required stamps to be placed on all published material (the revenue on the stamps would go to the Imperial coffers), and the **Quartering Act**, which stipulated that colonists had to house British soldiers on demand. These acts galvanized the opposition to the English government, a resistance based in Boston, where a group of revolutionary firebrands headed by Samuel Adams and known as the "Sons of Liberty" teamed up with more level-headed folks like John Hancock and John Adams to organize protest marches and petition the king to repeal the offending legislation. Though Parliament repealed the Stamp Act, in 1766 it issued the **Declaratory Acts**, which asserted the Crown's right to bind the colonists by any legislation it saw fit, and, in 1767, with the **Townshend Acts**, which prescribed more tariffs on imports to the North American colonies. This was followed by a troop increase in Boston; prior to this incident, there were between thirty and forty British soldiers for every colonist, whereas afterwards the ratio became a narrow one to one.

The tension erupted on March 5, 1770, when a group of British soldiers fired into a crowd of townspeople who'd been taunting them. The **Boston Massacre**, as it came to be known, was hardly a massacre – only five people were killed, and the accused soldiers were actually defended in court by John Adams and Josiah Quincy – but the occupying troops were forced to relocate to Castle Island, at the tip of South Boston.

▲ Statue of Sam Adams behind Faneuil Hall

The coming crisis was postponed for a few years following the Massacre, until December 16, 1773, when Samuel Adams led a mob from the Old South Meeting House to Boston Harbor as part of a protest against a British tax on imported tea. A segment of the crowd boarded the brig Beaver and two other ships and dumped the entirety of their tea cargo overboard in an act that's become known as the **Boston Tea Party**; Parliament responded by closing the port of Boston and passing the so-called Coercive Acts, which deprived Massachusetts of any self-government. England also sent in more troops and restricted access across the Boston Neck, the only land entrance to Boston. Soon after, the colonies convened the first **Continental Congress** in Philadelphia, with the idea of creating an independent government.

Two months after the province of Massachusetts was declared to be in a state of rebellion by the British government, the "shot heard 'round the world" was fired at Lexington on April 18, 1775, when a group of American militiamen skirmished with a company of British regulars; they lost that fight, but defeated the Redcoats in a subsequent incident at Concord Bridge, and the **Revolutionary War** had begun. The British troops left in Boston were held under siege, and the city itself was largely evacuated by its citizens.

The first major engagement of the war was the **Battle of Bunker Hill**, in which the British stormed what was actually Breed's Hill, in Charlestown, on three separate occasions before finally dislodging American battlements. Despite the loss, the conflict, in which the outnumbered Americans suffered fewer casualties than the British, bolstered the patriots' spirits and confidence.

George Washington took over the Continental troops in a ceremony on Cambridge Common on July 2, 1775; however, his first major coup didn't even require bloodshed. On March 16, 1776, under cover of darkness, Washington ordered much of the troops' heavy artillery to be moved to the top of Dorchester Heights, in view of the Redcoats. The British awoke to see battlements sufficient to destroy their entire fleet of warships; on March 17, they evacuated the city, never to return.

This was largely the end of Boston's involvement in the war; the focus soon turned inland and southward. After the Americans won the Battle of Saratoga in 1778, the French joined the war as their allies; on October 19, 1781, Cornwallis surrendered to Washington at Yorktown. Two years later, the United States of America became an **independent nation** with 1783's Treaty of Paris.

Economic swings and the "Athens of America"

Boston quickly emerged from the damage wrought by British occupation. By 1790, the economy was already booming, due primarily to the maritime industry. A merchant elite – popularly known as the "cod millionaires" – developed and settled on the sunny south slope of Beacon Hill. These were the original **Boston Brahmins** – though that name would not be coined until seventy years later – infamous for their stuffed-shirt elitism and fiscal conservatism. Indeed, the trust fund was invented in Boston at this time as a way for families to protect their fortunes over the course of generations.

The outset of the nineteenth century was less auspicious. Severe restrictions on international trade, notably Jefferson's Embargo Act in 1807, plunged the port of Boston into recession. When the **War of 1812** began, pro-British Bostonian Federalists derided the conflict as "Mr. Madison's War" and, as such, met in Hartford in 1814 with party members from around New England to consider seceding from the Union – a measure that was wisely, though narrowly, rejected. America's victory in the war shamed Bostonians back into their patriotic ways, and they reacted to further trade restrictions by developing manufacturing industries; the city soon became prominent in textiles and shoe production.

This industrial revival and subsequent economic growth shook the region from its recession. By 1820, Boston's population had grown to 43,000 – more than double its total from the census of 1790. The city stood at the forefront of American intellectual and political life, as well, earning Boston the moniker "Athens of America."

One of these intellectual movements had its roots back in the late-eighteenth century, when a controversial sect of Christianity known as **Unitarianism** – premised on the rational study of the Bible, voluntary ethical behavior, and (in Boston only) a rejection of the idea of a Holy Trinity – became the city's dominant religion (and one still practiced at King's Chapel), led by Reverend Ellery Channing. His teachings were the basis for **transcendentalism**, a philosophy propounded in the writings of Ralph Waldo Emerson and rooted in the idea that there existed an entity known as the "over-soul," to which man and nature existed in identical relation. Emerson's theory, emphasizing intuitive (a priori) knowledge – particularly in contemplation of nature – was put into practice by his fellow Harvard alumnus, Henry David Thoreau, who, in 1845, took to the woods just northwest of the city at Walden Pond in an attempt to "live deliberately."

Boston was also a center of literary activity at this time: historical novels by Nathaniel Hawthorne, such as *The Scarlet Letter*, tweaked the sensibilities and mores of New England society, and poet Henry Wadsworth Longfellow gained international renown during his tenure at Harvard. For more on these developments throughout the nineteenth century, see "Literary Boston in the 1800s", p.297.

This intellectual flowering was complemented by a variety of social movements. Foremost among them was the **abolitionist movement**, spearheaded by the fiery William Lloyd Garrison, who, besides speechmaking, published the anti-slavery newspaper *The Liberator*. Beacon Hill resident Harriet Beecher Stowe's seminal 1852 novel, *Uncle Tom's Cabin*, turned the sentiments of much of the nation against slavery. Other Bostonians who made key contributions to social issues were Horace Mann, who reformed public education; Dorothea Dix, an advocate of improved care for the mentally ill; Margaret Fuller, one of America's first feminists as well the editor of *The Dial*, a journal founded by Emerson; and William James, a Harvard professor who pioneered new methods in psychology, coining the phrase "stream of consciousness."

Social transformation and decline

The success of Boston's maritime and manufacturing industries attracted a great number of **immigrants**; the Irish, especially, poured in following Ireland's Potato Famine of the 1840s. By 1860, the city was marked by massive social divide, with overcrowded slums abutting beautiful mansions. The elite that had ruled for the first half of the century tried to ensure that the lower classes were kept in place: "No Irish Need Apply" notices accompanied job listings throughout Boston. Denied entry into "polite" society, the lower classes conspired to grab power in another way: the popular vote.

To the chagrin of Boston's WASP elite, Hugh O'Brien was elected mayor in 1885. His three-term stay in office was followed by that of John "Honey Fitz" Fitzgerald, and in the 1920s, the long reign of James Michael Curley began. Curley was to serve several terms as mayor, and one each as governor and congressional representative. These men enjoyed tremendous popularity among their supporters, despite the fact that their tenures were often characterized by rampant corruption: Curley was elected to his last term in office while serving time in a Federal prison for fraud. Still, while these mayors increased the visibility and political clout of otherwise disenfranchised ethnic groups, they did little to improve the lot of their constituents, which was steadily worsening – along with the city's economy.

Following the **Civil War**, competition with the railroads crippled the shipping industry, and with it, Boston's prosperous waterfront. Soon after, the manufacturing industry as well felt the impact of bigger, more efficient factories in the rest of the nation. The shoe and textile industries had largely disappeared by the 1920s; many companies had started to move south, where costs were much lower, and industrial production statewide fell by more than $1 billion during that decade. The **Great Depression** of the 1930s made a bad state of affairs even worse, as there were few natural resources the city provided that could keep it as an economic powerhouse.

On the heels of the depression, **World War II** turned Boston's moribund shipbuilding industry around almost overnight, but this economic upturn still wasn't enough to prevent a massive exodus from the urban center.

From the 1950s to the 1980s

In the 1950s, a more long-lasting turnaround began under the mayoral leadership of **John Collins**, who undertook a massive plan to reshape the face of Boston. Many of the city's oldest neighborhoods and landmarks were razed, though it's questionable whether these changes beautified the city. Still, the project created jobs and economic growth, while making the Downtown area more attractive to businesses and residents. By the end of the 1960s, a steady economic resurgence had begun. Peripheral areas of Boston, however, did not share in this prosperity. Collins' program paid little attention to the poverty that afflicted outlying areas, particularly the city's southern districts, or to the city's growing racial tensions. The demographic redistribution that followed the "white flight" of the 1940s and 1950s made Boston one of the most racially segregated cities in America by the mid-1970s: Charlestown's population was almost entirely white, while Roxbury was almost entirely black.

Along with other cities nationwide, Boston was ordered by the US Supreme Court to implement **busing** – sending students from one neighborhood to another and vice-versa in an attempt to achieve racial balance. More than two hundred area schools were involved, and not all reacted kindly: many Charlestown parents, for their part, staged hostile demonstrations and boycotted the public school system, which was especially embarrassing for Boston considering its history of racial tolerance. City officials finally scrapped their plan for desegregation after only a few years. The racial scars it left began to heal, thanks, in part, to the policies of Ray Flynn, Boston's mayor during the upbeat 1980s, helping to make the decade one of the city's healthiest in recent memory, both economically and socially.

The 1990s and into the twenty-first century

That resurgence spilled over into the 1990s, a decade that saw the job market explode and rents spiral upward in reaction to it. The increase in housing prices was further augmented by the 1996 state vote to abolish rent control in the city, a decision that pushed much of the lower-paid working class out to neighborhoods like Roxbury, and kick-started a **condominium boom**, especially in the South End, which was radically transformed from a near slum into the trendy hotspot it is today. In any case, it seems that anyone who can afford a posh apartment these days works for some biotech company – Boston's strength in this market spared most of its citizens from the dot-com crash that injured other major US cities' economies.

Indeed, the city has encountered little strife in the last decade. The most notable, and notorious, hubbub occurred in 2002, when the archdiocese of the local Catholic church, the Church of the Holy Cross, found itself at the center of a sex abuse scandal that prompted calls for an overhaul of the procedures concerning the handling of errant priests. While reforms remain undecided, the protesters who took up residency in front of the church doors during the heat of the scandal quieted down in short order, and the church quickly returned to business as usual – though with a tarnished reputation.

Of far greater impact on Bostonian life, Downtown's **Big Dig project** (see color intro, p.7) was, at over $1.6 billion per mile, the most expensive highway construction project in US history. Though the project was officially completed in 2005 (fourteen years after the first jackhammer sounded in Charlestown), the prettification portion of the Big Dig, namely the landscaping of the twenty-seven acres left in the wake of downtown's Central Artery, was still very much underway at the time of writing. In the meantime, the cleanup of Boston Harbor has had a great effect in reclaiming abandoned beaches and reinvigorating species of long disappeared fauna, many of which are making their homes on the Boston Harbor Islands, a group of idyllic offshore isles originally used as defense posts, but declared a national park in 1996 and subsequently opened to the public, accessible via regular ferries from Long Wharf.

The city's positive economic growth by the end of the twentieth century endowed a number of cultural institutions with funds to spruce up their digs; two of Boston's most intriguing libraries – the staid Boston Athenæum and the eccentric Mary Eddy Baker Library – reopened to the public in 2002, following substantial renovations. The most significant facelift, however, is taking place at the Museum of Fine Arts, where a recently inaugurated multi-million-dollar expansion project designed by renowned British architect Sir Norman Foster is slated for partial completion by 2009. Much to local fans' relief, Fenway Park, the country's oldest ballpark and home of the beloved Sox appears to have missed the chopping block, as plans to build a newer, more spacious stadium have been momentarily put to rest.

Architecture and urban planning

The land to which William Blackstone invited John Winthrop and his Puritans in 1630 bore almost no resemblance to the contemporary city of Boston. It was virtually an island, spanning a mere 785 acres, surrounded on all sides by murky swamps and connected to the mainland only by a narrow isthmus, "the Neck," that was almost entirely submerged at high tide. It was also very hilly: three peaks formed its geological backbone and gave it the name that Puritans used before they chose Boston – the Trimountain – echoed today in the name of Downtown's Tremont Street.

Colonial development

The first century and a half of Boston's existence saw a sleepy Puritan village slowly expand into one of the biggest shipping centers in the North American colonies. Narrow, crooked footpaths became busy commercial boulevards, though they retained their sinuous design, and the pasture-land of **Boston Common** became the place for public gatherings. By the end of the eighteenth century, Boston was faced with the dilemma of how to accommodate its growing population and thriving industry on a tiny geographical center; part of the answer was to create more land. This had been accomplished in Boston's early years almost accidentally, by means of a process known as wharving out. Owners of shoreside properties with wharves found that rocks and debris collected around the pilings, until eventually the wharves were on dry land, necessitating the building of more wharves further out to sea. In this way, Boston's shoreline moved slowly but inexorably outward.

Post-revolution development

Boston's first great building boom began in earnest following the American Revolution. **Harrison Gray Otis**'s company, the Mount Vernon Proprietors, razed Boston's three peaks to create tracts for new townhouses. The land from the tops of these hills was placed where Boston Common and the Charles River met to form a swamp, extending the shoreline out even farther to create what is now known as "the flat of the hill." Leftover land was used to fill some of the city's other coves and ponds, most significantly Mill Pond, near present-day North End. The completion of the Mount Vernon Proprietors' plans made the resulting area, Beacon Hill, the uncontested site for Boston's wealthy and elite to build their ideal home – as such, it holds the best examples of American architecture of the late-eighteenth and early nineteenth centuries, ranging in styles from Georgian to early Victorian.

This period also ushered in the first purely American architectural movement, the Federal style. Prime examples of its flat, dressed-down facades are prevalent in townhouses throughout Downtown and in Beacon Hill. **Charles Bulfinch** was its leading practitioner; his most famous work was the 1797 gold-domed Massachusetts State House looming over Boston Common, a prototype for state capitols to come. For more information on Bulfinch, see the box on p.85.

The expansion of the city

Boston continued to grow throughout the 1800s. Mayor Josiah Quincy oversaw the construction of a large marketplace, **Quincy Market**, behind the overcrowded Faneuil Hall building. These three oblong Greek Revival buildings pushed the Boston waterfront back several hundred yards, and the new surface area was used as the site for a symbol of Boston's maritime prosperity, the US Custom House. While Boston had codes prohibiting overly tall buildings, the Federal Government was not obligated to obey them, and the Custom House building, completed in 1847, rose a then-impressive sixteen stories.

Meanwhile, the city was trying to create enough land to match the demand for housing, in part by transforming its swampy backwaters into useable property. Back Bay, for example, was originally just that: a marsh along the banks of the Charles. In 1814, however, Boston began to dam the Charles, filling the resulting area with debris. When the project was completed in 1883, Back Bay quickly became one of Boston's choicest addresses, drawing some prominent families from their dwellings on Beacon Hill. The layout followed a highly ordered French model of city planning: gridded streets, with those running perpendicular to the Charles arranged alphabetically. The district's main boulevard, Commonwealth Avenue, surrounded a strip of greenery that terminated to the east in the Public Garden, a lush park completed by George Meachum in 1859, with ponds, statuary, weeping willows, and winding pathways that is the jewel of Back Bay, if not all Boston.

As if this weren't enough, Back Bay's Copley Square was also the site of numerous high-minded civic institutions built in the mid- and late-1800s, foremost among which were H.H. Richardson's Romanesque Trinity Church and the Public Library, a High Victorian creation of Charles McKim, of the noted firm McKim, Mead and White. But the most impressive accomplishment of the century was certainly Frederick Law Olmsted's **Emerald Necklace**, a system of parks that connected Boston Common, the Public Garden, and the Commonwealth Avenue Mall to his own creations a bit further off, such as the Back Bay Fens, Arnold Arboretum, and Franklin Park.

While Boston's civic expansion made life better for its upper classes, the middle and lower classes were crammed into the tiny Downtown area. The city's solution was to **annex** the surrounding districts, beginning with South Boston in 1807 and ending with Charlestown in 1873 – with the exception of Brookline, which remained a separate entity. Toward the end of the century, Boston's growing middle class moved to these surrounding areas, particularly the southern districts, which soon became known as the "streetcar suburbs." These areas, once the site of summer estates for the wealthy, were built over with one of Boston's least attractive architectural motifs: the three-decker. Also known as the "triple-decker," these clapboard rowhouses held a family on each floor – models of unattractive efficiency.

Modernization and preservation

New construction waned with the economic decline of the early 1900s, reaching its lowest point during the Great Depression. The streetcar suburbs were hardest hit – the white middle class migrated to Boston's nearby towns in the 1940s and 1950s, and the southern districts became run-down, low-rent areas. **Urban renewal** began in the late 1950s, with the idea of creating a visibly modern city, and while it provided Boston with an economic shot in the arm, the drastic changes erased some of the city's most distinctive architectural features. The porn halls and dive bars of Scollay Square were demolished to make way for the dull gray bureaucracy complexes of Government Center, while the West End, once one of Boston's liveliest ethnic neighborhoods, was flattened and covered over with high-rise office buildings. Worst of all, the new elevated John F. Fitzgerald Expressway (I-93) tore through Downtown, cutting off the North End and waterfront from the rest of the city. (Thankfully this eyesore – thanks to the Big Dig – is now underground.)

Following this period, the fury of displaced and disgruntled residents forced planners to create structures that either reused or integrated extant features of the city. The **John Hancock Tower**, designed by I.M. Pei and completed in 1975, originally outraged preservationists, as this Copley Square high-rise was being built right by some of the city's most treasured cultural landmarks; however, the tower managed a delicate balance – while it rises sixty stories smack in the middle of Back Bay, its narrow wedge shape renders it quite unobtrusive, and its mirrored walls literally reflect its stately surroundings. Quincy Market was also redeveloped and, by 1978, what had been a decaying, nearly defunct series of fishmongering stalls was transformed into a thriving tourist attraction. Boston's showiest architectural newcomer, the **Institute of Contemporary Art,** opened its glassy, cantilevered digs in 2006 and brought with it a whole slew of condo developers and restaurateurs eager to expand on the newly repackaged Seaport District. Subsequent development has, for the most part, kept up this theme, preserving the city's four thousand acres – and most crucially its Downtown – as a virtual library of American architecture.

Literary Boston in the 1800s

America's literary center has not always been New York; indeed, for much of the nineteenth century, Boston wore that mantle, and since then it has retained a somewhat bookish reputation despite no longer quite having the influence it once did on American publishing.

Puritanism and religious influence

John Winthrop and his fellow colonists who settled in the Boston area had a vision of a theocratic, utopian "City on a Hill." The Puritans were erudite and fairly well-off intellectuals, but religion always came first, even when writing: in fact, Winthrop himself penned *A Model of Christian Charity* while crossing the Atlantic. Religious sermons were the real literature of the seventeenth century – those and the now-forgotten explorations of **Reverend Cotton Mather** such as *The Wonders of the Invisible World*, a look at the supernatural that helped foment the Salem Witch Trials.

During the eighteenth century, in the years leading up to the Revolutionary War, Bostonians began to pour their energy into a different kind of sermon – that of anti-British sentiment, such as rants in radical newspapers like the *Boston Gazette*. Post-revolution, the stifling atmosphere of Puritanism remained to some extent – the city's first theater, for example, built in 1794, had to be billed as a "school of virtue" in order to remain open. But writers began to shake off Puritan restraints and explore their newfound freedom; in certain instances, they drew upon the repressiveness of the religion as a source of inspiration.

The transcendentalist movement

Ironically enough, Boston's deliverance from parochialism began in the countryside, specifically Concord, scene of the first battle of the Revolutionary War. The transcendentalist movement of the 1830s and 1840s, spearheaded by **Ralph Waldo Emerson**, was born of a passion for rural life, intellectual freedom, and belief in intuitive knowledge and experience as a way to enhance the relationship between man, nature, and the "over-soul." The free thinking the movement unleashed put local writers at the vanguard of American literary expression; articles by Emerson, Henry David Thoreau, Louisa May Alcott, Bronson Alcott (Louisa's father), and other members of the Concord coterie filled the pages of *The Dial*, the transcendentalist literary review, founded by Emerson around 1840 and edited by Margaret Fuller. Fuller, an early feminist, also wrote essays prodigiously; while Alcott penned the classic *Little Women*, and Thoreau authored his famous study in solitude, *Walden*. Meanwhile, a writer by the name of **Nathaniel Hawthorne**, known mainly for short stories like "Young Goodman Brown," published *The Scarlet Letter*, in 1850, a true schism with the past that examined the effects of the repressive Puritan lifestyle and legacy.

The abolitionist movement and literary salons

The **abolitionist movement** also helped push Boston into the literary limelight. Slavery had been outlawed in Massachusetts since 1783, and Boston attracted the likes of activist William Lloyd Garrison, who published his firebrand newspaper, *The Liberator*, in a small office Downtown beginning in 1831. Years later, in 1852, Harriet Beecher Stowe's slave narrative *Uncle Tom's Cabin* hit the printing press in Boston and sold more than 300,000 copies in its first year of publication. It, perhaps more than anything else, turned national public opinion against slavery, despite the fact that its writer was a New Englander with little first-hand knowledge of the South or the slave trade.

Another Bostonian involved with the abolitionist cause was John Greenleaf Whittier, who also happened to be among the founding members of Emerson's famed "Saturday Club," the name given to a series of informal literary gatherings that took place at the Omni *Parker House Hotel* beginning in 1855. Oliver Wendell Holmes and poet Henry Wadsworth Longfellow were among the moneyed regulars at these salons, which metamorphosed two years later into *The Atlantic Monthly*, from its inception a respected literary and political journal. One of its more accomplished editors, William Dean Howells, wrote *The Rise of Silas Lapham*, in 1878, a novel on the culture of commerce that set the stage for American Realism. Around the same time, more literary salons were being held at the Old Corner Bookstore, down the street from the Parker House, where leading publisher Ticknor & Fields had their headquarters. Regulars included not only the likes of Emerson and Longfellow, but visiting British authors like William Thackeray and Charles Dickens, who were not only published by the house as well, but also friends with its charismatic leader, Jamie T. Fields. Meanwhile, Longfellow was well on his way to becoming America's most popular poet, writing "*The Midnight Ride of Paul Revere*," among much other verse, while a professor at Harvard University.

The end of an era

In the last burst of Boston's literary high tide, sometimes resident **Henry James** recorded the sedate lives of the moneyed – and miserable – elite in his books *Watch and Ward* (1871) and *The Bostonians* (1886). His renunciation of hedonism was well-suited to the stifling atmosphere of Brahmin Boston, where well-appointed homes were heavily curtained so as to avoid exposure to sunlight; however, his look at the emerging battle of the sexes was in fact fueled by the liberty-loving principles of Emerson and colleagues in Concord thirty years before.

The fact that Boston's literary society was largely a members-only club contributed to its eventual undoing. **Edgar Allen Poe** slammed his hometown as "Frogpondium," in reference to the Saturday Club-style chumminess of its literati. Provincialism reared its head in the Watch & Ward Society, which as late as 1878 instigated boycotts of books and plays it deemed out of the bounds of common decency, spawning the phrase "Banned in Boston." To many observers, Howells's departure from *The Atlantic Monthly* in 1885 to write for *Harper's* in New York signaled the end of Boston's literary golden age.

Books

In the reviews below, publishers are listed in the format US/UK, unless the title is only available in one country, in which case the country has been specified. Highly recommended titles are signified by 🏃. Out-of-print titles are indicated by o/p.

History and biography

Cleveland Amory *The Proper Bostonians* (Parnassus Imprints US). First published in 1947, this surprisingly upbeat volume remains the definitive social history of Boston's old–money aristocracy.

Jack Beatty *The Rascal King: The Life and Times of James Michael Curley, 1874–1958* (Addison Wesley US o/p). A thick and thoroughly researched biography of the charismatic Boston mayor and Bay State governor; valuable too for its depiction of big-city politics in America.

David Hackett Fischer *Paul Revere's Ride* (University of Massachusetts Press/Oxford University Press US/ UK). An exhaustive account of the patriot's legendary ride to Lexington, related as a historical narrative.

Jonathan Harr *A Civil Action* (Vintage Books US). The story of eight families in the community of Woburn, just north of Boston, who took a major chemical company to court in 1981, after a spate of leukemia cases raised suspicion about the purity of the area's water supply; made into a movie starring John Travolta in 1998.

Sebastian Junger *The Perfect Storm* (HarperCollins US). A nail-biting account of the fate of the *Andrea Gail*, a six-man swordfishing boat from Gloucester caught in the worst storm in recorded history; later turned into a movie starring George Clooney in 2000.

🏃 **Jonathan Kozol** *Death at an Early Age: The Destruction of the Hearts and Minds of Negro Children*

in the Boston Public Schools (Penguin US). Winner of the National Book Award, this is an intense portrait of prejudice and corruption in Boston's 1964 educational system.

🏃 **J. Anthony Lukas** *Common Ground: A Turbulent Decade in the Lives of Three American Families* (Vintage US). A Pulitzer Prize-winning account of three Boston families – one Irish-American, one black, one white middle-class – against the backdrop of the 1974 race riots sparked by court-ordered busing to desegregate public schools.

Michael Patrick MacDonald *All Souls: A Family Story from Southie* (Beacon Press US). A moving memoir of growing up in South Boston in the 1970s among the sometimes life-threatening racial, ethnic, class, and political tensions of the time.

🏃 **Louis Menand** *Metaphysical Club* (Farrar, Strauss & Giroux US). Arguably the most engaging study of Boston heavyweights Oliver Wendell Holmes, William James, Charles Sanders Pierce, and John Dewey ever written, this Pulitzer Prize-winning biography links the foursome through a short-lived 1872 Cambridge salon (the book's title), and extols the effect of their pragmatic idealism on American intellectual thought.

Mary Beth Norton *In the Devil's Snare: The Salem Witchcraft Crisis of 1692* (Knopf US). Analysis of the witchcraft accusations and executions in and around Salem in 1692; collecting newly available trial evidence, correspondence, and papers, Norton argues that the crisis must be understood in the context of the horrors of the Second Indian War, which was being waged at the time in the area around Salem.

Mark Kurlansky *Cod* (Penguin). Does a fish merit this much obsessive attention? Perhaps only in New England, and Kurlansky makes a good case for viewing the cod as one of the more integral parts of the region's fabric.

Douglass Shand-Tucci *The Art of Scandal: The Life and Times of Isabella Stewart Gardner* (HarperCollins US). Astute biography of this doyenne of Boston society, who served as the inspiration for Isabel Archer in

Henry James's *Portrait of a Lady*. The book includes evocative photos of Fenway Courtyard in Gardner's Venetian-style palace – which is now the Gardner Museum.

Dan Shaughnessy *The Curse of the Bambino* (Penguin US). Shaughnessy, a Boston sportswriter, gives an entertaining look at the Red Sox's "curse" – no championships for 86 years – that began after they sold Babe Ruth to the Yankees. His *At Fenway: Dispatches from Red Sox Nation* (Crown Publishing US) is another memoir of a Red Sox fan.

Hiller B. Zobel *The Boston Massacre* (W.W. Norton US). A painstaking account of the circumstances that precipitated one of the most highly propagandized pre-Revolution events – the slaying of five Bostonians outside the Old State House.

Guidebooks

Charles Bahne *The Complete Guide to Boston's Freedom Trail* (Newtowne Publishing US). Unlike most souvenir guides of the Freedom Trail, which have lots of pictures but little substance, this one is chock full of engaging historical tidbits on the stories behind the sights.

John Harris *Historic Walks in Old Boston* (Globe Pequot US). In most cases, you'll be walking in the footsteps of long-gone luminaries, but Harris infuses his accounts with enough lively history to keep things moving along at an interesting clip.

Walt Kelley *What They Never Told You About Boston (Or What They Did*

Were Lies) (Down East Books US). Who would have guessed that in 1632, Puritans passed the world's first law against smoking in public? This slim book is full of such engaging Boston trivia.

Thomas H. O'Connor *Boston A to Z* (Harvard University Press US). This terrific, often irreverent, guide to the Hub will give you the low-down on local hotshots from John Adams to "Honey Fitz," institutions like the Holy Cross Cathedral and the L Street Bathhouse, and local lore on everything from baked beans to the Steaming Kettle.

Architecture, urban planning, and photography

Philip Bergen *Old Boston in Early Photographs 1850–1918* (Dover Publications US). Fascinating stuff, including a photographic

record of Back Bay's transition from swampland to swanky residential neighborhood.

Robert Campbell and Peter Vanderwarker *Cityscapes of Boston: An American City Through Time* (Houghton Mifflin US). An informative pictorial tome with some excellent photos of old and new Boston.

Charles Haglund *Inventing The Charles River* (MIT Press US). The past, present, and future of this artificially created river.

Jane Holtz Kay *Lost Boston* (Houghton Mifflin US). A photographic essay of long-gone architectural treasures.

Alex Krieger, David Cobb, Amy Turner, and Norman B. Leventhal (eds) *Mapping Boston* (MIT Press US). Irresistible to any map-lover, this thoughtfully compiled book combines essays with all manner of historical maps to help trace Boston's conception and development.

Barbara Moore and Gail Weesner *Back Bay: A Living Portrait* (Centry Hill Press US). If you're dying to know what Back Bay's brownstones

look – and looked – like inside, this book of hard-to-find photos is for you. They do a similar book on Beacon Hill.

Nancy Seasholes *Gaining Ground* (MIT Press US). A wonderful piece explaining just why Boston is 75 percent landfill. Marvel at how much was done in post-Puritan times to radically change the city's landscape.

🏃 Susan and Michael Southworth *AIA Guide to Boston* (Globe Pequot US). The definitive guide to Boston architecture, organized by neighborhood. City landmarks and dozens of notable buildings are given exhaustive but readable coverage.

Walter Muir Whitehill *Boston: A Topographical History* (Harvard University Press US). How Boston went from a tiny seaport on the Shawmut Peninsula to the city it is today, with detailed descriptions of the city's many land-reclaiming projects.

Fiction and drama

Margaret Atwood *The Handmaid's Tale* (Anchor Books US). Cambridge's Ivy League setting inspired the mythical Republic of Gilead, the post-nuclear fallout backdrop for this harrowing tale about women whose lives' purpose is solely reproduction.

James Carroll *The City Below* (Houghton Mifflin US). Gripping historical novel of later-twentieth-century Boston, centered on two Irish brothers from Charlestown.

Michael Crichton *A Case of Need* (Signet US). Written long before Crichton conceived of "ER" or even *Jurassic Park*, this gripping whodunnit opens with a woman nearly bleeding

to death on the operating table of a Boston hospital; she goes on to accuse her physician of attempted murder, and finds a trusty colleague trying to get at the truth of the affair.

Nick Flynn *Another Bullshit Night In Suck City: A Memoir* (W.W. Norton & Company). As well as having one of the best titles in literature (derived from a phrase used by Flynn's father to describe nights on the street), this book is an elegant depiction of the author's relationship with his homeless father, a sometime resident of Boston's *Pine Street Inn*.

🏃 Nathaniel Hawthorne *The Scarlet Letter* (Signet Classic US). Puritan New England comes to life, in all its mirthless repressiveness, starring the adulterous Hester Prynne.

William Dean Howells *The Rise of Silas Lapham* (Viking Press US). This 1878 novel was the forerunner to American Realism. Howells's less-than-enthralling tale of a well-off Vermont businessman's failed entry into Boston's old-moneyed Brahmin caste gives a good early portrait of a uniquely American hero: the self-made man.

Henry James *The Bostonians* (Viking Press US). James's soporific satire traces the relationship of Olive Chancellor and Verena Tarrant, two fictional feminists in the 1870s.

🏃 **Dennis Lehane** *Darkness Take My Hand* (Avon Books US). Perhaps the best in Lehane's Boston-set mystery series; two private investigators tackle a serial killer, the Boston Mafia, and their Dorchester upbringing in this atmospheric thriller.

Michael Lowenthal *The Same Embrace* (Plume US). A young man comes out to his Jewish, Bostonian parents after his twin brother disowns him for his homosexuality; courageous and complex.

John Marquand *The Late George Appley* (Buccaneer Books US o/p). Winner of the 1937 Pulitzer Prize, this novel satirizes a New England gentry on the wane.

Carole Maso *Defiance* (Plume US). A Harvard professor sits on death row after having murdered a pair of her own star students, in this fragmentary, moving confessional.

Arthur Miller *The Crucible* (Penguin US). This compelling play about the 1692 Salem witch trials is peppered with quotes from actual court transcripts and loaded with appropriate levels of hysteria and fervor.

Sue Miller *While I Was Gone* (Ballantine US). An emotional psychodrama centered on a middle-aged woman who spends time under an assumed name in a Cambridge commune, while on the run from her husband.

Susan Minot *Folly* (Washington Square Press US). This obvious nod to Edith Wharton's *Age of Innocence* is set in 1917 Boston instead of New York, and details the proclivities of the Brahmin era, in which women were expected to marry well, and the heartbreak that ensues from making the wrong choice.

🏃 **Edwin O'Connor** *The Last Hurrah* (Little, Brown US o/p). Fictionalized account of Boston mayor James Michael Curley, starring a 1950s corrupt politician; the book was so popular that the bar at the *Omni Parker House* hotel was named after it.

Ann Patchett *Run* (Harper US). An engaging tale that centers on Doyle, a widower and former Boston mayor, who raises three sons (including two adopted African American boys) on his own and pushes them to follow in his politicking footsteps. The novel contains a number of luminous Boston scenes, including a particularly evocative excerpt set in the Harvard Museum of Natural History.

Sylvia Plath *The Bell Jar* (Harper Perennial USA). Angst-ridden, dark, cynical – everything a teenaged girl wants out of a book. The second half of this brilliant (if disturbing) autobiographical novel about Esther Greenwood's mental breakdown is set in the Boston suburbs, where she ends up institutionalized.

🏃 **George Santayana** *The Last Puritan* (MIT Press US). The philosopher's brilliant "memoir in the form of a novel," set around Boston, chronicles the short life and education of protagonist Oliver Alden coming to grips with Puritanism.

C

Erich Segal *Love Story* (Avon US). This sappy story about the love affair between Oliver Barrett IV, a successful Harvard student born with a silver spoon in his mouth, and Jenny Cavilleri, a Radcliffe music student who's had to struggle for everything, has the uncanny ability to captivate even the most jaded reader; made into a movie in 1970.

Jean Stafford *Boston Adventure* (Harcourt Brace US). Narrated by a poverty-stricken young girl who gets taken in by a wealthy elderly woman, this long – but rewarding – novel portrays upper-class Boston in all its magnificence and malevolence.

Henry David Thoreau *Cape Cod; Walden* (Penguin US). *Walden* is basically a transcript of Thoreau's attempt to put his transcendentalist philosophy into practice, by constructing a cabin on the banks of Walden Pond, in Concord, Massachusetts, and living the simplest of lives based on self-reliance, individualism, spiritual enlightenment, and material frugality. Nature also plays a part in *Cape Cod*, an account of the writer's walking trips published after his death.

David Foster Wallace *Infinite Jest* (Little, Brown US). Sprawling magnum opus concerning a video that eliminates all viewers' desire to do anything but watch said video. Many of the book's best passages take place at Enfield, a fictional tennis academy set outside Boston; another plot line involves a Canadian terrorist separatist cell in Cambridge.

William F. Weld *Mackerel by Moonlight* (Pocket Books US). The former federal prosecutor and governor of Massachusetts turns his hand to writing, in this uneven – though not unworthy – political mystery.

Local accent and jargon

Boston has a language all its own, plus a truly unmistakable regional accent. One of Boston's most recognizable cultural idiosyncrasies is its strain of American English, distinguished by a tendency to drop one's "r"s, as on the T-shirts that exhort you to "Pahk the cah in Havvid Yahd" ("Park the car in Harvard Yard"). Enlightened readers take note – Harvard Yard is not a parking lot, and locals will be quick to school you if you utilize this locally annoying expression around them. Listen, too, for the greeting "How ah ya?" ("How are you?") or the genial assent, "shuah" ("Sure").

These lost "r"s crop up elsewhere, usually when words that end in "a" are followed by words that begin in a vowel – as in "I've got no idear about that." When the nasal "a" (as in "cat") is not followed by an "r", it can take on a soft, almost British tenor: "after" becomes "ahfta." And the "aw" sound (as in "body") is inverted, like "wa": "god" becomes "gwad."

If in doubt, the surest way to fit in with the locals is to use the word "wicked" as an adverb at every opportunity: "Joo guys see the Celts game lahst night? Theah gonna be wicked wasome this yeah!" What follows is a glossary of sorts for proper terms, slang, and jargon in and around Boston.

Terms and acronyms

BC Boston College

Beantown Nickname for Boston – a reference to the local specialty, Boston baked beans – that no one uses any longer.

The Big Dig The project to put the elevated highway I-93 underground.

Brahmin An old-money Beacon Hill aristocrat.

BU Boston University.

Bubbler Water fountain.

C-town/Chuck-town Nickname for Charlestown.

The Cape Shorthand for Cape Cod.

The Central Artery The stretch of I-93 that runs underground through Downtown; before the Big Dig, it was an elevated expressway that separated the North End and the water-front from the rest of the city.

Colonial Style of Neoclassical architecture popular in the seventeenth and eighteenth centuries.

Comm Ave Commonwealth Avenue.

Dot Ave Dorchester Avenue.

Federal Hybrid of French and Roman architecture popular in the late-eighteenth and early nineteenth centuries.

Frappe Milkshake (meaning milk, ice cream, and syrup) – the "e" is silent. Order a milkshake in Boston and you'll likely get milk flavored with syrup – distinctly devoid of ice cream.

Georgian Architectural style popular during the late-colonial period; highly ornamental and rigidly symmetrical.

Greek Revival Style of architecture that mimicked that of classical Greece. Popular for banks and larger houses in the early nineteenth century.

Grinder A sandwich made of deli meats, cheese, and condiments on a long roll or bun. Less used now as the more ubiquitous "sub" takes over.

Hamburg Ground beef sans bun. Add an "–er" at the end for the classic American sandwich.

Hub Like Beantown, a nickname for Boston not really used anymore.

JP Jamaica Plain.

Ladder District (formerly the Combat Zone). Just north of Chinatown, the once-busy strip of Washington Street designated for adult entertainment has been renamed the Ladder District, after its street grid's resemblance to a multi-runged ladder.

Mass Ave Massachusetts Avenue.

MBTA (Massachusetts Bay Transportation Authority) The agency in charge of all public transit – buses, subways, commuter trains, and ferries.

MGH Massachusetts General Hospital; also, "Mass General."

Packie Liquor store (many signs say "Package Store").

The People's Republic Another name for Cambridge, thanks to the liberal attitude of its residents.

The Pike The Massachusetts Turnpike (I-90); also, "Mass Pike."

Pissa Bostonian for "cool." Sometimes used with "wicked, ie "wicked pissa," meaning double good.

The Pit Sunken area next to Harvard Square where skaters hang out.

P-town Provincetown.

Scrod Somewhat of a distasteful generic name for cod or haddock. Almost always served breaded and sold cheap.

Southie South Boston.

The T Catch-all for Boston's subway system.

Three-decker Three-story house, with each floor a separate apartment. Also called a "triple-decker."

Townie Originally a term for residents of Charlestown, it now refers to long-term residents of Boston and its outlying suburbs, most readily identified by their heavy accents.

Victorian Style of architecture from the mid- to late-1800s that is highly eclectic and ornamental.

Wicked The definitive word in the Bostonian patois, still used to intensify adjectives, as in "wicked good."

Travel store

Small print and
Index

A Rough Guide to Rough Guides

Published in 1982, the first Rough Guide – to Greece – was a student scheme that became a publishing phenomenon. Mark Ellingham, a recent graduate in English from Bristol University, had been traveling in Greece the previous summer and couldn't find the right guidebook. With a small group of friends he wrote his own guide, combining a highly contemporary, journalistic style with a thoroughly practical approach to travelers' needs.

The immediate success of the book spawned a series that rapidly covered dozens of destinations. And, in addition to impecunious backpackers, Rough Guides soon acquired a much broader and older readership that relished the guides' wit and inquisitiveness as much as their enthusiastic, critical approach and value-for-money ethos.

These days, Rough Guides include recommendations from shoestring to luxury and cover more than 200 destinations around the globe, including almost every country in the Americas and Europe, more than half of Africa and most of Asia and Australasia. Our ever-growing team of authors and photographers is spread all over the world, particularly in Europe, the USA and Australia.

In the early 1990s, Rough Guides branched out of travel, with the publication of Rough Guides to World Music, Classical Music and the Internet. All three have become benchmark titles in their fields, spearheading the publication of a wide range of books under the Rough Guide name.

SMALL PRINT

Including the travel series, Rough Guides now number more than 350 titles, covering: phrasebooks, waterproof maps, music guides from Opera to Heavy Metal, reference works as diverse as Conspiracy Theories and Shakespeare, and popular culture books from iPods to Poker. Rough Guides also produce a series of more than 120 World Music CDs in partnership with World Music Network.

Visit www.roughguides.com to see our latest publications.

Rough Guide travel images are available for commercial licensing at www.roughguidespictures.com

Rough Guide credits

Text editor: Stephen Timblin
Layout: Nikhil Agarwal, Pradeep Thapliyal
Cartography: Animesh Pathak
Picture editor: Nicole Newman
Production: Rebecca Short
Proofreader: Andy McCulloch
Cover design: Chloë Roberts
Photographer: Susannah Sayler, Angus Oborn
Editorial: **London** Kate Berens, Claire Saunders, Ruth Blackmore, Alison Murchie, Karoline Densley, Andy Turner, Keith Drew, Edward Aves, Alice Park, Lucy White, Jo Kirby, James Smart, Natasha Foges, Róisín Cameron, Emma Traynor, Emma Gibbs, Kathryn Lane, Christina Valhouli, Joe Staines, Peter Buckley, Matthew Milton, Tracy Hopkins, Ruth Tidball; **New York** Andrew Rosenberg, Steven Horak, AnneLise Sorensen, April Isaacs, Ella Steim, Anna Owens, Sean Mahoney; **Delhi** Madhavi Singh, Karen D'Souza
Design & Pictures: **London** Scott Stickland, Dan May, Diana Jarvis, Mark Thomas, Chloë Roberts, Sarah Cummins, Emily Taylor; **Delhi** Umesh Aggarwal, Ajay Verma, Jessica

Subramanian, Ankur Guha, Sachin Tanwar, Anita Singh
Production: Vicky Baldwin
Cartography: **London** Maxine Repath, Ed Wright, Katie Lloyd-Jones; **Delhi** Jai Prakash Mishra, Rajesh Chhibber, Ashutosh Bharti, Rajesh Mishra, Jasbir Sandhu, Karobi Gogoi, Amod Singh, Alakananda Bhattacharya, Swati Handoo
Online: Narender Kumar, Rakesh Kumar, Amit Verma, Rahul Kumar, Ganesh Sharma, Debojit Borah, Saurabh Sati
Marketing & Publicity: **London** Liz Statham, Niki Hanmer, Louise Maher, Jess Carter, Vanessa Godden, Vivienne Watton, Anna Paynton, Rachel Sprackett; **New York** Geoff Colquitt, Megan Kennedy, Katy Ball; **Delhi** Ragini Govind
Manager India: Punita Singh
Reference Director: Andrew Lockett
Publishing Coordinator: Helen Phillips
Publishing Director: Martin Dunford
Commercial Manager: Gino Magnotta
Managing Director: John Duhigg

Publishing information

This fifth edition published April 2008 by
Rough Guides Ltd,
80 Strand, London WC2R 0RL
345 Hudson St, 4th Floor,
New York, NY 10014, USA
14 Local Shopping Centre, Panchsheel Park,
New Delhi 110017, India
Distributed by the Penguin Group
Penguin Books Ltd,
80 Strand, London WC2R 0RL
Penguin Group (USA)
375 Hudson Street, NY 10014, USA
Penguin Group (Australia)
250 Camberwell Road, Camberwell,
Victoria 3124, Australia
Penguin Books Canada Ltd,
10 Alcorn Avenue, Toronto, Ontario,
Canada M4V 1E4
Penguin Group (NZ)
67 Apollo Drive, Mairangi Bay, Auckland 1310,
New Zealand

Cover concept by Peter Dyer.
Typeset in Bembo and Helvetica to an original design by Henry Iles.
Printed and bound in China
© Rough Guides Ltd 2008
No part of this book may be reproduced in any form without permission from the publisher except for the quotation of brief passages in reviews.
320pp includes index
A catalogue record for this book is available from the British Library
ISBN: 978-1-84353-860-8

1 3 5 7 9 8 6 4 2

Help us update

We've gone to a lot of effort to ensure that the fifth edition of **The Rough Guide to Boston** is accurate and up to date. However, things change – places get "discovered", opening hours are notoriously fickle, restaurants and rooms raise prices or lower standards. If you feel we've got it wrong or left something out, we'd like to know, and if you can remember the address, the price, the hours, the phone number, so much the better.

Please send your comments with the subject line "**Rough Guide Boston Update**" to ©mail @roughguides.com. We'll credit all contributions and send a copy of the next edition (or any other Rough Guide if you prefer) for the very best emails.

Have your questions answered and tell others about your trip at
ⓦ community.roughguides.com

SMALL PRINT

ROUGH GUIDES

Acknowledgements

Sarah Hull thanks Stephen Timblin for being an all-around fantastic editor – funny, smart, and a begrudging friend of the Red Sox – and to Steven Horak for eternal patience and kindness. My never-ending devotion goes to Ranger Manson at the NPS, historic savior and a great guy; Carter Long, MFA friend and drinking partner; Nina Cassel in Cape Ann; Gabe at Straight Wharf in Nantucket, KG and LD in MV, Veronika V, Karen Goodno in Salem, my family, Dan

Shaughnessy, and David Ortiz. To my Stuart Smalleys: Amber, Ali, and Handel. And to Paul Snyder, for articulating the whale.

The editor wishes to thank Nikhil Agarwal and Pradeep Thapliyal for layout, Animesh Pathak for the maps, Nicole Newman for selecting the photos, Andy McCulloch for proofreading, and Jim Tressel for the mental hemorrhoids and premature graying.

Photo credits

All photos © Rough Guides except the following:

Full Page
Rowes Wharf Arch at twilight © Daniella Nowtiz /Corbis

Things not to miss
02 Symphony Hall © Michael J. Lutch/redferns
10 Fenway Park © Cindy Loo/Boston Red Sox
18 The Factory, by Preston Dickinson, Boston Museum of Fine Arts © Burstein Collection /Corbis

The sporting life color section
Fenway Park © Cindy Loo/Boston Red Sox
Paul Pierce of the Boston Celtics © Jeff Lewis/Icon SMI/Corbis
Harvard University rowing crew at the autumn regatta in Cambridge © Visions of America, LLC/Alamy

Yankee cooking (and drinking) color section
Glass of Samuel Adams Beer © Dave Bartruff /Corbis

Black and whites
p.192 Avalon dance club © John Coletti/ photolibrary
p.216 Boston Marathon © Timothy A. Clary/ AFP/Getty Images
p.224 Boston Gay Pride Parade © Darren McCollester/Getty Images
p.277 Nashaquitsa Pond on Martha's Vineyard © Walter Bibikow/Corbis

ROUGH
GUIDES

SMALL PRINT

Index

Map entries are in color.

Map symbols

maps are listed in the full index using colored text

▬ ▬ ···	State boundary	◉	Accommodation
▬▬▬	Expressway	⊠	Gate
═══	Main road	⊙	Statue
══	Minor road	ⵣ	Gardens
▬▬▬	Pedestrianized road	Ⓣ	T system station
▬·▬·▬	Railway	ⓘ	Information office
– – –	Ferry route	⊞	Hospital
────	Waterway	⊠	Post office
⌣⌣	Bridge	⚑	Church
𝍢	Lighthouse	▮	Building
✈	International airport	⊞	Church (town maps)
◆	Point of interest	▨	Park
🏛	Monument	▦	Beach
♀	Museum	⊡	Cemetery

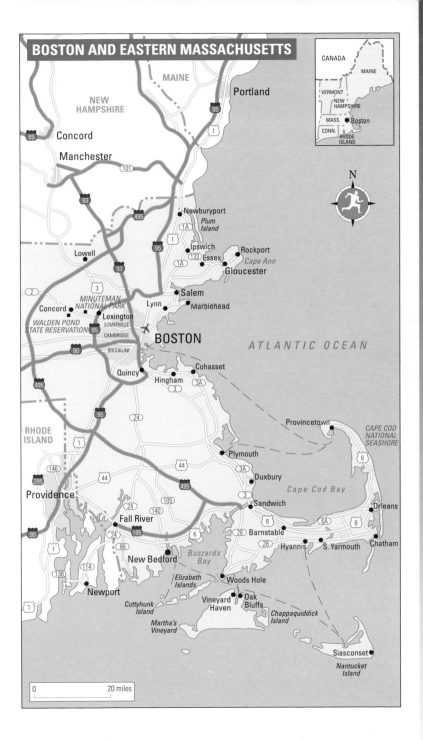

BOSTON AND EASTERN MASSACHUSETTS

CANADA

MAINE

VERMONT

NEW HAMPSHIRE

MASS. • Boston

CONN.

RHODE ISLAND

MAINE

Portland

NEW HAMPSHIRE

Concord

Manchester

89

95

1

101

95

93

Newburyport

Plum Island

1A

1

Ipswich

Rockport

Lowell

133

Essex

Cape Ann

93

1A

Gloucester

2

3

Salem

MINUTEMAN NATIONAL PARK

Lynn

Marblehead

Concord

Lexington

SOMERVILLE

WALDEN POND STATE RESERVATION

95

CAMBRIDGE

BOSTON

ATLANTIC OCEAN

90

BROOKLINE

Quincy

Cohasset

Hingham

3A

3

495

24

Provincetown

CAPE COD NATIONAL SEASHORE

95

Plymouth

6

RHODE ISLAND

44

3A

Duxbury

Providence

146

44

495

105

3

Sandwich

Cape Cod Bay

295

24

140

6

Orleans

Fall River

6

28

Barnstable

6A

6

1

195

New Bedford

24

88

Buzzards Bay

28

Hyannis

S. Yarmouth

Chatham

1

138

114

Elizabeth Islands

Woods Hole

Newport

Cuttyhunk Island

Vineyard Haven

Oak Bluffs

Chappaquiddick Island

1

Martha's Vineyard

Siasconset

Nantucket Island

N

0   20 miles

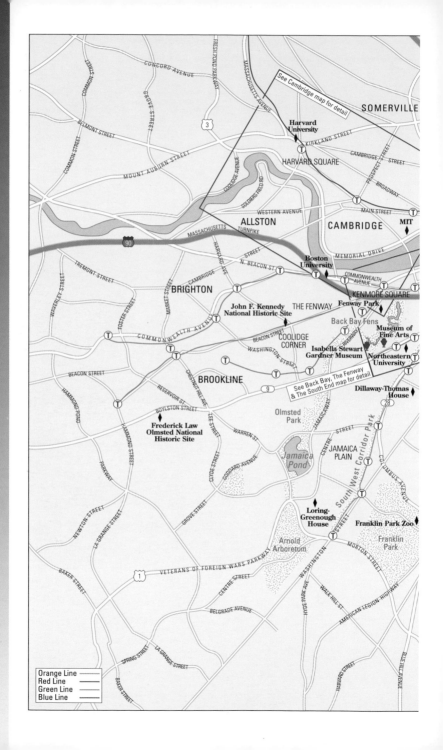

SOMERVILLE

See Cambridge map for detail

Harvard
University

KIRKLAND STREET

CAMBRIDGE STREET

HARVARD SQUARE

CONCORD AVENUE

FRESH POND PARKWAY

MASSACHUSETTS AVENUE

GROVE STREET

JAMES STREET

BELMONT STREET

COMMON STREET

COMMON STREET

3

MOUNT AUBURN STREET

SOLDIERS FIELD RD

COOLIDGE AVENUE

WESTERN AVENUE

MAIN STREET

PROSPECT STREET

BROADWAY

ALLSTON

CAMBRIDGE

MIT

MEMORIAL DRIVE

MASSACHUSETTS TURNPIKE

90

HARVARD AVE

N. BEACON ST

Boston
University

COMMONWEALTH AVENUE

TREMONT STREET

CAMBRIDGE STREET

BRIGHTON

KENMORE SQUARE

WAVERLEY STREET

FOSTER STREET

COMMONWEALTH AVENUE

John F. Kennedy
National Historic Site

THE FENWAY

Fenway Park

Back Bay Fens

Museum of
Fine Arts

BEACON STREET

COOLIDGE
CORNER

WASHINGTON STREET

Isabella Stewart
Gardner Museum

Northeastern
University

BEACON STREET

RESERVOIR ST

CHESTNUT HILL AVE

BROOKLINE

9

See Back Bay, The Fenway
& The South End map for detail

Dillaway-Thomas
House

28

HAMMOND STREET

HAMMOND POND

BOYLSTON STREET

LEE STREET

CLYDE STREET

WARREN ST

Olmsted
Park

JAMAICAWAY

CENTRE STREET

South West Corridor Park

COLUMBUS AVENUE

Frederick Law
Olmsted National
Historic Site

Jamaica
Pond

JAMAICA
PLAIN

PARKWAY

NEWTON STREET

LA GRANGE STREET

GROVE STREET

GODDARD AVENUE

Loring-
Greenough
House

SOUTH STREET

Franklin Park Zoo

Franklin
Park

MORTON STREET

Arnold
Arboretum

WASHINGTON STREET

HYDE PARK AVE

WALK HILL ST

AMERICAN LEGION HIGHWAY

BAKER STREET

1

VETERANS OF FOREIGN WARS PARKWAY

CENTRE STREET

BELGRADE AVENUE

SPRING STREET

LA GRANGE STREET

BAKER STREET

HARVARD STREET

BLUE HILL AVENUE

Orange Line
Red Line
Green Line
Blue Line

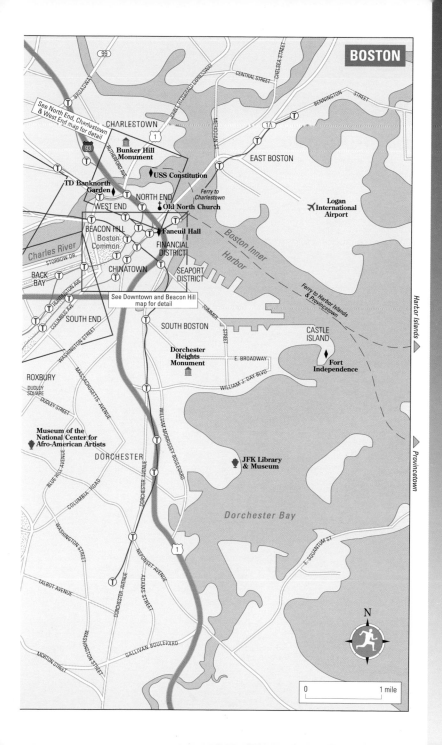

BOSTON

99

CENTRAL STREET

CHELSEA STREET

BENNINGTON STREET

See North End, Charlestown & West End map for detail

CHARLESTOWN

1

BROADWAY

Bunker Hill Monument

RUTHERFORD AVE

93

USS Constitution

EAST BOSTON

1A

MERIDIAN ST

TD Banknorth Garden

NORTH END

Ferry to Charlestown

WEST END

Old North Church

Logan International Airport

BEACON HILL

Faneuil Hall

Boston Common

FINANCIAL DISTRICT

Boston Inner Harbor

Charles River

STORROW DR.

CHINATOWN

SEAPORT DISTRICT

Ferry to Harbor Islands & Provincetown

BACK BAY

HUNTINGTON AVE

See Downtown and Beacon Hill map for detail

SOUTH BOSTON

CASTLE ISLAND

SOUTH END

COLUMBUS AVE

WASHINGTON STREET

SUMMER STREET

Dorchester Heights Monument

E. BROADWAY

Fort Independence

WILLIAM J. DAY BLVD.

ROXBURY

MASSACHUSETTS AVENUE

DUDLEY SQUARE

DUDLEY STREET

WILLIAM MORRISSEY BOULEVARD

Museum of the National Center for Afro-American Artists

BLUE HILL AVENUE

DORCHESTER

COLUMBIA ROAD

DORCHESTER AVENUE

JFK Library & Museum

WASHINGTON STREET

NEPONSET AVENUE

Dorchester Bay

1

E. SQUANTUM ST.

TALBOT AVENUE

WASHINGTON STREET

ADAMS STREET

N

MORTON STREET

GALLIVAN BOULEVARD

0   1 mile

Harbor Islands ▷

▷ *Provincetown*

WEST END

Massachusetts General Hospital

CARDINAL O'CONNELL WAY

NEW CHARDON STREET
BOWKER ST

T BOWDOIN

FRUIT STREET
PARKMAN ST

BRIDGE CT
ADAMS PL

Harrison Gray Otis House

CAMBRIDGE STREET

CHARLES
T

SMITH CT

Museum of African American History & Abiel Smith School

African Meeting House

Lewis Hayden House

George Middleton House

Community Boat House

BEACON HILL

Ashburton Park

Boston Athenæum

The Phillips School

Nichols House

Massachusetts State House

LOUISBURG SQUARE

Old Granary Burying Ground

Park Street Church

PINCKNEY STREET

MOUNT VERNON STREET

Church of the Advent

Charles Street Meeting House

Somerset Club

Robert Gould Shaw Memorial

PARK STREET

Hatch Shell

BRANCH STREET

BEACON STREET

Frog Pond

Visitor Center i

WINTER

Founder's Monument

Great Elm Site

TEMPLE PL

Flagstaff Hill

WEST STREET

Cheers

BEACON STREET

Soldiers and Sailors Monument

HARLEM PL

28

Public Garden

Boston Common

Boston Massacre Monument

The Opera House

Gibson House Museum

George Washington Statue

Swan Boats

Central Burying Ground

Millennium Place

AVERY ST

Baylies Mansion

COMMONWEALTH AVE

28

BOYLSTON
T

BOYLSTON

CHINATOWN
T

BACK BAY

Emmanuel Church of Boston

2

2 ARLINGTON
T

Colonial Theatre

LADDER DISTRICT

Cutler Majestic Theatre

KNEELAND

Church of the Covenant

Arlington Street Church

Boston Park Plaza

Massachusetts Transportation Building

THEATER DISTRICT

Wilbur Theatre

Charles Playhouse

Shubert Theatre

Wang Center for the Performing Arts

John Hancock Tower

BAY VILLAGE

NEW ENGLAND T MEDICAL CENTER

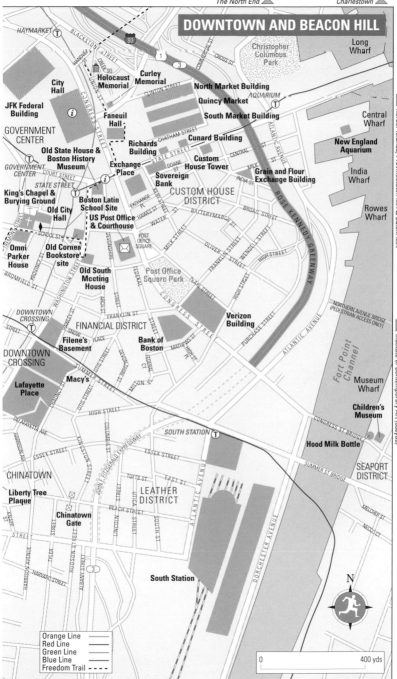

The North End ▲   Charlestown ▲

DOWNTOWN AND BEACON HILL

HAYMARKET Ⓣ

BLACKSTONE STREET

93

CROSS ST

COMMERCIAL ST

Christopher Columbus Park

Long Wharf

HANOVER STREET

CREEK SQ.

1

3

CONGRESS STREET

City Hall

Holocaust Memorial

Curley Memorial

North Market Building

CLINTON STREET

Quincy Market

AQUARIUM Ⓣ

ATLANTIC AVENUE

Central Wharf

JFK Federal Building

ⓘ

Faneuil Hall

South Market Building

GOVERNMENT CENTER

Richards Building

CHATHAM STREET

Cunard Building

CENTRAL ST

New England Aquarium

Old State House & Boston History Museum

STATE STREET

Exchange Place

Custom House Tower

MILK ST

Grain and Flour Exchange Building

India Wharf

GOVERNMENT CENTER

COURT STREET

DOANE ST

Sovereign Bank

INDIA ST

STATE STREET

ⓘ

EXCHANGE PL

CUSTOM HOUSE DISTRICT

King's Chapel & Burying Ground

Ⓣ

Boston Latin School Site

KILBY STREET

Old City Hall

US Post Office & Courthouse

WATER ST

BATTERYMARCH ST

BROAD STREET

ROSE KENNEDY GREENWAY

TREMONT STREET

SCHOOL ST

DEVONSHIRE ST

POST OFFICE SQUARE

OLIVER STREET

WENDELL STREET

HIGH STREET

Omni Parker House

Old Corner Bookstore site

MILK STREET

FRANKLIN STREET

PROVINCE ST

Old South Meeting House

Post Office Square Park

PEARL STREET

NORTHERN AVENUE BRIDGE (PEDESTRIAN ACCESS ONLY)

BROMFIELD ST

FEDERAL ST

CONGRESS STREET

HIGH STREET

DOWNTOWN CROSSING

WASHINGTON STREET

FRANKLIN ST

Verizon Building

Fort Point Channel

STREET

Ⓣ

FINANCIAL DISTRICT

PURCHASE STREET

ATLANTIC AVENUE

Museum Wharf

DOWNTOWN CROSSING

Filene's Basement

SNOW PLACE

HAWLEY ST

Bank of Boston

MATTHEWS ST

DEVONSHIRE ST

ATLANTIC AVENUE

Macy's

SUMMER STREET

MILTON ST

Children's Museum

Lafayette Place

OTIS STREET

HIGH STREET

CONGRESS ST BRIDGE

CHAUNCY ST

Hood Milk Bottle

DELAFAYETTE AVE

COLUMBIA STREET

SOUTH STATION Ⓣ

SUMMER ST BRIDGE

SEAPORT DISTRICT

HARRISON AVE

KINGSTON STREET

ESSEX STREET

ESSEX STREET

MELCHER ST

CHINATOWN

JOHN FITZGERALD EXPRESSWAY

TUFTS ST

EAST ST

LEATHER DISTRICT

ATLANTIC AVENUE

NECCO CT

Liberty Tree Plaque

BEACH STREET

LINCOLN STREET

SOUTH ST

DORCHESTER AVENUE

Chinatown Gate

KNEELAND STREET

STREET

HARRISON AVENUE

TYLER STREET

HUDSON STREET

ALBANY STREET

3

South Station

N

Orange Line ——
Red Line ——
Green Line ——
Blue Line ——
Freedom Trail - - - -

0   400 yds

Harbor Islands, Provincetown MA & Salem MA ▲

Institute of Contemporary Art (550yds) ▲

Phipps Street Burying Ground

THE NORTH END, CHARLESTOWN & THE WEST END

Charlestown Five Cents Savings Bank Building

Bunker Hill Monument

Breed's Hill

Charlestown Public Library

33 Cordis Street

WOOD ST

MONUMENT SQUARE

W SCHOOL ST

AUSTIN STREET

LAWRENCE ST

MAIN WARREN STREET

CORDIS STREET

PLEASANT STREET

MONUMENT AVE

SOLEY STREET

ADAMS STREET

Bunker Hill Community College

RUTHERFORD AVENUE

STREET

Warren Tavern

Winthrop Square

COMMON ST

UNION STREET

WASHINGTON STREET

Larkin House

DEXINS STREET

MAIN STREET

HARVARD STREET

CHARLESTOWN

T COMMUNITY COLLEGE

LYNDE STREET

HENLEY STREET

PARK STREET

John Havard Mall

NEW RUTHERFORD AVENUE

JOHN F. GILMORE BRIDGE

City Square

CONSTITUTION

NORTH POINT

Paul Revere Park (i)

LEONARD P. ZAKIM BUNKER HILL BRIDGE

CHARLESTOWN BRIDGE

Museum of Science

MSGR O'BRIEN HIGHWAY

NASHUA STREET

NASHUA STREET

Hayden Planetarium & Omni Theater

SCIENCE PARK T

LOMASNEY WAY

MARTHA ROAD

TD Banknorth Garden

North Station

NORTH STATION

O'Neill Federal Building

T

HAVERHILL STREET

WEST END

LOMASNEY WAY

CAUSEWAY STREET

LANCASTER STREET

PORTLAND STREET

FRIEND STREET

VALENTI WAY

CANAL STREET

BLOSSOM STREET

MERRIMAC STREET

CHARLES STREET

WILLIAM CARDINAL

+ Massachusetts General Hospital

State Service Center

BOWKER STREET

FRUIT STREET

PARKMAN STREET

N. ANDERSON ST

BLOSSOM STREET

O'CONNELL WAY

STANIFORD STREET

NEW CHARDON STREET

HAWKINS STREET

BULFINCH STREET

NEW SUDBURY STREET

CHARLES/MGH

T GEORGE WASHINGTON CIRCLE

Harrison Gray Otis House

BOWDOIN

CAMBRIDGE STREET

Ropewalk Building

TREMONT STREET

PROSPECT STREET

CHELSEA STREET

MT VERNON STREET

CHESTNUT STREET

3RD AVENUE

7TH STREET

1ST AVENUE

5TH STREET

6TH STREET

9TH STREET

8TH STREET

Orange Line
Green Line
Blue Line
Freedom Trail - - -

Pier 9

Pier 8

Shipyard Park

USS Constitution Museum

AVENUE

2ND

Charlestown Navy Yard

Boston National Historical Park

Pier 7

Pier 6

ROAD

i

USS Constitution (Old Ironsides)

Pier 2 Pier 3

Pier 5

Bunker Hill Pavillion

Constitution Plaza

Pier 1 USS Cassin Young

Pier 4

Mystic River

N

Boston Inner Harbor

Constitution Wharf

North End Playground

US Coast Guard Station

COMMERCIAL STREET

Copp's Hill Burying Ground

COPP'S HILL TERRACE

CHARTER STREET

FOSTER STREET

HENCHMAN ST

COMMERCIAL STREET

Battery Wharf

Fire Boat Dock

KEANEY SQUARE

PRINCE STREET

SNOWHILL STREET

HULL ST

SHEAFE

Narrowest House

SALEM STREET

Old North Church

GREENOUGH ST

BATTERY STREET

SALUTATION STREET

Lincoln Wharf

NORTH END

Clough House

TILESTON ST

Paul Revere Mall

HANOVER STREET

Union Wharf Building

Union Wharf

N WASHINGTON STREET

DONEGAL SQUARE

THATCHER STREET

LYNN STREET

N MARGIN STREET

N BENNET ST

HARRIS ST

St Stephen's Church

CLARK STREET

ENDICOTT STREET

St Leonard's Church

HANOVER STREET

FLEET STREET

HANOVER STREET

MOON ST

LEWIS STREET

HICHBORN STREET

Sargents Wharf

COOPER STREET

WIGET ST

PRINCE STREET

Paul Revere House

NORTH SQUARE

STILMAN ST

SALEM STREET

Pierce/Hichborn House

LEWIS STREET

Lewis Wharf

HAYMARKET SQUARE

MORTON ST

CROSS STREET

NORTH STREET

RICHMOND STREET

FULTON STREET

COMMERCIAL STREET WHARF WEST

COMMERCIAL

Lewis Wharf Building

Commercial Wharf

T

HAYMARKET STREET

NEW SUDBURY STREET

BLACKSTONE ROAD

HANOVER ST

WHARF EAST

ATLANTIC AVENUE

JFK Federal Building

CONGRESS STREET

Christopher Columbus Park

0   500 yds

MBTA Ferry to Long Wharf & Downtown

Downtown

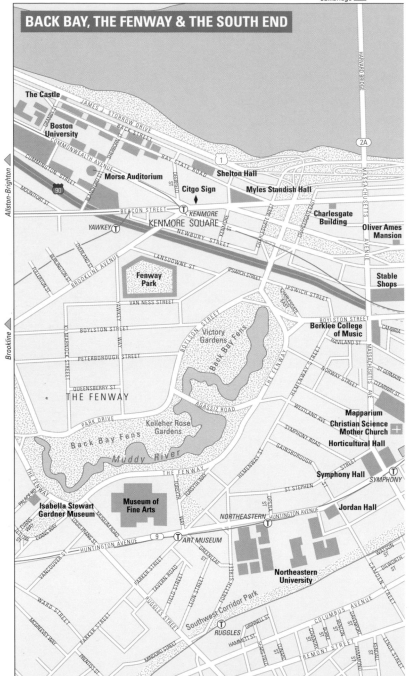

BACK BAY, THE FENWAY & THE SOUTH END

Cambridge

Alliston-Brighton

Brookline

The Castle

JAMES J. STORROW DRIVE

BACK STREET

Boston University

COMMONWEALTH AVENUE

BAY STATE ROAD

CUMMINGTON STREET

Morse Auditorium

Shelton Hall

Citgo Sign

Myles Standish Hall

MOUNTFORT ST

90

BEACON STREET

KENMORE

KENMORE SQUARE

YAWKEY

NEWBURY STREET

Charlesgate Building

Oliver Ames Mansion

HARVARD BRIDGE

2A

MASSACHUSETTS AVENUE

LANSDOWNE ST

Fenway Park

IPSWICH STREET

IPSWICH STREET

Stable Shops

BURLINGTON ST

CLEVELAND ST

BROOKLINE AVENUE

VAN NESS STREET

BOYLSTON STREET

Victory Gardens

Back Bay Fens

BOYLSTON STREET

Berklee College of Music

CAMBRIA

TOLLERTON ST

YAWKEY WAY

KILMARNOCK STREET

PETERBOROUGH STREET

HAVILAND ST

NORWAY STREET

HEMENWAY STREET

MASSACHUSETTS AVE

ST.GERMAIN

CLEARWAY ST

QUEENSBERRY ST

THE FENWAY

AGASSIZ ROAD

THE FENWAY

WESTLAND AVE

Mapparium

Christian Science Mother Church

PARK DRIVE

Kelleher Rose Gardens

SYMPHONY ROAD

Horticultural Hall

Back Bay Fens

GAINSBOROUGH

HEMENWAY ST

Muddy River

THE FENWAY

FORSYTH WAY

Symphony Hall

SYMPHONY

PALACE RD

THE FENWAY

Isabella Stewart Gardner Museum

Museum of Fine Arts

ST. STEPHEN

OPERA

ST.

JERSEY

NORTHEASTERN

Huntington Avenue

Jordan Hall

EVANS WAY

EVANS WAY

LOUIS PRANG ST

MUSEUM ROAD

FORSYTH WAY

9

ART MUSEUM

HUNTINGTON AVENUE

GREENLEAF STREET

WATSON ST

DILWORTH ST

VANCOUVER ST

PARKER STREET

TAVERN ROAD

FIELD STREET

LEON STREET

Northeastern University

CALUMET STREET

WARD STREET

RUGGLES STREET

Southwest Corridor Park

COLUMBUS AVENUE

BENTON ST

BANCROFT ST

KENDALL ST

MCGREEVEY WAY

PARKER STREET

PRENTISS ST

MINDORO STREET

RUGGLES

HAMMETT ST

GRINNELL ST

COVENTRY ST

LENOX ST

CUNARD ST

TREMONT STREET

HAMMOND ST

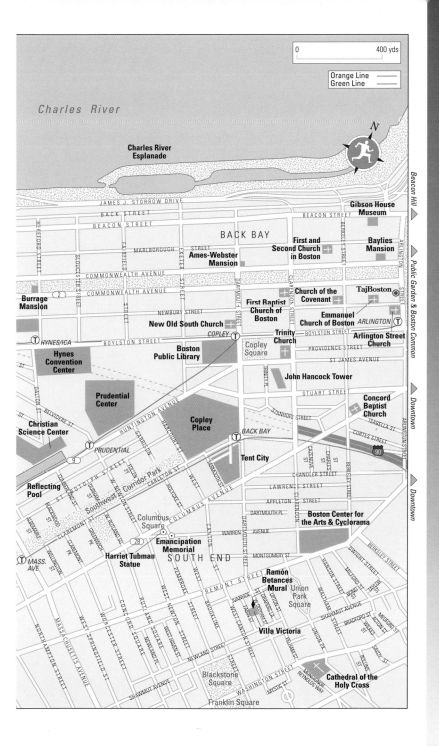

0   400 yds

Orange Line ———
Green Line ———

Charles River

Charles River
Esplanade

N

JAMES J. STORROW DRIVE

BACK STREET

BEACON STREET

BEACON STREET

Gibson House
Museum

BACK BAY

MARLBOROUGH STREET

First and
Second Church
in Boston

Baylies
Mansion

Ames-Webster
Mansion

COMMONWEALTH AVENUE

COMMONWEALTH AVENUE

Church of the
Covenant

TajBoston

Burrage
Mansion

2

NEWBURY STREET

First Baptist
Church of
Boston

Emmanuel
Church of Boston

ARLINGTON

New Old South Church

COPLEY T

Trinity
Church

Arlington Street
Church

HYNES/ICA

BOYLSTON STREET

BOYLSTON STREET

Copley
Square

PROVIDENCE STREET

ST JAMES AVENUE

Hynes
Convention
Center

Boston
Public Library

TRINITY PL.

John Hancock Tower

STUART STREET

Concord
Baptist
Church

Prudential
Center

Copley
Place

STANHOPE STREET

ISABELLA ST

CORTES STREET

Christian
Science Center

HUNTINGTON AVENUE

BACK BAY

90

9

PRUDENTIAL

CHANDLER STREET

Tent City

LAWRENCE STREET

Reflecting
Pool

Southwest Corridor Park

COLUMBUS AVENUE

APPLETON STREET

DARTMOUTH PL.

Boston Center for
the Arts & Cyclorama

Columbus
Square

WARREN AVENUE

28

Emancipation
Memorial

MONTGOMERY ST

MASS.
AVE.

Harriet Tubman
Statue

SOUTH END

Ramón
Betances
Mural

Union
Park
Square

TREMONT STREET

IVANHOE ST

Villa Victoria

Blackstone
Square

WASHINGTON STREET

Cathedral of the
Holy Cross

MONSIGNOR
REYNOLDS WAY

MYSTIC ST

Franklin Square

Beacon Hill ▷

Public Garden & Boston Common ▷

Downtown ▷

Downtown ▷

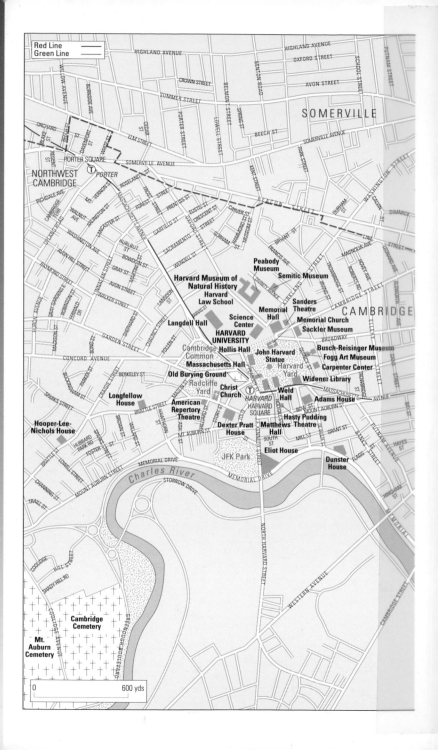

HIGHLAND AVENUE

OXFORD STREET

HIGHLAND AVENUE

AVON STREET

WILLOW AVENUE

BURNSIDE AVE

CROWN STREET

SUMMER STREET

BELMONT ST

SPRING ST

BEECH ST

SOMERVILLE AVENUE

SOMERVILLE

ORCHARD ST

ELM STREET

CEDAR

PORTER STREET

LOWELL STREET

KENT STREET

PARK STREET

PORTER SQUARE

SOMERVILLE AVENUE

SCHOOL STREET

PUTNAM STREET

DURHAM ST

WASHINGTON STREET

DIMMICK

NORTHWEST
CAMBRIDGE

T PORTER

RICHDALE AVE

WALNUT

MT. VERNON ST

ROSELAND ST

FOREST STREET

PRENTISS STREET

CARVER ST

BEACON STREET

LINE

MAGNOLIA AVE

HANCOCK STREET

CAMBRIDGE AVE

ARLINGTON

WASHINGTON AVE

AVON ST

HURLBUT

BOWDOIN ST

GRAY ST

EUSTIS ST

GARFIELD ST

CRESCENT STREET

OXFORD STREET

SACRAMENTO

WENDELL ST

GORHAM ST

FRANCIS AVE

BRYANT ST

CAMBRIDGE STREET

ELLERY STREET

CAMBRIDGE

LANCASTER STREET

LINNAEAN STREET

WALKER STREET

LANGDON ST

Peabody
Museum

Semitic Museum

BROADWAY

Harvard Museum of
Natural History
Harvard
Law School

Memorial
Hall

Sanders
Theatre

Memorial Church

RAYMOND STREET

BUCKINGHAM STREET

HURON AVENUE

MADISON ST

BOND ST

CHAUNCY STREET

FOLLEN ST

GARDEN STREET

Langdell Hall

Science
Center

HARVARD
UNIVERSITY

Sackler Museum

Busch-Reisinger Museum

Fogg Art Museum

GARDEN STREET

CONCORD AVENUE

Cambridge
Common

BERKELEY ST

Hollis Hall

Massachusetts Hall

Old Burying Ground

Radcliffe
Yard

John Harvard
Statue

Harvard
Yard

Carpenter Center

Widener Library

Adams House

MASSACHUSETTS

AVENUE

SPARKS STREET

Longfellow
House

BRATTLE STREET

American
Repertory
Theatre

Christ
Church

T

Weld
Hall

HARVARD

HARVARD
SQUARE

BOW ST

MT AUBURN STREET

Hasty Pudding
Theatre

DUNSTER ST

PLYMPTON ST

Hooper-Lee-
Nichols House

HAWTHORN ST

WILLARD ST

FOSTER ST

HUBBARD PARK RD

BRATTLE ST

Dexter Pratt
House

MT. AUBURN ST

SOUTH
ST

Matthews
Hall

GRANT ST

MILL ST

BANKS STREET

FLAGG STREET

HAYES STREET

CHANNING ST

LOWELL STREET

MOUNT AUBURN STREET

MEMORIAL DRIVE

JFK Park

Eliot House

Dunster
House

MINGHAM ST

TRAIL ST

Charles River

STORROW DRIVE

MEMORIAL DRIVE

NORTH HARVARD STREET

MEMORIAL DRIVE

COOLIDGE

HILL RD

SHADY HILL RD

COOLIDGE AVENUE

GREENOUGH BOULEVARD

Cambridge
Cemetery

WESTERN AVENUE

CAMBRIDGE STREET

Mt.
Auburn
Cemetery

0 _____ 600 yds

N

WALNUT STREET
COLUMBUS AVENUE
MCGRATH HIGHWAY
JOY STREET
SOMERVILLE AVENUE
MCGRATH HIGHWAY
GORE STREET

Cambridgeside Galleria Mall

WARD ST
MEDFORD ST
SOUTH STREET
WEBSTER STREET
WILLOW STREET
HARDING STREET
CAMBRIDGE STREET
BERKSHIRE STREET
CARDINAL MEDEIROS AVENUE
MEMORIAL WAY
FULKERSON STREET

OTIS STREET
SPRING ST
THORNDIKE ST
6TH STREET
5TH STREET
HURLEY STREET
CHARLES STREET
BENT ST
ROGERS STREET
BINNEY STREET
MUNROE ST
POTTER ST
LINSKEY WAY

EAST CAMBRIDGE

CONCORD AVENUE
PROSPECT STREET
SPRINGFIELD ST
OAK ST
HOUGHTON ST
TREMONT STREET
NORFOLK ST
LINCOLN ST
ELM STREET
COLUMBIA STREET
WINDSOR STREET
YORK ST
BRISTOL STREET
HAMPSHIRE STREET
PORTLAND STREET
DAVIS ST

INMAN SQUARE

Cambridge Firemen's Mural

ST MARY ROAD
INMAN STREET
AMORY ST
NORFOLK STREET
PROSPECT STREET
MARKET ST
ANTRIM STREET

BINNEY ST
Kendall Square Cinema

BROADWAY
KENDALL SQUARE
Ⓣ KENDALL

FAYETTE STREET
MAPLE AVENUE

BROADWAY
HARVARD STREET
WORCESTER ST
SUFFOLK ST
WASHINGTON ST
CHERRY ST
PINE STREET
SCHOOL ST
MAIN STREET
STATE STREET
OSBORN ST

MAIN STREET
CARLETON ST
WADSWORTH ST

WEST ST
ESSEX ST

Weisner Building

Ray and Maria Stata Center

MASSACHUSETTS INSTITUTE OF TECHNOLOGY

City Hall
Ⓣ CENTRAL
MASSACHUSETTS AVENUE
CENTRAL SQUARE
BISHOP RICHARD ALLEN DRIVE

MIT Museum

ⓘ
Pierce Laboratory

MEMORIAL DRIVE

GREEN STREET
FRANKLIN STREET
KINNAIRD ST
ROGERS ST
AUBURN STREET
WILLIAM ST
COTTAGE ST
PERRY ST
UPTON ST
KELLY RD
CHALK ST
FAIRMONT ST
PRINCE ST
HAMILTON ST
ERIE ST
BROOKLINE STREET
PACIFIC STREET
LANDSDOWNE STREET
BLANCHE ST
PURRINGTON STREET
ALBANY STREET
WAVERLY STREET

GREEN STREET
FRANKLIN STREET
LOPEZ ST
HOWARD ST
JAY ST
WESTERN AVENUE
RIVER STREET
PLEASANT STREET
MAGAZINE STREET

MIT Chapel

Kresge Auditorium

AMHERST ST
AMHERST ALLEY
MEMORIAL DRIVE

HARVARD BRIDGE

ALLSTON STREET
PUTNAM AVENUE
CHESTNUT STREET
FLORENCE ST
TUFTS ST
GLENWOOD AVE
HENRY ST
GRANITE ST
PUTNAM AVENUE
DRIVE
VASSAR STREET
AUBREY ST
AMESBURY ST

Charles River

The Castle
Boston University

STORROW DRIVE
BAY STATE ROAD
COMMONWEALTH AVENUE
MASSACHUSETTS TURNPIKE EXTENSION
BEACON STREET

KENMORE SQUARE
Ⓣ KENMORE

BROOKLINE EXTENSION
LANSDOWNE ST
Fenway Park

ELI BRIDGE
MEMORIAL DRIVE

Ⓣ BU EAST
BU CENTRAL
Ⓣ

Marsh Chapel
MOUNTFORT STREET

Ⓣ FENWAY

STORROW DRIVE

▶ **Back Bay**

CAMBRIDGE

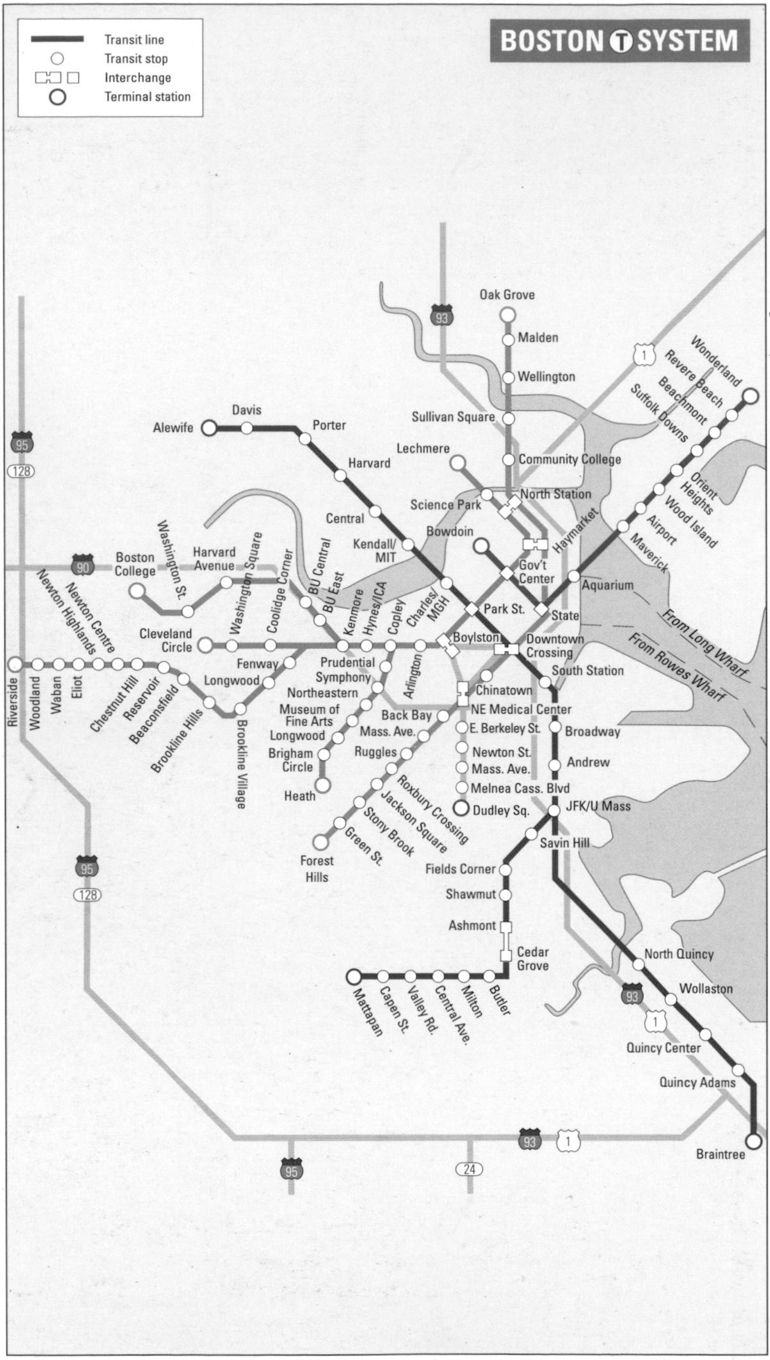

BOSTON T SYSTEM

Legend:
- Transit line
- Transit stop
- Interchange
- Terminal station

Stations and labels:

Oak Grove, Malden, Wellington, Wonderland, Revere Beach, Beachmont, Suffolk Downs, Orient Heights, Wood Island, Airport, Maverick

Davis, Alewife, Porter, Sullivan Square, Community College, North Station, Haymarket, Aquarium

Harvard, Lechmere, Science Park, Bowdoin, Gov't Center, State

Central, Kendall/MIT, Charles/MGH, Park St., Downtown Crossing

Boston College, Harvard Avenue, Washington St., Coolidge Corner, BU East, Kenmore, Hynes/ICA, Copley, Arlington, Boylston, South Station, From Long Wharf, From Rowes Wharf

Newton Centre, Newton Highlands, Cleveland Circle, Fenway, Longwood, Prudential, Symphony, Northeastern, Museum of Fine Arts, Longwood, Brigham Circle, Heath, Chinatown, NE Medical Center, E. Berkeley St., Broadway, Andrew

Riverside, Woodland, Waban, Eliot, Chestnut Hill, Reservoir, Beaconsfield, Brookline Hills, Brookline Village, Back Bay, Mass. Ave., Ruggles, Newton St., Mass. Ave., Melnea Cass. Blvd, JFK/U Mass

Roxbury Crossing, Jackson Square, Stony Brook, Green St., Forest Hills, Dudley Sq., Savin Hill

Fields Corner, Shawmut, Ashmont, Cedar Grove, North Quincy, Wollaston

Mattapan, Capen St., Valley Rd, Central Ave., Milton, Butler, Quincy Center, Quincy Adams, Braintree

US 95, 128, US 90, I 93, US 1, US 95, 128, US 93, US 1, 24

Harbour Islands, Logan Airport, Salem, MA & The USS Constitution in Charlestown — Logan Airport